LONDON'S TERMINI

'An absorbing book which traces the historical background and discusses general architectural matters of all London's main-line termini. It includes also a wealth of operating comment which gives the book a wide appeal and which is supported by track layouts of the stations described. The commentary is balanced and comprehensive, the author having included the early historical side of operations as well as describing the methods used up to the present time.' *Railway Magazine*

'Well-researched and immensely detailed with plenty of good stories about the financial and other troubles of the many railway companies' *The Daily Telegraph*

'Superb ... fully recaptures the special flavour of each station to perfection' *Railway Modeller*

'Illuminates not only their character but also railway history, architecture and social impact ... most enjoyable' *The Times Literary Supplement*

Cover illustration: Early evening scene at Kings Cross, 1926 (painted by V. Welch)

The David & Charles Series

LONDON'S TERMINI

ALAN A. JACKSON

UNABRIDGED

PAN BOOKS LTD : LONDON

First published 1969 by David & Charles (Publishers) Ltd.
This edition published 1972 by Pan Books Ltd,
33 Tothill Street, London, SW1.

ISBN 0 330 02747 6

Printed in Great Britain by
Richard Clay (The Chaucer Press), Ltd, Bungay, Suffolk

CONTENTS

ILLUSTRATIONS IN PHOTOGRAVURE

(between pages 76 and 77)

Euston looking south, c 1840
(*By courtesy of British Transport Historical Relics*)

Euston, portico and lodges, c 1901
(*Wrench*)

Euston, Platforms 4 to 6 looking north, c 1938
(*By courtesy of British Rail*)

Euston, the Great Hall, 1953
(*By courtesy of British Rail*)

St Pancras interior, looking north, c 1869
(*By courtesy of Vincent Brooks, Day and Sons*)

St Pancras, c 1885
(*By courtesy of National Buildings Record*)

Kings Cross, c 1853
(*By courtesy of R. B. Fleming and Co Ltd*)

Kings Cross, interior, 1958
(*Alan A. Jackson*)

Bishopsgate, c 1865
(*By courtesy of British Transport Historical Relics*)

Liverpool Street, c 1904

Fenchurch Street, 1853
(*By courtesy of the* Illustrated London News)

Fenchurch Street, interior, 1956
(*Alan A. Jackson*)

London Bridge Joint station, c 1845
(*By courtesy of British Transport Historical Relics*)

London Bridge signals, c 1864
(*By courtesy of the* Illustrated London News)

Cannon Street and approaches, 1955
(*Alan A. Jackson*)

Nine Elms, 1838
(*By courtesy of British Transport Historical Relics*)

(between pages 300 and 301)

Ludgate Hill, 1865
(*By courtesy of the* Illustrated London News)

Ludgate Hill, c 1898
(*George Potter*)

Holborn Viaduct, 1877
(*By courtesy of the National Buildings Record*)

Bricklayers Arms
By courtesy of the Illustrated London News

Waterloo, c 1900
(*By courtesy of British Transport Historical Relics*)

Waterloo, 1912
(*By courtesy of the Radio Times Hulton Picture Library and the Rev P. W. Boulding*)

Charing Cross signals and river bridge, c 1864

Charing Cross interior, 1864
(*By courtesy of British Transport Historical Relics*)

Victoria, LBSCR old station
(*By courtesy of British Transport Historical Relics*)

Victoria, SECR, c 1910
(*By courtesy of Rotary Photographic*)

The first Paddington Station, 1843
(*By courtesy of the* Illustrated London News)

Paddington interior, 1959
(*Alan A. Jackson*)

Paddington interior, 1912
(*By courtesy of the Radio Times Hulton Picture Library and the Rev P. W. Boulding*)

Marylebone, 1899
(*J. W. Wood, by courtesy of E. B. Woodruffe Peacock*)

Marylebone, 1967
(*Alan A. Jackson*)

IN TEXT

All these line illustrations, except those on pp xviii, 152 and 293, are
reproduced by kind permission of the editors of the *Railway Magazine*.

Born in North London almost halfway between the main railway lines to Edinburgh and to Cambridge, Alan Jackson left grammar school in 1939 to join the Civil Service. After a brief spell with the War Office he served in the RAF until 1946, travelling to Asia and following the German forces 'at a respectful distance all the way from the foot of Italy to Provence'. He married in 1949 and has three daughters. Although on most days still to be found in Whitehall, his interests, initially stimulated by London University Extension Courses, have turned increasingly to research and studies in London's recent transport and social history. Since the early 1950s he has made many contributions to the transport press and his books include a history of London's tube railways, *Rails Through The Clay* (with D. F. Croome), *Volk's Railways* and two books for boys. He is now working on a historical survey of London's modern suburban development.

PREFACE

London's railway termini fit awkwardly into the Motor Age. Designed for the steam locomotive and the horse cab, and built in profusion in the days of *laissez-faire* capitalism, when the railway was the main means of land transport, they now have to serve a unified and attenuated railway system operated by diesel and electric traction. The inevitable changes, long postponed, have at last begun. Surprisingly, none has yet been closed, but the days of Marylebone are surely numbered. Euston has been completely rebuilt; Holborn Viaduct and Cannon Street have undergone drastic modernization; the reconstruction of Victoria is under active consideration; a major upheaval is almost completed at Paddington; and there has been talk of discarding St Pancras after a proposed rebuilding of Kings Cross. With the passing of the steam locomotive from the great train sheds built to disperse its exhaust there has been a transformation; to those who knew them even ten years ago, stations such as St Pancras and Liverpool Street are now almost unrecognizable on a winter's afternoon.

Time then to set down a record. The original idea came from Mr Michael Higson, and when he offered it to me, I accepted with enthusiasm, eventually producing a far longer book than first envisaged. An attempt has been made to present the development of the existing main-line termini and their predecessors in a fairly straightforward and orderly fashion on a chronological base. After an introductory survey, a chapter is devoted to each station or station group, beginning with Euston, the first London terminus for long-distance traffic, and proceeding in a roughly clockwise direction to end with Marylebone, the last to be built. This arrangement, together with a

detailed index, is designed to render the book an easy and convenient source of reference.

It is perhaps as well to apologize in advance to those who
find their specialized interests skimped or neglected. Baker
Street has been left out because the Metropolitan Railway, for
all its pretensions, was never a main-line company. Train services have not received much attention because this topic has
been thrashed to exhaustion over the years in the amateur railway periodicals; where services are mentioned, the emphasis
has been placed on local workings – this is essentially a London
book. I am aware of the inadequacy of the signalling notes
which follow each chapter, but hope they will serve as a guide
until a specialist in this subject gives it the detailed treatment it
deserves.

There are many to thank for advice and assistance. The staff
of the excellent Westminster Public Libraries met my requests
with their customary calm efficiency; the public-relations officials of the London Midland, Eastern, Western and Southern
Regions of British Railways replied promptly to my inquiries
about current events and plans, and supplied statistics; the staff
at the Clapham Transport Museum, notably Mr Bob Cogger,
gave me the greatest assistance in my quest for illustrations.

Friends and fellow members of the Railway Club were, as
ever, generous with their time and help. Mr Charles E. Lee
went to much trouble to find illustrations from his own collection, and courteously allowed me to make use of his published
articles on some of the stations (detailed in Appendix VI); Dr
Edwin Course, of Southampton University, who has done so
much to foster my interest in London railways, looked through
the typescript and offered suggestions; Mr J. T. Howard
Turner contributed valuable advice from his extensive knowledge of railway engineering and the southern systems; Mr G.
T. Moody read the book as it was written, his lifelong study

of London railways providing a very substantial contribution of suggestions and comments; Mr H. V. Borley, Librarian of the Railway Club, another Londoner who knows his railways well, worked with his usual patience and care to check facts and dates. I am also grateful to the Rev P. W. Boulding for allowing me to use illustrations from his collection, and to Mr J. N. Slater, Assistant Editor of the *Railway Magazine*, for permission to use plans originally published in that journal.

My intention has been to provide a book that will be read and used not only by the railway minded, but by the student of nineteenth- and twentieth-century London. Should it prove helpful to both, stimulating further interest and inquiry, I shall be well content.

Ashtead, April 1969   ALAN A. JACKSON

ABBREVIATIONS

BR	British Railways
BUA	British United Airways
CCEHR	Charing Cross, Euston & Hampstead Railway (London Electric Railway, 1910; LT 1933)
CSLR	City & South London Railway (LT from 1933)
ECR	Eastern Counties Railway (GER from 1862)
ECS	Empty carriage stock
EKR	East Kent Railway (LCDR from 1859)
GCR	Great Central Railway (LNER from 1923)
GER	Great Eastern Railway (LNER from 1923)
GNR	Great Northern Railway (LNER from 1923)
GWR	Great Western Railway (BR, Western Region, from 1948)
L & BR	London & Birmingham Railway (LNWR from 1846)
L & CR	London & Croydon Railway (LBSCR from 1846)
L & SR	London & Southampton Railway (LSWR from 1839)
LBSCR	London Brighton & South Coast Railway (SR from 1923)
LCC	London County Council (now the Greater London Council)
LCDR	London Chatham & Dover Railway (SECR from 1899)
LGOC	London General Omnibus Company (LT from 1933)
LMSR	London Midland & Scottish Railway (BR, London Midland Region, from 1948)
LNER	London & North Eastern Railway (BR, Eastern Region, from 1948)

LNWR	London & North Western Railway (LMSR from 1923)
LSWR	London & South Western Railway (SR from 1923)
LTSR	London Tilbury & Southend Railway (LMSR from 1923, BR, Eastern Region, from 1948)
LT	London Transport (London Passenger Transport Board 1933–47, London Transport Executive 1948–62, London Transport Board 1963–9, London Transport Executive 1970)
Met	Metropolitan Railway (LT from 1933)
MS & LR	Manchester Sheffield & Lincolnshire Railway (GCR from 1897)
N & ER	Northern & Eastern Railway (leased to ECR from 1844)
NLR	North London Railway (LMSR from 1923)
SECR	South Eastern & Chatham Railway (SR from 1923)
SER	South Eastern Railway (SECR from 1899)
SR	Southern Railway (BR, Southern Region, from 1948)
VS & PR	Victoria Station & Pimlico Railway (SR from 1923)
WEL & CPR	West End of London & Crystal Palace Railway (LBSCR from 1860)

LONDON'S TERMINI

LONDON'S TERMINI

— Main Line.
–○– Underground Railways
(Tube Railways not shown)

CHAPTER ONE

SURVEYING THE SCENE

NOT ENTIRELY HAPHAZARD

It is at once clear, on looking at a map of central London, that the great railway termini were not arranged in accordance with any predetermined plan. Yet there is certain evidence (the array of northern stations along a more or less level line, and the strange shape of the Inner Circle railway) that development was not entirely haphazard. A closer examination reveals a distinct difference in pattern between the Northern and Southern lines; the latter are seen to probe much more closely to the centre, and to have the best sites.

At first, the most important, and almost the only restraints were the crude disciplines of finance. North of the river, Euston (1837), the first Paddington (1838), Shoreditch (1840), and Fenchurch Street (1841), were all sited either on the edge of the built-up area or on the outer rim of the higher-value property. In the south, where the property was neither valuable nor fashionable, the first terminus was brought close in, right up to the river at London Bridge (1836). It is true that the second, Nine Elms (1838) was farther out, but by 1844 the owning company was preparing to go forward to Waterloo Bridge and London Bridge. Bricklayers Arms (1844) was also distant, but as a passenger terminus it was but an expedient and really is a special case.

In the middle Forties the Railway Mania was in full flush. Capital was available for almost any scheme that seemed in the least hopeful, and for many that were not. A whole clutch of termini were daringly projected into the very heart of the metropolis, including a central terminus on what is now the Victoria Embankment, served by lines linking Paddington to

Fenchurch Street through Westminster and the City. At this, the Government took fright, and a Royal Commission (the Commissioners on Railway Termini within or in the immediate vicinity of the Metropolis, 1846) was appointed to review the various schemes affecting central London and to consider:

> whether the extension of railways into the centre of the metropolis is calculated to afford such additional convenience or benefit to the public as will compensate for the sacrifice of property, the interruption of important thoroughfares, and the interference with the plans of improvement already suggested.

Unable to foresee the importance that railway traffic into London would assume, the Commissioners were not impressed that the convenience of passengers weighed very heavily against the immense disturbance and expense which would follow a decision to bring the main-line railways into that central area, and to do so for the sake of short-distance passengers seemed to them quite unjustifiable. They saw no advantage in a single central terminus for all the railways, pointing out that the number of through passengers across the centre was negligible, and that the congestion which would arise both within and without such a station would be intolerable (they also rightly stressed the many difficulties that would stem from divided management).

GUIDANCE GIVEN

In their report, the Commissioners recommended that on the north side of the Thames, no railway should enter the central area as defined in their terms of reference (using modern names, the limits were: Edgware Road, Marylebone Road, Euston Road, Pentonville Road, City Road, Finsbury Square, Bishopsgate, Gracechurch Street, London Bridge, Borough High Street, Borough Road, Lambeth Road, Albert Embankment, Vauxhall Bridge, Vauxhall Bridge Road, Grosvenor Place, Park Lane). If in future it should be deemed advisable to admit railways to this area, the Commissioners thought this should be done in accordance with some uniform plan 'carefully laid down under the authority of Your Majesty's Government and sanctioned by the wisdom of Parliament'. On the south side of the river, the property to be disturbed was thought less valuable, the main roads to be crossed fewer and less important, and the street system better able to cope with the traffic created by railway termini.

Accordingly the Commissioners looked with favour upon the schemes then before Parliament for an extension from Waterloo to London Bridge, and an extension of the railway from the south-east (either the SER, or the North Kent Railway, whichever Parliament considered had the most merit) to a terminus at or near Waterloo. They noted that London Bridge and the proposed NKR terminus at Union Street were convenient for the City, both as regards passengers and goods, and that the authorized LSWR terminus at Waterloo Bridge would be equally convenient for the West End. Finally, they recommended the construction of a line outside their area which would connect all lines approaching London with each other, and with the docks, crossing the Thames at some point west of Vauxhall Bridge.

Further guidance was given by Select Committees of Parliament. That of 1855, the Select Committee of the House of Commons on Metropolitan Communications, decided that the termini ought to be connected with each other, with the river and the docks, and with the Post Office. It was to this Committee that Sir Joseph Paxton[1] proposed an imaginative if somewhat nebulous scheme for an Inner Circle railway in a glass arcade, which he called the Great Victorian Way. Another smaller railway boom occurred in 1863, with particular attention to London, and in that year, a committee of the House of Lords, the Select Committee on Metropolitan Railway Communication, 1863, considered the problem of the capital's communications. They reported against the idea of a large central terminus, said that any new lines in the central area should be underground, and proposed an 'inner circuit' north of the river to link the termini. It was also recommended that the limits of the 1846 Commission should be extended farther out, as far as ordinary railways were concerned. The Joint Committee on Railway Schemes (Metropolis) of 1864 endorsed the Inner Circle railway proposal.

Lines built from the north after 1846 respected the Royal Commission's forbidden zone. Kings Cross (1852), the second Paddington (1854), St Pancras (1868) and Marylebone (1899) all came up to or close to the frontier, but no farther. The 1863 Committee had considered that the Great Eastern Railway might be allowed to come nearer the centre, which it did in due course, opening Liverpool Street, just inside the central zone, in 1874. Meanwhile the North London Railway, aided and abetted by the London & North Western, had also put a foot across at Broad Street in 1865; but it was only a technical breach.

In the south, the position was altogether different. Accepting the freedom of action implied by the findings of the Royal Commission, the southern lines proliferated termini, each company striving to establish a station in both the City and the West End. In doing so, they spanned the river and entered the central zone on the north bank. In 1866 the London Chatham & Dover Railway even opened a link with the northern lines which passed right across the forbidden zone, mostly above ground, with a cheeky bridge over the bottom of Ludgate Hill, in the very shadow of St Paul's Cathedral.

There was good reason for all this activity. These southern companies had no great mineral or industrial traffics to keep them solvent; three-quarters or more of their revenues came from passenger traffic. Their main lines eked out a precarious living on a mixture of military, Continental and pleasure traffic, and such bread and butter as they could get came from the suburbs. For this suburban business, access to the City and

West End was of prime importance. And, by 1860, the authorities had begun to realize that transpontine termini for the southern lines would help to reduce congestion on the road bridges and in the narrow City streets.

Already established near the City at London Bridge, the LBSCR reached the West End at Victoria in 1860. The SER also managed the ideal, with well-sited termini in each part of the centre. Both inside the central zone, Charing Cross (1864) and Cannon Street (1866), were in bridgehead positions involving no serious destruction of valuable property. Even more successful (though at the cost of financial ruin) was the LCDR, with a West End station at Victoria adjacent to that of the LBSCR (1862) and a City establishment at Ludgate Hill (1864), later supplemented by two more, Holborn Viaduct (1874) and St Paul's (now Blackfriars) (1886), all well within the forbidden zone. As for the London & South Western, its new Waterloo terminus (1848) had already been deemed convenient for the West End by the Royal Commission, but it never succeeded in reaching the City on its own tracks, first making do with services projected over other companies' lines, then eventually constructing its own Tube railway from Waterloo to the Bank.

North of the river, the Great Western, Midland and Great Northern companies provided their suburban passengers with City access by linking their terminal approaches with the Metropolitan Railway and running through trains to Moorgate and beyond. The GWR also took a share in Victoria, but the approach was circuitous and of little practical value to its passengers. Some of the quite heavy GNR suburban traffic was siphoned off by North London trains running to the City at Broad Street, and the LNWR also made use of the NLR to carry its passengers to the City. But to none of these big northern companies was suburban traffic of anything but marginal importance; indeed it was often regarded as something of a nuisance.

With a heavy suburban traffic consisting largely of City

workers, the GER was content to stay at Liverpool Street and
Fenchurch Street, making no attempt to use its physical connexion with the Metropolitan at the former station after the
initial negotiations had broken down. However, from 1912,
GER passengers were offered direct access to the West End via
the Central London Tube railway. Fenchurch Street's other
user, the London Tilbury & Southend, obtained its West End
access by fostering a link with the District Railway (the Whitechapel & Bow Joint, opened in 1902).

FROM ONE TO THE OTHER

Those who advocated a combined central terminus were fond
of emphasizing the vagaries and difficulties faced by passengers
moving across London from one terminus to another. It was
many years before such journeys became reasonably convenient. From its opening in 1863, the Metropolitan Railway
afforded direct connexion between Paddington and Kings
Cross, and six years later, circuitous communication was available between those stations and Victoria, via Gloucester Road
and the Metropolitan District Railway. In 1870 the District
pushed east to a station near Charing Cross (sufficiently distant
to require a cab or outside porter were the passenger encum-
bered with luggage). The Metropolitan reached Liverpool
Street in 1875; Cannon Street received its District station in
1884.

It was not until that latter year that the officially-
recommended Inner Circle was finally joined, offering stations
adjacent to eight of the fourteen termini then existing, and also
serving Charing Cross, Fenchurch Street and Euston after a
fashion. Despite the congestion of the streets, journeys between termini at opposite points of the 'Circle' were more
expeditiously made by road transport, and most of the main-
line companies operated or subsidized cross-centre horse-bus
services, usually free of charge to passengers booked across
London.

Speedier and more convenient movement between the termini came in the 1900s with the arrival of the motor bus, the motor taxicab and the electric Tube railway (the Inner Circle was also electrically worked from September 1905). By 1913 all the termini except Fenchurch Street, Ludgate Hill and Holborn Viaduct were served by at least one underground electric railway route.

Although the Midland Railway introduced a motor-bus service between St Pancras and Victoria via Charing Cross in July 1905, the inter-termini services operated on behalf of the railway companies were gradually rendered superfluous by the expansion of the motor taxicab fleet and improvements in public transport.

During the 1920s, railway-inspired inter-termini services briefly flourished for the last time. In connexion with LNER Pullman trains, coaches were operated between Kings Cross and Victoria from July 1928; a year later, the GWR started a similar service using fifteen-seater buses between Paddington and Victoria, primarily for passengers booked through to Continental stations. About 1932 the operation of these services was handed over to a contractor. After the formation of the London Passenger Transport Board, they disappeared and a regular bus link was established between the major termini. From October 1st, 1936, the Board worked an inter-station service, using eight specially-built twenty-seater Leyland Cubs painted royal blue and cream, with large luggage boots beneath their raised rear seat decks. A flat fare of 1s single was charged. Withdrawn on the outbreak of war, these buses were revived in December 1943, working only in the evenings and at night. A remnant of the service still survives; on weekend nights normal double-deck buses provide an occasional connexion between Waterloo, Victoria, Paddington, Euston and Kings Cross–St Pancras.

For those who could afford the fares and the all but obligatory tip, cabs have always been a popular means of transport between the termini and to and from destinations in Town.

Their importance is demonstrated by the elaborate arrangements made to accommodate them; at all termini except Fenchurch Street, Broad Street, Blackfriars and Ludgate Hill, facilities were provided to enable cabs to set down passengers near the booking-offices and to collect them from alongside or near the arrival platforms. From the earliest days, most railway companies preferred to license certain 'privilege' cabs to pick up passengers at the termini. By so doing they could control the service, insisting that an adequate number of cabs meet all long-distance trains whatever the time of day, and that the best type of cab be used, driven by the most reliable men. The agents providing the privilege cabs had to leave a deposit for each vehicle and make a weekly payment. At Euston in 1877, the deposit was £2 per cab and the weekly toll, 2s. In case of complaint, the deposit would be forfeited. In 1897 all companies except the LSWR agreed to an interchange system whereby any cab privileged by one company could ply for hire at any other terminus without extra payment. At Waterloo, apart from a handful of cabs privileged to use the main-line departure cab yard, any cab could use the station on payment of one penny. The privileged cab system at London stations was generally abolished by Sec 2 of the London Cab and Stage Carriage Act, 1907, made permanent by the Expiring Laws Act, 1925. The Act did not affect the liability of cabs and drivers to comply with the railway companies' regulations as to conduct, fitness, numbers admitted at any one time, etc, and provision was made for continuation of the system if a company could prove to the satisfaction of the Home Secretary that without it an insufficient number of cabs would be available.

After its reconstruction in 1916, Paddington became a popular station among the cabbies. Its well-planned approach roads and ramps accommodated 127 cabs outside (over Platforms 11 and 12), with room for another forty in the roadway between Platforms 8 and 9. There was no toll, and the cabs entered the arrival side in strict order. A cab would take anything between twenty minutes and two hours to pass through the station, according to the time of day and state of traffic. As late as 1936 horse cabs were still occasionally seen in the rank and according to the *Great Western Railway Magazine*, July 1936, one was still meeting a 'regular' on his arrival from the country each Wednesday and Friday morning, as it had done for thirty-seven years.

DIRECT LINK ACROSS THE CENTRE

Only one direct railway link was completed across the centre of London. This was the LCDR–Metropolitan connexion of 1866, already mentioned. Severely restricted by sharp curves and steep gradients, it has not been used by regular passenger services for many years. Since the 1860s many more similar direct connexions have been proposed, but such schemes have always foundered on the grounds of high capital cost. As recently as 1966 British Railways offered two possible links for the London Transportation Study : Victoria to London Bridge, and Paddington to Liverpool Street. It was suggested that these might share intermediate stations at Covent Garden and Ludgate Hill, the latter also serving refurbished north/south facilities via the 1866 link.

SOCIAL EFFECTS

Once built, the termini with a predominantly long-distance traffic slowly influenced their immediate surroundings. A certain seediness crept up. This degeneration, sometimes all around, sometimes in a sector of neighbouring streets, was most marked at Paddington, Victoria, Waterloo and the Euston–St Pancras–Kings Cross complex. It was seen to a lesser extent alongside Charing Cross, but hardly at all at Marylebone, a sign perhaps of that station's distinct lack of success as a long-distance terminus.

It was not simply a matter of steam and smoke. Rather did

it arise from the nature of the traffic. Travellers far from the restraints of the family home were often easy, even willing victims to certain temptations, and these were made available. Shops were opened to dispense cheap souvenirs, contraceptives and provocative literature (though rarely all three at once), whilst public-houses were thick upon the ground, and of the large and noisy kind. Cheap little hotels provided shelter for commercial or clandestine lust. Near Waterloo, with its heavy naval and military traffic, a small brothel area grew up. Petty criminals of varying skills congregated to take advantage of the opportunities offered by the crowds, or by isolated and confused strangers to London. Others, who would consider themselves benefactors rather than criminals, preyed upon young country girls arriving to work in London, luring them to occupations more lucrative than domestic service.

But this was only part of the social impact. In constructing the termini and their approaches, the railway companies swept away some of London's worst slums, but nothing was done to rehouse those who were displaced until the mid 1880s, when Parliament eventually came to insist upon it,[2] and by then most of the destruction had been wrought. As the new lines swathed through the little houses and crowded tenements, consciences were eased by the provision of cheap trains at the beginning of each working day, sometimes voluntarily, sometimes by statute. These trains were not in practice much used by the displaced poor, who crowded into adjacent streets, aggravating the housing problem, but they did encourage a great exodus of clerks, artisans and shop and warehouse workers to new suburbs such as Tottenham and Walthamstow. This had been foreseen as early as 1861, when the Rev William Denton, of St Bartholomew, Cripplegate, in a pamphlet (*Observations on the displacement of the Poor by Metropolitan Railways and by other Public Improvements*), described the forcible eviction of the poor by the proposed new railways, and pointed out that cheap trains were no solution, as they were used only by artisans. He argued that the poor must live on top of their work, and the railways ought to provide dwellings for them, administered by trustees.

And what of the visual contribution; did the termini enhance the appearance of the great city they served? Alas, with a few notable exceptions, they cannot be described as a particularly inspiring collection of buildings. Foreign visitors, accustomed to monumental structures set in large open squares, must find the London termini rather an anti-climax. Almost all are hidden away behind main thoroughfares, or so placed that their architectural impact cannot be absorbed or appreciated. Waterloo is hopelessly strangled by the Charing Cross line viaduct, Marylebone skulks behind a huge hotel, the Siamese twins of Victoria hide shyly round a corner, and Liverpool Street, Broad Street, Fenchurch Street and Cannon Street abut on to streets little wider than country lanes. Where fine architecture did exist, it got scant respect. At Euston, Hardwick's screen, which must have looked splendid for a few years whilst it stood alone against the Hampstead ridge, was gradually suffocated by building all about, then mauled, to make room for dreary, straight-faced offices and finally, destroyed. Kings Cross, with a frontage of considerable merit, suffered for many years the indignity of a ghastly mess of forecourt buildings, provisional and permanent, from which it is only now being freed.

Appearance, internal design, and fitness for purpose are normally the business of the architect; but not so here. In the nineteenth century, architect and engineer lived in separate worlds, working with their backs to each other, almost literally so. Thus no London terminus emerged as a unified aesthetic concept, although perhaps Kings Cross, in its original state, with its honest functional frontage, spoilt only by a silly clock tower and grim side offices, can be said to have been a near miss. Euston's classical screen was magnificent, but behind it the railway buildings were from the first uninspiring and mean, and the Great Hall, splendid in itself, only succeeded in emphasizing the dichotomy.

Elsewhere, architects titivated the basic engineering structure (Paddington) or contributed offices or heavily ornamented hotels to close off one end of the train shed (London Bridge, St Pancras, Cannon Street, Charing Cross, Holborn Viaduct). In other cases there was no master architect; the frontage was designed by an engineer or builder, and ornamented by an 'architectural assistant' or consultant (Waterloo, Victoria, Liverpool Street, Broad Street, Fenchurch Street, Marylebone). Left alone to fulfil basic requirements, the great Victorian engineers often succeeded in creating functional beauty of a high order (the roofs at Paddington, St Pancras, Cannon Street and Liverpool Street, the concourse at Waterloo).

Requirements dictated the fundamental design. A primary requirement for the early terminus was ability to handle a departing and an arriving train simultaneously. To meet this, many of the first termini were built with a single departure and arrival 'stage' on opposite sides, the space between filled by spare tracks where carriages could be stored, cleaned, and examined under the shelter of the overall roof (the short, light coaches could easily be manhandled from one track to another by the use of turnplates). Nine Elms, Shoreditch, Bricklayers Arms, Euston, Victoria (LCDR), Paddington and Kings Cross were all of this pattern, the last five with their main offices alongside the departure platform, so that after walking through the booking-office, the passenger found himself facing the centre of his train. The main-line part of Liverpool Street, built as late as 1874, followed the same plan. Most of these stations, but not all, had separate carriage roadways for vehicles serving the departure and arrival sides, either within the station walls, or down one side.

When, with the growth of traffic from the 1870s onwards, the need for more platform accommodation arose, the empty carriage tracks in the middle of the station were abolished, and separate buildings were provided outside the terminus for the cleaning and storage of rolling stock. This created an operational problem because by then the nearest available land was often several miles away, and the shuffling of empty carriage trains to and from the depots congested already inadequate approach tracks. In some cases at least, the ECS traffic must have tipped the balance in making the expensive decision to widen terminal approaches.

When such widening works were undertaken, in the late-nineteenth and early-twentieth centuries, special tracks were occasionally provided for ECS working; and at all major termini complicated arrangements eventually existed for these movements.[3] Nowadays the problem has largely disappeared; many trains are turned round quickly in the terminus and sent out again in traffic after a perfunctory cleaning, whilst the remaining workings between termini and carriage depots no longer have to compete for line occupation with a procession of steam locomotives moving to and from their depots or yards.

Despite the increase in platforms, and the associated construction of cross-platforms behind the buffer stops, the rigid separation of arrival and departure 'sides', often with separate signal boxes, continued for many years. It survived at Paddington until 1967, and still continues to some extent at Kings Cross.

Most stations built after 1860 had their booking-offices and other amenities placed in a central position across the end, sometimes under a hotel which formed the frontage and closed the train shed. Stations of this type were Charing Cross, Cannon Street, Holborn Viaduct, Blackfriars, Broad Street, Fenchurch Street and Marylebone. St Pancras was an odd exception in that its booking-office and some other accommodation was placed at one side, although near the street frontage, whilst the remainder of the facilities and main gateways were positioned centrally under the hotel.

With the single exception of the original Greenwich terminus at London Bridge, all designers considered it proper to protect passengers and rolling stock from the weather by means of an overall roof. The early roofs were low and unprepossessing, but beginning with Kings Cross in 1852, the high arched roof gained favour. This not only assisted the dispersal of smoke, but clearly added grandeur. Two years after Kings Cross, the first modest single-span arch appeared at Fenchurch Street, and gradually this was developed into an almost monumental feature, far larger and grander than sober necessity required, through the riverine spans of Charing Cross and Cannon Street to a climax in 1868 with Barlow's noble 240-ft arch above St Pancras. After that, the column-supported roof returned to favour, but with variations and improvements such as Jacomb-Hood's column-free passenger concourse at Waterloo. Curiously, architects and the general public continued to regard the high arched roof as *de rigueur* for an important terminus, and the roofs at Marylebone and the rebuilt Waterloo were criticized as mean and ugly. As late as the 1930s, the 'modern' model terminus sold for Hornby Trains perpetuated the old tradition of the high segmented arch. Now economy dictates design, and with the disappearance of the smoke nuisance, a terminus can be built under an office block, or if that is lacking, passengers have to make do with individual umbrella canopies over each platform, or a roof only a little higher than the trains, as at the new Euston.

Only three of the termini (Victoria [LBSCR], Waterloo, and Euston) have been completely rebuilt. Elsewhere traffic growth, particularly suburban, enforced piecemeal expansion and reconstruction, extending as far as complete rebuilding of platforms at Fenchurch Street. A great deal more rebuilding and enlargement would have been inevitable but for the arrival of electric traction and the development of automatic signalling, two factors which afforded enormous increases in capacity without moving a brick. The underground loop termini below the main platforms which were on the drawing boards of several railway companies in the 1890s and 1900s were never needed.

CHANCES MISSED

For another type of rebuilding, the railways bestirred themselves too late. In the second half of the 1950s, central London experienced an office-building boom without precedent which made fortunes for an astute band of private developers. Holding at its termini some of the most attractive sites in the capital, the British Transport Commission remained virtually inactive. No effort was made to change the statutory restriction which prevented the Commission from developing its own property for other than operational purposes, leaving it only able to recoup ground rent from any land sold. Sites at three termini were leased to a private developer on extremely favourable terms without finding any way of taking an equity in his schemes. When other similar schemes (to be mentioned later in this book) were stamped upon by the LCC and the City of London, the Commission always gave in without much of a fight.

It was 1959 before the Minister of Transport was asked whether he would be willing to introduce legislation to enable the railways to develop their property on a commercial basis, and eventually, in the Transport Act of 1962, this freedom was given. Schemes existed, or were produced, for almost all the London termini, but alas, by the time they began to come forward, the planning permission tap was being turned off, and in November 1964 a virtually complete ban was imposed. Only the three schemes mentioned earlier came to reality; sold by their original owner to Town & City Properties Ltd in 1962, these were for offices on the York Road side of Waterloo (finally completed in 1969), in front of Holborn Viaduct (1963) and in front of Cannon Street (1965).

Reviewing what remains after the devastation of German bombs and post-war rebuilding, it is apparent that of the original structures, St Pancras, Paddington and Kings Cross are to be, or rather, should be, treasured – for different reasons.

The order of merit can be left to personal taste.

At St Pancras, Scott's hotel is an almost overpowering exercise in high Victorian Gothic, splendid in its roof line and profusion of ornament, its interior almost as intricate as the outside. Demolition would be a crime on the scale of Euston or the City Coal Exchange, a crime which with luck, it may already be too late to pull off. That said, I must confess that there is no joy for me in looking at the Midland Grand, perhaps because the bricks, now very dirty, were the wrong colour anyway, perhaps because it all comes from the drawing board, not from the heart. And its dreary surroundings depress the spirit: particularly Midland Road, with the goods depot on one side, and the dark bricks of St Pancras on the other, one of the most dismal vistas in London, looking for all the world as if it had been lifted bodily from the middle of some nineteenth-century northern town. But once inside the station, there is indeed unalloyed pleasure to be had from the triumphant spread of Barlow's great roof, a demonstration that superb architecture can be achieved through magnificent engineering.

In unique contrast alongside, Kings Cross presents its bold straightforward screen, perhaps still in danger from foreground clutter. Here the interior is a great disappointment. The accommodation is cramped, there is little to inspire. It is to me an unfriendly, cold-hearted place, but the front makes up for it.

Paddington's riches, not to be denied, all lie within, like those of a plain girl. The hotel fails to attract the eye, only a part of the train shed can be seen from the front. Enter and you are uplifted by Brunel's elegant perspective, gently curving, broken so happily by the 'transepts'. Closer scrutiny will reveal Wyatt's bizarre and delicate ornamentation, combining so nicely with the work of the master engineer.

These three are now firmly accepted as worthy of preservation, and although it is now unlikely that they will suffer the fate of Euston's screen and Great Hall, vigilance cannot be relaxed. Of the others, each has its redeeming features and special charms, and the reader will have his own favourites. Mine are Waterloo and Marylebone, still ignored by the architectural historian and the guide books. Edwardian-Imperial, blatantly extrovert, Waterloo has a fine, solid dignity; a spacious place, offering a perfect backcloth for marching troops and Great Occasions, it was built to a sensible design that still works well. A complete opposite is unassuming little Marylebone, a very feminine building. Nondescript architecture perhaps, but there is an almost domestic tranquillity about its well-cared-for appearance and appointments, a tranquillity which emanates a subtle, civilized charm. There is no bustle or confusion here. The trains serve only quiet suburbs and the beech-covered hill country beyond, where in the autumn, leaves cover the tracks. All this, together with its hopeless past and even more hopeless future, make Marylebone quite the most romantic of all the London termini.

CHAPTER TWO

EUSTON

THE FIRST MAIN-LINE TERMINUS

It is appropriate to begin with Euston, for it was London's first main-line terminus. Planned by the engineer Robert Stephenson, and graced by the noble architecture of Philip Hardwick,[1] the London & Birmingham Railway's terminus was opened to the public on July 20th, 1837. Hardwick's Doric portico and screen, and the Great Hall, designed by his son, Philip Charles,[2] were splendid monuments to the abounding confidence of the Railway Age. Surrounded and almost overwhelmed by the unworthy accretions of later years, they survived almost intact until 1961. Now the old Euston is gone, and in its place is a new terminus built to accommodate the slick electric trains which are affording London such excellent communication with Birmingham, Manchester and Liverpool that they have attracted many hundreds of new passengers from the motorways and internal airlines.

A number of sites were considered for the terminus of the London & Birmingham Railway. At first the intention was to finish up in Islington, conveniently near the Regent's Canal, for transhipments to and from the docks. Then Stephenson suggested another route into London, farther to the west, with a terminus at Marble Arch, but the provisional committee objected to this as unsuitable for freight traffic, agreeing a compromise site at Maiden Lane, near Kings Cross, from whence the line could later be extended to the docks. This proposal was rejected by the Lords in 1832. In his plans for the 1833 session, Stephenson took account of economy cuts ordered by the directors, achieving a saving by terminating the line at Camden Town, just north of the Regent's Canal. This was

authorized in 1833, but in the following year the board decided
to venture a little nearer London and agreed plans to go forward another 1¼ miles to Euston Grove.

This extension involved a crossing over the canal which
created a fairly severe gradient between there and the terminus
at 1 in 68 and 1 in 77. It was considered that the outward
climb might present difficulties to the light steam locomotives
then in use, and arrangements were made to haul the trains up
to Camden by continuous cable. Power for the cable was
supplied by two 60-hp Maudslay & Field condensing engines
placed underground beneath two tall chimneys either side of
the line.

At Camden the engines of incoming trains were detached
and the passengers' tickets collected. Trains then descended
the bank unaided, attached to the cable, and controlled by
'bankriders'. A complete section of the Rules & Regulations
was devoted to these men and their duties. From this we learn
that:

> The bankriders are to have the control, management and
> responsibility of the inclined plane and of the trains passing
> down it ... The speed on the incline must never exceed 10
> mph, but a lower speed is necessary when the train is heavy,
> or the rails in bad order.

On the outward run, the bankriders pushed the loaded
coaches to the 'Messenger', the rope which attached the train
to the winding cable, and fastened it. When all was ready, and
the policemen with their red, green and white flags had signalled the line clear, the men in the engine-house at Camden
were alerted by the 'wailing whistle', an organ pipe operated
by compressed air let into the connecting main at Euston. This
air main was also used to sound a similar pipe at the terminus,
giving warning of the approach of an up train. When the
whistle was heard, a bell was rung to carry the message on to
the porters and cabmen, and it is said that the noise would

cause the cab horses to raise their heads from their nosebags and preen themselves for action.

At first the cable was not ready, and until October 14th, 1837, trains were worked up to Camden with steam locomotives at front and rear. Cable working lasted until July 14th, 1844, but the coasting into the terminus continued for a few more years. Maudslay's engines found useful employment at a Russian flax mill.

Steam locomotives almost always needed assistance to bring trains out of Euston. In the early days this was given by a pilot engine, which was normally detached from the train near the Canal Bridge. Running forward, it was diverted to a short siding beyond the bridge, while the intrepid pointsman, with the second engine almost upon him, reset the points for the main line. This pointsman was enjoined by the regulations not to move the points unless he saw the engineman of the pilot locomotive 'motion to the left with his hand (by night with his hand lamp)'. Later, the LNWR adopted the conventional banking engine at the rear.

In these early years, passenger working was confined to the two easternmost tracks, and only they had the cable. The outer of the two western lines was used by engines moving between Euston and the engine yard at Camden in both directions, whilst the remaining line accommodated empty carriages, for which purpose it was roofed over south of the Park Street (now Parkway) Bridge.

This first Euston had but two boarded platforms, the 'arrival stage' and the 'departure stage', on the site of what were later Nos 3 and 6 in the old Euston. These platforms were about 420 ft long and between the platform tracks were two empty carriage roads. Small hand-worked turnplates were provided to move carriages from one line to another. Similar turnplates afforded access to a fifteen-road carriage shed in the north-east corner of the station yard.

The railway accommodation was on the eastern half of the large site that the company had purchased fronting Drummond

Plan of Euston Station 1837. From the Railway Magazine, July 1937

Street. To the west, beyond a central granite roadway, was the land reserved for the Great Western Railway's London terminus. That company planned to bring its Bristol line to a junction with the L & BR near Kensal Green, but there were arguments between the two parties about the terms of the GWR tenancy at Euston and the matter was further complicated by the GWR's determination to use the broad gauge. In the end, the Great Western withdrew and built a separate terminus at Paddington. The original Euston therefore presented a decidedly lop-sided appearance, with its railway tracks and platforms at one side behind the main frontage. Unlike Marylebone, which was also lop-sided, Euston eventually generated more than enough traffic to require all the empty space for railway use.

Approaching the station by road, the traveller saw from a distance the breathtaking vista of Hardwick's great portico, with its attendant lodges. This imposing 300-ft screen, viewed without obstruction from the new Euston Road, must have looked really splendid on a summer's day, with the sunlight catching the pristine albescence of its Bramley Fall stone all against the verdant backcloth of Hampstead Heath. One lodge was joined to the portico on each side, and there were detached lodges, with detached piers, on each side beyond. The spaces in the portico and those between the lodges and beyond were closed with lofty wrought-iron gates decorated with the company's coat of arms, cast by J. J. Bramah to Hardwick's designs.

A GRAND BUT SIMPLE PORTICO

The 72-ft high portico, a true *propylaeum*, had four hollow Doric columns 44 ft 2 ins high and 8 ft 6 ins in diameter, thus exceeding in magnitude the Athenian *propylaea*. It was completed in May 1838 at a cost of some £35,000. Full of pride at the achievement represented by the completion of the London & Birmingham Railway, the directors had decided that nothing but architecture of the highest classical order was good enough to commemorate it, as they thought, permanently. In a report to the shareholders in February 1837, they explained: 'The entrance to the London passenger station, opening immediately upon what will necessarily become the Grand Avenue for travelling between the midland and northern parts of the kingdom, the directors thought that it should receive some architectural embellishment. They accepted accordingly a design of Mr Hardwick's for a grand but simple portico, which they considered well adapted for the national character of the undertaking.' The Hardwick portico was not only a 'Gateway to the North', but a great triumphal arch to mark the arrival of a wonderful new means of transport, a symbol of the solidity and endurable nature of the railway, representative of the successful marriage of steam and progress.

It did not meet with universal acclaim. Augustus Welby Pugin, architect of the Gothic Revival, was snappy:

> The architects have evidently considered it an opportunity for showing off what they could do instead of carrying out what was required. Hence the colossal Grecian portico or gateway, 100 ft high, for the cabs to drive through and put down a few feet farther, at the 14-in brick wall and sash window booking-office. This piece of Brobdingnagian absurdity must have cost the company a sum which would have built a first-rate station, replete with convenience, and which would have been really grand for its simplicity.[3]

Perhaps he would have approved of the new Euston.

Beyond the screen, a granite-paved roadway led into the station yard, to the east of which was a two-storey stuccoed building containing the waiting-rooms, offices and lavatories, with separate entrances and accommodation for first-class passengers, to ensure they had no distressing contacts with the lower orders. Second-class customers had a combined waiting-room and booking office, but nothing was provided for the third class. At the roadway side, this building had a one-storey-high colonnade to shelter the first- and second-class passengers arriving by carriage, omnibus or cab.

The double train shed, designed by Charles Fox,[4] was about 200 ft long, its 40-ft spans supported on cast-iron columns. At the east side was the arrival platform, flanked by a roadway for cabs and omnibuses, which passengers could reach under the protection of the roof. The various destinations of the buses were indicated on boards fixed to the columns opposite their stands. A strict control was kept over the cabs. Only forty-five were allowed inside the station at any one time, the proprietor paying the railway company a £2 deposit for each 'privilege' cab. In case of complaint the deposit was forfeited, the driver dismissed from the yard. As cabs left the station, their destination and number were noted by the railway police as a precaution against lost property and an aid in the investigation of crime and complaints.

Facilities were provided for loading the private carriages of the wealthier clients on to flat wagons whilst their horses were led into a box. This was the 1837 equivalent of Motorail, with one small difference – the passengers could if they wished remain in their own carriage throughout the rail journey. It was a tiresome business for the railway staff, as passengers using the service would often arrive at the last minute, causing delay to the train while the loading procedure was carried through.

At first, the resources of the new station were not overtaxed. There were but three outward trains and an equal number of arrivals each day, serving Harrow, Watford and Boxmoor and covering the $24\frac{1}{2}$ miles in just over an hour. On April 9th, 1838, the line reached Watling Street at Denbigh Hall (just beyond Bletchley). Through passengers to Birmingham were then conveyed from Euston, travelling over the uncompleted section between Denbigh Hall and Rugby in the road coaches of Chaplin & Horne. The rail link was completed on September 17th, with nine trains each way daily between Euston and Birmingham, covering the $112\frac{3}{4}$ miles in five and a quarter hours or more, against one and a half hours today.

At Birmingham, rail connexions were available to Liverpool

and Manchester. Before the London & Birmingham Railway became part of the London & North Western Railway in 1846, the opening of new lines had given Euston access to Preston, Derby, York and Edinburgh. The west-coast line to Scotland was completed on February 15th, 1848.

Soon after the opening of Euston, a second and larger office building, containing an open Doric colonnade of eight bays, was erected north of the first. This was subsequently included in the core block around the Great Hall, and the columns, which were in its east wall, survived on platform 6 until the demolition of the old station in 1962.

THE FIRST RAILWAY HOTELS

Two railway hotels, the first of their kind in London, were opened at Euston in September 1839. Simple in style and stucco-covered, they were designed by Philip Hardwick Sr, and placed in front of the portico, one either side, thus initiating the destruction of the vista and the crowding-in of the classical screen. On the west side was the Victoria, unlicensed and unpretentious, officially described as 'dormitory and coffee room'. The superior establishment on the opposite side, the Euston, catering for first-class passengers, was managed by the aptly-named Mr Bacon, a former steward of the Athenaeum.

These two four-storey buildings were linked in 1881 by a new block in 'the modern French style', detailed by J. Maclaren, a very second-rate affair which utterly destroyed the view of Hardwick's screen from the Euston Road. But by this time the 'embellishment' of which the London & Birmingham directors had been so proud was out of fashion, regarded as little more than a nuisance. As if to mock it, the hotel was supported over the roadway by four rows of horrible cast-iron Doric columns stuck in a poky opening which extended only to first-floor level. There were some compensations; the £30,000, 141-bedroom hotel soon earned a good name among travellers. Writing of it in the *Railway Magazine* early in

1914, Basil Mercer said, 'comfort is studied rather than display, and the fact that English waiters are employed ought to gladden the heart of every patriotic Englishman'. After suffering some damage in the Second World War, the Euston Hotel was finally closed in May 1963 when it was demolished to make room for the new station.

By 1845 some 140 staff were employed at Euston to attend to the needs of the passengers and mails using the twenty-two trains in and out each day. Some strain on the original platform accommodation was already becoming evident. George Carr Glyn, the L & BR chairman, told the Royal Commission on Metropolitan Termini that in the summer and autumn of 1845, 'the Post Office were so late that the 8.30 PM Lancashire Mail was frequently delayed until the 9 PM departure time of the Yorkshire Mail; the confusion was very great, and the company decided to separate the Yorkshire traffic'.

This separation was achieved in 1846 by the provision of new departure and arrival platforms (later numbered 9 and 10) on the vacant land originally reserved for the GWR, to the west of the 1837 station and cab yard. Platform 9 remained 'the York' to railwaymen until it finally disappeared in 1963, although the main flow of York traffic was diverted to the more direct route of the Great Northern Railway after that line had reached London in 1850. At the same time as the construction of the new platforms, houses in Whittlebury Street, on the extreme western boundary of the original Euston site, were demolished to make room for a long railway office block, running north from Drummond Street. By 1849 the original arrival platform had been lengthened to 900 ft and a third carriage siding had been added between the 1837 platforms.

THE GREAT HALL

The second splendour of old Euston, the Great Hall, opened on May 27th, 1849, was a combined concourse and waiting-room which set the pattern for many similar halls in large stations abroad. It formed part of a 220-ft by 168-ft block erected in 1846–9 by William Cubitt & Co at a cost of £150,000. Despite the employment of an eminent architect, this large complex of buildings was erected with virtually no regard either to the future development of the station or its existing layout. By the nature of its plan and position, it could not but distort the future growth of the station, virtually splitting the whole area into separate parts, and, owing to the shape of the site, making it quite impossible to build anything but short platforms behind it. Given that it was to be a central feature of the terminus, it is also odd that it was not placed symmetrically with the portico, but a little to the west of it.

After passing through the portico and the yard behind, passengers alighted from their conveyances under an awning at the south end of this new building and entered through one of five doorways. These led into an outer vestibule, 64 ft by 22 ft, floored with a mosaic pavement of patent 'metallic lava'. Five more entrances opened into the Great Hall.

This huge chamber was 125 ft 6 ins long by 61 ft 4 ins wide, and 62 ft high. At its northern end, a curved double staircase in stone led up to a central flight serving a 16-ft wide vestibule and a gallery round the walls. Beyond the vestibule were a shareholders' meeting-room, board room, various committee rooms and the suites of the company's principal officers.

The meeting-room, with space for some 400 shareholders, was a beautiful apartment in the Renaissance style, with pairs of marble pillars around the walls. The main features of the board room were a sculptured plaster ceiling and a great yellow pine table.

Few other English buildings could offer anything to match the deeply-coffered ceiling of the Great Hall, embellished with massive curved consoles and plaster bas-reliefs in each corner, the whole beautifully lit by attic windows. The bas-reliefs, measuring 10 ft by 7 ft, were in pairs; with busty, long-thighed women and muscular men, they symbolized London, Birming-

ham, Northampton, Chester, Manchester, Carlisle, Lancashire
and Liverpool.

Above the Doric portal of the meeting-room was a stone
group incorporating a judicious Victorian mix – Britannia, a
lion, a ship, Mercury, the Arts and the Sciences. Both sculpture and bas-reliefs were the work of John Thomas.[5] The
decoration was completed by mock columns, four double ones
at the north end, four single ones at the south, all 24 ft 7 ins
high. Contemporary accounts described the style as 'Roman-
Ionic'. Modern architectural writers have found other influ-
ences. Whatever it was, it was undoubtedly impressive, and no
other London station had anything to match this huge room.

Such display was inevitably expensive. Every effort was
made to cut the cost where this could be done without dimin-
ishing the effect. The walls were decorated with grey Martin's
cement to simulate granite, and the columns were of plaster,
marbled to suggest red granite. In 1852 a Carrara marble
statue of George Stephenson by E. H. Baily was placed at the
foot of the staircase. Over the years, clutter accumulated, including slot machines and a number of railway models in large
glass cases.

To the east of the hall was the main booking-hall, 60 ft by
40 ft, matched on the opposite side by a smaller booking-hall,
56 ft by 33 ft, for the midlands and the branch lines. West of
the Great Hall block, on the other side of what was later
Platform 10, a new building, long and narrow, housed the
parcels office. In line with it, to the south, were the Queen's
Apartments, an early example of the VIP lounge, intended to
afford privacy and comfort to royalty and other notables using
the railway. There were two rooms, one an antechamber, both
decorated in the 'Greek' style, with white and buff walls
'painted in large panels with the most fairy-like scroll orna-
ments and flowers'. The windows of the main room stretched
from floor to ceiling, and when they were opened, the
privileged users could step straight on to the departure platform.[6] These facilities were apparently scorned, as within a few

years the premises were devoted to more practical purposes, becoming an extension of the parcels office.

After the splendours of the portico and the Great Hall, the rest of Euston came as something of an anti-climax. A writer of the 1850s commented:

> ... as is common in this country ... the spirit of the pro-prietors evaporated with the outworks ... We cannot bestow unqualified praise upon the station arrangements at Euston. Comfort has been sacrificed to magnificence ... the waiting-rooms, refreshment stand, and *other conveniences* are as ill-contrived as possible; while a vast hall with magnificent roof and scagliola pillars appears to have swallowed up all the money, and all the light of the establishment. The first-class waiting-room is dull to a fearful degree, and finished in the dreariest style of economy. The second-class waiting-room is a dark cavern, with nothing better than a borrowed light ...[7]

Apart from the addition of a small bay platform on the east side, behind the Great Hall (later No 7), to accommodate the Kensington (Addison Road) trains in 1863, there were no further substantial changes until 1869-74. Then, stimulated by the arrival in London of its competitor, the Midland, the LNWR set about adding a little grandeur and some more plat-forms.

A strip of ground was acquired between the hotels and Euston Road to accommodate an 80-ft-wide approach drive. At the south end of this, J. B. Stansby, the company's architect, provided square two-storey entrance lodges, faced with Port-land stone, panelled and rusticated. Incised and gilded letters on the quoin stones proclaimed the names of the principal stations of the LNWR, many of them, such as Peterborough, Leicester and Swansea, to be reached much more expeditiously from other establishments up and down the road.

In the west lodge, the guide-book publishers and tourist agents Norton & Shaw established a branch office, whilst the other was used as a small parcels office. This new entrance, opened in 1870, was graced by a bronze statue of Robert

Stephenson by Baron Carlo Marochetti, presented to the LNWR
by the Institution of Civil Engineers, in whose vaults it had
been gathering dust for some years. Behind Stephenson, the
LNWR later erected a memorial to the 3,719 employees killed
in the 1914–18 War.

For eleven years, until the enlargement of the hotel
destroyed it, the drive enhanced the vista of Hardwick's screen
from the Euston Road. A touch of emphasis was added by
placing the station name in incised gilded letters on the
architrave of the portico.

In the station itself, extensive improvements were carried out
on the east side. New platforms (1 and 2) were completed in
1873, together with a cab entrance from Seymour Street (now
Eversholt Street) at the north end leading to a cab road between them. The space for this enlargement was obtained by
demolishing a row of small houses on the west side of Seymour
Street and by removing the 1837 carriage shed (a new shed
was built on the up side at Willesden). Whilst this work was
going on, in 1872, the original 1837 roof was raised 6 ft to
provide more room for the dispersal of smoke, not to mention
a little more grandeur. An area 900 ft by 130 ft was jacked up
hydraulically and all the new pedestals were inserted in the
course of a week.

ADDING DREARINESS

From 1881 onwards, new offices were constructed east and
west of the station yard and along the Drummond Street front
on the west side. These added greatly to the heavy dreariness
of the old Euston and continued the process of destroying
Hardwick's work. The westernmost pier and lodge were
demolished to make way for them. So difficult was the lodge
to remove, that the contractors were forced to blow it up. The
London & Birmingham had been built to last.

A continuing growth of long-distance traffic made it necessary to expand the western side of the station to the fullest

possible extent, and this was accomplished between 1887 and
1892. It was a major project, involving the diversion of Cardington Street over the burial ground of St James's, Westminster. In disturbing the dead, care was taken that there would
be no cause for the kind of public outcry that had arisen during
the construction of the approaches to St Pancras. Each corpse
was provided with a new coffin and reinterred at St Pancras
Cemetery, Finchley, at the expense of the LNWR. Acworth
records in *The Railways of England*, that 'a doctor and an
inspector were constantly present at either end on behalf of
the company, to see that nothing was done which might offend
against either due reverence for the dead or due regard for
the health of the living'. When it was all over, the ground was
probed to make sure nobody was left behind.

The lengthy western departure platforms (12–15) were
brought into use on July 1st, 1892, together with a separate
booking-office and cab entrance in Drummond Street. This
station within a station caused much confusion, so much so,
that in the heat of the moment, comparisons were drawn with
the old Waterloo, though it was never as bad as that. Eventually the situation was put right by extending the main cab
yard westwards under the office block and by opening a new
booking-office near Platform 12, in a better position to serve
all parts of the station. A casualty of the west-side alterations
was the down-side carriage shed, replaced by an additional
shed at Willesden in 1888. On the east side, the 'wooden
platform' for local trains (Nos 4 and 5) was completed in 1891
on the site of the carriage roads remaining from the original
station.

Euston had now reached its maximum extent of fifteen platforms, numbered from east to west. Arriving trains used 1 to
3, suburban trains 4 and 5. Platform 6 handled both arrivals
and departures, including royal trains, and (until the very end
of the old Euston), the famous 'West Coast Postal'. Number
7 was another local platform, whilst 8 to 10 were used for
parcels and occasionally for local trains. Served from Carding-

ton Street by an approach road over Platforms 13 to 15, Platform 11 was used only for parcels, milk and fish traffic. Platforms 12 to 15 were allocated to main-line departures. Between 5 and 6 was a third road, 'the horse-box line'.

The area behind the Great Hall, too cramped for passenger platforms, was known as 'the field' and contained several short reception sidings. At the outer end of Platforms 10 and 11 were a carriage dock and an engine siding (later another siding, 'B', was put in between platforms 10 and 11). Between 11 and 12 was the 'brake pit road' and between 13 and 14, 'road No 2'. Alongside Platform 15 were engine sidings, and, at the outer end, an engine turntable. The enlargement works were rounded off in 1898 by the demolition of the two-arch Ampthill Square bridge and its replacement by a girder structure, permitting the arrival platforms to be extended and the approach curves to be eased.

All this patching and stretching of the 1837 station only served to emphasize Euston's unworthiness as the London terminus of the self-styled 'Premier Line'. At least some of the directors were ashamed of it, and in 1898–9 the board considered a scheme for complete reconstruction, with the frontage brought up to Euston Square Gardens. An Act was obtained in 1900, but the financial disruptions of the South African war enabled the company to postpone what must have looked like a very difficult decision. Piecemeal development was to continue for another sixty years.

Until this time, there was but one down running line between Camden and Euston, a state of affairs that caused much difficulty and delay and had to be put right, whether or not a new station were built. Work began in 1901 on the widening of the cutting and approach lines, continuing until 1906. Some half-million tons of clay were removed, making room for the new lines and two new carriage sheds, one each side of the tracks. These sheds provided cover for some 350 coaches, and with the additional sidings put in at the same time, eliminated many of the unprofitable 11-mile return workings to the Willesden depot. (In 1953 carriage servicing was transferred from Willesden depot to a large new installation at Stonebridge Park.)

A new double line was provided in the cutting for engine movements to and from the Camden depot, and a subway with a gradient of 1 in 50 was constructed to carry an up engine line and down empty carriage line from the arrival side to the carriage sidings and shed on the west side. 'Backed out' by their own engines through this subway, the carriages of arriving trains, after servicing in the west yard, could be moved direct to the departure platforms without interfering with other traffic. Upon the completion of this work, four running lines were available for passenger trains in and out of the terminus.

From the down to the up side, the arrangement was:

eleven-road carriage shed
four 'backing-out' roads
up engine line No 1
down fast
down slow
up slow
up fast
up engine line No 2
down empty carriage line
five-road carriage shed

The last work carried out by the LNWR improved the amenities of the terminus. In 1913–14 a new booking concourse was formed south of the Great Hall by using a 150-ft by 30-ft section of the cab yard. The old booking-offices were converted to refreshment rooms. When this work was complete, in 1915–16, the hall was renovated and repainted. Electric light had been installed throughout the station in 1905, but the gas globes in the hall were left undisturbed.

Euston has always been predominantly a main-line station; suburban traffic was sparse for many years, but an hourly service to Watford was started on June 1st, 1879, after completion of quadrupling between Camden and Willesden Junction. There was no connexion with the Underground system until May 12th, 1907, when the City & South London Tube railway opened its extension from the Angel. This was followed on June 22nd by the opening of a second Tube station, on the Charing Cross, Euston & Hampstead Railway. At the insistence of the LNWR, both Tube lines had street stations, the CSLR in Eversholt Street (Euston House is now over the site), and the CCEHR in Drummond Street, but there were also lifts to a small booking-hall beneath the eastern side of the terminus, with stairs up to Platforms 3 and 6. The Metropolitan was a good five minutes' walk away, at Gower Street, renamed Euston Square (a misnomer) on November 1st, 1909, as a late reaction to the opening of the Tube stations at Euston. The arrival of the Tube railways, in particular Parliamentary approval for Tube extensions from Golders Green to Edgware and Watford, spurred the LNWR into some serious thinking about suburban traffic.

In 1906 plans were announced for a new electric line alongside the main lines as far as Watford, with a terminal loop in Tube beneath Euston. After the LNWR had taken over the management of the North London Railway in 1909, and following negotiations with the Underground company, this scheme was wisely modified. In 1911 it was agreed that the incoming traffic from the new suburban line would be split into three streams: LNWR electric trains to Euston and Broad Street, and Bakerloo Tube trains to the West End via a new Tube connexion between Queen's Park and Paddington. The electric trains into Euston were to run into the existing station instead of an underground loop. To segregate them from the main-line traffic, there were to be further improvements to the approaches, including new twin tubes of 16-ft 4-in diameter through Primrose Hill, and a system of burrowing junctions at Chalk Farm. There would also be a new 955-yd single-track tunnel passing under all lines and the Regent's Canal, carrying the up empty carriage road from the north side of the line at Camden to

the west carriage yard, on the other side some way down the
bank. These works were delayed by the First World War, and
were not finally completed until 1922. A public service of 630-
volt dc third- and fourth-rail electric trains between Euston and
Watford began on July 10th, 1922. In the terminus, Platforms
4, 5 and 7 were electrified.

At the 1923 grouping, the LNWR was absorbed into the London Midland & Scottish Railway, a company soon proud to
call itself the largest private enterprise in the British Empire.
Despite this boast, it did not make any very impressive changes
at Euston, at least not until 1935, when it proposed to tear the
whole place down and rebuild.

During 1927 the Great Hall was renovated for a second time.
On this occasion the advice of Sir Edwin Lutyens, the eminent architect, resulted in the walls and pillars being coated
with 'imitation red Egyptian porphyry'. Electric light replaced
gas in the original globes. Three years later, 'as a further step
forward in its modernization',[8] the hall received in its midst a
large and hideous inquiry and reservation bureau. Very little
else happened. Platform loudspeakers were installed in 1934
and a year later, Platforms 12 and 13 were lengthened.

RUMBLINGS OF RECONSTRUCTION

But behind the scenes great plans were being made. As early as
1933, at the annual dinner of the Royal Institute of British
Architects, Sir Josiah Stamp, chairman of the LMSR, had
flown the kite, mentioning the difficulty of rebuilding Euston
without demolishing the Great Hall, and wondering whether
he would be accused of vandalism if he scrapped Scott's St
Pancras 'obsolete as an hotel and useless as offices' (the significance of this last point will be seen in a moment). At the
end of 1935 it was announced that Euston Station, hotel and
offices would be rebuilt with the aid of a Government loan
guarantee under the Railways (Agreement) Act of 1935.
Percy Thomas, president of the Royal Institute of British

Plan of Euston 1953. From the Railway Magazine, March 1953

Architects, was appointed consulting architect to cooperate with the company's architect and chief civil engineer in preparing plans and designs. These duly emerged, and showed that the vast new terminus would have a hotel and office frontage on the Euston Road. Helicopters would be accommodated on the roof (a suburban service for directors?) and there would be sufficient room for the traffic of St Pancras. The Great Hall, which stood in the way, would have to go, but it might prove possible to re-erect Hardwick's portico along the Euston Road front.

On July 12th, 1938, Sir Josiah sat down in the shareholders' meeting-room of the doomed Great Hall complex to throw a switch which set off charges at Caldon Low quarries, releasing 100,000 tons of limestone to build the new station. After this little drama, nothing more was done apart from the erection of some flats at Kentish Town to accommodate those who would be displaced by the new works. Once again a war had intervened.

Air raids in 1940 damaged the roof of the Great Hall, and a bomb which landed between Platforms 2 and 3 wrecked offices and part of the hotel. All in all, the Germans made a pretty poor job of demolishing the old place. Battered by heavy wartime use, the shabby hole-and-corner muddle that was Euston passed into the hands of British Railways with a great deal of other property in similar state. Unable to obtain the capital necessary for complete reconstruction, BR continued the patching-up policy. Surprisingly it spent over £500,000 on this.

One of the first of BR's gifts to Euston was a large train-arrival bureau erected at the south end of Platforms 1 to 3 in June 1951. Here, in almost cinema-like atmosphere and comfort, ninety-two people could sit, watching train information back-projected on to a twelve-panel screen, savouring the widespread disruption, railway and personal, that lay behind the bland announcements that the train from X and Y was seventy minutes late at Rugby, and that from A and B, ninety minutes late at Watford.

The next step was to get the awkward track layout sorted out. Long trains standing in an arrival platform fouled access to other platforms, holding up incoming trains outside. Nothing could be done about this until the Ampthill Square bridge at the north end of the station and the old No 2 signal box were moved out of the way. The offending bridge was demolished in January 1952 and the signal box disappeared when the signalling was modernized later in that year. This done, the track layout was simplified, and the number of diamond crossings reduced from eighteen to five. At the same time, Platforms 1 to 3, 6, 7 and 15 were lengthened, the extensions varying from 40 ft on 15 to 190 ft on 1. In 1954–5, Platforms 12 to 15 were repositioned and widened, the siding between 14 and 13 becoming 13 platform road after 13 had been widened; 12 was moved similarly, the old Platform 12 line becoming a siding. New cantilevered supports for the building on the extreme western side of the station provided room for the new Platform 15 road.

In view of what was to come, it is poignant to record that the Great Hall and shareholders' meeting-room were carefully redecorated to Hardwick's original designs during 1951–3. The general appearance of the hall was much improved by the removal of the intruding LMSR inquiry bureau.

A 'Continental refreshment terrace' was opened at the south end of the departure platforms in September 1958. Here passengers were able to sip BR tea amidst coal smuts and diesel fumes – a scene worthy of the pencil of Osbert Lancaster.

Attention was next directed to the ticket-issuing facilities. A new suburban booking-office, equipped with a Westinghouse-Garrard ticket-printing and issuing machine, was installed on Platforms 4 and 5 in 1958. Two years later, new main-line booking-offices, with ten AEG Multiprinter machines, were opened either side of the main entrance to the Great Hall. Euston thus became the first London terminus to have fully-mechanized ticket-issuing equipment.

These improvements did little to alleviate the dreary, soot-begrimed squalor of the old station. To the ordinary passenger, it was a place to get away from as quickly as possible, yet for those with hearts to feel and eyes to see it was heavy with history, a station of character. There was still a thrill to be had as one stood at the buffers of Platforms 1 and 2 watching powerful locomotives rolling in round the sweeping curve with well-filled expresses from the north; and the redecorated Great Hall seized the imagination, evoking as it did the awesome dignity of the 'Premier Line' and the great Victorians who built it up. But the portico, with a tobacco kiosk wedged incongruously into its east side, was filthy and sad; crowded about, it could not be properly seen and many must have passed through the station unaware of its existence.

When we heard in 1959 that all this was to disappear, that at long last a new Euston was to be built, no one was much troubled. The old place would go without many tears, and everyone assumed without a second thought that some way of saving the Great Hall and the portico would be found.

OLD GLORY DESTROYED

An integral part of a great scheme for the electrification of the lines to Birmingham, Manchester and Liverpool, the new station was to be a terminus worthy of what was virtually a new railway. As the LMSR planners had already realized, Euston could not be enlarged without removing the Hardwick screen and the Great Hall, for the only possible space for expansion was to the south, and the historic buildings were in the path of new platforms. So it was that late in 1959 BR gave the London County Council the required two months' notice of its intention to demolish the portico and the hall; both were on the statutory list of buildings of achitectural and historical interest. The LCC gave permission, provided the screen was re-erected in an appropriate dignified and open setting, but their consultants could find no way of preserving the Great Hall without impeding the operational requirements of the railway.

Half its battle won, BR strongly opposed the LCC's re-erection stipulation, pointing out that the portico could not be moved and rebuilt for less than £190,000, whereas the cost of demolition was but £12,000. The baby was then placed firmly in the Government's lap, with the LCC bravely promising financial help if others would do likewise. In July 1961, the Minister of Transport, Ernest Marples, announced that the preservation of the portico did not justify the expenditure involved; but this was not the end of the story.

A strong opposition was organized. Many experts questioned the estimate of £190,000, and it was said that a Canadian firm would undertake to move the portico on rollers for less than half that sum. The Earl of Euston, the Earl of Rosse, John Betjeman, and many eminent architects led the battle against what the Conservative *Daily Telegraph* had called 'a disgraceful action'. On October 16th, 1961, with scaffolding already erected around the great Doric columns, seventy-five architects and students demonstrated inside the Great Hall, hanging placards on the portico. Eight days later, a fifteen-man deputation, led by the president of the Royal Academy, Sir Charles Wheeler, attended upon Prime Minister Harold Macmillan in his room at the House of Commons. But it was all to no avail.

In his reply to Sir Charles, the Prime Minister pointed out that not only would the removal cost £190,000, but even if it were thought right to spend such a sum, there was no suitable site where the re-erected portico would not look incongruous. It could not be placed in front of the new station, as this was to come right up to the Euston Road. Its fate sealed, the 'Arch' felt the first blows of the breakers on November 6th, 1961. Four months later, it had disappeared from sight. In case of a miracle, the contractor carefully numbered the stones.

REBUILDING BEGINS AT LAST

Taylor Woodrow Construction Ltd was awarded the contract for stage one of the new Euston in the summer of 1962. Slowly, the process of platform reconstruction proceeded across the station site from east to west; down came the Great Hall and its less worthy surroundings. With that wonderful calm ingenuity that is a professional characteristic of railway civil engineers, a new station was erected amidst the ruins of the old while train services continued through it all.

An 11,000-sq-ft temporary building, containing ticket offices, waiting-room, shops, a post office and an inquiry office, was opened on April 1st, 1963, to serve the needs of passengers during the rebuilding period. There was some inconvenience, and many passengers were diverted to other stations, but Euston remained very much alive throughout the whole operation.

By 1966, fifteen passenger platforms had been completed, together with parcel and restaurant-car docks on the Cardington Street side, twenty platforms in all. Lengths varied from 1,300 ft to 700 ft, the main platforms being 37 ft wide. The first regular workings of main-line electric trains began in November 1965, to be followed on January 3rd, 1966, by the full electric service. In conjunction with the construction of the new platforms, the approach tracks were rearranged to give complete interchangeability of routes.

Platforms 8, 9, 10 were fitted with conductor rails as well as overhead wires to accommodate the Watford suburban trains (the conductors were removed from 8 in 1967). Most main-line electric trains were turned round at the platforms, only night-trains, Pullmans and certain day expresses going out to Willesden carriage depot. It was soon found that there was insufficient stabling space for the electric locomotives and some use was made of Platform 11 for this purpose.

Above Platforms 3 to 18 in the northern part of the station was a fully-mechanized parcels depot, 5 acres in extent, opened on August 7th, 1966. Road vehicles reached this from Barnby Street via elevated roadways, leaving at the north end of Cardington Street. Parcels were moved to and from the platforms by ramps and goods lifts.

At the bend of Cardington Street, on the site of the locomotive turntable, a four-storey Signals and Telecommunica-
tions Centre was opened in September 1965.

From the time the new station was first planned in the late
1950s, BR had hoped to find a large part of the expenditure
from the proceeds of commercial lettings, but the LCC frowned
on the idea of offices over the station. The BR plan involved four
tower blocks, one 365 ft high, together with a 300-ft-high hotel
between the station frontage and Euston Road. It was unfortunate that the final proposal went to the LCC just one week
after the Government had issued a White Paper stating that
the rate of office growth in central London could not be
allowed to continue without more effective control, and that
in future, most new offices would have to be outside the
central area. A few weeks later, in March 1963, the LCC
told BR there could be no offices at Euston other than for BR
staff.

A NEW GREAT HALL

Fresh plans were then prepared, with the possibility of a hotel
tower block still in mind, and Taylor Woodrow began work on
the passenger building in May 1966. Designed by R. L. Moor-
croft, the London Midland Region architect, this long, low
unassuming structure flanked Euston Square, just south of
Drummond Street, part of which was covered. Between the
building and the square was a paved open space, known as the
piazza, above a parking area for 230 cars.

Completed in large part by September 1968, the new passenger building was opened by the Queen on October 14th. On
the Euston Square frontage, passengers approached a 647-ft
colonnade through which they passed from the piazza to the
concourse hall. This colonnade was a neat link with the Euston
of 1837, which had a similar feature on the street side. Har-
monizing with the great grey mass of the station behind, the
frontage elevations were in black and white, polished black

granite cladding on the rectangular columns, and white mosaic horizontal facings, with glazed screens between.

The passenger hall, some 200 ft wide by 150 ft deep under a 36-ft-high main roof, was quickly named the Great Hall, after its predecessor. Well lit and air-conditioned, it was entirely free from the trolley traffic that is such a great nuisance to passengers at some other termini. The ticket barriers to Platforms 1 to 15 were on the north side, at the head of gently sloping ramps; also on this side, below the clerestory, was a large electro-mechanical departure indicator set between illuminated advertisement panels. To the west of the hall was the self-contained 'Travel Centre', with its information, reservation and booking facilities. Along the north and east sides were various shops, refreshment rooms and lavatories, some of those on the east at first-floor level. Shops were also to be found in the colonnade either side of the hall, altogether offering a greater variety of services than at any other British station, including a tailor, a hairdresser, a bank, book and record shops, an off-licence, a travel agency, a betting shop, and a photographic shop. The post office however was not replaced although there were posting and postal-vending machines in the hall.

Immediately below the concourse was the large new Underground booking-hall, reached by escalators, but also linked directly to the suburban platforms by subway. From December 1st, 1968, Victoria Line service was available from Euston, in addition to the Northern Line. No connexion was made to the Metropolitan and Circle Lines at Euston Square; should a subway eventually be built, it will need a travolator, as the Euston platform ends are still a long way back from Euston Road.

Apart from the parcels facilities already mentioned, all vehicular traffic was confined to basement level. Taxis and private cars entered from the west side, and after setting down at a platform with direct access to the concourse, could leave for the outgoing station taxi rank, the basement car park, or the street, as appropriate. In the northern part of the basement, reached by a service road from Eversholt Street, were unloading docks for mail, newspapers, and shop and catering supplies.

Two relics of the old Euston were preserved in the new. The Stephenson statue adorned the piazza, and John Thomas' Britannia group from the doorway of the shareholders' meeting-room was to be found just inside the entrance to the Sprig Buffet.

At the time of writing, the last of the old buildings on the west side are being demolished, for the completion of the new station in 1969. Now that the final dispositions can be seen, there is no doubt that room could have been found for the portico between the frontage and the main road. We can only imagine how it might have looked, cleaned and restored, its noble lines adding strength and significance to the unpretentious new frontage.

SIGNALLING AND ACCIDENTS

Until the last decade of the nineteenth century the signalling arrangements at Euston were distinctly primitive, but on April 27th, 1891, as part of the general improvements to the west side, a new main signal cabin, Euston No 2, was opened in the yard, opposite Platforms 7 and 8. This contained 288 levers in two long frames, at which the men worked face to face. The old No 1 box, or 'bell house', with twenty levers, strung above the cab road between Platforms 2 and 3, dated from the 1870s. It remained in use to control the workings of Platforms 1 to 5. Communication between Nos 1 and 2 boxes was effected by means of a ringing code and describers; the former was necessary as the signalman in No 2 could not see the arrival roads, and there was no track circuiting.

With the approach lines improvements of 1901–6, subsidiary boxes Nos 1, 3 and 4 were converted to electric power signalling, with point motors and solenoid-worked semaphores and discs. No 3 box ('Port Arthur') was situated at the station end of the backing-out roads on the down side, and No 4 was between up engine line No 1 and the subway. Later, many of the signals controlled from the main No 2 box were changed to the same electrical system, and in March 1906 this box was given two new tappet-locking frames designed by A. M. Thompson, arranged along the windows at either side of the cabin, 255 levers in all.

A serious accident occurred in 1924, shortly after the inauguration of the suburban electric services. At 7.53 AM on April 26th, a six-car up electric train struck the rear of the 5.30 AM Cup Final excursion from Coventry, made up to fourteen coaches. Five passengers were killed in the main-line train, which was standing at the up slow home signal for Euston No 4 box. The motorman of the electric train was trapped in his cab for five hours. As a result of what the Ministry of Transport inspecting officer described as a 'false mental impression', the signalman had given *train out of section* for an up Scots express, which had been standing on the up fast line alongside the excursion, on his up slow instead of his up fast instrument, subsequently accepting the electric train on the line already occupied by the excursion. Owing to smoke and steam under Park Street bridge, the motorman had not been able to see the tail light of the excursion until he was within 16 yd of it.

Although some colour-light signalling was installed by the LMSR in 1934, this was on a very limited scale, and Euston's signalling remained crude for the working of such a large and important station.

Just how crude was illuminated by the inspector's report of an accident which took place fifteen years later, on August 6th, 1949. On the morning of that day, empty stock was being propelled from one of the backing-out roads into Platform 12 when it was wrongly directed into Platform 13, occupied by stock for the 8.37 AM Manchester train, which it ran into at about 5 mph. The inspector noted that there was no track circuiting and nothing in No 2 box to show which platforms were occupied, apart from a slate on which the signalmen were supposed to chalk up platform occupation, rubbing out the entry when the train left. Track circuiting was installed on Platforms 12 to 15 soon after this accident.

Modern signalling came at last in 1952. The new box, opened on October 6th, had 227 all-electric levers in a Westinghouse frame (61 point levers, including 2 ground frame releases, 126 signal levers, including 50 for ground signals, and 40 spares). The box, on the up side just north of the Hampstead Road bridge, replaced Euston Nos 1, 2 and 3, and the main-line controls in Euston No 4. It worked the station's whole new complex of colour-light signals and electro-pneumatic points (the first at any London terminus) as far out as Camden No 1 box. There were 32 long-range multi-aspect colour-light signals, 26 position-light subsidiary signals, 21 short-range yellow-aspect signals (for movements from running signals to sidings without track circuits) and theatre-type route indicators.

This expensive equipment remained in use for only thirteen years. The new box, opened in September 1965 as part of the rebuilt station, was on the west side between Cardington Street and Ampthill Square. It had a Westinghouse control panel split into two rings, allowing two signalmen each to set up a route simultaneously. Working with Ericsson train-describer equipment, the panel was of the entrance-exit type, combining operating controls and indications for 755 routes. Signalmen and panel were in an air-conditioned room. Control of the main lines extended as far as South Hampstead, that for the dc lines as far as Queen's Park No 3, and that for the North London route as far as Primrose Hill. In all, the station and control area contained 67 colour-light signals (only 4 of them automatic), 82 ground signals, and 84 sets of points. Euston No 4, which had become Euston Carriage Shed box in 1952, and Camden Nos 1 and 2 were all closed, as was the 1952 box.

CHAPTER THREE

ST PANCRAS

MISTAKEN FOR A CHURCH

It is said that an American tourist staying at a Bloomsbury hotel once asked for the nearest place of worship, and was directed to St Pancras Church. Taking a wrong turning, he found himself confronted with St Pancras Station, which he duly entered, sufficiently deceived to doff his hat. On meeting a resplendently-attired individual whom he took to be some sort of beadle, he inquired the time of the next service, and was somewhat abashed to be given the departure times of half a dozen trains. This story does not strain credulity too far; St Pancras is a most impressive building, with Gothic architecture that imparts a distinctly ecclesiastical flavour. Its structure provides undeniable impact, for not only is there the intricate, imposing frontage, but inside, and in some ways more precious, is a beautifully-engineered train shed, one of the finest in the world. In truth a worthy temple for the steam locomotive, St Pancras was the Midland Railway's contribution to the London railway scene. Its splendours were not surpassed by any terminus built subsequently.

The Midland had reached Hitchin in May 1857, and from February 1st following, its trains ran into London over the Great Northern main line. Freight and minerals were flowing south in increasing quantity over the Midland, but because the GNR jealously imposed a cruel toll of 1s 9d a ton on coal carried over its line, compared with 2d for other minerals, most Midland coal continued to come south over the London & North Western, which had handled the Midland's London traffic for many years.

Little satisfaction was to be had from these arrangements.

The coal was delayed at Rugby, and over the single pair of tracks between Hitchin and London, the GNR naturally gave priority to its own trains. Matters came to a head in 1862, when both Midland and GNR were handling a very heavy excursion traffic into London for the Great International Exhibition in South Kensington. Most of the special exhibition trains, including those of the Midland, were accommodated in the GNR goods yard at Kings Cross, where amenities were sketchy, and platforms inadequate or non-existent. This, and the delays were bad enough, but as summer came and the pressure on track space grew, the GNR demanded that the Midland make use of their own coal depot, which they had all but finished nearby. There was some hesitation on the Midland's part as to whether this was feasible, when, to show their temper, the GNR summarily cleared a number of Midland wagons from their yard.

Utterly himiliated by the events of 1862, the Midland board confirmed a decision already half-made – that the railway must have its own access to London. A Bill was prepared for a 49¾-mile line southwards from Bedford, presented to Parliament in the following year, and passed, despite not unexpected opposition from the GNR and the LNWR.

Mention has been made of a Midland coal depot at Kings Cross. Even before the decision was taken to build the London extension, the Midland was busy providing itself with extensive facilities for its metropolitan goods traffic, which had outgrown the accommodation the GNR was able to offer. Opened in stages between 1862 and 1865, the Midland goods and coal depot was sited between the North London Railway and the Regent's Canal, immediately to the west of the GNR yards, and to the north of Agar Town, a slum area from which it took its name. Naturally, in consenting to these arrangements, the GNR had hoped to stave off any ideas for a separate main line to London.

Despite the fact that coal and goods traffic provided the greater part of the Midland's revenues and the main incentive

for the London extension, the prestige value of a well-sited passenger terminus was not overlooked. To be fully competitive
with its rivals, the LNWR and GNR, the Midland realized it must
bring its passengers to the Royal Commission boundary at
Euston Road, despite the necessity to cross the canal and break
open an already built-up area. The matter was clinched when
the company was able to obtain for a moderate price the
eastern part of Lord Somers' estate, on the north side of
Euston Road.

William Barlow,[1] the Midland's consulting engineer, decided
to bring the line south from Camden Square on the level,
passing under the North London Railway, through the reeking
slums of Agar Town, and over the canal and the Fleet River.
This meant that the platforms of the terminus were to be some
20 ft above the Euston Road, despite a slight falling gradient
into the station, which was to cause a number of buffer-stop
collisions over the years and require shunting engines to assist
outgoing trains from the rear. During the first half of 1866,
several thousand houses in Agar Town and Somers Town,
almost all of them mean and squalid, were demolished to make
way for the railway. Evicted without compensation of any
kind, some 10,000 people crowded into adjacent areas, making
new slums and breeding grounds for epidemic disease. At the
southernmost point, seven streets were demolished to make
room for the $4\frac{1}{2}$-acre terminus. Also on the site of the station
was St Luke's, Kings Cross, a brand new church, which had
to be rebuilt in Kentish Town at the Midland's expense.

A corner of the much overcrowded burial ground of the old
St Pancras Church stood in the path of the works, and the
human remains, which existed in stratum to a considerable
depth, were reinterred in other cemeteries. Working conditions
amid the foetid ground, saturated as it was with decomposing
matter, were indescribably repulsive and difficult. At first, little
reverence was shown; bones were left lying about to become
the playthings of street urchins, and open coffins were seen on
the working site. A great furore arose in the newspapers, and

after protests in high quarters, more care was taken.

This havoc among the dead was largely the result of a decision to construct a double-track link between the Midland and the Metropolitan Railway, leaving the main line on the east side, just north of the North London Railway, at a point later known as St Paul's Road junction. Almost at once the line divided into a tunnel at 1 in 75, and it was the cut and cover work for this tunnel that broke into the graves. After passing diagonally under the main line, the tunnel recrossed it beneath St Pancras, joining the widened Metropolitan Railway just west of that company's Kings Cross Station. The widening of the Metropolitan (City Widened Lines) extended from Kings Cross to Farringdon Street, and was opened, for GNR passenger trains, on February 17th, 1868.

Another tunnel was built beneath the frontage of St Pancras Station, parallel with Euston Road, in anticipation of a widening of the Metropolitan westwards to Paddington. No such widening took place, and this work remained unused until March 15th, 1926, when a track was laid in it, connecting the Circle Line with the City Widened Lines, to afford some relief to the former. The spur was closed in 1935, and the tunnel incorporated in the new Metropolitan and Circle Lines station at Kings Cross, brought into use in 1941.

BASIS OF A FINE DESIGN

Work on the new terminus began in 1866, an early task being the enclosure in an iron pipe of the Fleet River, then virtually an open sewer.

Barlow's first plans for the station were for a double- or even triple-span roof above the elevated platforms; he intended to fill the air space below the rails with spoil from the tunnels. Discussions with James Allport,[2] the Midland's general manager, brought forward the suggestion that this basement area offered valuable storage space, readily accessible from the surrounding streets, and it was then decided that the whole area beneath the station should be vaulted and available for cellar-age.

It was this decision that led Barlow to think of a single-span roof, so it is perhaps not too great an exaggeration to say that St Pancras owes much of its grandeur to Burton beer. The problems and solutions were lucidly expounded by Barlow in a paper read to the Institution of Civil Engineers on March 20th, 1870. In order to make the best possible use of the base-ment space, columns and girders were employed instead of brick piers, and the spacing between the columns was that in the Burton beer warehouses, that is to say, the beer barrel became the unit of measurement. A roof of two or more spans would need to be supported by columns of large diameter which would penetrate the basement and thus interfere with this neat plan. Moreover, such columns would require extra strong foundations, presenting great engineering difficulties where they came over the tunnel beneath the station. Barlow realized that the station floor would form a ready-made tie for a roof of single span, and dared to propose this. Although the cost of a 240-ft-span roof would be higher than that of a double-span, he was encouraged by Allport's desire to have the maximum freedom of movement within the station, with flexibility to alter the platform and track plan to meet changes in traffic needs.

St Pancras was thus provided with its magnificent roof, still admired today as an outstanding piece of engineering. Barlow created the main design, but he left much of the detail to R. M. Ordish, an engineer who specialized in cast-iron roofs and suspension bridges. This breathtaking roof was 689 ft long, towering 100 ft above the rails at the apex of its ribs. At the crown, the arch was slightly pointed, as this was thought to offer some advantage in resisting the lateral action of the wind; by curious coincidence, this feature anticipated the Gothic architecture of the frontage. Each of the twenty-five channel and plate-iron ribs weighed almost 55 tons, and each was 29 ft 4 ins from its neighbour. No support was provided by the

SITE OF WAGON LIFT TO
PASSENGER STATION LEVEL

MIDLAND ROAD

SOMERS TOWN GOODS DEPOT AND POTATO MARKET

PANCRAS ROAD

Plans of St Pancras c 1958. From the Railway Magazine, *October 1968*

(*above*) *street level*
(*right*) *platform level*

PANCRAS ROAD

SIGNALBOX

to GOODS
DEPOT

GOODS WAY

PHOENIX ROAD

SITE OF WAGON LIFT TO LOWER LEVEL

TO ST.PAULS ROAD JUNCTION AND KENTISH TOWN

M I D L A N D   R O A D

P A N C R A S   R O A D

FORMER CAB APPROACH

PLATFORM NO.1   No.2

No.3   No.4

No.5

No.6

PARCEL OFFICE

No.7

CLOAK RM

LAV. UNDER

BOOKING
HALL

KITCHEN

DINING &
REFRESH

REFRESH
MENTS

KITCHEN

O F F I C E S

RAMP UP

RAMP DN.

EUSTON   ROAD

Metropolitan Line

PASSAGE
UP

TO METROPOLITAN
WIDENED LINES
AND MOORGATE

0   100   200   300 f

side walls, the ribs being held to their brick piers by massive
curved iron anchor plates, and tied by the main floor and 3-in-
diameter rods below. The tops of the brick piers were level
with the platforms. To give the maximum headroom near the
walls, the curvature of the roof arch was diminished from 160
ft to 57 ft radius at the haunches. The result of all this was a
clear space of 245 ft 6 ins across the station.

Before St Pancras was opened, the strength of the new structure was amply tested. As there was some delay in obtaining
bricks, the partly completed roof, boarded, slated and glazed,
was left for a time without the protection of the side walls.
During this period it withstood severe buffeting by the wind
without any perceptible movement. When erecting the frame-
work of the roof, the Butterley Company used two large timber
stages; with a load of two iron ribs, workmen and impedimenta,
these imposed a deadweight of some 350 tons on the station
flooring. Again there were no ill-effects.

After the opening of the station, an iron and glass windscreen
was completed across the outward end of the roof. At the other
end, the plan had been to close the roof off with the frontage
block, but later, to avoid any risk of smoke and steam entering
the hotel, a second gable and another glazed screen were provided to form a barrier.

When finished, the roof was painted dark brown, which did
not please Allport. He thought it looked 'exceedingly dull and
heavy, and ... marred, to some extent, the grand appearance
which the station would otherwise have exhibited';[3] it should,
he considered, be the colour of the sky (presumably he did not
mean the dark yellow so frequently seen in NW1 in the long
winters of the Steam Age). Allport's suggestion was taken up;
in 1877, F. S. Williams wrote in *The Midland Railway, Its
Rise and Progress*, that the roof had 'recently' been repainted
and decorated with 'a blue sky-like appearance'. Blues and
greys were used for subsequent repaintings.

We have already seen something of the strength of the
station floor. Carried on girders and 720 cast-iron columns, it

was formed of Mallet's buckle plates, and strong enough at any point to carry a locomotive, thus providing the maximum flexibility of track and platform arrangement. Beneath were the beer vaults, served by a network of tracks and turnplates, over which the wagons were moved by capstan and rope after descending in an hydraulic lift at the north end of the platforms. For many years the beer traffic flourished, requiring daily trains to the terminus, but road vehicles gradually eroded it after the 1920s, until it ceased altogether in the early 1960s. By 1967, all track and other salvageable material had been removed from the vaults so that they might be let for other uses, or perhaps filled in.

As the London extension approached completion little more than the bare bones of the terminus were ready to receive it. The first regular freight trains on the all-Midland route reached Agar Town goods station on September 9th, 1867. Next came passenger trains on local service between Bedford and Moorgate, using the tunnel under the terminus from July 13th, 1868. Finally, in the early hours of October 1st, 1868, without ceremony of any kind, St Pancras itself was opened to traffic. Booking-offices and other amenities were incomplete. Of the hotel which was to form the frontage only the foundations could be seen.

THE MIDLAND GRAND HOTEL

This hotel was to be the grandest, plushiest of its kind, a veritable palace to pamper and flatter the self-esteem of the industrial tycoons from the burgeoning midlands and north. Above it the Midland intended to place offices for its headquarters' staff. An architectural competition was held for this building in 1865.

'After more than once declining', Sir George Gilbert Scott[4] was persuaded to enter by his friend Joseph Lewis, a Midland Railway director. In September 1865, whilst the family were at a small hotel on Hayling Island, Scott's son fell ill;

the architect stayed on with his family throughout that month and the following one, putting the time to good use by preparing his design. His entry was successful, but in the interests of economy various modifications were later made to his lavish plans. Of these, the most important was the elimination of the top storey, no longer necessary after it had been decided to leave the headquarters' staff at Derby.

Economies and deferments were the result of financial pressures arising from the need for heavy expenditure on the London extension; not only did this far exceed the estimates, it had to be met during the difficult times which followed the failure of the Overend & Gurney discount house in May 1866. For these reasons the work was taken in sections and progress was slow. Work did not begin until 1868 and it was not until May 5th, 1873, that the first part of the seven-storey hotel could be opened. Another three years elapsed before the completion of the west wing.

With its castellated fringes, scores of dormer windows (each with finial, its myriad pointed-arch windows below the cornice, the multitude of chimneys on its steeply-pitched roofs, and its every corner marked by spirelet or pinnacle, the Midland Grand Hotel was one of the finest and largest examples of high Victorian secular Gothic. From the elaborate *porte cochère* at the west end, the 565-ft frontage curved back and round to parallel the Euston Road, terminating in a 270-ft spire-capped clock tower which was a worthy rival to that of Barry and Pugin at Westminster. The clock was supplied by John Walker of Cornhill in 1872; after showing increasing signs of old age, it stopped altogether in 1967. Over the elevations, Edward Gripper's patent bricks were varied with dressings in several different kinds of stone, and red and grey Peterhead granite. Frontage and skyline together offered a treasury of delights and surprises in which the erudite could find details of Salisbury and Winchester, the merely patient discover a statue of Britannia crowned by a lightning conductor.

Seen from close quarters, it was perhaps a little overwhelming, but from the heights of Pentonville on a winter's afternoon, with a low sun behind to enhance the magic and disguise the excesses, it could be superb. John O'Connor captured something of this in his 1881 painting, now in the London Museum.

The outward extravagance of the Midland Grand was matched inside, where Scott was assisted by F. Sang and others. From the main entrance hall in Euston Road, a pointed arch led into a Minton-tiled corridor round the curve of the west wing. On the right, following the line of the building, was the general coffee and dining-room, which overlooked the cab roadways and steps up to the station. This room, 100 ft long, 30 ft wide and 24 ft high, was later to be despoiled by partitioning and changes in décor. At the far end of the corridor, on the left, was the double intertwined grand staircase, decorated with iron scrollwork and ascending to the third floor under a beautiful vaulted ceiling 80 ft above the ground. Tucked into the well of this staircase was a tiny Moorish-style booth where Turkish coffee was dispensed. On the first floor was a vast reading- and drawing-room, with its own arcade and windows overlooking the Euston Road. Nearby a smaller coffee room was kept 'select' by the imposition of higher tariffs. Altogether there were some 400 sitting-rooms and bedrooms. Everywhere were pointed arches, carved oak doors, marble-faced walls.

Scott had opened all the stops, for he was venting a powerful frustration:

It is often spoken of to me as the finest building in London; my own belief is that it is possibly *too good* for its purpose, but having been disappointed, through Lord Palmerston, of my ardent hope of carrying out my style in the Government Offices, and the subject having been in the meanwhile taken out of my hands by other architects, I was glad to be able to erect one building in that style in London.[5]

There is little doubt that Scott made good use of the many studies in fourteenth-century Gothic detail that he had pre-

pared for the Whitehall offices, but St Pancras was, of course, a
completely fresh design. No expense was spared in providing
all the latest devices, such as gasoliers, electric bells, dust
chutes and hydraulic lifts. Following complaints, rubber sur-
faces were placed in the cab roadways to deaden the noise
at night.

Under the management of R. Etzensberger, late manager of
the Victoria Hotel, Venice, and of the commissariat of the Nile
steamers, the Midland Grand prospered. Baedeker thought it
one of the best of London's railway hotels, and noted in 1911
that bed and breakfast prices started at 7s, compared with 8s
at the Euston and 12s 6d at the Ritz. Carefully choosing his
words, George Augustus Sala declared it to be 'the most sumptuous and the best-conducted hotel in the Empire'. Service and
amenities were always up to date, even in advance of the times,
and in many ways a pattern was set for other big hotels to
follow. As early as the 1890s there was a ladies' smoking-room,
a very daring innovation at a time when it was considered
positively *fast* for a woman to smoke, even in secret. At the
turn of the century, it had the first revolving door to be installed in London, and a curious type of telephone enabling
guests to listen in to theatre and concert performances.

Although some businessmen remained faithful, the hotel's
serious lack of modern comforts (notably central heating and
an adequate number of bathrooms) caused patronage to decline steeply after the First World War. In 1935 the LMSR gave
up the unequal struggle and converted it to railway offices.

Within what is now prosaically known as St Pancras Cham-
bers, some of the original splendour survives. The grand staircase, with its 1873 carpet held in with great brass rods, amid
dark red walls patterned with gold fleurs-de-lis, remains a
showpiece; and there are other surprises, such as an alcove
mural of the *Garden of Deduit – Roman de la Rose* by T.
W. Hay, great mirrors, marble mantelpieces and fine mahogany
panels at the lift landings. Light modern colour schemes no
doubt brighten the working day for the clerks and typists, but

they have drowned the dignity of the interminable, dead-straight corridors that stretch out from each landing of the grand staircase. Today British Transport Hotels Ltd occupies most of the building, not inappropriately, as their main office.

UNDER BARLOW'S ROOF

The station itself was entered through an imposing archway under a 55-ft-wide tower where the frontage block joined the west wing. Incoming cabs went through this arch, and after unloading, left down a ramp parallel with the platforms. Along the front of the hotel, serving another of its entrances, the cab road continued as far as a second arch, used by cabs coming away from the arrival side (these had their own separate entrance at the back of the station). Here the front roadway bent back on itself and descended to an exit gate next to the entrance. At the eastern end, by the bend in the cab road, a small staircase, greatly widened and improved in 1895, led down to Pancras Road and Kings Cross Station.

Once through the entrance arch, the passenger alighted from his vehicle in a glass-roofed yard, where waiting porters attended him. Through one of three doorways, he then entered a handsome booking hall, completed in 1869, lit by six pairs of pointed arch windows and panelled with oak in linenfold. Secreted in the capitals of the columns around the walls, as if to demonstrate that it was not a church after all, were some charming little carvings of railwaymen.

Two doorways led from this hall to the cross-platform between the buffer stops and the hotel. Now, at last, the traveller was under the great roof. He was a dull man if his imagination was not stirred. For let there be no doubt, St Pancras before the Diesel Age was an experience never to be forgotten. Entering it on a foggy afternoon, the visitor received the full impact of the steam railway, assaulting all his senses at once. Smoke and steam rose slowly to a roof almost out of view, whilst at the far end the atmosphere concentrated to a muddy dark yellow, obscuring the gasometers. In the great cavern between, where the electric lighting always seemed to fight a losing battle with the murk, all locomotive sounds were amplified. When, as often happened, a safety valve could restrain itself no longer, and sent a roaring blast of steam to cleanse the Butterley ironwork, women and children would all but jump from their skins, and many a man would flinch.

Originally there were eleven roads and five platform faces: the short local platform (now No 1) faced the west wall, its opposite face was the full-length main departure platform; then came six carriage storage roads between the present Nos 2 and 5, followed by the main arrival platforms (now 5 and 6) either side of a 25-ft-wide cab road; against the east wall was the excursion platform, now No 7. In 1892, a wooden platform, the present Nos 3 and 4, was inserted in the carriage roads, giving the final total of six 800-ft platforms and a short bay. There were now two sidings between Platforms 2 and 3, and another, ending in the hoist to the beer vaults, between 4 and 5. Platforms 1 and 2 were used for both arrivals and departures, including local trains, while 3 and 4 were allocated to departures and 5 to 7 to arrivals.

Beyond the ends of the platforms were four tracks, east and west departure, east and west arrival, merging quickly to form an up and two down passenger lines which continued as far as Cambridge Street junction, the end of the first block section. From this point there was only a plain double passenger line as far as St Paul's Road junction, where the two tracks from the Metropolitan came in on the up side. To the west of the passenger lines there was now a double goods road, also used to work empty carriage trains to and from the sidings at Kentish Town or the carriage depot at Cricklewood. Although there were engine sidings and a turntable on the up side near the gasometers, the main locomotive depot was at Kentish Town, about 1½ miles out, also on the up side. Despite improvements carried out in 1907–8, when some coal bays on the up side were removed and the layout over the canal widened, these arrangements remained troublesome to operate, not least in crossing empty trains from the arrival platforms to the down goods road and bringing them over to the up side again at Cricklewood to reach the depot. Another cause of delay came with increased train lengths in later years; it was physically impossible to lengthen the platforms without costly engineering works, and any train longer than twelve coaches would block movements to other platforms.

Arranged along the sides of the station at platform level were various offices, notably on the west side, where a parcels depot was later added. Here, too, was the splendid gentlemen's court, one of the most impressive in any London terminus, with its stalls arranged in tasteful clusters around the roof columns. At street level, along the front and sides of the buildings, shops and coal offices provided a useful rent income.

TRAIN SERVICES

Apart from the additional platforms already mentioned, no alterations of substance were made to the original structure, which remained more than ample for the traffic. In 1902, there were 150 trains in and out daily: 'At no time of the day can St Pancras be called a busy station in the sense in which the word is understood at Waterloo or Liverpool Street. The long-distance expresses leave at stated – and stately – intervals, the only approach to bustle being at midnight, when three important trains leave within five minutes of each other.'[6]

For many years suburban traffic was virtually non-existent, almost all the local trains working to and from Moorgate. In 1903 only fourteen suburban trains arrived between 5 and 10 AM, but from 1910, some attempt was made to develop outer suburban traffic to St Albans and beyond by accelerating and augmenting the service.

In pre-grouping days St Pancras offered variety to the railway observer, with Great Eastern, and London Tilbury & Southend engines mixing with those of the Midland. The GER ran trains as far as Yarmouth, Norwich and Lowestoft via Kentish Town and South Tottenham between 1870 and 1917, St Pancras serving tenuously as that company's 'West End' terminus in exchange for Midland running powers over the GER to the London docks. In the years immediately before 1914, St Pancras had the fastest service to Cambridge (seventy-one min). The GER trains were suspended in 1917 as a war-time economy measure, and never restored, apart from a brief revival in the summers of 1922 and 1923 when one express daily ran to Hunstanton and back. This GER route was patron-ized by both royalty (to Sandringham) and racegoers (to New-market), and the company maintained its own booking-office at the Midland terminus.

Opened in 1894, the LTSR connexion provided St Pancras with boat trains, which conveyed passengers via South Totten-ham, Barking and Tilbury to Australia and Scandinavia. The link was made possible by the opening of the Tottenham & Forest Gate Railway (promoted by the Midland and the LTSR), from South Tottenham to a junction with the LTSR at Wood-grange Park, on July 9th, 1894. Previously the Tilbury boat trains had worked from Liverpool Street or occasionally from Fenchurch Street. From 1895 the Midland also ran a few through trains daily from St Pancras to Southend via Barking, at first using their own locomotives, but from April 1899 LTSR engines worked Midland coaches from St Pancras. Boat trains were also operated from St Pancras for the short-lived (1930–32) Tilbury–Dunkirk service. Hauled in LMSR and early BR days by the ubiquitous Fowler 4F 0–6–0 tender locomotives, the Australian and Scandinavian boat trains lasted until 1963 when they returned to Liverpool Street or Fenchurch Street.

One of the most serious air-raid incidents at any London terminus in the 1914–18 War occurred at St Pancras on Feb-ruary 17th, 1918. A stick of five bombs fell across the station, most of them causing no great harm, until one exploded in the cab court outside the booking-office. Here a crowd of people were sheltering under the entrance arch, and twenty were killed. There was no interruption to rail traffic.

BOMBS AND RENEWAL

Despite their greater destructive power, the bombs and mines of the 1939–45 War failed to shake the rock-solid construction of St Pancras, although there was some serious damage. A land mine wrecked a large part of the roof on the night of October 15th–16th, 1940, closing the station for five days whilst the debris was cleared. In the night of May 10th–11th, 1941, a bomb penetrated the station floor at the inner end of Platform 3, passing through the beer vaults to explode near the railway tunnel below. Again the main structure and foundations were unharmed, but the station was closed for eight days until local damage was made good, Platforms 2 and 3 remaining out of use until the first week of June.

British Railways spent a great deal of money on St Pancras after years of near-neglect by the LMSR. Apart from the signalling modernization to be mentioned later, the track in the station approaches was rearranged and reconstructed in 1947, new refreshment facilities were opened in 1959, and in 1963 a brave attempt was made to smarten up the somewhat gaunt platform entrances by erecting a 240-ft barrier screen with train indicators. Shortly before this, in 1958–9, the glazed area of the roof was enlarged to bring more natural light to the concourse, and the roof structure was repaired and repainted (the glass in the end screens was not replaced after the war). During 1957, the woodwork of the booking-hall was cleaned up, restoring much of its former splendour; at the same time, the ceiling was lowered and reconstructed. This work, which was reasonably successful, was later sadly marred by an ugly clutter of aluminium luggage lockers around the wall.

The desultory suburban service inherited from the Midland and LMSR was livened up a little. From September 28th, 1959, multiple-unit diesel sets took over partially, and steam was entirely replaced from January 11th, 1960, when an improved and regular service began (half-hourly off peak to Elstree and beyond, hourly for the inner stations). Despite a series of alarming train fires, the diesels, perhaps the most intensively-worked in the world, did well, increasing traffic by over twenty per cent. Even so, suburban movements at St Pancras remained very light in comparison with those at Liverpool Street and the Southern termini. Steam also disappeared from the main-line trains in the early 1960s.

During 1966, BR began to talk about 'combining' St Pancras and Kings Cross, threatening to replace Scott's hotel with an office tower. This was probably kite-flying, as the memory of Euston was still fresh in all minds. In answer to a question in the House of Lords, Lord Kennet, for the Government, said he was aware of the strong feelings about the destruction of Euston's portico and that his minister 'would take any step open to him to avoid a repetition of any such destruction'. This was followed, in November 1967, by the inclusion of the terminus in the statutory list of buildings of special architectural or historic interest. During 1967, proposals were made for using the terminus as an exhibition or sports centre, or as a transport museum, whilst BR published a somewhat half-baked scheme for rebuilding Kings Cross, closing St Pancras, and diverting the Midland services to Euston or the City Widened Lines. This BR plan was ill-received and much criticized on practical grounds, and eventually, in December 1968, scrapped, as it had not been found cost-effective. Saddled with its historic monument on a potentially lucrative site, BR swallowed hard and retreated, muttering that the interior of the hotel would have to be modernized.

Although the continuing pressure for rationalization and economy still threaten the long-term future of the railway facilities at St Pancras, it now seems most unlikely that the train shed and hotel frontage will be denied to posterity. Nuclear explosions aside, just what will happen to it in its second century remains an interesting question.

SIGNALLING

From the outset, St Pancras signalling was interlocked with
block working. The first signal box, designed to harmonize
with the station building, stood at the north end of the turntable siding, to the east of the station yard. This box was
closed in 1873 and replaced by the Station or East box, which
was just to the north of the outer ends of Platforms 3 and 4.
It had two frames, the east with 32 levers, and the west with
38 (later increased to 41), both parallel to the tracks, and was
in fact two signal boxes placed back to back.

After the opening of the Somers Town goods depot on the
west side of St Pancras in 1887, a principal box, St Pancras
Junction, was erected in the neck of the junction between the
lines to the depot and that to the carriage siding on the western
side of the passenger station. This cabin was 82 ft long and
12 ft wide and had an 84-lever passenger frame and a 48-
lever goods frame, the former facing east, the latter west, and
north of the other. A gantry carrying 42 up home and advance
starting semaphore arms on 21 dolls spanned the four roads
leading out of the platforms, but in 1914 this was replaced by
another which had only 16 arms and 8 dolls, each doll with
an illuminated route indicator at its base.

The proximity of these two boxes, and of Cambridge Street,
the end of the first block section, combined with the nature of
the track layout, led to a large amount of signal slotting and a
great many signal movements for each train. Despite this, St
Pancras was one of the last of London's termini to receive
modern signalling.

A scheme was eventually drawn up which provided two- and
four-aspect colour-light signalling and electro-pneumatic
points at the terminus, and in the approaches as far out as the
country end of Belsize tunnel. Work began in the middle 1950s.
On October 7th, 1957, a new box was opened on the west side
of St Pancras Station, at the end of Platform 1, replacing the

Station, Junction and Cambridge Street cabins. The relay-interlocking route setting installation, with its dc track circuits, was controlled from a console with 205 route switches, thirty-three switches for individual emergency point operation, and others for ground frame releases. Below the main operating-room was a room with 1,400 relays, a battery room, and a linesmen's mess room. Westinghouse supplied the signalling equipment, Standard Telephones & Cables the train describers.

In the modernization, St Pancras lost a third box, known only to the enlightened few, as it was hidden some 46 ft below the station. St Pancras Tunnel box was a tiny four-lever affair scooped out of the west wall of the tunnel between Kings Cross (Metropolitan) and St Paul's Road junction. Opened in 1889, after a mishap the previous year, it was a block post inserted to shorten the long section between Midland Junction box (Metropolitan Railway) and the Midland's box at St Paul's Road. At first, the tunnel signals controlled from the box were of the armless type, worked mechanically, but eventually colour lights were installed. To reach the box, the signalman entered a small door at the bottom of the cab ramp on the west side of the terminus. On the other side of the door was a small room, with a claustrophobic iron spiral staircase leading down from the middle of the floor. Arrived at the bottom, he could see the lights of the box across the tracks, dimly shining through the soot-begrimed panes of its semicircular window. Although signalmen are used to lonely vigils, Tunnel box must have been an unusual, even eerie duty. In later years, trains were relatively infrequent; between them, a deep silence reigned in these sooty depths, broken only by the distant rumble of the Metropolitan and the hum of the ventilation fan at the back of the box. Eight hours there could never have been much fun. When the box was closed on February 2nd, 1958, the operation of the signals in the tunnel was taken over by London Transport's Kings Cross C box.

CHAPTER FOUR

KINGS CROSS

TWO SIMPLE TRAIN SHEDS

In common with some of the other termini, Kings Cross is more than one station. The main and original part consists of two simple train sheds closed across the street end by a plain screen. Once derided, but now, with changing tastes, much admired despite its gloomy stock bricks, this screen conceals railway and passenger facilities greatly in need of reconstruction. Accretions of later years, collectively known as the Suburban station, are a drab untidy mess, mercifully hidden round a corner.

When the Great Northern Railway arrived in London in 1850, its trains were accommodated in a temporary station adjacent to Maiden Lane (now York Way) whilst the line was being pushed under the Regent's Canal to the permanent terminus at Kings Cross, through the 528-yd Maiden Lane or Gas Works tunnel. Referred to in the timetable as 'Kings Cross', this temporary terminus, opened on August 7th, 1850, consisted of two timber platforms on the down side between Gas Works and Copenhagen tunnels. Its spartan amenities had to cope with the excursion traffic of the Great Exhibition of 1851, and, in August of that year, with the embarkation of Queen Victoria and Prince Albert on a journey by rail and road to Scotland.

Built over a 10-acre site formerly occupied by the Small Pox and Fever Hospitals and a number of houses, the permanent terminus was sufficiently advanced to permit opening for public traffic on October 14th, 1852. At first, there were twelve down trains between 7 AM and 8 PM, only three of them expresses, and a similar up service, with a last arrival at 10 PM.

Buses connected with all trains to convey passengers to Paddington, Waterloo and London Bridge at a fare of 6d, which included up to 40 lbs of luggage.

Lewis Cubitt,[1] working with the engineers William and Joseph Cubitt[2] designed a straightforward, elegant and economical station. At the south end, two train sheds were closed by a 216-ft façade of London stock bricks incorporating two arches which revealed the cross-section of the interior. Almost devoid of ornament, this south front was crowned by a central square clock tower 112 ft high, the clock set in an Italianate turret which spoiled the stark simplicity of the design. Dent's clock had been exhibited at the 1851 Exhibition; it had four 9-ft-diameter dials, but the north one was blocked off as it could not be seen from the ground after erection at Kings Cross. The minute hands moved every half-second instead of the more customary thirty-second jerks, although this hardly explained why it rarely if ever agreed with Walker's clock on neighbouring St Pancras. Also in the tower were a tenor, a bass and a treble bell, the largest weighing 1 ton 9 cwt. Silenced in 1914, the chimes were heard again between 1924 and 1927, then stopped for good; twenty years later they were taken away.

The two arches of the south front were flanked by quite plain square buttress piers finished on top with flat brick fascias. Along the front, at street level, was a projecting porch with six arched openings (the ugly iron and glass canopy was a later addition). On the east side, a wide arched entrance led to the cabway alongside the arrival platform. To the west, there was an undistinguished masonry block containing offices and the usual station amenities.

Each train shed was 800 ft long and 105 ft wide, and 71 ft above the rails at centre. They were joined down the middle of the station by a strong brick wall carried on abutments. Along the west side of the station was a departure platform (now No 10), and along the east, the arrival platform (now No 1); between them were fourteen carriage roads.

About three-quarters of the roof area was glazed. The roof arches, at 20-ft intervals, were supported by laminated wood girders which exerted a very powerful thrust on the outside walls. This pressure was of no great moment on the west side, which was thoroughly buttressed by the office block, but on the east, the flying-buttress arrangement over the cab road was much weaker. By the late 1860s this east wall was showing signs of strain. During 1869–70 the timber trusses on the east side were replaced with wrought-iron girders. A similar operation was carried out in the departure shed in 1886–7.

The long building between the departure platform and the outside carriage road on the west of the station contained a refreshment room, first- and second-class waiting-rooms, first- and second-class ladies' rooms (there were no third-class *ladies*), parcels office, and the general offices and board room of the GNR. No facilities were provided for third-class passengers, who had only one train a day each way in the initial service. About one-third of the way down the platform was the 'pay office' or booking-hall, 100 ft long by 40 ft high, and occupying the full 40-ft width of the building.

At the time of its opening, Kings Cross was the largest station in Britain, and much admired. So much so, that some GNR shareholders were moved to complain of extravagance. Their grumbles were answered by Edmund Denison, the chairman, who told them that it was 'the cheapest building for what it contains and will contain that can be pointed out in London'. For a construction cost of £123,500, Denison thought the company had done well, as indeed they had, for the Euston portico and Great Hall had alone cost much more.

Lewis Cubitt also designed the five-storey Great Northern Hotel, which was opened in 1854 and is still in use. A plain, uninteresting building in white stone and brick, arranged on a curved plan, it is set apart from the station, to the south-west.

USING THE CAPACITY

Denison's suggestion that the capacity of the terminus would be put to good use was soon borne out. There was a steady growth of traffic. When Kings Cross opened there were only four stations (Hornsey, Colney Hatch & Southgate, Barnet, and Potters Bar) on the 17¾-mile stretch between London and Hatfield, but additional stations were opened at Holloway Road in 1856, at Wood Green in 1859 and at Seven Sisters Road (now Finsbury Park) in 1861. From February 1st, 1858, room had to be found for the London trains of the Midland. In 1863 connexions were established with the Metropolitan Railway (which had opened on January 10th, 1863, with a station at Kings Cross slightly east of the GNR terminus). All GNR local trains were diverted to Farringdon Street from October 1st. On reaching the surface at Kings Cross, down trains had to set back into the departure platform of the terminus, but in the up direction, before descending to the lower regions, the local trains stopped at a specially-provided platform called York Road, just outside the terminus.

An additional arrival platform was inserted into the main station during 1862, one face (later No 2) of full length, but the other with a short platform stepped into the northern end, forming a bay (later No 3). The full width portion at the inner end was sufficient for a short train.

Further strains were imposed on the Kings Cross approaches by the construction of a connexion between the Metropolitan and the LCDR in 1866. From thenceforward a heavy coal traffic left the GNR at Kings Cross bound for south London and beyond via Ludgate Hill and Herne Hill. Also, from January 1st, 1866, passenger trains were worked between Kings Cross and Herne Hill, and from January 3rd, between GNR suburban stations and Ludgate Hill. A Hatfield to Herne Hill service started on August 1st. GNR trains across London were diverted to Victoria from March 1st, 1868. Ten years later, from June

1st, 1878, through services were established over the same cross-centre route between Enfield and Muswell Hill and Woolwich Arsenal, initially worked by the GNR, but taken over by the SER on August 1st, 1880.

A year after the inauguration of through services between north and south London, on August 22nd, 1867, another thirty-six trains were added to the daily tidal flow by the opening of the Finchley and Edgware branch.

All trains had to be worked over the single up and down tracks in Gas Works tunnel. An additional impediment was present at the north end of the tunnel, where all up goods trains had to cross over the running lines on the level before they could reach the Kings Cross yard. It was small wonder that the Midland trains were delayed.

When the City Widened Lines were constructed alongside the Metropolitan, new junctions had to be made at Kings Cross and to enable the work to proceed, the GNR service was suspended from July 1st, 1867. These alterations were completed early in 1868, and a limited passenger service resumed on February 17th. In the following year, on June 1st, the GNR suburban trains were extended eastwards to Moorgate.

Although some relief was felt when the Midland trains departed for their own line after September 30th, 1868, this was short-lived. With the opening of branches to Enfield in 1871, to High Barnet in 1872 and to Alexandra Palace in 1873, suburban traffic continued to expand. From a mere nineteen in 1855, the number of departures from Kings Cross had grown to eighty-nine in 1873, all but twenty of which were suburban, almost all off the Metropolitan.

SUBURBAN ACCRETIONS

All this time, Kings Cross had been worked with a single departure platform used not only by main-line and local trains, but backed into by every passenger train leaving the Metropolitan. This somewhat absurd situation was now gradually

put right. First came the opening, in August 1875, of what was
rather longwindedly known as 'Kings Cross Main Line (Local)
Station', consisting of three short platform faces and two
tracks outside the western wall of the terminus, under its own
overall roof. This local station, used only for departures, was
opposite the north end of the main departure platform, occupying the site of a carriage repair shop. A small yard for turning
and coaling locomotives was built at the same time between
the local station and the down line to the Metropolitan.

This Metropolitan connexion remained without a platform
until February 1st, 1878, from which date the tedious backing
into the main-line station was at last ended by the opening of
'Kings Cross (Suburban)'. Yet this created new difficulties,
for great was the anxiety (and embarrassment) of the less skil-
ful drivers as they struggled to start well-loaded trains from its
sharply-curved steeply-graded platform. Traffic from the
Metropolitan was heavy, and it was usual for the tunnel mouth
to be wreathed in smoke; although a repeater signal was provided at that end of the platform, it was necessary after dark
to assist drivers of through trains by giving hand-lamp signals.

The tunnel, known as Hotel Curve, was detested by all
engine crews, who no doubt had their own picturesque names
for it. Not only was there a wicked curve of 7-chains (154-yd)
radius, but part of the climb was at 1 in 35. An unfortunate
GNR employee was obliged to spend his working hours within
this fearsome hole, spreading sand on the rails after the passage
of each train. Freight trains could not be banked except in
special circumstances, as the second engine had to be crossed
over all the busy lines into the terminus before it could return.
Double-heading was out of the question, as the loading gauge
of this single-line tunnel was so tight that the crew of the
second engine would be unable to work in the fumes and
smoke from the pilot. Some light was thrown on conditions in
Hotel Curve by the Ministry of Transport report of an accident
which took place in July 1932 (the passing of time had led to
no improvement). A train had slipped back so badly on the

upward climb that it had run into another in its rear. The inspector commented: 'The signals only become visible just as the engine reaches them, and it is only by touching the tunnel lining with an outstretched hand that trainmen can be certain they are travelling in the right direction. Even breathing is at times difficult, and drivers have little or no chance of rectifying an error.' After this, following the inspector's recommendation, lights were provided at short intervals to help drivers preserve their sense of location, speed and direction.

Between 1867 and 1873 the number of GNR season-ticket holders had increased from 2,500 to over 6,000, and there was every sign of continued growth. As most of the local trains still went through to the Metropolitan, the congestion was experienced in the double-track approach tunnel rather than in the terminus itself. The difficulties of working the approaches further increased with the opening of a GNR goods depot at Farringdon Street in 1874. At this time, it was not uncommon for rush-hour trains to take up to thirty minutes to cover the $1\frac{1}{2}$ miles between Holloway and Kings Cross. In those days there was no *Evening News* to give publicity to 'troubled trains' and the passengers' protests were formally summarized in 'memorials' which they presented to the GNR directors.

The harassed management rested its hopes on a connexion to the North London Railway at Canonbury, permitting diversion of many GNR suburban trains to Broad Street. Alas, the LNWR-dominated North London would not have GNR passenger trains on its tracks, and the only acceptable solution was for the North London to run over the GNR suburban lines on a mileage basis. This began on January 18th, 1875, mopping up much of the traffic, and enabling Henry Oakley, the GNR general manager, to boast that his suburban trains were 'running with improved punctuality'. But as traffic continued to grow, optimism was quickly dispersed. The remaining land around the inner stations was rapidly covered with new houses designed to attract the Pooters and the Cummingses. By 1881 the season-ticket army had swollen to 14,400.

Plan of Kings Cross 1905. From the Railway Magazine, March 1905

Great efforts were made to improve the terminal approaches. A skew bridge and duplicate Copenhagen tunnel were provided in August 1877 to keep trains entering Kings Cross goods yard out of the way of passenger movements. In the following year, a second Gas Works tunnel was completed beneath the canal, to be opened, together with a resited York Road platform, on March 4th. A third Copenhagen tunnel, on the east side, was ready for traffic on June 20th, 1886.

SERIOUS·DELAYS

Despite these works, up trains were still subject to serious delays, especially in the rush hours. There were several reasons why this was so: tickets were collected and examined while trains stood for this purpose at Holloway (until 1896, when the Holloway ticket check was abandoned. York Road and Kings Cross [Metropolitan] were 'open' stations and many a small boy enjoyed a free ride between them); there were only two roads through Gas Works tunnels, and all empty stock for down departures had to be worked through them with the passenger trains; and finally, as some Moorgate trains had coaches for Kings Cross terminus, delay built up whilst the portion was detached at York Road.

The inevitable third tunnel under the canal was finished in June 1892. Situated on the west side, it accommodated two down roads (down slow and down main No 2), the western-most road in the 1852 tunnel becoming down main No 1, and the other a shunting road. This latter line was converted to an up line for empty passenger trains and light engines on August 29th, 1898, enabling empty trains to run direct into the departure platform for the first time. After this, shunting from the arrival to the departure side was usually accomplished by using the down roads.

As the tracks in the station yard were still an inflexible muddle, these shunting operations presented a considerable hazard. It only needed the derailment of a single coach in the cramped space between the tunnel mouths and the platforms to cause more or less complete chaos. Such incidents were apt to occur at holiday times when the station staff were always under great strain. Another handicap was the down-under-and-up alignment of the Gas Works tunnels and the subsequent 1-mile climb at 1 in 107. Not only were run-backs to be expected (some are mentioned at the end of this chapter), but the tunnels and yard were liable to flooding after heavy rain. A typical incident occurred on July 25th, 1901, when all traffic was completely suspended for $4\frac{1}{2}$ hours after a flood. Such indignity was suffered by no other major London terminus.

Towards the end of the nineteenth century, Kings Cross was handling some 250 passenger and freight trains daily, as well as empty carriage workings and other movements, the total load being near to saturation point for the layout with traditional signalling methods. (Empty carriage trains were worked to and from sidings at Holloway, Finsbury Park, Hornsey, and later, Bounds Green. There were also light-engine movements to and from the locomotive depot, situated on the west side of the Kings Cross goods yard.) Although much of this traffic was on and off the Metropolitan, as late as 1892 the terminus was still being worked with only one main-line departure platform. As there were over forty departures daily, the situation was becoming intolerable.

In 1893 new platforms (later 5 and 6) were built either side of the central wall between the two train sheds. These were opened on December 18th, the westernmost one at last giving a second platform for departures. At the same time, an iron girder footbridge was erected, connecting all platforms in the main station about halfway down their length, and linking the old general offices on the departure side with new offices built in the early 1890s over the cab road on the arrival side.

This cab road was a rather sinister place, and as at Euston and Paddington, the number and destination were recorded by a railway policeman as the cab left. 'A precaution against the

"When a train arrives it stops close to the parade at the up side and passengers step out upon it, and may, if they are disposed to ride to any part of the town enter the omnibusses, cabs, or cars that are waiting for them."

(Osborne's London & Birmingham Railway Guide, 1840)

Euston, looking south c 1840. The outline of the portico is seen behind the train shed, right. A train has just arrived, with a private carriage on a flat truck at its rear. From a watercolour by E. Duncan

Euston, portico and lodges, c 1901. The western lodge has been demolished to make way for offices, and the arrival train shed can be glimpsed at the extreme right

Euston, Platforms 4, 5 and 6 looking north, c 1938, with Watford electric train in Platform 4

Euston, the Great Hall, after restoration by British Railways in 1953, looking north. The entrance to the shareholders' room is seen at the top of the stairs

St Pancras interior, looking north, c 1869. At left, by the Spiers &
Pond refreshment cabin, a local train awaits departure. Girders for
the hotel screen are seen in the centre road, whilst an express
arrives on the right

St Pancras in pristine splendour, about 1885, shortly after the completion of the west wing and cab ramps. Kings Cross is seen at the
extreme right. The site for the Somers Town goods depot has been
cleared at the extreme left

Kings Cross in its early simplicity, c 1853. From a watercolour
published by R. B. Fleming & Co Ltd

Kings Cross in the last days of steam; left to right 60131 *Osprey*, 'A1'
Pacific; 61379, 'B1' 4-6-0; 60064 *Tagalie*, 'A3' Pacific. February 15th,
1958

Bishopsgate, c 1865

Liverpool Street West Side, about 1904

Fenchurch Street as rebuilt, 1853, to the design of George Berkeley. From a drawing by T. Gilks for the *Illustrated London News*, December 10th, 1853

Fenchurch Street interior, March 24th, 1956, BR 2-6-4T, 80080 backing on to special train for the Railway Correspondence and Travel Society's East London Railtour No 2

London Bridge Joint Station, as completed c 1845

London Bridge SER approaches c 1864. The 'AB' signal cabin is seen in the foreground. 'CD' cabin is in the background, right. An engraving for the *Illustrated London News*

Cannon Street Station and approaches, July 12th, 1955, before the demolition of the bomb-damaged roof

Nine Elms, 1838

kidnapping of children' a child would be told, only to receive
a further shock on peering out of the back of the cab, where
he would almost certainly see an unkempt, unshaven figure
loping along behind, following it all the way home, and sometimes stealing a precarious ride on the bar at the back. Could
this be a kidnapper, or was it perhaps a burglar? The truth was
less romantic. In those hard days, men were prepared to go to
all this trouble for the few pence to be earned in carrying bags
from the cab to the house.

MORE ADDITIONS

Alterations were made to the local station in 1895, when an
additional track was placed between the platform and a new
island platform, 500 ft long and 20 ft wide. To make room for
this, the locomotive yard, with its 50-ft turntable and coaling
stage, was moved west, and the curve from the Metropolitan
somewhat flattened. The platform on the Metropolitan connexion was rebuilt, and a short terminal platform constructed
at a higher level on its west side. This, together with new milk
and horse and carriage docks, filled the triangular space
between Cheney Street and the back of Culross Buildings. The
new platforms were opened on April 4th, 1895.

The local platforms were now designated A to E, from west
to east, A and B being known as 'suburban' platforms to dis-
tinguish them from C to E in the local station. Platform E,
which was accessible from the main-line departure platform,
both at its north end and through an intermediate passageway,
was sometimes used for main-line departures. The local station
had its own booking-office, circulating area and refreshment
room, all fronting Cheney Street. There was also a small buffet
on Platform B, offering a refuge from the discomforts of that
smoke-bound outpost. In the main station, the arrival and
departure sides were still rigidly separated, even to the extent
of separate platform numbering (1 and 2 departure, and 1 to
5 arrival), a situation which was to persist until 1921.

When Kings Cross was first opened, both the station and hotel were in line with the St Pancras Old Road. About 1872 that road was diverted to run alongside the new St Pancras Station, bringing it to a right angle junction with Euston Road, and leaving an open space in front of the terminus. This space remained unoccupied for a time, but it was later used by a vendor of garden furniture, who filled it with a display of rustic seats, arches and summer houses designed to catch the eye of the homegoing suburbanite. Subsequently, permanent and semi-permanent buildings were erected, including a left-luggage office. On Sunday May 11th, 1902, fire broke out in one of the wooden buildings. Fanned by a north-east wind, it spread rapidly, destroying a large part of the garden furniture, the left-luggage office and some GNR road vans and buses.

After this, more buildings were erected, and by 1914 the area was thoroughly cluttered. There were the mail office, the Jubilee cloakroom (used for heavy parcels), the emigrants' transit shed, the excursion office, a timber office for railway staff, a cab shelter, and, plonked right at the front, the 1906 station of the Piccadilly Tube railway in the standard dark-rhubarb terracotta blocks. As if this wasn't enough, the LNER added some crudely-designed single-storey shops either side of the Tube station in 1934, and shortly after that, Laing's erected a specimen of a desirable suburban residence in front of the Great Northern Hotel.

In addition to the through services to Metropolitan Railway stations, access to the Metropolitan platforms at Kings Cross was available through a long subway from the main-line concourse, opened on June 20th, 1892. Subways from the southern end of the departure platform gave ready access to the underground booking-hall of the City & South London Tube railway, which was extended from Angel to Euston on May 12th, 1907. The Piccadilly Tube station, already mentioned, was opened on December 15th, 1906, and connected to the Metropolitan-GNR subway.

During the First World War, it was the practice to draw

main-line trains into the tunnels as far as possible when enemy
aircraft were overhead. In fact no damage was inflicted on the
station, which was fortunate, as it had considerable strategic
importance. Very heavy freight traffic was passing south almost
continuously through the Metropolitan connexion, so much
so that the slack-hour trains between the Metropolitan and the
GNR were taken off in January 1915 to provide more paths. A
large amount of high explosive was carried through Kings
Cross, much of it by passenger train, and a special store for it
was constructed on the main departure platform.

LAST MAJOR CHANGES

The last major changes to Kings Cross were made in 1922–4.
They were largely designed to facilitate the working of the
increased number of local trains terminating there instead of
running through to the Metropolitan (with a few exceptions,
the slack-hour cancellations of 1915 were never restored).

As the up carriage road in the centre Gas Works tunnel was
mainly reserved for the working of empty carriages and light
engines into the terminus, it was not always available for
shunting local trains from the arrival side to the local station,
and the down lines then had to be used instead. This also
applied when engines were moved from the arrival side to the
engine yard on the down side. The remedy adopted involved
the conversion of the permissively-worked up carriage road to
an up relief running line, together with signalling improvements. From January 22nd, 1922, up trains could be directed
into all the departure platforms except the present 16 and 17
and up suburban trains began to use 11 to 13.

Although providing considerable benefits, this change by no
means cured the basic defects of the Kings Cross layout.
Departures from Platforms 1 to 5 (present-day numbers) still
blocked all inward movements, those from 6 all inwards movements to 7 to 15, those from 7 all movements into 8 to 15,
and so on. The up slow line was only usable for the Metro-

politan connexion and Platform 1, and the up main for Platforms 1 to 5. All trains destined for Platforms 6 to 15 had to
use the up relief road. This sorry state of affairs still applies,
but is a little difficult to explain to passengers when things go
wrong, or when they want to know why trains often *leave*
behind time at Kings Cross. The extremely costly works that
would be necessary to rectify the situation have been avoided
for sixty years only because much of the pressure was taken
out of the Kings Cross suburban traffic by the arrival of Tube
railways and improved street transport in the first decade of
the present century.

Relief to suburban and cross-London traffic was first felt in
1906–7; and in the latter year the through trains to south
London were withdrawn for lack of patronage. In 1906 the
GNR felt sufficiently relaxed to indulge in a publicity campaign
extolling the virtues of residence on the 'Northern Heights'
and encouraging new traffic to 'Bracing Barnet' (16 minutes
from Kings Cross; season rate 6*d* a day), 'Healthy Southgate'
(13 min; 4½*d*), 'Breezy Highgate' (13 min; 2½*d*), and 'Picturesque Finchley' (17 min; 4*d*). The extension of the Piccadilly
Tube to Wood Green, Bowes Park and Southgate in 1932–3
made heavy inroads into the Kings Cross suburban traffic, and
another large section of it was removed when the Tube trains
of the Northern Line took over the working of the High Barnet
and Mill Hill branches in 1939–41.

When the Gresley Pacific locomotives came into use after
the First World War, it was decided to install a 70-ft turntable
at Kings Cross to eliminate wasteful light-engine running.
Before the war, the GNR had bought 5¾ acres of the gas works
site, and a new engine coaling and turning yard was now constructed on this. An interesting feature of the yard, which came
into use in December 1923, was the provision of an underground steam pipe which fed steam from a locomotive standing
in the yard to heat carriages waiting at the departure platform,
thus freeing pilot engines which had formerly been used for
this purpose.

The new works of the immediate post-war era were completed on December 15th, 1924, when a 400-ft island platform (Nos 14 and 15) was opened on the site of the old engine yard. Since July 11th, 1921, the platforms had been numbered from east to west right across the station, including the local and suburban stations, but with 7 to 9 omitted. This gap was partly filled on September 19th, 1926, by the opening of a 945-ft by 12-ft concrete island platform on the departure side, numbered 7 and 8. In 1938 the width of this platform was doubled after the removal of the No 9 carriage road; at the same time, it was connected to the central footbridge. To provide further room for main-line arrivals and add to the mystery and complications of Kings Cross platform numbering, the LNER abolished Platform 3 in 1934, extending No 4 to full length.

Like Waterloo and Charing Cross, Kings Cross experienced a grisly cloakroom incident in the between-war years. The depositor of the female legs which were found in a case in the cloakroom in 1934 was never discovered; all that the police were able to ascertain was that they neatly fitted a female torso entrusted about the same time to the care of the left-luggage office at Brighton station.

During the 1920s, the LNER carried out various improvements in the passenger amenities, building new lavatories, bath and dressing-rooms under the main departure platform (No 10), and opening a Georgian tea room, a new refreshment room and an inquiry office at the side of this platform. In 1927 Platform 10 was extended at the outer end by 45 ft to accommodate the longer trains then coming into use.

More work was done in the 1930s when all the lettering of the station signs was changed to Gill Sans, a type fount designed by Eric Gill (1882–1940) and adopted in 1932 by the LNER as standard for every form of lettering and printing. New platform barriers with illuminated blinds showing departure times were erected in the main station. A large inquiry and reservation office was opened on Platform 10 in 1936, and in

1938–9 a subway was constructed to connect all the platforms in the main station with a new parcels and mailbag depot on the west side.

A HECTIC WAR

Kings Cross had a hectic war, handling a very heavy traffic in troops and civilians. Engine shortages caused trains to be made up to twenty or more coaches, some of which would be outside the platform, necessitating additional shunting movements and loss of time. Some trains carried as many as 2,000 passengers.[3] Severe damage was inflicted on the station by two 1,000-lb bombs, chained together, which fell on the west side on May 11th, 1941, removing a slice of the general offices, the grill room and bar, and wrecking the booking-hall. A large section of the roof was blown out. It was fortunate that the explosion occurred in the small hours of a Sunday when the station was deserted, but even so, twelve men were killed. Temporary booking and refreshment facilities were soon organized, and there was no necessity to cancel any trains. As a result of bombing on the Metropolitan lines, services to Moorgate were suspended from December 30th, 1940, until October 1st, 1945 (to Aldersgate), and May 6th, 1946 (to Moorgate).

The post-war period has seen no restoration of the once-intense suburban services. In 1937 there were twenty-one departures in a typical peak hour, ten of them from Moorgate; now there are but nine, three from the City. But since 1958–9, these trains have been worked by diesel locomotives and railcars, and there has been a slight increase in traffic associated with population growth in the outer country area. In 1959, 6,953 passengers left between 4.30 and 7.0 PM, but in 1968 the corresponding figure was 8,919. Main-line workings at Kings Cross went over to diesel haulage in the early 1960s.

DRAUGHTY AND CHEERLESS

Today Kings Cross is neither a pleasing nor impressive station. The form of the original design, with its separate arrival and departure sheds, and all amenities alongside the departure platform, is ill-suited to modern needs. The little cross-platform that emerged from this design is utterly inadequate as a concourse; hardly wide enough for comfort on the west side, it narrows down even more on the east, where Platforms 1 to 4 extend farther south than the others. At the front of the station, large openings allow a generous breeze to blow through the train sheds, a feature which does not make for passenger comfort, even if it did help to disperse the smoke and steam, and now dilutes the more insidious exhaust of the diesels.

The main-line booking-hall is bleak and uninviting, and the heart of the station, the long Platform 10, is an untidy and cheerless place in comparison with the similarly situated Platform 1 at Paddington. A large bookstall is almost its only bright spot. An exploration of the other end of this platform reveals an increasingly gloomy scene. Near the end, a strangely-isolated waiting-room is usually inhabited by layabouts and string-belted tramps; on reaching daylight, one stumbles upon a grim-looking huddle of train-spotters, still mourning steam, yet trying very hard to summon interest in the unromantic manoeuvres of diesel engines and cars. A similar walk down the original arrival platform, permanently barricaded with parcels, is recommended only to the athletic.

Equally depressing, despite smart new platform barriers and information displays, is the Suburban station, as the extra-mural platforms are now collectively known. Here but two amenities remain, a buffet in the veneers and chrome of the 1930s, and a tiny bookstall, open only at peak hours.

In the early 1960s, the construction of the Victoria Line Tube station at Kings Cross offered a fine opportunity to give Cubitt's noble frontage a worthy setting. Up went the hoardings and the hopes of those who cared about such things; down came the ugly terracotta Tube station and the even uglier 1930s shops. Then, as the Underground men pursued their complicated engineering out of sight, British Railways produced a plan for rebuilding Kings Cross which would retain the original front but erode some of its impact. Across the Cubitt screen were to be slashed the searing horizontals of a two-storey concourse building, projecting at least 40 ft. Within there would be escalators, subways and travolators affording connexion with the Underground and City Widened Lines, the latter carrying St Pancras short-distance services after the closure of the Midland terminus. To the west and slightly to the north of the main-line station, a 300-ft tower would provide a new home for BR headquarters' staff.

As mentioned in the St Pancras chapter, this scheme, which never had seemed realistic or acceptable, was torn up by BR towards the end of 1968. Just what can be done with the sad jumble that is Kings Cross within the limits of BR'S restricted capital resources remains to be seen. Electrification of the surburban lines, promised off and on for over sixty years, may come before much longer, but will not in itself go far to solve the troubles of this terminus.

SIGNALLING AND ACCIDENTS

At first Kings Cross had no block working. Points were worked by hand levers, and signals from pull-over levers operated from a small fenced-off area at the west side of the southern tunnel portal. The main line was equipped with semaphore signals with perforated arms, moved to three positions (stop, caution and clear) to control time-interval working.

This primitive equipment had been replaced by the early 1870s, when block working was in operation. A new box, later called West, was opened in 1881, with 140 levers (10 spare). This was supplemented in 1886 by East box, with 100 levers (21 spare). West box, which was at the north end of what are now Platforms 5 and 6, dealt with departure movements and station shunting. East box, situated near the north end of Platform 1, controlled arrivals and York Road. Both boxes had tappet-interlocked frames supplied by McKenzie & Holland.

It was not feasible to provide ground signals to cover all possible moves over the complicated and difficult layout in the station yard, and it was not unusual for a shunting move into one of the tunnels to be signalled back by a gang of shunters with hand lamps.

Owing to the presence of two road bridges over the station yard, the signalmen in East and West boxes did not have a clear view of the tracks they controlled, and a form of track circuiting (the first in Britain) together with electric fouling bars, was installed on some lines in the tunnels as early as 1894. The bridge immediately north of the station carried Battle Bridge Road, the other an access drive into the gas works. The latter was removed in 1912, but Battle Bridge Road survived until 1921, when it was demolished and replaced by Goods Way, constructed over the tunnel.

As part of the departure-side rearrangements mentioned in the main text, power-operated three-position upper quadrant signals were brought into use in six places on January 22nd, 1922. These signals had illuminated roller-blind route indicators showing at front and rear, and were supplied by Siemens. Full track circuiting was completed in 1923.

On October 3rd, 1932, all the semaphore signals in the station area were replaced by Siemens colour lights. The new signalling, which also included seventy-three point motors, was controlled from an all-electric power frame of 232 levers. This frame was in a new box, which replaced East and West and was centrally situated at the north end of Platforms 5 and 6. Precautions were taken against flooding; signal cables were run overhead on light gantries, some point motors were mounted on concrete blocks clear of the usual flood level, and point detector boxes were made watertight.

Situated at the bottom of a long gradient, Kings Cross could hardly hope to avoid accidents of a particular kind. The first occurred in 1860, when an excursion train from Manchester mounted the buffers after a tipsy guard had overlooked the need to give additional assistance by applying his handbrakes. Fortunately no one was killed, but the mess was considerable. This incident was followed on November 2nd, 1865, by a spectacular affair involving a coal train. During the passage of Copenhagen tunnel, a portion of this train broke away, rolling down into the terminus, where the guard managed to escape by jumping on to the platform. Some trucks spilled over the end of the track, charging into the roadway, where they spent their load in final undignified collapse. A hurried digging over of the coal was organized for fear that someone might be buried, but there were no casualties.

More serious were the events of Sunday February 4th, 1945. On that day, the 6 PM for Leeds and Bradford, composed of Pacific locomotive 2512 and seventeen coaches, in all about 590 tons load, met trouble in the middle Gas Works tunnel. Here *Silver Fox* slipped so violently that she stalled, allowing her train to run back. A signalman in the Kings Cross cabin, seeing what was happening on his diagram, tried to divert the runaway into Platform 15, as the road was set for Platform 10, occupied by the 7 PM for Aberdeen. Unhappily, one of the bogies of the last coach had passed over the points before they began to move; two passengers were killed in the subsequent derailment and signalling equipment was extensively damaged. It was not until February 23rd that train services and signalling were completely restored. The inspector's report revealed that the track was new, the engine tyres practically unworn – a good combination for low adhesion, causing the heavily-taxed locomotive to perform as it did on the 1 in 105 gradient at the other side of the dip under the canal.

CHAPTER FIVE

BROAD STREET

VAST EMPTINESS TODAY

Penetrated by occasional trains, which creep in with an apologetic air, the vast emptiness of Broad Street is a reminder that this was once the City terminus of the busy North London Railway, with more daily train arrivals than Euston and Paddington together, more indeed than any other London terminus except Liverpool Street and Victoria. Now sustained outside the rush hours by only one train service, it is a station that has seen little glory and a great deal of hard work. The original building was no jewel of architecture, and the crude accretions in the forecourt have almost succeeded in suffocating it. Yet here and there, compensations are offered to the seeing eye.

The North London began life as the East & West India Docks & Birmingham Junction Railway, a title intended to express its purpose, which was to carry freight between the London & Birmingham Railway and the London docks. Still burdened by this weighty title, the line was opened in September 1850, under the aegis of the London & North Western Railway, who always controlled its main policy. By the time the name was changed to the neater North London Railway in 1853, passenger traffic had assumed an unforeseen importance. Cheap fares and frequent trains encouraged patronage, despite a 44-mile detour round east London before the City was reached at Fenchurch Street, by courtesy of the London & Blackwall Railway.

CITY ACCESS FOR THE NORTH WESTERN

More direct access to the City was an obvious next step, and became possible with the assistance of the LNWR, which was

anxious to have a goods depot in the City, and agreed to contribute the larger part of the cost of a new terminus. This was to
be at the junction of Broad Street and Liverpool Street, and
reached by a 2-mile line running south from the North London
at Kingsland.

Many humble houses had to be demolished in Shoreditch
and Haggerston before the approach line could be built and,
to secure Parliamentary approval, the North London undertook to provide one morning workmen's train from Dalston
and a return working in the evening, at a fare of one penny.
Few of the displaced took advantage of this generous con-
cession; most of them crowded into nearby streets, continuing
to walk to such employment as they had.

Terminus and extension together cost £1,200,000. Southwards from east and west junctions at Kingsland, three tracks
were carried on viaducts to the edge of the City of London. A
new station, Dalston Junction, was built at the northern end,
and there was one intermediate station, at Shoreditch (a second,
Haggerston, was added in 1867). The construction and design
of the terminus and approach tracks was the responsibility of
William Baker, the first chief engineer of the LNWR, which was
to own the western side of Broad Street Station, as well as
the approach tracks on that side south of Skinner Street junction, the approaches to its goods depot from New Inn Yard
junction, and a goods depot at Shoreditch.

At the site of the terminus, after the demolition of houses
and other property, excavations revealed the existence of
human remains in stratum several feet thick. This was thought
to be either a plague pit or the burial pits of the old Bethlehem
Hospital.

The frontage was 250 ft long by 110 ft wide, situated at
the western end of Liverpool Street, opposite the end of the
street whose name the station took. No architect is mentioned
in the account in the *Illustrated London News* of February
3rd, 1866, which describes the elevations as of 'mixed Italian
style' and 'rather more decorated than most stations of similar

kind'. Baker probably roughed out the details himself, perhaps employing one or two minor architectural draughtsmen to finish them off. The materials were white Suffolk bricks, with columns of Peterhead granite, and capitals, medallions and other decorations in terracotta. In the centre of it all was a 75-ft clock tower, quite swamping its small clock. Altogether it was really rather horrid, the only redeeming feature a pleasing arcaded external staircase on the east side.

Inside, at street level, were two booking-halls, one for each railway company, 60 ft high, and either side of the clock tower. The two conjoint train sheds together measured 460 ft by 200 ft. High above the street, they at first contained only four tracks, the principal platform being some 50 ft wide.

After a ceremonial breakfast for the Lord Mayor and Sheriffs of the City on October 31st, the terminus was opened to ordinary mortals on November 1st, 1865. Trains ran every fifteen minutes to Chalk Farm, at the same interval to Bow (for Fenchurch Street; from August 1st, 1866, this service was diverted to Poplar) and every thirty minutes to Kew (via Hampstead Heath; there were connexions to Kingston via Mortlake, and some through trains; the service was alternated to Kew Bridge and to Richmond from January 1st, 1869). Passengers to and from Dalston and points west were better off by a saving of twenty minutes each way. A Watford service was begun on September 1st, 1866, and some of the Chalk Farm trains were extended to Willesden Junction on June 3rd, 1879, but withdrawn from January 1st, 1917.

The LNWR goods depot, opened on May 18th, 1868, was at ground level, some 60 ft below the passenger station, and on the west side of it. Wagons were raised and lowered from the yard above by means of hydraulic lifts. Everything was arranged as compactly as possible to make the best use of the highly priced land; passenger terminus and two-level goods station together occupied only 2½ acres.

A GREAT SUCCESS

It was all a great success. Both passenger and freight traffic flourished. The North London's own traffic more than doubled in a very short time, to be supplemented from January 1875 by some forty or so trains each way daily between Broad Street and Great Northern suburban stations. During the last quarter of the nineteenth century this modest terminus became one of the busiest in London.

A fourth approach track, known as No 2 down, was finished in 1874 (the bridge over Great Eastern Street was delayed until 1876 by negotiations with the Metropolitan Board of Works). This work was followed by a rearrangement of tracks and platforms on the western side of Broad Street, completed in 1877. In an endeavour to improve the passenger flow through the station, the interior was rearranged, a new central booking-office at platform level coming into use on September 4th, 1890. At the same time, the appearance of the frontage was marred by the erection of two covered footbridges over the forecourt, with stairs to the street at one end, and platform-level entrances at the other. The east side of the station was rearranged in 1891, when a further track was added, making eight in all.

Varying in length from 419 to 480 ft, and numbered from east to west, the platforms were of stone, ill-lit by ponderous gas lamps. The rails of the platform tracks ran over engine pits, full length on Nos 1 to 4, and extending as far as the crossovers on Platform 5 to 8.

At the turn of the century, Platform 1 was the home of the Chalk Farm stopping trains. Poplar and Bow services used 2 and 3; both 3 and 4 were patronized by the North London trains to and from the GNR suburban stations; 5 was used by the Outer Circle and 6 and 7 by services to LNWR suburban stations and the NLR fast trains to Richmond and Willesden. Platform 8 accommodated the stopping service to Richmond and Kew Bridge. The Outer Circle service was operated by the LNWR, first between Broad Street and Kensington (Addison Road) from September 1st, 1867, then onwards to Victoria (LBSCR) from January 1st, 1869. It was diverted from Victoria to Mansion House (Metropolitan District Railway) from February 1st, 1872. After the electrification of the District, it was cut back to Earls Court from January 1st, 1909. It ceased in 1914 when a shuttle service of electric trains began to work between Earls Court and Willesden Junction (High Level).

Each pair of platforms shared a coaling stage, and there were two more stages just outside the station. On the east side, the engine of an arriving train would wait at the buffers whilst another locomotive was brought from the coaling stage to be coupled to the other end of the train, ready for departure. Once the train had left, the incoming engine moved to the coaling stage for coal and water and was then ready for the next departure. On the west side (Platforms 5 to 8) there were scissors crossovers, allowing the immediate release of the train engine, which could leave with the same train after visiting the coaling stage. A ninth platform was added outside the western wall in 1913.

When the Central London Railway extended its Tube line from the Bank to Liverpool Street in 1912, a booking-hall was built under the forecourt of Broad Street Station. Served by two escalators, it was brought into use on October 10th. Access to the main concourse of the terminus was provided from February 23rd, 1913, when two lifts began to operate between the Tube station and the North London platform level. A Tube railway booking-office was opened by the upper lift landing and through tickets were issued between NLR stations and the Tube. Later in 1913, these works were completed by the erection of a Portland stone frontage to the Broad Street Station courtyard, surrounding the old footbridge staircases and incorporating a new central entrance for the main station, with entrances to the Tube booking-hall either side.

Until 1910, Broad Street's traffic was entirely local in charac-

Plan of Broad Street 1906. From the Railway Magazine, September 1906

ter. The services provided in the 1900s worked to Chalk Farm and to Poplar every fifteen minutes, to Richmond hourly and to Kew Bridge hourly. In addition there were the Outer Circle trains to Mansion House, half-hourly, and two trains an hour to GNR stations. (The stations served were those on the lines to High Barnet, Alexandra Palace, Enfield [Gordon Hill after 1910], and Potters Bar. For short periods, Hatfield and Cuffley were also served. In the peak year of 1906 there were sixty-five trains each way daily to and from GNR stations, all worked by NLR engines and stock.) At peak hours there were additional trains and also LNWR services to Watford and Tring. In 1906 Broad Street was handling 712 trains a day, with some 80,000 passengers.

As a challenge to the improved GWR service to Birmingham via that company's new main line, the LNWR introduced a Monday to Friday restaurant-car express to and from Broad Street. This 'City to City' train began on February 1st, 1910, between Wolverhampton and Birmingham and Broad Street, stopping only at Coventry on the up working and additionally at Willesden on the return run. It was designed to attract businessmen and carried a lady typist who would tap out letters to order during the journey. The down train was withdrawn from July 13th, 1914, and the up train from February 22nd, 1915, and the service was not revived after the war.

CHILLY WINDS

Broad Street's suburban trains early felt the effect of electric tramcar, motor bus and Tube railway. The chilly winds of their competition were first noticed about 1901, and despite brave efforts to publicize the doubtful pleasures of travelling by the 'open-air route' and the operation of non-stop trains between Broad Street and Gospel Oak, the graphs of revenue and passengers slid downwards. By 1911 the annual total of passengers carried was the lowest for forty years.

Electrification was first considered in 1904 as a means of

stopping the rot, but it eventually came as part of the LNWR scheme of 1911, a scheme drawn up two years after that company had taken over the management and working of the North London. LNWR electric trains, operating on the four-rail system, first left Broad Street on October 1st, 1916, when the Richmond and Kew Bridge workings were taken over by the new trains. Rush-hour services to Watford via Hampstead Heath followed on April 16th, 1917. An all-day electric service to Watford via Primrose Hill began on July 10th, 1922. At Broad Street, Platforms 5 to 9 were equipped with conductor rails, the electric trains running in and out on the No 2 up and down roads between the terminus and Dalston.

Between the wars there were electric trains to Richmond every fifteen minutes and to Watford every thirty minutes, with additional trains in the peak including one to Croxley Green. Steam trains ran every half-hour to Poplar (five in the peak hour). Rush-hour services included one steam train an hour to Tring and six to LNER (ex GNR) stations. In the 1920s, Broad Street's traffic continued to decline, particularly that over the former GNR lines, reduced to rush hours only since 1915. More attractive alternatives were provided by motor bus and Tube railway, the LMSR assisting the process by retaining in use the old North London four-wheel carriages until 1935. Unheated and gas-lit, with hard-back seats and open top partitions, these veterans survived even longer on the Broad Street – Poplar service, where one set was still running, in newly-varnished North London livery, as late as 1938.

To afford some relief to the cramped accommodation in the old Fenchurch Street, the LMSR lengthened Platforms 1 and 2 at Broad Street, operating regular services from them to Southend, Grays and Tilbury from 1923 onwards. These trains continued to run until the Fenchurch Street enlargement was completed in 1935.

Broad Street suffered minor damage in the First World War. On September 8th, 1915, bomb explosions shattered a thousand panes of glass, demolished a wall and injured some horses in the goods station. More serious disturbances were created twenty-five years later. The lines into the terminus were put completely out of action on the night of October 3rd–4th, 1940, and the station was closed for several days. Similar interruptions were experienced on October 13th and November 11th. Services over the former GNR lines, which had been suspended between September 11th and December 3rd, 1939, to make room for essential war traffic, were taken off altogether on October 4th, 1940, after the previous night's bomb havoc. LNER stock had been used from February 5th, 1940, causing much initial confusion among passengers. Heavy air attacks on the East End of London, with subsequent evacuation of many of the residents, finally extinguished the poorly-patronized service east of Dalston Junction, which was not worked after May 14th, 1944. Shoreditch and Haggerston Stations had closed in 1940. Although the Poplar service was never resumed, the LNER revived the Broad Street trains after the war, using its own locomotives and stock; trains ran to and from Hertford North and Welwyn Garden City from July 30th, 1945, in rush hours only.

Main-line trains reappeared briefly at holiday times in 1950 and 1951 when some short-distance main-line services to Cambridge and other places were diverted to relieve Kings Cross.

A POST-WAR PROBLEM

Apart from the electric rush-hour services between Broad Street and Watford and Croxley Green via Primrose Hill, and peak-hour diesel trains to and from Stevenage, Hertford North and Welwyn Garden City, the only trains which now use this terminus are the electrics to and from Richmond via Hampstead Heath, three an hour each way until mid-evening. At slack times, the traffic is so light that one ticket collector and a booking clerk are sufficient to staff the whole terminus. On weekdays they have for company a tailor and a few office workers who inhabit the old shops round the concourse. At the turn of the century there were almost 50,000 passengers arriving in the rush hours, but in 1968 the daily user was only 9,000, falling to 3,000 on Saturdays and only 1,250 on Sundays.

Traffic thinned out so much that British Railways closed off the main station block altogether in the late 1950s, erecting two small buildings on the concourse, one for the stationmaster and ticket booking, the other for inquiries and 'gentlemen'. These were completed in 1957. Unable to operate the refreshment room profitably, the railway authorities passed it over to private enterprise, who in turn gave up the struggle in 1963. Now there is little to divert the waiting passenger, apart from a charming one-eighth scale model of NLR 4-4-0T No 60. A feature of Broad Street for many years, this model was built at Bow Works in 1888. It once ran on live steam, but now suffers the indignity of being powered by an electric motor, which responds when a penny is dropped for the Railway Benevolent Institution. At the opposite end of the concourse is a sad little cenotaph which the North London Railway erected to commemorate those of its staff who were killed in the 1914–18 War.

In 1967–8 Broad Street was stripped of most of its remaining grandeur when part of the train shed was removed to reduce maintenance costs. What is now left is but a poor thing indeed, just one more of BR's many under-used assets. Perhaps one day the site will be put to more lucrative commercial use, something which should have been done in the 1950s when everyone but BR was cashing-in on the central London office-building boom, but now much more difficult to achieve. Whatever is done with it, room ought to be available somewhere for the two tracks which would be sufficient to carry the remaining rail traffic.

SIGNALLING

From the outset, Broad Street had interlocked signalling, provided by McKenzie & Holland, in two boxes, one for each side of the station. No 1 box was situated north of the platforms on the east side and worked the NLR platforms. No 2, at the north end of Platform 8, was the LNWR box. In the 1891 rearrangement mentioned in the main text, the original No 1 box was replaced by a new seventy-five lever box opened in May 1891. This had NLR standard tappet interlocking, and was situated north of the coaling stage serving Nos 2 and 3 platforms.

Each cabin had an inner home signal to maintain locking and prevent reversal of points in front of an approaching train. Further protection was given by a Park & Pryce train-protection bar in each platform road, which locked the inner home at danger while a train was standing in the platform on the bar.

North of the station, Skinner Street Junction box marked an intermediate block section and New Inn Yard Junction box the end of the first section. These two cabins were also needed to control the freight working in and out of the LNWR goods depot on the west side of the terminus.

CHAPTER SIX

LIVERPOOL STREET

NOT AS BLACK AS PAINTED

A gloomy low-level situation, uninspired architecture, and a confusing, disjointed layout all contributed to Liverpool Street's past unpopularity. In steam days it always seemed to have more than its fair share of smoke and grime, not being an easy place to ventilate or keep clean. Suffering the austerities of wartime travel, Tom Driberg had been moved, in the winter of 1944, to describe it in *Reynolds News* as 'almost completely squalid ... tiringly chaotic ... this hell hole ...' setting off an interesting correspondence in the *Railway Gazette*; but it was never as bad as *that*, even in its worst days, and those wartime years were among the worst. Electrification provided the opportunity of keeping the interior clean and bright, making Liverpool Street a much more pleasant place for the ordinary passenger. But many a railway enthusiast now passed through with a heavy heart, sadly missing the impatient beat of Westinghouse brake pumps and the soft smoke that lingered so long, mixed so romantically with summer sunlight or winter fog.

SHOREDITCH, OR BAD CHARACTERS GOT RID OF

Whatever the real or imagined disadvantages of Liverpool Street, it was a vast improvement upon its predecessor, the Shoreditch terminus of the Eastern Counties Railway. That line had been opened from a temporary station at Devonshire Street, Mile End, on June 20th, 1839, after the formal opening of June 18th, reaching the permanent terminus just south of the junction of Bethnal Green Road and Shoreditch on July

1st, 1840. As the engineer John Braithwaite[1] had cut through the built-up area by bringing the ECR in from the Lea Valley over a viaduct of brick arches, the platforms were above street level. Passengers arriving in London by this route for the first time must have wondered how they would make their escape, for the line terminated in one of the capital's poorest and most unpleasant quarters. Six years after the opening, the station was renamed Bishopsgate, probably in the hope that it might be thought nearer the City than it was.

Its situation was in truth unfortunate. Within a stone's throw of Old Jago, one of London's foulest slums, inhabited almost entirely by criminals, the terminus was built on the site of Webb Square, 'a sort of receptacle for pickpockets, house-breakers and prostitutes, great numbers of whom were removed; and the same along St John Street, one side of which was taken down, and several bad characters were then got rid of'.[2] As early as 1845 the ECR was proposing to construct an alternative terminus. In supporting a Farringdon Street scheme before the Royal Commission of 1846, George Hudson spoke of the inconvenience of Shoreditch, both for the City and the West End. Nearly twenty years later the terminus was still there, and the *Railway News* was commenting acidly that the site 'has always been an unsavoury and unsuitable locality, and not even the change of name from Shoreditch to Bishopsgate has ever made it one whit more attractive'.

Designed by Braithwaite, the Shoreditch building contained the offices of the Eastern Counties Railway and of the Northern & Eastern Railway, which used the line inwards from Stratford. Incorporated in 1836, this company proposed to build a line from Islington to York via Bishops Stortford, Cambridge and Lincoln. Finding the cost of a London terminus and approaches too much for its financial resources, it made arrangements with the ECR to run over that company's line between Stratford and Shoreditch at a toll of 4*d* per passenger and a rent of £7,000 a year. The first section of the N & ER, from Stratford to Broxbourne, was opened on September 15th,

1840, and the line had only reached Bishops Stortford before the company was leased to the ECR in 1844; it was vested in the Great Eastern Railway, the ECR'S successor, in 1902.

Behind a 125-ft frontage were single departure and arrival platforms each 265 ft long, separated by three empty carriage roads. Above the tracks and platforms was a corrugated wrought-iron roof with a 36-ft centre span and 20-ft 6-in side spans. Water from it drained through thirty-four cast-iron columns which ran in two rows down its 230-ft length. At each end of the platforms, all five 5-ft-gauge tracks were linked by turnplates. Both the N & ER and the ECR were converted to standard gauge in 1844.

On the up side, to the east of the station, were two ticket platforms, and, in the yard, a horse and carriage dock. The down side of the station yard contained horse and carriage docks, a 32-ft turntable, an engine pit, a water crane, and a coke platform. In St John Street, on the north side of the line, and east of the passenger station, was a goods yard.

Such a small station inevitably required enlargement before it was very old. A modest rebuilding, incorporating a new frontage in the Italian style by Sancton Wood, was carried out in 1848-9. But it was still inadequate and poorly-sited.

In 1862, the ECR became part of the Great Eastern Railway, and consideration was at once given to the question of a London terminus. Attempts to obtain use of the proposed station at Broad Street were unsuccessful, and in a report to the board, dated December 17th, 1862, the manager and engineer recommended the construction of a new passenger terminus inside the City of London, the development of suburban traffic by the construction of new lines, and the conversion of Bishopsgate to a goods station. They described the terminus as 'objectionable in almost every feature. In locality it is remote; its approaches are inconvenient; and as regards space, it is so restricted that your traffic can only be carried at great cost, with great delay, and with an absolute restriction on the number of trains which can be dispatched'. The extension into the City received the blessing of a House of Lords Select Committee on London's Railways in 1863.

Various proposals were made; first for a terminus at Finsbury Circus, then as far south as Wormwood Street, with approach tracks above street level; but the scheme sanctioned by Parliament in 1864 was for a low-level station in Liverpool Street, alongside and to the east of the North London Railway terminus then under construction. Ten years were to elapse before the project was realized. It was a difficult time to raise capital, especially for the GER, then going through an anxious period of financial stress. When a move could at last be made, there were long delays before the necessary properties were acquired.

It was decided to bring the approach tracks down from the old ECR viaduct at Tapp Street (just west of the present Bethnal Green Station), maintaining a gradient of 1 in 70 until they were below street level. This provided some saving in land acquisition, allowing the lines to pass under one side of the original terminal site. Beyond, the alignment was to go under Commercial Street and Shoreditch High Street before turning south to enter the terminus, on a site once occupied by the gardens of the old Bethlehem Hospital. Among the major buildings to be demolished were the City of London Theatre and the City of London Gasworks. When giving evidence on May 16th, 1884, to the Royal Commission on the Housing of the Working Classes, William Birt (general manager of the GER) mentioned the destruction of 450 tenement dwellings, sheltering some 7,000 people. Some of the houses had been occupied by as many as seven families and were perhaps some of the worst of their kind in London. Their destruction had been anticipated in a clause of the 1864 Act requiring the GER to run a 2d return daily from Edmonton and another from Walthamstow. In practice the GER provided many more cheap trains but, as elsewhere, most of those thrown out of their homes were too poor to afford new houses in the suburbs. Instead, they spent the few shillings 'compensation' on a bottle or two of gin and the hire of a cart and squeezed themselves into adjacent streets, increasing the already pitiable overcrowding of the Shoreditch area. Birt claimed that the GER always compensated tenants, paying from 30s to 50s according to the circumstances of each family, but whilst this may have been strictly true at the time he gave evidence, such payments as were made a decade earlier did not always reach those levels.

AT THE FOOT OF AN INCLINE

Many years later, in the *Great Eastern Railway Magazine,* of February 1923, Lord Claud Hamilton[3] related how the GER directors were prevented from taking any interest in the design of the new terminus. Planning and construction were in the hands of Samuel Swarbrick, the general manager, who had the chairman, Lightly Simpson, under his thumb. Swarbrick, who was more interested in financial matters than traffic and operating considerations, had agreed the low-level plan. Hamilton thought this a serious error, and wanted to see the platforms at street level, but he and his fellow directors were not allowed to interfere. 'The result,' wrote Hamilton, 'has been a great inconvenience to the travelling public ... every one of our heavily-laden trains has to commence its journey at the bottom of an incline.'

A part of the new station was opened on February 2nd, 1874, for the Enfield and Walthamstow services, the remainder coming into use on November 1st, 1875, when the old Bishopsgate terminus was closed to passengers. Converted to a goods depot, it reopened in 1881 and survived in use until December 5th, 1964, when it was totally destroyed by fire.

Liverpool Street, as opened in 1874–5, occupied an area of 10 acres, and had 10 platforms, numbered from west to east. At the extreme west side, the tracks serving Platforms 1 and 2 were extended in tunnel beneath the station buildings and under the street to a junction with the Metropolitan Railway, just west of what was later to be that company's Liverpool Street Station.

The main buildings of the terminus consisted of a 90-ft-high block on Liverpool Street, another block attached to this, running back 320 ft from the street, and a third block, 146 ft long, joined to the second at its north end, at right angles to it, and terminating in a massive spired clock tower. Apart from the clock tower, on the west, and a 90-ft-high central section in the middle block, these last two buildings were 67 ft high. In the open space formed by the angle of the buildings were four roadways for pedestrians and vehicles. The westernmost of these was above the tunnel to the Metropolitan and led to the separate suburban booking-office. This office was later closed, and a five-storey office block erected over it, west of the clock tower.

For many years the pedestrian way remained open, with access to a new low-level suburban booking-office, but it is now closed and used as a car park for the Great Eastern Hotel. Next to the suburban approach, descending from the street to platform level, was the entrance way for cabs bound for the main-line departure side. This roadway had a pavement at the west side and formed the most popular entrance and exit for those not using the subways under the street to and from the Metropolitan station. After this came the exit ramp for cabs leaving the departure side, and finally, alongside the west block, a small yard serving the general offices which were situated in this building. At the extreme eastern side of the station, along-side the easternmost platform, there was another vehicle road-way, running the full length of the station from Pindar Street to Liverpool Street, serving main-line arrivals.

Behind the north block and the clock tower was the suburban section of the station, ten platform faces and eight tracks under a 450-ft roof in spans of 46 ft and 109 ft. The main-line departure and arrival platforms (later 9 and 10) were to the east of the middle office block; 900 ft in length, they extended almost up to Liverpool Street under a 730-ft roof in spans of 109 ft and 45 ft.

The train shed, shaped like an inverted 'L', with its four

spans of iron and glass reaching up to 76 ft above the tracks, had roof trusses of wrought iron, with cast-iron ornamental details and spandril fittings. The roof is one of the best points of Liverpool Street; lofty and delicate-looking, it imparts grace to the interior. Later the roofscape was enhanced by two enormous four-faced clocks, which were suspended above the platforms. Despite their Gothic appearance, they were electrically operated.

In the centre of the long west block, at platform level, was the main-line booking-office, 90 ft long and 50 ft wide, conveniently situated between the cab road and the departure platform. After the First World War, the GER erected a large mural memorial at the north end of this hall. It was unveiled on June 22nd, 1922, by Field-Marshal Sir Henry Wilson (Chief of the Imperial General Staff, and an Ulster MP), and a plaque next to it recalls that on returning from the ceremony, Wilson was assassinated on his doorstep by two members of the Irish Republican Army. Another plaque on the same wall forms a memorial to the heroic GER marine officer, Captain Fryatt, who was executed by the Germans in 1916.[4]

Either side of the booking-hall were waiting and refreshment rooms. Above, all along this middle block, were the general offices of the GER.

The frontage buildings, in white Suffolk brick, with Bath stone dressings and ornamentation, are uninteresting, even dreary in appearance. Edward Wilson, an engineer, drew up the designs for the terminus, and any architectural assistance was at a humble level. The style is a restrained Gothic, the features seemingly taken straight from a copy book of do-it-yourself architecture.

The platforms behind the north block, now numbered 1 to 8, were allocated to suburban services, apart from the two easternmost, which shared main-line departures with the long platform now numbered 9. Against the western wall was No 1, reached by a footbridge, spanning the entrance to the Metropolitan junction tunnel, which received the platform tracks of

Nos 1 and 2. The remaining suburban platforms were set farther back, the two easternmost tracks having a platform face either side. These faces are now known as 7 west, 7 east, 8 west and 8 east, but at earlier periods were variously known as 6, 7, 8 and 9, or 6, 7, 7 and 8. This confusion is the reason why some accounts give the number of platforms at the original Liverpool Street as nine, others ten. There were in fact twelve platform *faces*. Next came the long departure platform, and opposite it, on the extreme eastern side of the station, the arrival platform (now 10), of similar length.

From February 1st until July 12th, 1875, when its own station was completed, Metropolitan Railway trains used Platforms 1 and 2 of the GER station. The proposed through workings between the two railways were suffocated by tedious arguments about charges, and after the opening of the Metropolitan station (on the opposite side of Liverpool Street, and known as Bishopsgate until January 1st, 1909), the connecting tunnel was used only for special workings. The last of these, a Metropolitan excursion train from Rickmansworth to Yarmouth, ran in 1904. Three years later the junction was removed.

Although the tenemented poor had received little or no recompense, the landowners required suitable rewards. The cost of construction and materials was heavy, notably high prices being paid for the roof ironwork. Altogether the terminus cost some £2,000,000, and in an endeavour to recover some of it, the GER obtained powers in an Act of 1869 to charge fares over the 1¼-mile extension at the 2-mile rate.

In conjunction with the opening of Liverpool Street, a three-pronged group of suburban lines was constructed north of Bethnal Green, as recommended in the report mentioned earlier. These new lines ran through Hackney Downs and Tottenham to Lower Edmonton, where a junction was formed with the original Enfield branch; and from Hackney Downs through Clapton to junctions with the Cambridge line and the 1870 Walthamstow branch from Lea Bridge. Both were opened

in August 1872. The Walthamstow branch was extended to
Chingford in 1873, and the Tottenham and Edmonton line
was given a branch to Palace Gates (Wood Green) in 1878. As
these new direct routes to Walthamstow and Enfield were
ready before Liverpool Street, and there was no room for more
trains at Bishopsgate, a new station, Bishopsgate Low Level,
was opened on the approach line to Liverpool Street on
November 4th, 1872. This was directly beneath the original
terminus, and as there was little or no room for smoke to escape, it was decided to fit condensing apparatus to the whole
interchangeable fleet of suburban tank engines; the possibility
of through running on to the Metropolitan Railway may also
have been a factor in this decision. Bishopsgate Low Level
station remained open after the completion of Liverpool Street,
but was closed as a wartime economy on May 22nd, 1916, a sad
day for the knowing rush-hour passengers who would assure
themselves of an evening seat by boarding incoming trains
there.

During the 1880s, the suburban services over these new
lines, with their very cheap fares and frequent trains, developed
a heavy traffic, and it became clear that the accommodation at
Liverpool Street would be insufficient for all the GER services,
despite the continued use of Fenchurch Street for some routes.
As early as 1884, the chairman of the GER told shareholders that
the company could fill a thousand trains daily in and out of
Liverpool Street, but the existing premises could handle only
two-thirds that number.

EAST SIDE EXTENSION

For some time the GER had been acquiring land between the
eastern boundary of the terminus and Bishopsgate. This area,
188 ft wide, and some 6 acres in extent, was now cleared, and
in 1890 construction of what was to be the East Side station
was begun. This time, Parliament had insisted that the displaced inhabitants be rehoused by the railway company at low

fixed rents. Alternative accommodation was found for 137 in existing property; the remaining 600 went into tenements completed in 1890 at GER expense.

As part of the new works, a third pair of approach tracks was provided between Bethnal Green and Liverpool Street, coming into use in 1891. The westernmost lines, reserved entirely for the Enfield Town, Palace Gates and Walthamstow services were then known as the Suburban lines, the middle pair as the Local and the eastern pair as the Through. These last four tracks continued beyond Bethnal Green, eventually to Romford. Between Bethnal Green and Hackney Downs North junction were four tracks, the Suburban, and, on the east, the Fast lines, the latter joining the Local lines at Bethnal Green.

At Liverpool Street, Platforms 1 to 5 (West Side Suburban) were connected to both the Suburban and Local lines, Platforms 7 to 14 were served by both Local and Through, whilst 15 to 18 were connected to the Through lines only. The East Side, with its eight 30-ft-wide platforms, all slightly longer than Nos 1 to 8, was opened to public traffic on April 2nd, 1894. During the time when the new platforms and signal boxes were being connected, no trains were cancelled, but from March 27th to April 2nd, 132 flagmen worked 800 trains a day, and from June 25th to July 2nd, when the new West Side signal box was installed and certain alterations made to the West Side platforms, 140 flagmen managed 871 daily trains without serious incident.

If the number of platforms is taken as a measure of size, Liverpool Street, with eighteen, was the largest London terminus until the opening of the new Victoria in 1908, but both before and after that date it held supreme place as regards the number of passengers handled daily. In March 1907 there were 851 passenger trains in and out each twenty-four hours, together with 224 empty coach trains, 10 goods trains and 5 light engines, a total of 1,090 movements every day.

At this time the normal platform allocation was as follows:

West Side

1 Palace Gates and Enfield Town and all workmen's trains on the Suburban lines
2 Palace Gates and Enfield Town
3 Chingford
4 North Woolwich and evening trains on the Enfield and Chingford lines
5 Loughton and North Woolwich
6 Loughton, North Woolwich; Cambridge line departures as required
7 & 8 Cambridge line departures
9 Cambridge and Colchester main-line departures
10–12 Main-line arrivals
13 Main-line arrivals as required. Suburban and stopping trains on the Colchester line

East Side Suburban

14 New Cross and Croydon via East London Railway
15–17 Ilford, Romford and Southend lines
18 Barking via Forest Gate junction
Ilford, Romford and Southend as required
Horse box and other specials as required

The services to south London through the Thames Tunnel which used Platform 14, and sometimes 18, and before that, the original station, had an interesting career. After the completion of the East London Railway from Wapping to East London junction (just east of Bishopsgate) on April 10th, 1876, the LBSCR started a service from Croydon to Liverpool Street on the following July 1st. This was joined by SER trains, which worked into Liverpool Street from Addiscombe Road (now Addiscombe) between April 1st, 1880, and March 2nd, 1884. From January 1st, 1886, the GER had taken over the workings to the LBSCR stations, operating a service to New Cross, and, from February 1st, 1887, to East Croydon. These trains did not run beyond New Cross from June 1st, 1911, and ceased altogether when the East London Railway was electrified from March 31st, 1913. Apart from these local trains, there had been a daily return working between Liverpool Street and

Brighton from 1876 to 1883, with through carriages for a further year.

The frontage of the East Side was formed by the Great Eastern Hotel, which had been completed in May 1884. Designed by C. E. Barry in a vaguely French Renaissance style, this red-brick structure was somewhat more impressive than the earlier station buildings. Now the largest, if not the only major hotel in the City of London, the Great Eastern contains the Abercorn Rooms, entered from Bishopsgate, and used for banquets, dances and other functions.

MYSTERIOUS AND MURKY

Beneath the hotel was an area known as the 'backs', penetrated by the tracks of Platforms 9 and 10 and one of the two sidings between them, thus providing the building with a railway-served basement. A mysterious and murky place, the 'backs' were the introduction to an equally grim subway which led to the eastbound Metropolitan platform. As a child, the author was often taken this way when visiting relatives in south-east London, never passing through without a shudder, as both subway and 'backs' had entered his subconscious and formed the scenery of many a frightening dream.

There always seemed to be a few trucks in the 'backs', or on the sidings between 9 and 10, known as the 'yard'. We later discovered that Liverpool Street had a night goods train, the 12.7 AM from Stratford, which brought in permanent-way material, coal for the hotel and the engine docks, and truck traffic for the hotel and other departments. This 'ghost train', as it was known to the staff, returned with a load of hotel refuse and ashes from the engine docks. In the heyday of steam, the coaling stages of the engine docks at the platform ends needed as much as 15,000 tons a year. The terminus also saw parcels trains from the Southern lines via the East London Railway, which were brought into the yard for splitting and reversing before moving on. Interchange freight trains were also worked in and out of the terminus.

Along Bishopsgate, the East Side was penetrated by in and out cab roads ending in a small yard opposite Platforms 11 and 12. Next came an office block, later known as Harwich House, and this was followed by the rather plain façade which contained the pedestrian entrances to the booking-hall, concourse and platforms of the East Side. Beyond this was a large block of offices with shops at ground-floor level, stretching almost the whole length of the platforms, and containing the entrance to the parcels depot. This building was later named Hamilton House after Lord Claud Hamilton. The parcels depot extended over Platforms 11 to 18, with a parcels bridge as far as Platform 8. Flanked by roadways, it was connected by lifts to the platforms, and to a parcels subway below.

Entering the East Side from Bishopsgate, the passenger either descended a stairway into the large concourse at the head of the platforms, or passed into the East Side booking-office from which doorways led out on to the footbridge which ran right across the station. The train shed of the East Side consisted of a four-span roof (51 ft 6 ins, 42 ft 3 ins, 42 ft 3 ins and 51 ft 11 ins), with red-brick walls, and a cross-span over the 15,000-sq-ft concourse. There was a pleasing lightness and spaciousness about this new section of the terminus, which was designed by W. N. Ashbee,[5] head of the GER architectural section.

When the station was first planned, it was apparently not realized that if there were any expansion in the only possible direction, eastwards, the extra length of the main-line Platforms 9 and 10 would split the station in two just as effectively as the Great Hall split Euston. When the East Side was built, it was necessary to make the best of this situation and erect footbridges not only across the south ends of 9 and 10, but across the full width of the combined East and West Sides, to provide ready access to all parts of the station. This main footbridge was by no means straight, none too wide, and at two different levels. It was the scene of much confusion at busy times as people struggled to get from one side of the station.

to the other; from it many a curse must have been uttered, because of it, many a train missed.

But it did have one redeeming feature, for three little tea rooms jutted out from it, offering refreshment and relaxation for the weary. There were two on the West Side, opposite Platforms 3 to 6, and one on the East Side, facing 12 and 13. These delightful Gothic gazebos provided many a pleasant half-hour for the railway-minded station saunterer and those given to watching the social scene. Sitting here, with the aroma of tea and buttered toast subtly mixing into the smoke and steam wafting through the open window, it was possible to enjoy a particularly cosy contemplation of the bustle and activity always present below. One of these rooms, now inevitably a self-service cafeteria, and that much less attractive, remains open on the West Side; the others are used as a store and as a stationmaster's office.

Communications across the station were somewhat improved in July 1912 when the Central London Tube railway was extended to Liverpool Street. A booking-hall was then built for the Tube beneath the West Side, and a subway opened to connect it to Bishopsgate, across the station. Taking the view that the Central London would bring extra traffic, the GER made the space required for the Tube station available free of charge. In more recent years, the area at the end of Platforms 9 and 10 has been tidied up, the 'backs' sidings abolished, and level communication around the ends has replaced the smaller footbridge.

In addition to the passenger facilities provided by the Central London Tube railway, Liverpool Street was one of the two London termini to be served by the Post Office Tube railway, opened between Paddington and Whitechapel in December 1927. A station was provided at the south end, under the hotel, with two 315-ft parcel and letter bag conveyors to Platforms 10 and 11. Normal traffic in the 1930s reached some 10,000 bags daily, with 690 GPO trains calling.

SUBURBAN JAZZ

The suburban and outer suburban network was completed by the opening of the Southend branch (1889), the Churchbury loop, from Edmonton to Cheshunt (1891) and the Hainault loop from Ilford to Woodford (1903). Neither of the loops was immediately successful, and the Churchbury line was closed to passengers in 1909. By the 1900s, the GER suburban service was the most lavish and the busiest in the world. In 1912 the three pairs of approach tracks were carrying around a thousand trains daily, with a passenger load of some 200,000 in and out, mostly in suburban trains of fifteen to seventeen four-wheel carriages. From the earliest days, Liverpool Street suburban traffic had been deliberately encouraged, particularly on the West Side. The two cheap trains required by the 1864 Act had been increased to twenty-three by 1883 and to thirty by 1900, five of them to Enfield Town, providing a return run of 21½ miles for 2*d*. Supplementing the 2*d* trains were twelve 3*d* trains operating between 7 and 7.30 AM and following these, until 8 AM, there were about a dozen trains at half the ordinary fare. The 2*d* and 3*d* fares remained in force until 1920, when the cheap fares were revised on a mileage scale. By 1927 the cheapest return fare from Enfield Town or Wood Street was 6*d* (arriving by 7.2 AM). In the evening, all cheap tickets were available on any train after 4 PM (after noon on Saturdays), excluding some fast trains. A half-hourly all-night service, the first in Britain, was introduced on June 21st, 1897, between Liverpool Street and Walthamstow.

This frequent, punctual and cheap train service encouraged artisans, clerks, and shop and warehouse workers to move out from the inner belt, and private enterprise provided thousands of small houses for them to rent in Tottenham, Edmonton and Walthamstow. In Walthamstow, the population grew from 11,092 in 1871 to 95,131 in 1901, and there were similar increases in Tottenham, Edmonton and parts of Wood Green.

Prompted by the existence of Tube railway schemes for north-east London, electrification of the suburban lines was considered, and powers were taken in 1903. But although the traffic continued to grow, nothing was done, nor were any Tube railways built. After the First World War, the suburban problem became more burdensome, as the increasing concentration of the rush hours brought severe overcrowding. From 200,000 passengers a day in 1,250 trains in 1912, Liverpool Street's traffic had grown to 229,073 in 1921, with only fourteen more trains. Between 7.30 and 9.30 AM, 66,488 passengers arrived, 68,017 leaving in the evening between 5 and 7.

It was impossible to enlarge the terminus any further without enormous expenditure and disruption; electrification seemed the only way of increasing capacity. A scheme for electric services to Palace Gates, Enfield, Broxbourne, Chingford, Ongar, North Woolwich and Gidea Park was drawn up, but the directors hesitated, appalled at the amount of capital required, money which they knew would be difficult, if not impossible, to raise, in view of the small return that could be expected. Yet something had to be done for the heavily over-crowded Enfield and Chingford services, and it was agreed in 1919 to make the best of the existing equipment by spending £80,000 (less than a fortieth of the cost of electrification) on track and station rearrangements, resignalling and other measures that would permit the steam trains to be run at maximum possible intensity. This scheme was planned by F. V. Russell, the GER superintendent of operation.

Although very successful, this was only an expedient, and everyone in authority knew that they were merely putting off the difficult decision of electrification as long as possible. Known officially as the *Intensive Service*, the new arrangements which came into operation on July 12th, 1920, were quickly christened the *Jazz Service* by an evening newspaper. An increase of fifty per cent was achieved in the Monday to Friday service between 5 and 7.30 PM and of seventy-five per cent in the corresponding up service between 8 and 10 AM. At the height of the rush period, there were twenty-four sixteen-coach trains, each with 848 seats, passing each hour along one track between Liverpool Street and Bethnal Green. (Six ran to Chingford, six to Wood Street [fast to St James Street], nine to Enfield Town [three with Palace Gates connexions at Seven Sisters] and three to Palace Gates.)

This was a remarkable achievement with manual signalling and motive power largely consisting of 0–6–0T of an 1886 design weighing only 32 tons empty, engines with 4-ft wheels and cylinders $16\frac{1}{2}$ ins by 22 ins. Off-peak and Sunday services were also improved by the introduction of shorter, faster and more frequent trains which provided a basic ten-minute service on the Enfield and Chingford lines.

Every possible step was taken to cut terminal delays. Independent engine docks and layouts were provided for Platforms 1 to 4, allowing incoming engines to be shunted without fouling the other lines beyond platform limits. With these and other alterations, trains could be moved into a platform every ten minutes, staying only four minutes. At the busy hours, trains started in sequence from Platforms 4 (Wood Street fast), 3 (Enfield), 2 (Chingford) and 1 (Enfield or Palace Gates), at two-minute intervals, followed by a four-minute gap to accommodate arrivals. Each incoming engine, as released, worked the next departure, and extra men were on duty to assist with the uncoupling and servicing of arriving engines.

Additional circulating space was made on the platform side of the barriers of 2 to 6 by demolishing a bookstall, staff offices and lavatory entrances. This gave passengers a choice of exit gates, thus speeding up the clearance of the platform. Access to Platform 1 was made easier by finally closing up the Metropolitan branch tunnel (it had been used for stabling stock), making it possible to reach it on the level. After removal of the tracks, the tunnel was converted to staff recreation and dining-rooms. The entrance can still be seen from Metropolitan Line trains entering Liverpool Street on the eastbound line.

To obtain longer headways and provide paths for down

Plan of Liverpool Street 1924. From the Railway Magazine, May 1924

main-line trains which might be running late, it was necessary to have 'non-stop' working in various combinations. A code number was allocated to each train according to its stopping pattern, and leaflets explaining the numbers were left on the seats of trains some weeks before the new service started. These numbers were prominently displayed on the side of the brake vans and at the Liverpool Street barriers, together with a list of stations passed. Later, 'pedestal' departure indicators with departure-time dials and station-name displays were placed at the head of each platform (similar indicators were installed on Platforms 11 to 18). Finally, to speed up loading, second- and first-class compartments were temporarily picked out by yellow- and blue-coloured bands painted between the windows and the roof.

As a consequence of the Jazz Service track alterations, trains using Platforms 1, 2 and 3 now ran on the Local lines only in emergencies, and Enfield and Chingford line trains were confined to Platforms 1 to 4. Trains using Platform 4 still occasionally ran on the Local lines, but usually on the Suburban lines. Platforms 5 and 6 were connected only with the Local lines. Through services to Palace Gates were reduced to rush hours only, but the branch was worked with a frequent push-pull service, connecting with Enfield line trains, which left Liverpool Street carrying on their smokebox doors the lengthy legend: ENFIELD TOWN CHANGE FOR PALACE GATES AT SEVEN SISTERS.

After a temporary suspension during the 1921 coal strike, the Jazz Service lasted until the 1926 general strike. When that had passed, the slack-hour timetable was modified, and the pressure on the West Side began to abate. People moved to new houses farther out, took up local employment in the expanding Lea Valley industrial area, or used more attractive forms of transport into the centre (until 1925, when the Gresley 'quintuplet' articulated sets were slowly introduced, all trains were composed of gas-lit four-wheelers with a very spartan atmosphere in the third class).

Activity at Liverpool Street generally declined. In 1923, 244,000 passengers were passing through daily, but this had fallen to 209,000 by 1938 (and was to go down to 171,000 in 1959). The number of ticket collectors decreased from 76 in 1924 to 63 in 1935, and the complement of porters in the same period fell from 134 to 90.

We must now return for a moment to complete the story of the station in the GER years. Liverpool Street was one of the few London termini to suffer serious air-raid damage in the First World War. On the night of September 8th, 1915, several bombs fell on the approaches, wrecking the Suburban and Through lines, and splitting a water main which flooded the Local tracks. Repairs were quickly effected, and a full service of trains was working by 11 the next morning. During a daylight raid on June 13th, 1917, three bombs fell at the outer end of the platforms just before noon, wrecking several carriages of the midday train for Hunstanton, which was standing in No 9. Two carriages in the dock between Platforms 8 and 9, in use for medical examinations, were also smashed up. Sixteen people were killed and thirty-six injured. During the war years, the extensive cellars under the station and hotel were fitted up as air-raid shelters for the staff and public, and an emergency office provided in them for the staff handling military-traffic control.

Almost the last act of the GER at Liverpool Street was to erect a large main-line train indicator on the footbridge above Platform 9. Put into use on December 17th, 1922, this showed the times, platform numbers and stopping points of departures in fourteen columns, each with a maximum of twenty indications. Details of arrivals were also displayed.

Nothing of great moment happened to Liverpool Street under the LNER régime. In May 1935 the East Side booking-office was modernized and equipped with Westinghouse ticket-issue and accounting machines (since removed), the rapid printers being of a type similar to those which had been in use for some years on the Underground. During 1938-9, after

years of neglect and public criticism, some attempts were made
to clean and brighten the station. Surburban and East Side
booking-offices were panelled with vitriolite, a smooth yellow
composition that provided an easily cleaned surface; the steelwork and masonry inside the station lost some of their in-
grained dirt; the lighting was improved; and advertisements
and notices were regrouped. A new snack bar was provided,
together with enlarged waiting- and refreshment-rooms. The
'backs' had their walls tiled and their lighting brightened up,
removing something of their nightmare quality. It was all bits
and pieces, good-intentioned perhaps, but it really did not
make much difference; the dear old place soon lapsed into
its normal grimy, grey state, and the wartime blackout helped
no end.

A good deal of damage was suffered by Liverpool Street
during the Second World War,[6] but at the end, there it was,
still looking very much the same. High-explosive bombs fell
on Platforms 1 and 4, the first wrecking a train, which took
several days to remove. On the East Side, there was damage to
the booking-office and Platform 18 at the concourse end. A
delayed-action bomb which landed in the engine sidings beyond Platform 10 exploded on the following day and killed two
men, even though it had been surrounded by four trucks filled
with ballast. A bomb which fell on the Broad Street viaduct
whisked an LMSR wagon on to Liverpool Street's roof, where
it had to be dismantled before it could be removed. The office
blocks were badly mauled; Hamilton House lost a large chunk
in January 1941 and in the following May, the West Side
block and part of the clock tower were burnt out. The tower
remains in decapitated state, now further disfigured with tele-
vision aerials, but BR did provide a new clock in 1961.

EASTERN ELECTRICS

Even before the First World War, the suburban traffic of the
East Side had shown a vigorous growth following the rapid

development of Forest Gate and Ilford between 1880 and 1905. The line from Stratford to Romford was quadrupled between 1895 and 1902, with two new stations in the Ilford area. After 1919, building north and east of Ilford proceeded rapidly, and the pressure of suburban traffic shifted from the West to the East Side of Liverpool Street. Overcrowding and the lack of rail transport for the sea of new housing in North Ilford, including the City of London Corporation estates, brought strong pressures on the LNER for electrification and extension, rising to a peak in the 1930s. But the company was financially impotent when it came to expenditure of this order. Quadrupling from Romford to Shenfield was completed in 1934, with Government aid.

A far-reaching plan of cooperation between London Transport and the main-line railways was initiated in 1935 as a result of the London Passenger Transport Act of 1933 and an LPTB/main-line railway pooling scheme, which released the necessary financial support. The 1935 scheme provided for new railway construction in west, north and east London. Designed to relieve unemployment as well as the travel situation, it was to be financed by Government guaranteed loans. Included in this plan was the electrification of the Liverpool Street–Shenfield line on the then British Standard overhead-wire system at 1,500 volts dc and the tapping of the Loughton and Hainault line traffic by an extension of the Central Line Tube from Liverpool Street, with cross-platform interchange to the District at Mile End and to the surface lines at Stratford. A great deal of work was done from 1937 onwards, but the demands of war caused operations to be suspended between 1940 and 1945. Central Line trains reached Leystonstone on May 5th, 1947, and through workings from Liverpool Street to the Loughton line ceased. A partial electric service between Liverpool Street and Shenfield started on September 26th, 1949, and the electric trains took over all local workings from November 7th.

An important part of the Shenfield scheme was the inter-

change of the positions of the Local and Through lines west of
Ilford to permit cross-platform transfers with the Tube trains
at Stratford and to segregate the types of traffic approaching
Liverpool Street. The Through approach tracks became the
Electric lines and main-line and Southend trains were transferred to the Local tracks, renamed the Main. Both pairs of
tracks were electrified. The long lead from the old Through
(now Electric) lines to Platforms 7 and 10 was taken out, and
the electric trains served only Platforms 13 to 18, although 11
and 12 were also wired for emergency use.

A considerable realignment and widening was undertaken
on the East Side approaches, including a new retaining wall
which provided up to 40 ft more width south of Worship
Street. Overline bridges in the approaches had to be reconstructed to cover the extra width, and to obtain the necessary
clearances for electrification.

Extensions of this electrification to Chelmsford and Southend were opened on June 11th and December 31st, 1956, but
meanwhile further work was announced as part of the British
Railways Modernization Plan of 1955. Under this scheme,
some 45 route miles of the Liverpool Street suburban network
were to be electrified – Liverpool Street to Enfield Town and
Chingford, and a restoration of passenger services over the
Churchbury Loop with electric workings over it and beyond
to Hertford East and Bishops Stortford. Shortly afterwards it
was decided to adopt the 6.25- or 25-kV 50 cycles ac system
as standard and to convert to that system the other Liverpool
Street electric lines. Platforms 1 to 10 were wired up, and the
last steam suburban trains left Liverpool Street on the evening
of November 20th, 1960. By the end of 1962 all other steam
workings had given way to diesel-electrics or diesel multiple-
unit sets.

In 1963 express electric working was introduced between
Liverpool Street and Clacton, the multiple-unit trains calling at
important intermediate stations. Already, some years earlier,
London office workers had been encouraged to live at Clacton

by the operation of special fast steam services backed with energetic publicity. By the middle 1960s, this Essex seaside town was on the way to becoming as much a London dormitory as Southend or Brighton.

A peak-hour suburban and outer suburban timetable introduced on September 9th, 1963, brought the Liverpool Street electrification programme to fulfilment. There were sixty-seven departures between 5 and 6 PM, twenty-seven to the Enfield, Chingford and Bishops Stortford lines and forty along the Ilford and Romford line. There were fast, semi-fast and stopping trains to most electrically-served stations, the fast trains often leaving after a stopping train and making connexions with it farther out. To accommodate twelve-car trains for the Southend line, Platforms 11 to 15 were extended at this time.

British Railways thoroughly cleaned Liverpool Street and installed fluorescent lighting high in the roof. Amongst a number of improvements and alterations in recent years, the most important has been the straightening and widening of Platforms 9 and 10 by the removal of the siding known as 9a road, together with one of the two long sidings between these platforms. In 1962–4 the 'backs' were closed in, and a post office and a lost-property office constructed opposite the end of Platforms 9 and 10. The post office did not last long – it was closed in 1968. A most successful modernization of the main-line booking-hall was completed in 1965. Except at the end containing the war memorial, the ceiling was lowered, the space above being used for a Continental travel office. The well-lit booking-hall included a long ticket office with large plate-glass windows which afforded an excellent view of the new ticket-issuing and printing machines.

Some economies have been effected. The West Side Suburban booking-office was closed from October 16th, 1967. Beginning on November 5th of the same year, Platforms 1 to 9 were closed on winter Sundays.

Few complaints are now heard about Liverpool Street, which

is once again London's busiest terminus, although the daily passenger load is still well below the peak reached in the early 1920s. (Waterloo has a larger number of trains, but Liverpool Street has more daily passengers.) Now that the smoke and soot have gone, it is an altogether brighter, smarter place, although to call it clinical, as some steam devotees have done, is to exaggerate. Its future seems assured by its convenient location and healthy traffic, and with electric working there is ample capacity for future growth, restricted only by the limited width of the approaches.

SIGNALLING AND ACCIDENTS

Signalling at the 1874–5 station was interlocked, and controlled from a cabin with 139 levers. After the opening of the East Side in 1894 there were two main boxes, both fitted with Sykes' lock and block apparatus in its most complete form.

The larger of the two cabins, West Side box, had 244 levers in two frames extending the full 70-ft length of the interior, facing east and facing west. This was the largest box on the GER, continuously manned by four men and a boy, and needing five men at peak periods. Sited beyond the end of Platform 6, under Primrose Street bridge, it controlled Platforms 1 to 10, and all arrivals and departures.

The East Side was provided with a box containing a 136-lever frame, located under the Pinder Street bridge at the end of Platform 11. Subsidiary to the West Side box, this controlled the eastern platforms, 11 to 18.

As all the platforms could not be seen from the East and West boxes, there were observation boxes for the platform lines, equipped with electrical plungers and switches. These were East Platform box, at the end of 14 and 15, and West Platform box at the end of Platform 5. When a train arrived in a platform road, the Platform box signalman turned over the switch hook on his plunger instrument for that line, maintaining the corresponding block indicator in the main box at danger. On the platform road becoming clear, the Platform box man took off his switch hook and could also then plunge the main box to free the latter's home signal for another train to enter that platform. The main box home signal became front-locked after use, in the normal Sykes' manner, until another plunge was given from the Platform box. These arrangements were necessary because there was no track circuiting or similar device.

In 1919, in connexion with the introduction of the Jazz Service, route indicators were installed for incoming trains on the West Side, and sixty-five signal arms were abolished. Electrically-worked banner or repeating signals were also provided at strategic points.

Four-aspect colour-light signalling was installed between Liverpool Street and Gidea Park with the Shenfield electrification. At Liverpool Street, a new signal cabin was built out from the east wall, just south of Worship Street, and carried over the electric lines on cantilevers. This cabin, opened on September 25th, 1949, controlled all the approach tracks and station working. Three signalmen operated a three-section route-setting panel, one for each set of approach tracks, controlling 318 routes. Liverpool Street thus became the first London terminus to be completely equipped with relay interlocking controlled signalling.

There have been few serious accidents. On December 13th, 1963, the last car of a down rush-hour suburban electric train was derailed near the closed Bishopsgate Low Level station by a broken axle. An eighteen-year-old girl was killed in the overturned coach, but there were no serious injuries to other passengers.

CHAPTER SEVEN

FENCHURCH STREET

FIRST IN THE CITY

Tucked away in a side street, the little terminus of Fenchurch Street is one of the least known in London. It has never housed great expresses, and the farthest point reached from its platforms is a mere $39\frac{1}{2}$ miles away. Yet, despite a seeming dullness, it has a long and interesting history, and was the first railway terminus within the City of London. Situated in the midst of the shipping quarter, and serving the docks and the estuary, it naturally acquired a maritime flavour, but nowadays this is less evident.

By the 1830s, steamer services on the Thames were well developed. The acknowledged route from London to Kent was by steamer to Gravesend, thence by road. The river was also the best way to Woolwich, to the pleasure gardens at Rosherville (near Gravesend), and to the seaside resorts of Southend and Thanet. Larger vessels worked passenger services between London and the Continental ports. Almost all these steamers called at Brunswick Wharf, Blackwall, at the entrance to the East India Dock, a long $6\frac{1}{2}$ miles by river from London Bridge round the pendulous Isle of Dogs.

In 1836, a $3\frac{1}{2}$-mile railway was sanctioned between the Minories in the City of London and Blackwall, with the dual object of providing a short cut to river passengers and connecting the principal London docks (the East and West India) with the City. Dissatisfied with a terminus on the extreme eastern edge of the City, the railway's promoters tried in the following year to obtain powers for an extension to Lime Street, but their Bill was thrown out on the opposition of the City Corporations, which feared street congestion. However, in

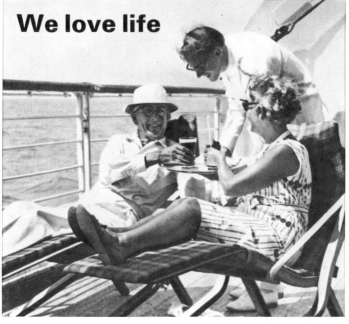

We love life

When you've got time really to enjoy life
you need the money to do so.

£10,000 when you retire
by taking out now a Prudential Endowment
Assurance. For more details, complete
and return this card.

Some examples
The value of Prudential policies has been
amply demonstrated over the years, as
is shown by these examples of payments on
claims under Ordinary Branch with-profits
endowment assurances for £5,000 taken
out in the U.K., and which matured at age
65 on 1st April, 1971.

Age at entry	30	40	50
Sum assured	£5,000	£5,000	£5,000
Bonuses*	£6,445	£5,155	£3,370
	£11,445	£10,155	£8,370

*Bonuses on future maturities cannot be guaranteed

DO NOT AFFIX POSTAGE STAMPS IF POSTED IN
GT. BRITAIN, CHANNEL ISLANDS OR N. IRELAND

BUSINESS REPLY SERVICE
LICENCE No. K.E. 1511

The Chief General Manager
THE PRUDENTIAL ASSURANCE CO. LTD.

142 HOLBORN BARS
LONDON EC1N 2NH

POSTAGE WILL
BE PAID BY
LICENSEE

1839, while the railway was being built, approval was given for a terminus at Fenchurch Street, on a $\frac{1}{4}$-mile extension which was to cost £250,000.

The London & Blackwall Railway was one of the first to be constructed through a built-up area. To minimize demolitions and eliminate the necessity for a large number of level crossings, it was decided to place most of it on a brick viaduct. No fewer than six intermediate stations were to be opened over the $3\frac{1}{2}$ miles completed in 1841, and as it was thought that steam locomotives would be unsuitable for working such closely-spaced stops and might in any case present a fire hazard to the many small houses nestling against the viaduct and the sailing ships in the Limehouse Basin, alternatives were considered. At this time, the only practical ones were horse and cable traction, and the latter was chosen. The gauge of the line was 5 ft or thereabouts, approximately that of the nearby Eastern Counties Railway, to which there was as yet no connexion.

When the line first opened on July 6th, 1840, it was single track, the second track being added on August 3rd. The temporary terminus at the Minories was a simple two-road shed, with an all-over roof. Construction of the extension to Fenchurch Street was completed in the following year, and the terminus came into use on August 2nd, 1841. It was sited just to the south of its namesake, a little to the east of Mark Lane, and a new street called Railway Place was cut to give access to it. As it was so close to the terminus, Minories quickly lost importance, and after a temporary closure, it was finally shut in October 1853.

Fenchurch Street resembled Minories, with its two platforms and overall wooden roof, but although a little larger, lacked any architectural pretensions. Perhaps its one claim to fame was that it sheltered the first railway bookstall, operated by William Marshall, the founder of Marshall & Son, a firm of newspaper distributors who became close rivals to the famous W. H. Smith & Son.

The stationary engines which moved the continuous cables were at Minories and Blackwall and the extension had no cable. Incoming coaches, released from the rope at Minories, moved forward to the terminus under their momentum, the 1 in 150 upward slope tending to slow them down as they approached the platform, which was convenient. Departing coaches needed only a slight push from the platform staff.

A provision in the 1839 Act excluded trains from Fenchurch Street on Sundays, Christmas Day and Good Friday. Sunday trains left from Minories until this was repealed in 1842. The new Act explained the reason for the relaxation:

> ... whereas the company in the construction of the extension have caused the same to be completely enclosed so as to prevent annoyance to the neighbourhood by the noise arising from the working of the said railway, which was apprehended at the time of the passing of the said Act ...

It seems that as long as the trains could not be seen or heard, their working on the Sabbath, even if sinful, was permissible – an interesting illustration of Victorian moral attitudes. For the whole distance between the Minories and Fenchurch Street the line was enclosed by fenestrated walls and roofed with slate (iron on the Minories bridge).

Although traffic increased by fifty per cent after the opening of Fenchurch Street, the London & Blackwall was only a moderate success. Through bookings were offered to the Woolwich and Gravesend steamers, but whilst some were attracted by the forty-five minute saving in journey time, many remained faithful to the water. In an attempt to obtain the traffic, the railway purchased three boats, working an hourly service to Gravesend in competition with the seventeen or so vessels operated by the five river companies.

On the railway, a fifteen-minute service was provided all day, each line being used alternately for up and down trains. Various patterns of operation were employed, but apart from Stepney, the intermediate stations were always served by a form of slip working and travel between any two of them was impossible without going on to the terminus and moving back. Separate coaches were worked between Blackwall and Stepney in both directions. The movement of the ropes was controlled by messages passed through Cook and Wheatstone single-needle telegraph apparatus.

LINKED TO THE OUTSIDE WORLD

As may be imagined, there were many mishaps and muddles, and with two guard-brakemen on each coach, the system of working was to say the least somewhat staff-expensive. Plans were soon made to connect the line to the ordinary railway system, with operation by conventional means.

A turning point in the history of Fenchurch Street came on April 2nd, 1849, when a 1¾-mile branch was opened from Stepney to a station alongside the Eastern Counties Railway. At first there was no junction with the larger company, and the Blackwall was obliged to operate a shuttle service between Bow and Fenchurch Street. As the ECR had converted to standard gauge in 1844, the L & B branch had been built to that gauge and the rest of the Blackwall Railway was converted to it. From February 15th, 1849, cable traction had been discarded and a small stud of 2-2-2 well tanks with 5-ft 6-in driving wheels acquired to take its place.

A physical link with the outside world was finally established on September 26th, 1850 when the East and West India Docks and Birmingham Junction Railway opened. This line (North London Railway from 1853) formed a junction with the Blackwall at Bow and ran north and west to Islington. From its opening, a fifteen-minute service was worked between Fenchurch Street and Islington and the L & BR shuttle to Bow, Eastern Counties, was taken off. The newcomer's trains were extended from Islington to Camden Town (now Camden Road) on December 7th, 1850, and to Hampstead Road (near Primrose Hill) on June 9th, 1851.

The additional traffic brought by the new service, with the prospect of further business from a proposed London Tilbury & Southend Railway, led the Blackwall Railway to enlarge and rebuild Fenchurch Street. This work was undertaken to the designs of the engineer, George Berkeley, and was completed in February 1854.

The new station had a single-arch all-over roof with a closed end, a design common enough in America, but virtually unknown in Europe at this date. In the street frontage there were eleven bays of white brick, each with a tall arched window. Above was a pediment, its top revealing the curve of the roof. At street level were six small double doorways, protected by a flat canopy extending the full width of the station and covering the pavement. When this canopy eventually collapsed, it was replaced by a tooth-edged see-saw wooden awning of the pattern used over many GER station platforms. Adjoining the main front, to the north, was a small office building with three floors, coming up to the lower edge of the pediment.

Beyond the street doors were two gloomy booking-halls, one allocated to the proposed London Tilbury & Southend Railway. From these halls, passengers ascended stairs at the north and south ends of the building to reach the concourse, which was at the level of the viaduct. A third stairway at the north end provided direct access from street to concourse.

As later at Broad Street and St Paul's, there was no platform access for vehicles; hydraulic lifts were installed to carry parcels and luggage to rail level. The small concourse extended the full width of the station, and was partly over the booking-halls. From its north-east corner, a passage into the office block led to the L & BR board room, which had a high ornamented ceiling, and was later converted into a waiting-room for first-class ladies. There were four short platforms under the 300-ft long, 101-ft span of the crescent truss roof. Along the south wall, at platform level, were small rooms for staff use.

All this, together with a third approach track (for up services,

completed in 1856) was very largely for the benefit of the
London Tilbury & Southend Railway, a scheme sponsored by
the Blackwall and the ECR in an attempt to obtain some of the
heavy river traffic between London, Gravesend and Southend.
The first section of the LTSR, from Forest Gate to Tilbury (for
Gravesend) was opened on April 13th, 1854, and on the same
day, a connexion was at last made between the ECR and the
Blackwall Railway at Bow. Eleven LTSR trains each way then
worked between Fenchurch Street and Tilbury via Barking, a
Bishopsgate portion being attached or detached at Stratford.
(The LTSR was leased to the contractors, Peto, Brassey & Betts
for twenty-one years from July 3rd, 1854, but its train services
were operated by the ECR, who provided both engines and
stock.) To relieve congestion at Stratford, a more direct line
was constructed for the LTSR between Bow and Barking, and
put into use on March 31st, 1858. LTSR trains now entered
the junction with the North London Railway, and the Tilbury company was given perpetual running powers over the
$2\frac{1}{4}$ miles into Fenchurch Street.

At the beginning of 1866, the Great Eastern Railway, which
had succeeded the ECR in 1862, took over the working of the
London & Blackwall on a 999-year lease, with a rent equivalent
to four and a half per cent on the Blackwall's ordinary capital.
It was shortly after this that the sinecurist Blackwall directors
felt able to give up their board room to the first-class ladies.
They did, however, continue to meet elsewhere twice a year
until the 1923 grouping, to receive their guaranteed rent and
declare a dividend, and then, weakened by these exertions, to
dine and wine together.

When Broad Street opened in 1865, the North London
Railway started an almost circular fifteen-minute service between its old and new termini via Bow and Hackney, but this
did not last for long, and on August 1st, 1866, was altered
to run Broad Street–Poplar, with a fifteen-minute connecting
shuttle service between Bow (NLR) and Fenchurch Street. This
shuttle was taken over by the GER on January 1st, 1869, until

its termination in 1892, and NLR passenger trains were seen
no more at Fenchurch Street. The terminus was now virtually
owned by the GER, with the LTSR very much the tolerated
lodger.

Until the opening of Liverpool Street in 1874, Fenchurch
Street was the GER suburban-line terminus, and apart from the
Bow shuttle already mentioned, that company ran trains to
North Woolwich (from June 1st, 1854), and to the Loughton
branch (opened in 1856 and extended to Ongar in 1865). By
the late 1860s, City merchants were moving into sumptuous
new villas along the Loughton line and Fenchurch Street was
handling a preliminary trickle of first-class season-ticket
holders. In the 1900s, the Loughton line trains had a good proportion of first-class coaches, altogether a different type of
traffic from that handled on the West Side of Liverpool Street.

In 1872 there were 18 trains daily to the Loughton branch,
26 to North Woolwich, 18 to the LTSR (only 6 to Southend),
as well as the fifteen-minute services all day to Blackwall and
Bow (NLR).

The LTSR, which had reached Southend via Tilbury on
March 1st, 1856, became an independent company by an Act
of 1862 and independence was completed by an Act of 1882
which rescinded the GER and Blackwall powers to appoint
directors. It acquired its own coaches in 1876–7, and locomotives three years later. As early as 1881 a fast business train was
started between Fenchurch Street and Southend, taking one
hour for the 42 miles via Tilbury. A direct line from Barking
to Southend was completed on June 1st, 1888, and a suburban
business was gradually built up, encouraged by the offer of
cheap season tickets. By the end of the century, Fenchurch
Street was very busy indeed, but some of the pressure was
taken off in 1902, when a connexion was opened between
the Metropolitan District Railway at Whitechapel and the
LTSR at Bow. Traffic from the inner suburban stations of the
LTSR was then mopped up by District trains working as far out
as East Ham and, after quadrupling, by District electric trains

(Upper plan) *Old layout at Fenchurch Street before remodelling.*
(Lower plan) *New layout and station as reconstructed 1935.*

From the Railway Magazine, July 1935

to East Ham (August 20th, 1905) and Barking (April 1st, 1908). The Tilbury company contributed electric stock to these trains.

In addition to the growing traffic of the LTSR, the Fenchurch Street approach tracks had to carry an increasing number of freight trains, serving the six goods depots and branches which had been opened within half a mile of the terminus. These were on the north side: *Goodman's Yard* (GER), *Haydon Square* (LNWR), and *Commercial Road* (LTSR); on the south: *Royal Mint Street* (GNR), *Royal Mint Street* (Midland) and the GER London Docks spur. A fourth approach track became a necessity, and this was completed in March 1896.

At the turn of the century, Fenchurch Street had five platforms, of varying lengths. Against the south wall was the 380-ft No 1, the home of the Blackwall trains, still leaving every fifteen minutes throughout the day. Patronage was falling off; the first depletion had come with the decline of the steamer traffic (ironically a consequence of the opening of the Thames-side railways); then, after the adoption of the telephone in City offices, the messengers passing between the City and the docks had disappeared (and the ships themselves, now larger, moved to new docks farther down the river); and finally, electric trams and motor buses had taken most of what was left. Sunday trains to Blackwall ceased from October 1st, 1908, and the weekday service was reduced to three an hour about the same time. In the First World War, a thirty-minute service was sufficient, but afterwards the fifteen-minute frequency was recklessly restored. By then, the trains were running almost empty, and in 1926 the decision was taken to abandon the service. It ceased on May 3rd as a result of the General Strike, never to be resumed. Platform 1 was also used by the NLR trains when these were operating to Fenchurch Street, but as mentioned, this had ceased long before, in 1869.

Platforms 2 and 3 were on a 555-ft island, protected beyond the overall roof by umbrella awnings. GER trains on the Ilford line used 2, and those to Loughton and Ongar were seen at 3.

On Sundays, North Woolwich trains also used 3, and LTSR trains were occasionally seen there. Next came an engine road, with a crossover at the buffer-stop end, and then, the pride of Fenchurch Street, the 765-ft Platform 4, the only one which could accommodate the bogie stock trains of the LTSR, and exclusively used by that company. This face, which could take thirteen coaches and the inevitable Tilbury 4–4–2T, was the busiest in the station. At its far end, on the north side, and entirely beyond the overall roof, was No 5, a 470-ft bay. Here were found the North Woolwich and Gallions trains. (Trains ran from Fenchurch Street to Gallions over the Royal Albert Docks Railway from July 1881 onwards.) A footbridge from the outer end led to the signal cabin on the south side of the station. Stairs from Platforms 4 and 5 linked them with a separate entrance and booking-hall in John Street (now Crosswall). This was in a five-storey building erected in 1881 to house the offices of the L & BR and the LTSR.

Conditions on Platform 4 during the evening peak hour were described by W. Ivey, chairman of the West Ham Tramways and Electric Lighting Committee, in evidence to the Royal Commission on London Traffic in 1904. Ivey thought the most popular train was the 5.58 PM:

> That is a very long train ... when it draws in there is a great rush of people before it stops, to get seats in the carriages, and I have seen people knocked over; and it is not altogether decent, in fact, to see sixteen or seventeen people inside one compartment ...

He went on to describe how a fellow councillor had

> counted in a first-class carriage as many as twenty-six passengers, among whom were two females (shame).

He added that passengers for the GER trains in the bay were occasionally unable to reach them, owing to the crowded state of Platform 4.

Between 1902 and 1909, the LTSR season-ticket traffic almost doubled. Fast trains and the exceptionally generous rates –

an average of 6 miles for one penny – encouraged London office
workers to live at Westcliff and Southend in increasing numbers. By 1909, seven full train loads were being brought into
London from Southend in two hours each morning with an
average running time of fifty-nine minutes.

Some hope of relief came in 1912 when the Midland, needing better access to the docks, succeeded in pulling off a
diplomatic coup, acquiring the LTSR under the very nose of the
GER. The new owners undertook to electrify the Southend line
and to apply for powers to do so by 1914. For their part, the
GER agreed to enlarge Fenchurch Street and to electrify the
approach tracks to receive the LTSR trains. It did not prove
possible to make a start on these works before the outbreak of
the First World War, which caused a further postponement.
After 1918, the financial difficulties of the private railway
companies ruled out capital expenditure of the order required
on a scheme likely to provide such a small return, and electrification of the LTSR had to await nationalization. However, long
before that, as we shall see, the other promise was kept.

LNER OVERSHADOWED BY LMSR

At the 1923 grouping, the LNER inherited Fenchurch Street,
and the LMSR took over the LTSR services. By the late 1920s
when there were some 50,000 passengers on the 300 trains
handled daily, the LMSR presence was overshadowing that of
the rightful owners, whose Ilford, Ongar and North Woolwich
services were but poor things beside the still-burgeoning traffic
of the Southend line. Such was the growth of the latter, and
so inconvenient the layout of Fenchurch Street, that something
just had to be done, and a £250,000 scheme to increase the
capacity of the terminus was started in 1932.

It would have been impossibly expensive to add to the number of platforms by widening the station site, owing to the
high value of the surrounding property, so the scheme merely
tried to make the best use of the existing area. By far the

greatest defect of the layout was that there was only one platform long enough to take the Southend trains, and that to reach
or leave this and the adjacent No 5 bay, all trains using the
fast road had to share a short stretch of single track in the immediate approach. It was therefore decided to provide an island
platform of suitable length for the Southend trains, with an
independent approach road to each face. For the LNER, there
was another island platform, slightly shorter, placed between
the up and down slow lines. The reconstructed station thus had
two platforms of 750 ft (3 and 4) and two of 550 ft (1 and 2),
instead of five of assorted lengths, all but one of which had
been too short for modern requirements.

To relieve pressure on the main entrance and exit, each
island platform was given two sets of stairs to a new subway
through the viaduct, linking them with a new Crosswall entrance. Beyond the main roof, both islands were protected for
their whole length by umbrella awnings.

In the approaches, the tracks required a considerable amount of
rearrangement, and this involved reconstruction and strengthening of the bridges over Minories, Vine Street, Cooper's Row
and Crutched Friars. At the far end of the station, the old
telegraph office and tea room, backing on to 3 and 4, and the
bookstall, backing on to 1 and 2, were demolished to increase
the circulating area at the head of the platforms. A combined
cafeteria, buffet and waiting-room was erected at the back of
the concourse. The platform ends were given an elegant
wrought-iron barrier, arranged to give alternative exits from
all platforms on the plan adopted at Liverpool Street West Side
some years before. New indicators, with departure-time clocks
and station-name displays on the Liverpool Street pattern
were installed at the barriers. At ground level, the LTSR and
GER booking-offices were combined in 1932, when the concourse parcels office was moved there.

When the reconstruction, which included signalling
modernization, was completed in April 1935, additional trains
were introduced on the Southend line. New Stanier 2–6–4T

arrived during the same year to operate all the Southend trains. At the evening peak, departures for the LTSR lines now left at four-minute intervals, incoming train engines taking the next train out. In an effort to equalize loading, each train served a different pattern of stations in the Southend area. There were now 370 trains a day, with some 70,000 passengers, most of them on the former LTSR lines.

On the LNER side, it was a different story. For a few more years, things remained much the same; but by 1949, all the services had disappeared, leaving the former LTSR line trains in sole occupation. First to go was the North Woolwich service, which ceased during the bombing of October 1940. When Tube trains reached Leytonstone on May 5th, 1947, services to the Loughton lines came off, and the remaining Ilford line trains vanished when the Liverpool Street to Shenfield line was fully electrified on November 7th, 1949. Platforms 1 and 2 were taken over by trains to and from Tilbury.

A feature of the Liverpool Street–Shenfield electrification as planned by the LNER had been a shuttle service of electric trains between Fenchurch Street and a terminal bay at Stratford, affording cross-platform interchange at the latter station with down electrics from Liverpool Street and eastbound Central Line Tube trains. The 1500-V dc overhead wires were duly erected for this service over all four tracks out of Fenchurch Street, where Platforms 1 and 2 were wired up. The bay was built at Stratford. This done, it was decided that whilst the shuttle service would offer some convenience, it would largely duplicate existing Underground facilities, and the project was abandoned. Empty trains ran over the line regularly to keep the wires clean, as it was realized it would have strategic value in an emergency. And so it proved in February 1953, when the LTSR line was cut by floods between Benfleet and Leigh. A special service of electric trains was then worked for five days between Fenchurch Street and Shenfield in connexion with steam trains thence to Southend (Victoria).

During the mid 1950s, the LTSR steam services suffered a

sad decline. Locomotive breakdowns and mishaps of various kinds became everyday events. As is not unusual with London railway matters, the situation was greatly blown up in the Press, especially when, after a period of severe weather in the winter of 1956–7, a Congregational minister was moved to refer to the railway service as 'an illustration of inhuman wickedness'. The difficulties arose largely from an acute shortage of experienced men, especially locomotive fitters and firemen, the consequent lack of proper maintenance playing havoc with the heavily-worked locomotives.

UNDER THE CATENARY AT LAST

By this time, approval had been given for electrification of the line, under the British Railways modernization plan. The engineering works associated with electrification were extensive, and another five years were to pass before all was ready for the new trains. In the meantime, by dint of strenuous efforts on the part of management and staff, there had been some improvement in the standards of steam working. At this period, Fenchurch Street was dealing with about 37,800 passengers a day, in some 175 trains.

The LTSR line electrification was carried out to the new British Railways standard of 6·25- or 25-kV 50 cycles ac. The existing 1500-V dc line into Fenchurch Street was converted at the same time as an emergency route, and to provide access to Ilford depot, though there was still no intention of running a public service to Stratford. Some electric trains began to run in steam timings in the slack hours on November 6th, 1961, but all services were not worked electrically until June 17th, 1962. The new timetable, which has since been modified, provided six trains an hour from Fenchurch Street in the off-peak period, four of them via Upminster. Fast trains reached Southend Central in forty-five minutes. There were 17 departures between 5 and 6 PM, all of twelve-car trains, each offering a total of 57 first-class and 1,032 second-class seats.

At Fenchurch Street, Platforms 3 and 4 were wired. The track layout was simplified by removing the engine spurs and modifying complicated point formations. From April 1st, 1963, Swedish Lloyd boat trains were transferred from St Pancras, as electric trains covering the 22½-mile run to Tilbury in thirty minutes, could offer a faster run.

As is usual with electrification, traffic soon began to increase. In 1968, 30,728 passengers arrived in the morning peak hours on the October census day, compared with 18,606 in 1959, and the total number of passengers passing through the terminus daily had increased to 67,300 from 43,000 in 1959.

Apart from the introduction of electric services, BR made a number of improvements. Fluorescent lighting was installed throughout the station in 1953; on the whole it was well arranged, but it still left the booking-hall rather gloomy. In 1959 new departure indicators were erected at the platform barriers, with linked displays in the two booking-halls, controlled either by the train announcer or the ticket collectors. This apparatus did not have a happy life, and in 1967 was modified to work with the standard train-describer system.

Fenchurch Street is one of the two London termini that lack Underground connexions. The nearest station is Tower Hill (District Line), a few minutes' walk to the south. On February 5th, 1967, the London Transport station was resited, providing a more convenient interchange for passengers able to use the Crosswall entrance to the terminus (open only from 6 AM to 9.45 PM, Mondays to Fridays). So popular did this prove, that the Crosswall entrance had to be widened in the following year.

A plan for rebuilding Fenchurch Street incorporating an office block above the platforms was put forward by private developers in 1959, but was refused by the City Corporation on the grounds that offices should be restricted to sites already zoned for them. Berkeley's stern frontage therefore still remains, increasingly out of place amidst a forest of modern office blocks and towers.

There is now a proposal to divert all Fenchurch Street traffic to Liverpool Street except in rush hours, running the trains on and off the old GER main line at Forest Gate, the junction of the original LTSR line. As Liverpool Street could not cope with the additional rush-hour load, or at any rate could not do so without substantial rearrangement, Fenchurch Street is likely to remain open for a few more years yet; but its future is by no means assured.

SIGNALLING

The mechanical signalling at Fenchurch Street was controlled from a cabin situated on the south side of the station over the up slow line. This was provided with lock and block instruments and 115 working levers in a Saxby & Farmer frame.

Together with eight other cabins, it was replaced on April 14th, 1935, by a new 140-lever box at Fenchurch Street and modernized cabins at Stepney East and Gas Factory junction. These three boxes controlled the Siemens & General Electric Railway Signal Company's four-aspect colour lights and point motors installed in the station area and as far east as Bow junction.

As part of the electrification scheme of the early 1960s, an SGE NX push-button panel was installed in the 1935 box to provide remote control of the junctions at Stepney East and Gas Factory. At the same time, the 1935 track circuiting was changed from 50 to $83\frac{1}{2}$ cycles/sec ac. No other alterations were made to the LMSR colour-light signalling.

CHAPTER EIGHT

LONDON BRIDGE

DOYEN OF THEM ALL

Oldest of the permanent termini, London Bridge dates back to the opening of London's first passenger railway in 1836. After this came the development of an untidy sprawl of separate stations, all on arches above street level. The complex underwent two major operations in the nineteenth century, but since 1902, things have settled down and there have been no important structural changes. If allowance is made for the bomb damage of the last war, the physical appearance of most parts of the station, if not the atmosphere, remains much as it was in the early years of the present century. Like the old Euston, London Bridge holds much of interest to the perceptive railway student, but prompts no affection in the heart of the ordinary passenger, to whom it offers little comfort or convenience. Thanks to its hybrid origins, subsequent neglect, and German bombs, it is indisputably the most hideous of all the termini in external appearance.

In 1832, a $3\frac{1}{2}$-mile railway was proposed between Greenwich and Tooley Street, London Bridge. Some 2,000 people were moving daily over the $5\frac{1}{2}$-mile road between the two places, and it was hoped to attract most of these as well as develop new traffic. The promoters adopted a scheme drawn up by Lt Col G. T. Landmann, a retired Royal Engineer, who had suggested that the line be placed on a brick viaduct of 878 arches. This scheme not only solved the problem of the many roads and lanes intersecting the route in Bermondsey, but also offered the possibility of additional revenue from the letting of the arches as warehouses, stables, or even dwellings.

The first section of this London & Greenwich Railway, the

first passenger railway and the first steam railway in London, was opened on February 8th, 1836, from Spa Road, Bermondsey, to Deptford. If one really wishes to be pedantic, Spa Road was therefore the first railway terminus in London, but it was a very temporary affair.

Ten months later, on December 14th, 1836, the Lord Mayor of London, attended by the Sheriffs, the Common Council and some 2,000 other guests, arrived for the formal opening of the first London Bridge Station. Trains began to run at midday, and with a band of musicians dressed as beefeaters riding on the roof of one of the carriages to provide a suitable accompaniment, the Lord Mayor travelled to Deptford and inspected the installations. Two years later, the railway finally reached Greenwich.

Approximately on the site of the present Platforms 9 and 10, the station was a very spartan affair with three tracks and two platforms, reached by an incline and steps from the street below. In short, it was the stub end of the long viaduct, entirely unprotected from the weather (later an old sail was put up to give some shelter). The ticket office and the company's offices were in a very plain three-storey block on the south side of the viaduct. A design was prepared for a triumphal arch to stand across the entrance, but this was never erected, no doubt through lack of funds.

It seems that the low platforms caused lady passengers some distress, because the conductors were rather lax in letting down the carriage steps to the fullest extent, thus exacting a display 'of the beauty of their legs and ankles'. It is just possible that this neglect of duty was deliberate, as the same account (in the *Kentish Mercury* for March 31st, 1838) relates that when helping the weaker sex into the carriages, these officials were apt to press the ladies' fingers and stare them 'full in the face'.

From the start, the Greenwich company had dreamed of greater things, aware for some time that other more important railways had their eyes on London Bridge as a terminus. In preparation, they had wisely acquired more land than they needed for immediate requirements, and had spread out the viaduct at the London end to take eight tracks. In 1835 a London & Croydon Railway had been authorized, and this was to enter London over the Greenwich tracks, which it would join at Corbett's Lane, Bermondsey, a privilege which was to cost it 3*d* for every passenger carried. A year later, the South Eastern Railway obtained its Act. This was to form an extension of the London & Croydon Railway through Coulsdon and Redhill to Tonbridge and Dover, and would also use the Greenwich line on payment of a toll.

When the L & CR opened on June 5th, 1839, it ran twelve trains each way daily, using a separate three-track terminus at London Bridge immediately north of the Greenwich company's premises. All Croydon trains therefore had to cross the Greenwich line on the level, and when questioned about this by a Parliamentary committee, the Greenwich representative confessed that it suited them, as it gave them a hold over the London & Croydon. The Croydon's station was about 300 ft long and 100 ft wide with a train shed 170 ft long by 48 ft wide, supported on one side by fourteen cast-iron columns and on the other by a brick wall with piers and arches. The booking-office was in Joiner Street below, and separate stairs were provided for first- and second-class passengers. The remaining space on the viaduct was occupied by a small goods station between the train shed and Tooley Street.

It was first intended that the Croydon's station should accommodate not only the trains of that company and those of the SER, but also give shelter to a third user of the Greenwich Railway, the London & Brighton Railway, incorporated in 1837. Parliament now required extra tracks to be provided into London Bridge, preferring a widening of the existing viaduct to the construction of separate lines, which would have been more destructive of property. The Greenwich accordingly obtained powers to build a second pair of tracks on the south side of the viaduct, and agreed with the Croydon company that it would exchange stations at London Bridge to avoid crossing over by the trains of the user companies. In 1840 the four companies were authorized to make agreements for the apportionment and management of the London Bridge terminal area and to construct new works, while the Greenwich was given powers to build a new station for the three user companies.

THE JOINT STATION

The first section of the London & Brighton Railway opened on July 12th, 1841, and the additional tracks into London Bridge were ready on May 10th, 1842. Sixteen days later, the SER trains began to run between London Bridge and Tonbridge (Dover was reached on February 7th, 1844). Building of the Joint station was pressed ahead, and it was possible to open it in February 1844. The Croydon then moved in, and the Greenwich company's own trains began to use the Croydon train shed on the north side of the viaduct.

This new Joint station, designed by Henry Roberts[1] had a very pleasant two-storey frontage building in the 'Italian palazzo style', with a pretty campanile at the southern end, carrying clock and weathervane. An 80-ft-wide approach road came up from Borough High Street, skirting the northern boundary of the St Thomas's Hospital grounds. In the ground floor of the 250-ft block were booking-hall, parcels offices and waiting-rooms. To the south, facing Joiner Street, was a smaller, triangular block for the offices of the Brighton, Croydon & Dover Joint Station Committee which had been formed to manage the new terminus, and functioned only in 1844–5. Behind these buildings, the engineer William Cubitt provided three tracks in a new train shed on the site of the old Greenwich Station, and departure and arrival sheds, each with a main and subsidiary platform and three tracks. The platform on the south side of the northernmost shed (intended for the North Kent Railway) was 240 ft long, whilst the main departure platform was 338 ft and the main arrival stage 531 ft. At the rear of the triangular office blocks was a four-road carriage shed, connected to the Joint station by traversers.

This was splendid, but never finished, and very soon to be proved far too small for the rapidly increasing traffic. And there was another cloud on the horizon, for all was not well between the Greenwich and its customers. Ever alert for the quick penny, the Greenwich had raised the toll as soon as the second pair of tracks was ready, obliging the three companies to pay $4\frac{1}{2}d$ a passenger, irrespective of class. This was particularly painful for the Croydon, on which journeys were much shorter than those of the Brighton and the SER, and where relatively smaller fares were quite disproportionately inflated by the new toll.

Attempts were made to force the hand of the Greenwich company by starting a bus service between the Croydon's station at New Cross and the West End, with fares cheaper than those to London Bridge. The Croydon also refused to carry third-class passengers between New Cross and London Bridge. These measures failed to move the Greenwich.

BRICKLAYERS ARMS, OR THE WEST END IN BERMONDSEY

As a more dramatic ploy, the Croydon and South Eastern companies conspired to erect their own terminus on the east side of the Old Kent Road, just south of its junction with what is now Tower Bridge Road. This station, laughably referred to as a 'West End terminus' was known as Bricklayers Arms, after a nearby coaching inn, and was opened on May 1st, 1844. In just one sense was the wild claim to serve the West End within sight of the truth: the direct roads to the river bridges at Waterloo and Westminster gave a shorter journey time than that from London Bridge.

Although partly fashioned as a rod to beat the Greenwich company, Bricklayers Arms had other uses. It was to provide accommodation for the traffic in sheep, cattle and goods which could not be conveniently handled in the cramped conditions at London Bridge; it offered room for a locomotive yard; and, finally, it projected the South Eastern part of the way towards a *real* West End terminus. Some 26 acres were available for cattle and goods traffic, and the Croydon and South Eastern companies at once deserted the goods facilities on the north side of London Bridge. J. P. Fearon told the Royal Commission on Metropolitan Termini in 1846, 'It is no doubt too far from Town for a West End terminus, but it is most efficient and most complete for a goods station'. The approach was made by a 1¾-mile branch from the Croydon's line just before it met the Greenwich viaduct. A third of the cost was contributed by the Croydon, the SER finding the rest, but in 1849, the latter used power given in the authorizing Act to purchase the Croydon's share. Thereafter, the Croydon had to pay a toll of 1¼d a passenger over the branch.

Bricklayers Arms was a neat and compact little terminus with a layout and arrangement similar to that of the original Euston. Architectural gloss, in the fashionable Italian-villa style, with some Baroque details, was provided by Lewis Cubitt (see Chapter 4, note 1, p 382). His main contribution was a screen across the end, penetrated by 22-ft archways with exaggerated keystones and by doorways protected by pantiled hoods on heavy stone brackets. Above the central arch was a clock, and above that, a little arcaded campanile topped by a weathervane. Contemporary drawings exaggerate the height and dignity of this screen and do not accurately portray the arrangement of the openings.[2] It was a poor thing in comparison with the front of Kings Cross.

Along one side of the station was a tiled colonnade where passengers alighted from their vehicles, passing through to the first- and second-class booking-offices and waiting-rooms alongside the departure platform. At the other side of the train shed was an arrival platform and carriage way, and at the outer end, a two-track loading dock for private carriages, with its own waiting-room. Between the departure and arrival tracks

were two empty carriage lines. Across the end, a narrow platform connected the departure and arrival sides behind the
screen. Beyond the offices on the departure side, at the outer
end, was a four-track carriage shed. At inner and outer ends of
the station tracks were sets of turnplates for moving carriages
and vans, the set at the outer end also providing access to the
carriage shed and private carriage loading dock. Three parallel
iron roofs sheltered the platforms and tracks, but they suffered
some basic defect in design, as they collapsed soon after opening, and again in 1850, when a train collided with a supporting
pillar.

An hourly service was at once started to and from the Croydon line; this was not only more frequent, but cheaper than the
London Bridge–Croydon trains. At last moved from its inflexible attitude, the Greenwich agreed in July 1844 to charge
the Croydon varying tolls, based on the same proportion of the
overall fare as the length of its viaduct bore to the overall journey mileage. For its part, the Croydon agreed to equalize the
fares and train service as between London Bridge and Bricklayers Arms, and at once did so. It was quickly realized that
there was little point in terminating half the Croydon trains at
the remote Bricklayers Arms Station, and the Croydon company gave up serving it in March 1845.

The South Eastern ran about half its main-line trains to
Folkestone and Dover from Bricklayers Arms, and from 1845
also ran some excursion trains. Some confusion occurred at
first.

> . . . the Dover Railway Company, finding the inconvenience of
> two stations (namely, the *Bricklayers Arms* and the *London
> Bridge*), ceased to split the trains at Deptford, and now run
> alternately, for this very reason, that a man never knew which
> station he was going to in London; and therefore if he said to
> his servant, 'You will meet me at the Dover Railway on
> Friday,' he said, 'Which station am I to go to, the Bricklayers
> Arms or the London Bridge?' . . . the present Dover com-
> pany run one train to the Bricklayers Arms and one other
> to London Bridge on purpose to obviate this difficulty . . .

(B. W. Horne, evidence to the Royal Commission on London Termini, 1846.)

Despite the omnibuses, arranged to meet all trains and carry passengers to the City for 3*d* and to the West End for 6*d*, Bricklayers Arms was a complete failure as a passenger terminus. By May 1846 the SER trains had been reduced to a couple up and down daily, and in October even these disappeared. All that remained was the curious practice of attaching a first-class coach to the 11 PM down goods 'at the special request of travellers desirous to reach Folkestone or Dover in time for the morning steamer' as *Bradshaw* stated in January 1846. Who were these 'travellers'? Probably diplomatic couriers and the occasional newspaperman, but what a convenient and inconspicuous means this must have offered of leaving the country in those days of no passports. One likes to imagine that the facility was sometimes used by young bloods escaping from gaming debts or respectable merchants decamping with trembling mistresses.

A brief new life of passenger activity came to Bricklayers Arms in 1849 after a connexion had been made between the branch and the new North Kent line of the SER. From September 1st, a fifteen-minute shuttle service was operated between the terminus and exchange platforms built at this junction, the SER claiming that this provided '. . . a West End terminus for every train to the North Kent and Greenwich traffic' (report read at the meeting of the SER, September 20th, 1849). But once again, the 'West End terminus' was spurned by an ungrateful public, and the service, reduced in March 1850, was withdrawn altogether early in 1852. No more regular passenger trains were seen at Bricklayers Arms, and the train shed was handed over to the goods department. Shortly after the opening of Bricklayers Arms, the Croydon company had to return to the goods station at London Bridge because the SER wanted its site for a locomotive yard, but following an agreement between the two companies in 1847–8, the SER con-

structed a new 5-acre goods depot for the LBSCR (the Croydon's
successor) at Willow Walk, on the north side of the Bricklayers
Arms branch. This was opened in July 1849. The sheds at
Bricklayers Arms itself were exclusively used by the SER.

With its direct road access to the West End, Bricklayers
Arms was convenient for royal traffic and continued in use for
this purpose, suitably cleaned up and decorated, until the even
more accessible Charing Cross was opened. One of its last
royal patrons was Princess Alexandra of Denmark, who arrived
in March 1863 to marry Edward (later Edward VII). In 1913
the royal and first-class waiting-rooms were converted to offices
for the goods invoice clerks and cashiers. A brief revival of
passenger activity came between 1932 and 1939, in which years
the Southern Railway ran a few summer excursions from the
old terminus. Cubitt's frontage was severely damaged in a fire
during 1936, and was afterwards demolished.

PARTITION AT LONDON BRIDGE

We must now return to London Bridge, and the affairs of the
little Greenwich company. Like the similar Blackwall line
across the river, the Greenwich had much to offer the larger
companies, and it was only a matter of time before it fell into
more powerful hands. Under the shadow thrown over its business by the construction of goods and passenger facilities at
Bricklayers Arms, the London & Greenwich entered into negotiations with a confident SER, and it was soon agreed that the
main-line company should take it over on lease from January
1st, 1845. It remained a separate undertaking until 1923, when
it was absorbed into the Southern Railway.

With Big Brother now that much more firmly established at
London Bridge and the new Joint station already proving too
small, squabbles quickly developed between the users, and it
was finally decided to divide up the site. So it was that the
pretty Joint station was demolished after a mere five years' use.

In 1850 the SER erected a boundary wall down the centre of

the London Bridge terminal site and set about building its own terminus on the north side. A three-storey frontage was designed by the SER architect, Samuel Beazley.[3] This building had a flat roof and curved inwards to the station at the south end, the last short section being set back a little from the rest. A flat canopy, supported by iron pillars ran along the entire length, curving gracefully at the southern corners. The *Illustrated London News* of February 15th, 1851, did not think much of the new block, observing that it was 'of less merit than its predecessor'. Almost the only feature of note was the chiming clock which projected above the cornice, decorated birthday-cake fashion with cement 'in a manner by no means advantageous to Mr Beazley'. Sadly mauled by German bombs of World War II, and the necessary demolitions for the Charing Cross extension, a very small part of this building still survives.

Supplementing the frontal block was a 150-ft-long three-storey building flanking the Tooley Street side of the inclined approach road. This had a ground floor of shops in Tooley Street, and an arcade of shops and a refreshment room on the incline side. There were offices on the top floor, under a flat roof. Completed in August 1851, the shops in 'London Bridge Arcade' remained empty for some time as the rents were thought too high.

Inside the main block were separate booking-offices for the Greenwich, North Kent and Dover lines. Behind, in a narrow shed of their own (the old Croydon terminus) were the three Greenwich lines. Immediately south of these were the North Kent lines, an arrival and departure road, with an empty carriage track between. The southern part of the premises, known as the 'Dover station' was adjacent, an arrival and a departure track, with empty carriage road between, under a single-span roof on the site of the 1836 station. In 1853, two years after the completion of this SER station, there were thirty departures daily on the Greenwich line, and about fifty on the various SER lines (North Kent to Gravesend and Chatham via Woolwich, and to Margate, Ramsgate, Dover, Folkestone and Hastings).

The Croydon and Brighton companies had combined in 1846 to form the London Brighton & South Coast Railway, and in the following year there had been an important agreement between thte LBSCR and the SER. With certain exceptions, the LBSCR was to cease paying tolls over the Greenwich viaduct and Bricklayers Arms lines, and the SER was enabled in return to run free, also with exceptions, over the LBSCR between Corbett's Lane and Croydon. The exceptions related mainly to future lines and effectively marked out the 'legitimate territory' of each company.

Although the SER was prepared to offer its neighbour accommodation, this would obviously have been inadequate, and the new company decided to build its own terminus on the southern side of the wall. In 1850 things were still in a state of flux, but a booking-office had been erected, with a temporary screen on each side, that on the left of the gateway to the SER station's carriage road, that on the right forming the entrance to the arrival-side carriage road of the new Brighton station. A three-storey 'Italian style' frontage block was erected in 1853–4. This had a flat roof like its neighbour, and was decorated with stone dressings and rusticated pilasters and quoins. A narrow, flat canopy, supported by iron wall brackets, ran along the front over the footway and entrances (after about thirty years this was replaced by a much larger affair which covered part of the cab yard). Behind, the departure and arrival platforms were covered by a 700-ft-long train shed of about 100-ft span, glazed with rough plate glass.

The half-finished station had to cope with the heavy traffic arising from the Great Exhibition of 1851, an event not without significance for the LBSCR. Sir Joseph Paxton's remarkable glass exhibition building was purchased in the following year by a company closely associated with the LBSCR and moved from Hyde Park to the 300-acre Penge Park, which had been sold without pain by Leo Schuster, an LBSCR director. A railway station on a new branch was opened for passenger traffic on June 10th, 1854, the same day that Queen Victoria opened the re-erected building, now known as the Crystal Palace. Two short platforms were added at London Bridge about the same time to handle local trains, including those serving Crystal Palace. As had been hoped, the Palace proved a useful source of additional traffic for the LBSCR, so much so that the company's stock of locomotives and carriages was often taxed to the limit to meet the demands of the public. On one day in 1859, 112,000 were conveyed up to the Palace, some 70,000 of them from London Bridge. Normal LBSCR service in 1858 at London Bridge comprised fourteen trains daily each way on the main line, and forty-eight on the local routes to Croydon, Crystal Palace and Epsom.

A third pair of approach tracks was added to the Greenwich viaduct to carry the additional traffic created by the opening of the North Kent line in 1849. These were situated on the north side and came into use on February 24th, 1850. Another track was built at the same time beyond Corbett's Lane junction to the point where the North Kent diverged (just south of the Surrey Canal). To avoid crossing the down line on the level at North Kent East junction, the self-contained Greenwich line was then changed over to right-hand running, the six tracks on the viaduct being worked as follows:

Greenwich up
North Kent and Greenwich down
North Kent and Dover up
SER and LBSCR down
SER and LBSCR up
Croydon up local[4]

Three more tracks were provided on the south side of the viaduct for the opening of the South London line from London Bridge to East Brixton on August 13th, 1866. These became:

down South London
up South London
up South London

Plan of Approaches to London Bridge. 1, London & Greenwich. 2, South Eastern. 3, London & Croydon. 4, London Brighton & South Coast. 5, East London. 6, East London (abandoned). 7, Passenger stations. 8, Closed passenger stations. A, Foreign Cattle Market. B, Surrey Commercial Docks

and were worked and owned by the LBSCR, whose trains could now for the first time enter London Bridge under the control of the company's own signalmen.

In connexion with the opening of the South London line, the LBSCR side of London Bridge was enlarged. A new train shed was erected, and a group of additional platforms (now 19 to 22) provided on the south side, making a total of nine.

A hotel was built on the Brighton side of the station by private enterprise in 1861. It was placed as near as possible to the station, at its south-west corner, against the viaduct, fronting St Thomas and Joiner Streets, with its second floor at platform level. Designed by Henry Currey,[5] the architect and surveyor to St Thomas's Hospital, the Terminus Hotel had about 150 public rooms in seven storeys. It never proved very popular and was purchased in 1893 by the LBSCR, which converted it to general offices. After suffering grievous bomb damage, it was demolished in 1941.

PRESSURE TO GO WEST

Around the middle of the nineteenth century, strong pressures were developing for railway extensions farther into the City and West End to accommodate the rapidly increasing passenger traffic of the Southern lines. Reporting in 1855, the Commons Select Committee on Metropolitan Communications revealed that the number of people using the London Bridge stations had increased from some five and a half to over ten millions in the five years 1850–54. Sir Joseph Paxton pointed out in evidence that it took longer to go from London Bridge Station to Paddington than to travel from London Bridge to Brighton. Two years later, as the price for refusing the East Kent Railway access into London, a Commons committee extracted a promise from the SER chairman that his company would produce a scheme for a West End terminus for the lines from Kent and the Channel ports. After its secretary, Samuel Smiles, had thoroughly investigated the matter, the SER, working through a subsidiary, obtained powers in 1859 for a terminus at Charing Cross, to be reached by an extension from London Bridge.

Almost as soon as it left the north side of London Bridge, this Charing Cross extension was made to swerve south-west by the presence of Southwark Cathedral across its path. In so swerving, the alignment cut across a small corner of the grounds of St Thomas's Hospital, at that time situated immediately east of London Bridge Station. Although the amount of land required was a mere one-sixth of an acre, for which the railway company offered £20,000, the governors of the hospital used powers given to them in the Act authorizing the extension and compelled the purchase of the whole of the hospital and grounds. For this they coolly demanded £750,000, a sum which represented ninety per cent of the Charing Cross company's capital. After arbitration, the railway paid £296,000, which went a long way towards the £500,000 cost of the new Albert Embankment hospital of 1868–71.

Before it could be converted to a through station, the north side of London Bridge required substantial alterations. The London Bridge Arcade was swept away and a railway viaduct built above. This viaduct carried the extension on to an ugly plate girder bridge over the station approach, which was followed by another similar bridge over Borough High Street. The Greenwich terminus (the original Croydon station) disappeared, and the tracks off the Greenwich viaduct into London Bridge on this side were lifted at 1 in 103 into a High Level Through station with five platforms (two down and three up). These platforms, alongside and above Tooley Street, came into use with the extension on January 11th, 1864. At first only the Greenwich and Mid-Kent line trains used the extension, the lines being opened to all traffic on May 1st, 1864. The southern part of the SER station became a Continental goods depot, with eight roads under an overall roof.

As traffic continued to increase in the 1870s, the LBSCR considered enlargement of its station, but dismissed it as too costly. As an alternative, it was decided to secure the maximum capacity from the existing site by rearranging tracks and improving the signalling. Platforms were extended at the outer ends and in and out roads provided so that they might be used for either departures or arrivals. The new signalling allowed two trains in the same platform simultaneously if desired. By shortening the cab road at its eastern end, room was found for two more short platforms (the present 17 and 18), making eleven platforms in all, numbered from north to south. This work was finished in 1879.

Pressure from increasing traffic was also felt on the SER side, and in 1893–4 this was rebuilt, with an additional platform face on the north. These platforms were now numbered south to north 1 to 7, omitting 3 (there was a No 3 road between the platform lines of 2 and 4, of which more presently). At the time of this rebuilding, new railway offices were provided for SER staff in the narrow space between Platform 7 road and Tooley Street.

The last major changes in the London Bridge layout were made at the turn of the century. After many years of intense competition, the South Eastern and the London Chatham & Dover companies had come together, from January 1st, 1899, under a managing committee consisting of four directors from each board, using the name South Eastern & Chatham Railway. In 1901, continuing widenings begun by the SER, the managing committee opened two extra tracks on the north side of the viaduct as far as Spa Road, the Greenwich trains resuming normal left-hand running as a consequence of this on May 26th. The displaced poor were rehoused in Folkestone Gardens, a gaunt collection of tenements south of the line's bridges over the Surrey Canal.

A vast sweep of eleven parallel tracks, the approaches to London Bridge now formed one of the most impressive stretches of railway in Britain, alive with trains for most of the twenty-four hours. From north to south the various lines were:

SECR No 1 down
SECR No 2 down
SECR No 3 down
SECR No 2 up
SECR No 1 up
SECR down main (also used by LBSCR)
SECR up main (also used by LBSCR)
SECR up local (also known as up Croydon) (also used by LBSCR)
LBSCR South London down
LBSCR South London up main
LBSCR South London up local

Beyond Spa Road three new roads were laid on the north side of the viaduct, and the working of the first six roads from that side was:

SECR No 1 down
SECR No 2 down

SECR No 3 up
SECR No 2 up
SECR No 3 down
SECR No 1 up

On October 19th, 1909, in preparation for electric working, the middle South London line was resignalled for reversible operation as far as South Bermondsey junction and over the 'Spur' to Bricklayers Arms junction. This was intended to relieve the congested down main, which in 1912 was carrying fourteen LBSCR and five SECR trains between 5 and 6 PM.

During 1899 the Continental goods depot was moved to Ewer Street, Southwark, on the Charing Cross extension (Ewer Street closed in 1960 upon the opening of a new and larger Continental freight depot at Hither Green). On the Continental depot site four Low Level terminal platforms (now 8 to 11) were constructed; 8 and 9 were 660 ft long, 10 was 510 ft, and 11 only 393 ft. The old wooden overall roof was removed and umbrella canopies provided for the new passenger platforms. Separately numbered 1 to 4 from south to north, these platforms came into use on June 2nd, 1902, with a covered footbridge joining them to the High Level station.

ELECTRIFICATION

London Bridge now had its final total of twenty-one platforms, fifteen terminal, six through, but its capacity was to be vastly increased in later years by electrification and the installation of colour-light signalling.

The first electric trains appeared on the Brighton side on December 1st, 1909, providing the service over the South London line to Victoria, via Denmark Hill. They were operated on the 6,600-V single-phase ac system with overhead-wire distribution and bow collectors on the trains. The six most southerly platforms (now 17 to 22) were wired, but 17 was rarely used by the electric trains. In 1912 the electrification was extended to the other services: Crystal Palace (LL) via Tulse

Hill (March 1st) and Streatham–Victoria via Tulse Hill (June 1st). Electric trains also ran to Norwood Junction when working in and out of Selhurst depot. In 1912 the number of trains using the Brighton station daily was 901, compared with 663 before electrification.

No damage was inflicted upon London Bridge during the air raids of the First World War, but precautionary measures included the provision of office accommodation in the Tooley Street arches and under the Brighton station, with special facilities for staff controlling military traffic. The SECR air-raid control centre, which gave instructions for the working of traffic during air raids, was also located at London Bridge.

At the grouping of 1923 the London Bridge stations passed to the Southern Railway which at once determined to electrify all the former SER suburban lines, using the 600-V dc third-rail system. The services through London Bridge to Bromley North, Orpington, Beckenham Junction, Hayes and Addiscombe were electrically operated from February 28th, 1926, and those to Dartford via Blackheath and Charlton, via Bexleyheath and via Sidcup, as well as the Plumstead via Greenwich service, followed on June 6th. Full services on all these routes began on July 19th. The Caterham and Tattenham Corner services were electrified from March 25th, 1928, with a full service from June 17th.

On the Brighton side, the overhead wire was replaced by third rail, whilst other services were electrified on the new system, and by the early summer of 1928, all the platform lines in this part of the station were fitted with conductor rails. The first dc electric trains ran on March 25th, 1928, to Crystal Palace (LL) via Sydenham, and on June 17th, the services to Coulsdon North (peak hours only), to Epsom Downs via West Croydon, South London line to Victoria, to Crystal Palace via Tulse Hill, to Streatham Hill and to London Bridge via Selhurst and Sydenham (and vice versa) were electrified on the dc system. Finally, on March 3rd, 1929, it was the turn of the services to Dorking North and Effingham Junction via

Mitcham, and from the same day, the Streatham Hill trains were extended to Victoria.

After the conversion of the suburban network, electric working was extended to the south-coast resorts, whose stations already provided a considerable business traffic to London Bridge. Platforms 14 and 15 were lengthened to 800 ft, and from January 1st, 1933, electric trains ran to Brighton and West Worthing (previously, from July 17th, 1932, there had been electric working as far as Reigate and Three Bridges). The Seaford, Eastbourne and Hastings services were electrically operated from July 7th, 1935, and then from July 3rd, 1938, the Bognor and Littlehampton rush-hour trains.

Long-distance season traffic had been a feature of the Brighton side of London Bridge for many years, and indeed without too much exaggeration, one could say that the whole of the LBSCR was virtually a suburban system. Perhaps the most impressive sight that London Bridge could offer was the nightly departure of 'the Fives' from adjacent platforms. In steam days these were:

5.0 PM 'City Limited', Brighton non-stop (a train dating from the 1840s)
5.5 PM Eastbourne
5.8 PM Hove and Worthing

all using the same main line for a considerable distance. Just before the main-line electrification, the Brighton train would consist of ten corridor coaches and a first-class Pullman car (252 first- and 224 third-class seats), drawn by a handsome Billinton 4–6–4T; the Eastbourne, which included a slip coach for Horley and stations to Forest Row, also had a first-class Pullman, and would probably be hauled by a U or U1 2–6–0; and the 5.8 would have a two-coach slip portion for Haywards Heath and stations to Brighton and be headed by another 4–6–4T. Three minutes later, another train would leave for Brighton, semi-fast, and in this eleven minutes seven electric suburban trains would also have left the

Brighton station. Translated into electric working 'the Fives' became:

5.00 PM	Brighton (12 cars including buffet)
5.02 PM	Eastbourne and Seaford (12 cars)
5.05 PM	Hove, Worthing and Littlehampton (12 with buffet)
5.11 PM	Brighton and Littlehampton (10 cars)

There have been changes since, but the timetable current at the time of writing still shows four similar main-line departures between 5 and 5.14 PM.

CHANGES OF 1928

We must return for a moment to 1928, which was an important year in the history of London Bridge. Perhaps the most momentous change, symbolic of the unification of the Southern lines, was the making of an opening in the wall between the two sides of the station, now known as the Eastern Section (ie, the former SER) and Central Section (former LBSCR) stations. With the hole in the wall came a second footbridge over the Low Level and Through platforms to facilitate interchange across the station. In part these alterations were designed to make things a little easier for the increased number of rush-hour passengers forced to change trains at London Bridge, an unfortunate consequence of the more frequent service provided by electrification. As early as 1867 some trains from the Brighton side had run through the High Level platforms into Cannon Street; this had not lasted very long, but for many years a few trains on the SER Caterham and Tattenham Corner services had crossed over from the far side to reach Cannon Street and Charing Cross, as had three or four business trains from the Reading–Redhill and Redhill–Tonbridge lines. When intensive electric services were introduced on the Brighton side in 1928 it was clear that such crossing movements, fouling three other lines, could no longer be tolerated in the rush hours. Caterham and Tattenham Corner electric trains were therefore terminated in the Low Level platforms at rush hours and the steam business services mentioned suffered the same fate.

Another important change of 1928 also followed electrification on the Brighton side. This was the conversion of the middle South London road out of London Bridge from reversible to down working, and consequent rearrangement of the approach tracks. The old down South London line became up local, and from June 17th, the eleven approach tracks were used as follows: Eastern Section numbers 1, 2 and 3 down, Eastern 2 and 1 up, Central Section down local, Central down through, Central up through, Central up local, South London down, South London up.

Following these changes on June 17th, the twenty-one platforms were numbered consecutively from north to south, apart from the 'missing' Platform 5. There never had been such a platform, but a number 5 (formerly 3) through road existed between the platform roads of 4 and 6. This was used as a light-engine line and also as a refuge for freight trains awaiting a path to the Northern lines via Ludgate Hill and Farringdon. After the opening of the Lewisham loops in 1929 the number of these cross-London freights through London Bridge was substantially reduced. The middle road was removed in 1952 to facilitate the extension of Platforms 3 and 4 in the ten-car scheme.

LAYOUT

This is a convenient point to offer a description of this complicated station, which has changed but little since 1928. In the Through, or High Level station were the curved island Platforms 1 and 2, 3 and 4, 6 and 7. As well as the connexion offered by the footbridges already mentioned, there were subways from the London ends of these platforms to a very cramped circulating area beneath the viaduct of the Charing Cross extension. Here was found a wooden booking-office and a buffet, the latter inside the old SER frontage block. Platforms

1, 2 and 3 were served by down trains, and 4 could be used for down working in foggy weather or other special occasions by trains which had terminated in it. Main-line trains serving the Kent coast used Platform 3 in the down direction, 6 and 7 when coming up; the sharply curved, up-tilted 7 provided steam drivers with many an embarrassing start. The six Through platforms varied in length from 602 to 745 ft before they were extended in 1954 at the country end to accommodate ten-car trains. Opposite Platform 7, sharing the same road, was a short low platform used for postal traffic. Known as 'the Mount', its surface was shiny from the constant friction of mailbags. A roadway through the old SER building led to a small yard behind this platform which was used by the Post Office vans. Amenities at platform level were few; 1 and 2 boasted bookstalls and 1 had a tiny buffet at the country end where homegoing commuters drowned the day's troubles or prepared to face their wives.

Alongside the Through station were the Low Level terminal Platforms 8 to 11, used for parcels traffic and the rush-hour workings already referred to. Platform 11, not electrified and only 393 ft long, was normally used for stabling vans and locomotives, although it saw the occasional slack-hour passenger train in steam days. Its other face, 10, was full length, sheltered at its inner end by the first floor of the long and narrow office block that abutted on to the south end of the old SER frontage.

Passing through the hole in the wall, the passenger reached the concourse of the former LBSCR station opposite the ends of the northernmost platforms, 12 and 13, which were of medium length and used for suburban services. Between 13 and 14 were two non-electrified sidings, one of which disappeared in a widening and lengthening of 14 and 15 in 1931. At the buffer stops was a bookstall of which more will be heard.

South-coast main-line trains used the three long Platforms 14, 15 and 16, the only ones capable of taking twelve-car electric trains, 16 being the longest in the station at 827 ft. On the opposite face of 16 was the shortest platform, the 518-ft No 17.

Plan of the 1937 layout of London Bridge Station, Southern Railway. From the Railway Magazine, February 1937

Between 17 and 18, another short platform, there was an incline off the end of the carriage roadway, leading down to the old lamp room. At the far side were Nos 19 to 22, usually referred to as the South London line platforms.

A waiting-room and a booking-hall were to be found in the ground floor of the frontage building, and in a passage through it, on the north side, were some shops. At the north side of the concourse was a buffet, with a tea room above, the latter now a staff canteen. On the St Thomas Street side, between the old hotel and the South London platforms, there were a cloakroom, parcels office and staff rooms; the South London platforms had their own buffet and bookstall, at the back of 19 and 20. All this was under a three-section roof, with a central arch of 80-ft span over Platforms 15 to 18, carried on elegant fluted iron columns and decorated brackets, and a series of gambrels, forming horizontal sections either side, on lattice girder supports.

In 1936, with the reduction in steam operation, the 46-ft 5-in turntable opposite the ends of 15 and 16 was removed, and the remaining engines were turned at New Cross Gate sheds. In its place, the Southern erected a giant nameboard, floodlit at night, presumably to reassure dazed commuters of their whereabouts.

As may be surmised, this somewhat confused cluster of platforms and stations was not conducive to smooth passenger flow. At rush hours, the footbridges over the Eastern Section platforms were the scene of some confusion, and the various currents of passenger movement on the Central side not only conflicted with the flow to and from the Eastern Section, but tended to tangle with the road vans and other impedimenta of a healthy parcels, newspaper and mail traffic centred around the carriage roadway alongside Platform 16.

By 1936 the combined stations were handling about 250,000 passengers a day, but only 170,000 passed through the barriers. There were 2,407 train movements at London Bridge in each twenty-four hours, and in the busiest morning peak hour, 94 trains arrived, 29 continuing to Cannon Street, 19 to Char-

ing Cross, and 46 terminating. To assist rush-hour crowds
and supplement the destination indicators worked from the
signal box, the SR experimentally installed loudspeakers on
Platforms 1 and 2 in 1927, probably the first equipment of its
kind on a major London station.[6]

Apart from its predominant suburban and business traffic,
London Bridge saw special workings for events at the Crystal
Palace, race days at Epsom, and the September picking season
in the Kentish hopfields. Over 33,000 travelled each year to
and from the hopfields during the 1930s, carried in special
trains made up from the oldest available stock. Vans were
provided to accommodate the various household accoutre-
ments – a line was drawn at tables and chairs, but most other
essential domestic equipment was accepted. These trains
usually left very early in the morning or from the Low Level
platforms after the Saturday rush hours. Now hop pickers'
traffic has entirely disappeared (the last special train ran in
1960), partly owing to the adoption of machines, but largely
because those attracted to a free country holiday now enjoy a
vastly improved standard of living. The new generation flies
to Majorca for fish and chips in the sun.

In contrast to its treatment in the First World War, London
Bridge received severe punishment in the Second. On December 9th, 1940, the signal box had a narrow escape when a
parachute mine, entangled in a signal girder, settling against
the wall of the cabin. Whilst the three men inside continued
with their work, two sailors defused the mine. In the great fire
raid on the City (December 29th–30th, 1940), bombs rained
on the station. The large clock on the end wall of the Central
Section building stopped at 12.27 as the hotel and the top
floors of both frontage buildings were gutted by fire. The Central Section parcels office was destroyed. Parcels work was
moved to the booking-office and tickets were sold from a
wooden hut on the concourse. A quarter of a century later,
this splendid piece of wartime improvisation was still there.
Another casualty was the Eastern Section buffet at the entrance

to Platforms 6 and 7, but this was repaired and reopened in May 1948. After the damage to the Central Section side, Platforms 18 to 22 shared a common entrance and exit.

Between 1958 and 1964, the remaining steam services disappeared. The Hastings via Tunbridge Wells trains, which passed through the Eastern platforms, were worked by diesel-electric multiple-unit sets from June 9th, 1958; the remaining steam trains through this side of the station vanished with the completion of the Kent coast electrification in June 1961. The last steam workings at London Bridge, to the Oxted, East Grinstead, Eridge and Uckfield lines, were replaced by diesel-electric multiple-unit sets or locomotives, and the final regular steam run was made in 1964. The sole remaining train to the Redhill–Reading line (the 5.25 PM) last ran in February 1963.

After 1945 peak-hour traffic continued to grow, becoming still more concentrated in time. In 1958, 37,000 left London Bridge in the heaviest hour, compared with 24,000 in 1939. There has since been a slight decline: the corresponding figure for 1967 was 30,900. (These figures do not of course include those in trains through the Eastern Section platforms.) In the peak evening hour there are now 61 trains through the Eastern Section station, including those not stopping, and 44 leave the Central Section platforms. Although this total of 105 is only 14 higher than 1939, it must be remembered that today's trains are longer and more capacious than those of the immediate pre-war period. A typical pre-war eight-car suburban electric train offered a total of 652 seats (112 first class), but a modern eight-car electric train as used on the Central Section has 772 seats (an increase of seventeen per cent), whilst the ten-car trains introduced on the Eastern Section in 1955–7 have a total of 958 seats (forty-six per cent increase).

To date, BR has not done a great deal for London Bridge. The war-damaged frontage blocks have been left in a semi-ruined state but part of the remains of the SER frontage was demolished in 1966 to provide a van yard in front of the Low Level station. Wooden platforms have been replaced with concrete and asphalt (a job begun by the SR in 1942) and new barriers were erected on Platforms 12 to 19 in 1953. The post office in the Eastern Section frontage, which had been open for over fifty years, suffered a loss of business, and was closed on August 31st, 1963.

When the City and South London Tube railway was extended to Moorgate on February 25th, 1900, an Underground station was provided near London Bridge Station, at the bottom of the approach road. Communications were improved on December 2nd, 1901, by the opening of a 180-yard subway from the Tube station to lifts and a small booking-hall at the southern corner of the Brighton station forecourt, but the SER passengers still had a tiresome walk in the open air. In December 1940 this Brighton side Tube entrance was damaged by bombs and closed. Reopened on July 9th, 1945, it was only available in peak hours from April 8th, 1957. A new, larger Tube booking-hall, with three escalators replacing lifts, and generally more convenient for the main station, was opened by London Transport on November 19th, 1967.

This new Tube station is eventually to be connected to a series of overhead walkways which will be built to connect London Bridge Station with the City Corporation's new river bridge, and with Guy's Hospital. British Railways produced plans for a new London Bridge Station in July 1961, proposing a 210-ft seventeen-storey office block, with subsidiary four-storey wings of offices and shops, all connected to the new walkways and Tube station. Car parks were to be provided under a central pedestrian concourse, and at last, parcels, newspaper and mail traffic would be segregated from the passenger flow. But the Government no longer looked with favour on new offices in central London by the time this £4 million scheme got off the ground. As the office rents were to help pay for the station rebuilding, BR has now postponed the latter 'indefinitely', and remembering the planning muddles at Euston, LT has provided no direct access to the terminus from its new Tube station.

A RUSH-HOUR STATION

Today, London Bridge is very much a rush-hour station. In 1967 86,300 passengers arrived daily, 61,400 between 7 and 10 AM. Between times there is only a moderate flow of short-distance passengers in the High Level and Central Section stations. The Low Level platforms have been closed between 10 AM and 3 PM and at weekends since October 1st, 1966, and from the same date, apart from Platforms 18 to 22, the Central Section station has been closed on Saturday afternoons and Sundays. Newspaper traffic, especially evenings for south-east England, is heavy. Mail has been carried from London Bridge since 1837 and is still an important activity, notably at 'the Mount' platform and Platform 16, which sees the nightly departure, at 11.50, of the London–Dover Travelling Post Office (there is a late fee letter box for this train by the Central Section buffet).

Each weekday morning, between 8 and 9, huge crowds flow out of London Bridge, forming a human tide, which washes into the City offices across the river. In the evening, the footways over the bridge are swamped again, in the reverse direction. Thousands more pass through the station, whilst others move to and from the Tube platforms and the buses which terminate in the station forecourt.[7] All these people, the vast majority of the station's users, know their way about, which is just as well, for its untidy, disjointed layout, inherited from the railway politics of the nineteenth century, and smashed about by wartime bombs, offers many a hazard to the stranger, and cries out for rationalization and rebuilding.

SIGNALLING AND ACCIDENTS

Not surprisingly, London Bridge has a varied and interesting signalling history. At first, the Greenwich Railway used hand flags and lamps, but later they installed 15-ft posts carrying square iron plates showing red on one side and green on the other, controlled by hand levers at the base. The London & Croydon used a primitive form of semaphore from about 1842, and a contemporary illustration of the Joint station shows a double arm signal. The block bell system invented by C. V. Walker, the SER telegraph superintendent, was installed outside London Bridge in 1852.

With the opening of the Charing Cross extension in 1864, an entirely new signalling installation was provided by Saxby & Farmer. Two cabins, AB and CD, were erected over the approach tracks to the south of the station, with semaphore signals in splendid array on their roofs. Each box had three posts carrying three double semaphores, up and down arms for each set of approach tracks. 'Stop' was indicated by the horizontal position, 'caution' by a lowering of the arm, but the 'all clear' indication (arm hidden in a slot in the post), was not given in this busy area. Each arm carried a letter code indicating the route to which it referred. Both boxes were manned by a crew of three; signalman, telegraph clerk and signal lad. At the suggestion of Captain H. Tyler, the block bells were replaced by miniature semaphores in the signal boxes.

For the reconstructed through station of 1894, there were three boxes on the SER side; A, with 41 levers, at the west end of the present Platforms 1 and 2, B, with 148 levers, an overhead box at the other end of the station, and C, sited at the crossover junction to the Croydon lines, with 47 levers. These boxes had Sykes' lock and block apparatus, and, in common with other boxes in the inner area, were fitted with Walker's clock-face train describers.

After the construction of the South London line in 1866, the LBSCR operated its own signals at London Bridge, opening three boxes, South, East and West, a total of seventy-two levers. All had Saxby & Farmer's 'striking' interlocking, and in 1879 some of this equipment was taken to Epsom Downs Station, where it survived in use until quite recent times.

As part of the scheme for increasing the capacity of the

Brighton station, the East and West boxes were closed in 1879, and replaced by a large North box situated opposite the ends of what are now Platforms 17 and 18. This new cabin, which straddled the turntable siding, was to remain in use and until the colour-light installation of 1928. It was 71 ft 4 ins long and 26 ft 4 ins wide, containing 280 levers in two Saxby & Farmer back-to-back frames. The 'grid iron' interlocking initially installed was later replaced by the more conventional tappet system. North was really a yard box, as the Sykes' lock and block working began at South box, situated on the south side of the South London line, just outside the station. This was a mere 9 ft wide and 53 ft long, with ninety-eight levers.

The 1879 installation included route indicators on the signals controlling the six in and out roads (A to C on the South London side, D to F on the main-line side). They were enamelled discs, numbered and lettered, placed on the posts, and illuminated at night by oil lamps. Sheathed when not in use, they were worked by separate levers in the signal box. The discs on the outer home showed the road to which the train would run, those on the inner home the platform it would use, a pattern followed in the later colour-light installation. Starting signals showed the road to be taken to the advanced starters.

Another interesting feature of the 1879 equipment was the use of fish-tailed arms to indicate platform occupation, permitting the working of two trains into one platform when required. If the distant and home arms were both lowered, the platform was fully clear to buffers, but if only the home arm was off, the driver knew he must enter with great caution as the platform was partly occupied. In later years it seems doubtful whether the distant arms were ever pulled off, even when the platform was completely empty, probably because the signalmen could not see the platform ends and preferred to err on the side of safety. During the First World War, the platform distants were replaced with conventional calling-on arms which were pulled off under a level home arm to indicate partial occupation of the platform.

Colour-light signalling, with track circuiting and power-operated points was introduced by the Southern Railway for the dc electrifications of the 1920s. The tracks in London Bridge Station and the approaches, together with the through lines to Borough Market junction, were changed over to the new signalling on June 17th, 1928. A power signal box, 113 ft by 14 ft 9 ins, containing a Westinghouse & Saxby frame of 311 miniature levers, controlled all the platform lines and approaches. There were two 'spotlight' track diagrams, each 18 ft long. So extensive was the mechanical interlocking of this frame that it rested on the floor below that used by the signalmen.

Four-aspect colour lights were used on the Eastern Section lines between Borough Market and Spa Road, but as there was no freight traffic on the Central side, three aspects were considered sufficient between the Central platforms and Bricklayers Arms junction (main line) and Old Kent Road junction (South London line).

Unfamiliarity with this new signalling was the probable cause of the first serious accident at London Bridge, which occurred just east of the signal box on July 9th, 1928. Observing a signal changing to green, the driver of a light engine moved off, ignoring a ground signal at danger, and colliding with the front of the 7.22 PM electric for Epsom Downs, which was proceeding under clear signals. The engine, and two cars of the passenger train left the rails, killing one passenger immediately and fatally injuring another. Twenty years later, on January 23rd, 1948, at 9.30 AM, an up electric from Seaford and Ore over-ran the up inner home signals, to enter Platform 14, which was already occupied by an empty train. The motorman on the passenger train and a learner with him were trapped, dying in the arms of a priest from Southwark Cathedral, who had climbed into the wrecked cab. The empty coaches were forced up over the buffers, killing a man on the concourse and wrecking the bookstall. A third accident, fortunately without fatalities, occurred about 8.30 PM on October

22nd, 1956, under hand signalling during a track-circuit failure. A down train was wrongly allowed out of the station, and collided with an incoming train at a crossover about 500 yd outside. Fortunately both motormen saw what was inevitable, and braked hard.

In 1967, in conjunction with a new timetable giving a larger number of trains through the High Level stations in peak hours, additional signals were provided between London Bridge (Eastern Section) and Cannon Street and Metropolitan junction.

CHAPTER NINE

CANNON STREET

A SPECIAL AURA

A great train shed yawning over the Thames, high brick walls, proud towers, and a wedding-cake hotel across the street frontage combined to give the old Cannon Street a special aura. Now, thanks to German bombs, and the requirements of longer trains, this architectural magic has all but vanished. Only the towers and part of the walls remain in sad, soot-blackened splendour, to form an incongruous frame for the monotonous new office blocks and smart modern concourse at the north end. Opened in 1866 as the City station of the South Eastern Railway, Cannon Street now handles little else but season-ticket business, its long-distance services confined to a few rush-hour trains.

At first the SER had been content to serve the City from London Bridge and two proposed intermediate stations on the Charing Cross extension (at the south end of Southwark Bridge and at Blackfriars Road), but in 1860, a year after the Charing Cross Act, the London Chatham & Dover, the SER's great rivals, were authorized to extend into the City as far as Ludgate Hill. Spurred by this, the SER-backed Charing Cross company decided to complement the West End terminus with a City station on the north bank of the river. There was as yet no Metropolitan District Railway, and street congestion, even in those days, was decidedly tiresome. In 1846 William Hosking told the Royal Commission on Metropolitan Termini that in the summer of 1845 it had taken him one and a half hours to come up from Brighton by train and a half-hour more to reach Trafalgar Square by any road; he added 'I have walked as quickly as I could go by any other mode'. There was every reason to hope then that a useful local traffic might be built up between this City station and Charing Cross, to supplement the suburban and long-distance business. An Act was obtained in 1861 for a station in Cannon Street, opposite Walbrook and St Swithin's Lane, just two minutes' walk from the Bank and Mansion House.

This was to be reached by a 60-chain branch from a triangular junction with the Charing Cross line just west of London Bridge. The station, river bridge and viaducts of the approaches were all designed by John Hawkshaw,[1] consulting engineer to the SER. Work began in July 1863.

On its east side, the triangle south of the river had three tracks, one down and two up; a fourth line, for down traffic, was added in 1896. On the west, there were three tracks, two towards Charing Cross, one towards Cannon Street, and across the 'base', only two, one up, one down, because it was planned to run almost all trains between London Bridge and Charing Cross in and out of Cannon Street. All three sides were on a brick viaduct and at the north end of the layout was an engine shed, turntable and coking stages (space was so tight that engines had to run on to the turntable before they could get in or out of the shed).

ACROSS THE RIVER TO THE CITY

Carrying the five approach tracks across the river was an 80-ft-wide bridge, 706 ft long, supported on four piers, each pier of four cast-iron columns, with cast-iron moulded caps. The two shore spans were each 125 ft long, and the three centre ones 136 ft. At Trinity high-water mark, there was a minimum clearance of 24 ft 8 ins to the soffit. The columns were filled with concrete below the river bed and with brickwork in cement above. They were 18-ft diameter below water line, 12 ft above it. In contrast to the Charing Cross bridge, all main girders ran longitudinally, and there were no high girders above rail level. The four running lines and the engine road rested on a plate girder superstructure.

On the north side, the bridge widened out into a 202-ft fan to carry the nine roads into the station, the platform ends and engine sidings. Footways were provided on each side of the bridge between ornamental parapets and the railway. That on the west side was opened to the public, on payment of a $\frac{1}{2}d$ toll, between 1872 and 1877, whilst that on the east was used by railway staff to reach the installations on the south shore.

Hawkshaw's station abutted immediately against the bridge. To gain the necessary height, it was built on a substructure of brick piers and arches. Over Upper Thames Street, the rails and platforms were carried on wrought-iron girders, the span being 37 ft.

Over the platforms towered a vast roof of 190-ft span. Surmounted by a 22-ft-wide lantern which ran nearly the full length of 680 ft, this roof was 106 ft 6 ins above the rails at the apex of the arch, and was glazed over two-thirds of its surface area. Solid brick walls, averaging 6 ft 6ins in thickness, and relieved by arched bays, supported this pretentious canopy. On the inside, these walls were later disfigured by scores of advertisement panels, including one which tempted sober City men with the delights of the Bal Tabarin. At the river, the walls terminated in arcaded towers which rose to the level of the roof lantern and were surmounted by weather vanes dutifully marked SER in the tails of their arrows. These towers, which were relieved by rusticated stone quoins, contained water tanks providing hydraulic power for the lifts to and from the station's vaults, and later, water for carriage cleaning. Across the river end, the roof was closed by a gable windscreen glazed in wooden frames made to fit between the iron struts and ties.

Inside the well-lit train shed, despite the advertisements, there was an air of spacious dignity. West to east, the arrangement was as follows:

single track

Charing Cross platform (480 ft)

two tracks

west arrival platform (721 ft) (carriage loading dock at north end)

cab roadway (empty cabs entered from Upper Thames Street via a U ramp at the south end and left with their fares through the frontage block and yard)

east arrival platform (721 ft)

three tracks (the middle road for spare stock and standing room, with carriage loading dock at north end)

general departure platform (665 ft)

two tracks

Greenwich platform (522 ft)

single track

The Charing Cross and Greenwich platforms were 13 ft 6 ins wide, the overall width of the arrival platforms and cab road was 30 ft, and the general departure platform was 19 ft wide. The Charing Cross platform, as the name implies, was used by the shuttle service between the two termini. Greenwich trains terminated at Cannon Street from its opening day; later, when Greenwich was linked to Maze Hill, a half-hourly service was operated to Charlton Junction, extended in peak hours to Plumstead. Mid-Kent, and some North Kent line trains, also used the Greenwich platform.

The ends of the general departure platform and the east and west arrival platforms projected beyond the shelter of the train shed on to the bridge. Widths of the platforms varied from 12 ft 6 ins to 19 ft.

Beyond the buffer stops was a circulating area across the full 187-ft width of the station, and north of this were waiting-rooms, booking-office, refreshment room, and cloakroom. On the street side, steps led down to a 90-ft-deep forecourt between the station building and Cannon Street, with further flights of steps at the north-west corner and in the centre, and a cab gateway at the north-east corner. Before the forecourt was laid out, a tunnel was constructed 28 ft below the surface for the future District Railway.

The frontage block was a five-storey hotel, the City Terminus, opened in May 1867 by an independent company, but later taken over by the SER. A high Victorian jumble of Italianate and French Renaissance styles, it was the work of Edward Middleton Barry.[2] Its north-east and north-west corners, each crowned with a mansard rooflet and a spirelet, were brought forward a little from the main building line; between them, the steeply-pitched main roof was spattered with banks of chimneys and a row of arched-top dormer windows. An Italianate water tower marked out the south-east corner. First, second and third floors had balconies along the front, the two lower ones with flower bowls marking each window division. Much use was made of Blanchard's artificial stone as facing, and of white glazed terracotta.

The Cannon Street Hotel, as it was later renamed, has a small place in history, for it was in these unlikely surroundings that representatives of various revolutionary bodies met in July 1920, to set up the Communist Party of Great Britain. A decline in business led to the closure of the hotel in 1931, but the large licensed public rooms were kept open for meetings and banquets. The remainder was converted to offices and let under the name of Southern House.

Opened on September 1st, 1866, Cannon Street was served by almost all trains proceeding to and from Charing Cross, including the Continental boat expresses. In addition, a shuttle service was worked every twenty minutes (later every ten minutes), providing, with the other trains, an average frequency of five minutes between the City and the West End. For the seven-minute run, the SER charged 6d first class, 4d second, and 2d third, compared with 3d for a horse-bus ride between Bank and Charing Cross. During 1867, Cannon Street handled some eight million passengers, of which three and a half million were local between West End and City.

The westernmost track of the river bridge was used ex-

clusively by the inter-terminal service; the neighbouring track
was for up trains from both London Bridge and Charing Cross,
whilst the centre track was used by up trains from London
Bridge; next came the main down line to London Bridge or
Charing Cross, and lastly, the engine road, used by locomotives
entering or leaving the depot on the south bank, or awaiting
their trains. All trains entering Cannon Street had to be
supplied with another locomotive for the outward journey, this
being called forward from the engine sidings on either bank,
or from the engine road. Any available engine was used for
taking trains on to Charing Cross, and for bringing trains from
there to Cannon Street. In general, main-line locomotives
worked to and from Cannon Street, and not to Charing
Cross.

CURIOSITIES OF SERVICES

Local traffic between the two termini slumped badly as soon
as the District Railway opened from Westminster to Blackfriars
in May 1870, and even more so when it reached Mansion
House in July 1871. Upon the completion of the Inner Circle
on October 6th, 1884, a station was provided under the Cannon Street forecourt. Attempts were made to advertise the
'open-air route', but the Underground was more reliable as
well as more direct. Even before the opening of the Underground line, one special type of traffic on the City–West End
route had largely disappeared. Some ladies of the streets had
found that the SER's first-class compartments, combined with
the uninterrupted seven-minute run, provided ideal conditions
for their activities at a rental that represented only a minute
proportion of their income. The number of drawn blinds on
these trains noticeably decreased after the opening of an intermediate station at Waterloo, at which most trains stopped, on
January 1st, 1869.

A curious service of the early days was that worked from
Cannon Street to Kensington (Addison Road) (with carriages

through to Euston), via Waterloo Junction, Latchmere Junction and Battersea. This had begun in July 1865 between London Bridge and Euston, but was diverted to Cannon Street from February 1st, 1867. Cut back to Waterloo for the month of January 1868, it was withdrawn from February 1st. Another 'foreign' service was that operated by the LBSCR, two business trains from Brighton to Cannon Street, and back again in the evening, lasting only from September 2nd, 1867, to July 31st, 1868.

However unsuccessful these experiments, and the local service to Charing Cross, the general suburban traffic to and from the City increased steadily, as did that of the main-line services working through to Charing Cross. In 1878 there were 165 trains in the busiest two and a half hours, more than one train a minute. By the middle 1880s it became necessary to increase the capacity of the approaches, and to this end, the bridge was widened to 120 ft, to accommodate ten tracks, including sidings. Two more cast-iron columns were added to each pier on the western side, and the rebuilt bridge was completed on February 1st, 1892. The bridge layout now had a siding on each flank, and the remaining eight tracks, west to east, were: No 1 out (Charing Cross), Nos 2 and 3 in, No 4 out (London Bridge or Charing Cross), No 5 (dead-end siding), Nos 6 and 7 in, and No 8 out (London Bridge). Engine facilities were provided on each side of the layout on the south bank, with a turntable at each side, and an engine shed and coaling stage on the east side.

In the station, another platform was added by inserting a single-track bay between the east and west arrival platforms, in space gained by shortening the cab roadway and blocking up the entrance from Upper Thames Street. The platforms were now numbered 1 to 9 from west to east, with the bay described as No 4 on both its faces. Platforms 3, 4 and 5 were extended on to the bridge as far as the first pier.

Although the weight of locomotives and the volume of traffic had increased considerably since 1866, a thorough examina-

tion of the bridge in the 1900s disclosed no signs of settlement
in the piers. But it did reveal that the superstructure had received heavy punishment from both the load and the weather,
and it was necessary to impose restrictions until it had been
strengthened. Carried out without any interruptions to traffic
over a period of four and a half years, this work was completed
in 1913. Six new main girders, each 443 ft long, were inserted
between the existing ones. The flooring was renewed and re-
inforcing plates were attached to the old girders at the points
of greatest strain.

War brought important changes. From November 15th,
1914, all the SECR Continental services were transferred to Victoria, and apart from specials to be mentioned later, boat trains
were never seen again at Cannon Street. The practice of running Charing Cross trains through Cannon Street ceased
almost completely on December 31st, 1916, a severely reduced
passenger timetable coming into force on the following day.
Cannon Street was then closed on Sundays, and from May 1st,
1918, it was also shut from 3 PM on Saturdays and between
11 AM and 4 PM Mondays to Fridays. These closures allowed
the use of the terminus as an engine and crew exchange point
for the large number of goods trains which were moving war
supplies between the Northern lines and the Channel ports via
Farringdon and Ludgate Hill. The GNR and Midland trains
were dealt with at Cannon Street in alternate weeks; the consequent speedier return of the Northern engines and crews to
their parent systems and the reduction in the number of pilot-
men provided a welcome increase in productivity. Between

*Layout of Cannon Street Station platforms before reorganization of 1926.
From the* Railway Magazine, *August 1966*

May and November 1918, when the normal weekday opening of Cannon Street was resumed, some 175,000 goods wagons and vans in 5,803 trains were worked through Cannon Street under this arrangement.[3]

Air raids provided few problems. Minor damage was inflicted on July 7th, 1917, when some 500 panes of glass were smashed and a bomb which fell outside No 2 cabin failed to explode. On January 28th, 1918, an empty carriage train leaving the station was damaged by an anti-aircraft shell.

Suburban traffic had grown appreciably in the first years of the new century, becoming an increasing burden to operate. The SECR had obtained powers for electric working as early as 1903, and in 1922 produced a plan which obtained a Treasury guarantee of principal and interest under the Trade Facilities Act, 1921, but this was overtaken by the formation of the Southern Railway. In the meantime, the SECR endeavoured to improve operation by the adoption of parallel working in the rush hours. Introduced on February 12th, 1922, in the morning peak, this arrangement involved no track or signalling changes, merely timetable revision to secure the simultaneous passing of up and down trains on the same route at junctions, and parallel running on multiple tracks. In this way, many conflicting movements were eliminated, and the experiment was so successful that similar arrangements were later introduced for the evening business traffic.

REMODELLING THE TRACK

As mentioned in Chapter 8, the first of the former SER suburban services were electrified on the third-rail dc system in 1926. To obtain the best results from electrification, the track layout, platforms, and signalling at Cannon Street were completely remodelled. The old layout was designed to facilitate the reversal of trains proceeding to and from Charing Cross, and allowed trains coming in from London Bridge to cross over on the river bridge and reach a central or western platform where they would be ready to depart for Charing Cross, and vice versa, in the opposite direction. There was little space for light engines, and those waiting to take trains out had often to be held on a running line.

The major aim of the new layout was to allow as many parallel and non-conflicting movements as possible. On the south bank there were four electrified tracks towards London Bridge, down local, down through, up through, up local. On the Charing Cross side of the triangle there were two electric lines, 'Out Met' and 'In Met', and a third track, in the form of a non-electrified loop, known as 'Met Siding'. ('Met' was an abbreviation for Metropolitan junction, where the lines from Cannon Street towards Charing Cross joined the direct tracks from London Bridge.) At the northern tip of the triangle, Stoney Street junction was abolished, as were the engine sidings, coaling stages and turntable on the eastern side of the line. The small engine shed was demolished and a sub-station built over its site. Facilities for engines were retained on the western side and the new layout allowed engines to run from the west side of Cannon Street into the Ewer Street depot or to Charing Cross without fouling the running lines from London Bridge. There was no access from the up local line to No 1 platform, but apart from this, all platforms could be reached from all up roads, and all platforms had access to all down roads. A link between No 1 and the up local would have needed very sharp curves, and the balance of advantage was given by omitting this connexion. A considerable simplification was effected, and the number of sets of points in the new layout was seventy-seven, twenty-four fewer than in the old.

The new track for the approaches was delivered to a field alongside New Cross Gate goods yard, where it was patiently assembled, adjusted to get the best alignment, and fitted with point locks, point machines, conductor rails and cables. This eliminated all cutting and adjusting of rails on site, but even so, removal of the old track, erection of the new, resignalling, and testing, required the complete closure of Cannon Street station

Cannon Street Station as rearranged in 1926, in connexion with electrification. From the Railway Magazine, August 1966

from 3 PM Saturday, June 5th, until 4 AM Monday, June 28th, 1926. Most of the 56,000 passengers who used Cannon Street each day were dealt with at London Bridge under emergency arrangements which must have been somewhat trying for all concerned.

In the station, the bay platform was abolished, and the remaining platforms rearranged to provide a total of eight, all more or less in line at buffers, and numbered from east to west. Each platform was faced with concrete blocks and surfaced with mastic asphalt. As before, there were single tracks against each outer wall, with a platform face on the inner side; all other faces had a pair of tracks between them. Platforms 1 and 2 were 569 and 567 ft long; 3 and 4, 580 and 574 ft; 5 and 6, 675 ft, and 7 and 8 752 and 745 ft. Numbers 1 to 5 were electrified, the others being left for the main-line steam trains, which also used 5. The concourse was enlarged, the booking-hall rearranged, and new iron railing barriers and gates provided at the platform entrances in place of the former very ugly timber screens.

A provisional service of electric trains to Orpington, Bromley North, Addiscombe, Hayes and Beckenham Junction had begun from the old Platforms 5 to 8 on February 28th, 1926, and with the new layout on June 28th, electric trains began to run between Cannon Street and Dartford via all four routes. Full electric services on all nine routes were operated from July 19th.

In a typical slack hour, there were eight electric departures; in the peak hour, seventeen. There were thirty-six steam departures daily, mostly to Chatham and beyond, via the North Kent line, ten of them between 5 and 6 PM. Since July 12th, 1925, the whole of the residential service to and from the Kent coast had been concentrated at Cannon Street (previously the best down train, the 5.10 PM, had started from Holborn Viaduct, running non-stop from St Paul's to Margate West).

Further electrification took place on July 2nd, 1929, when the Gillingham and Maidstone services were converted. At

Cannon Street, Platforms 6 and 7 were then fitted with conductor rails.

In spite of the sparse traffic on offer, it was decided to reopen the station on Sundays from July 6th, 1930. Another
facility restored in a very small way was the resumption of a
few workings through Cannon Street to Charing Cross from
July 17th, 1933. Some of these survived unadvertised until
1956. Continental trains were also seen again in the summer
of 1936, when some agency specials were diverted on Saturdays
to relieve Victoria, a practice which was repeated each summer
up to 1939.

From October 16th, 1939, the station was again closed outside rush hours (between 10 AM and 4 PM and after 7.30 PM
on weekdays, and at weekends after 3 PM on Saturdays). Services were reduced, and by 1944 there were only twenty-four
departures between 5 and 6 PM, five of them steam main-line
trains. The Kent coast had but one fast train, at 5.45 PM.

German bombs made their mark on this prominent riverside structure, notably on the night of May 10th-11th, 1941,
when Southern House was burnt out, and both the station roof
and the river bridge were hit. As the roof burnt, and blazing
timbers and molten glass fell on the platforms, railwaymen
bravely hauled trains out on to the bridge in an effort to save
them, only to be bombed again in this exposed position.
'Schools' class 4-4-0 *St Lawrence* received a direct hit, but
was eventually repaired. The bridge was not seriously damaged.[4] Some time later, all the remaining glass in the roof was
removed for safety.

NEVER ON SUNDAYS

After the war, Southern House was patched up, and the two
top floors rebuilt. An inspection of the station roof revealed
that it was in no state to carry new glass, but would be safe
enough in skeleton form for a few years. From May 31st, 1948,
the station was again open all day, also on Sundays, from Octo-

ber 3rd; this lasted until September 15th, 1958, when economy measures enforced weekend closure. At the time of writing, the doors are closed at 1.45 PM each Saturday, not to reopen again until 4.35 AM on Mondays. A stranger arriving at the street entrance on a Saturday afternoon might reasonably assume the worst, as a tattered notice announces unhelpfully, STATION CLOSED.

British Railways has wrought great changes at Cannon Street, both in the structure and in the train services. Steam-hauled business trains to Hastings were completely replaced by diesel-electric multiple-units on June 9th, 1958. The last regular steam train left Cannon Street for Ramsgate a year later, on June 13th. Full electric services to the Kent coast came into operation on June 18th, 1962.

As at the other Southern termini, rush-hour traffic became increasingly concentrated. In 1939 the heaviest evening peak hour saw about 16,500 passengers leaving, but by 1959 the number had grown to 23,500. It was 26,300 in 1967. One measure to meet this problem was the ten-car train scheme for the Eastern Section. For this, Cannon Street's platforms had to be lengthened, a job which raised a few problems. For operational reasons the eastern platforms could not be further extended on to the bridge, and the only alternative was to push the concourse back under the old hotel. The other platforms, 5 to 8, which could be built out on to the bridge were lengthened to take twelve-car trains. In 1955 it was announced that the platform extensions would be undertaken as part of a major reconstruction of the station, including a new concourse in the ground floor of Southern House and the replacement of the old roof by one of the ridge and furrow pattern similar to that at Charing Cross. This scheme, costed at £1,250,000, was started on November 17th. Three of the extended platforms (1, 4 and 5) were ready on March 4th, 1957, when the first ten-car trains ran, and the remainder were put into use early in 1958.

ALL BUT REBUILT

In April 1958 the contractors began to take down the ironwork of Hawkshaw's arched roof whilst passengers sought their way through the various demolitions and temporary buildings below. From April 10th to June 30th, as the major part of the roof dismantling proceeded, the station was closed from 10.45 AM to 3.15 PM on weekdays, and on Saturday afternoons and Sundays. By the end of January 1959, the roof had gone, but in response to pleading from the President of the Royal Academy, the Fine Art Commission and others, the walls and towers were left, although they were meaningless and more than a little absurd without the graceful curve of the roof to unite them.

In 1956, soon after the reconstruction work had started at the northern end of the station, structural faults were discovered in Southern House. It was decided to demolish it, and erect new office blocks across the northern part of the terminus. Expensive models were produced and elaborate plans prepared for a twenty-storey block with a fourteen-storey wing, but the City Corporation refused permission on grounds of excessive height (220 ft), alleging that the view of St Paul's would be obscured. Revised plans were then submitted for a fifteen-storey frontal block, another lower one over the northern ends of the platforms and a third in Bush Lane alongside the station. A flat roof was to be built over the platforms, adaptable as a car park or heliport. This met with approval, but the roof was later omitted on the grounds of cost. At last, in April 1963, work began on the demolition of the old hotel, in preparation for what the Southern Region's publicity leaflets described as 'London's First Big Rail Terminal of the Sixties'.

The Bush Lane building and the podium block over the eastern part of the new concourse and the inner ends of Platforms 1 to 5 were completed in 1962. A flat slab roof was extended westwards to shelter the remaining part of the con-

Layout of Cannon Street Station 1966. From the Railway Magazine, September 1966

course and the inner ends of the other platforms. Across the
front of the station, a fifteen-storey block, 220 ft long and 170
ft high, was finished in 1965. Both buildings had the feature-
less and sterile appearance common to most contemporary
office architecture.

A pleasant and spacious concourse, floored entirely in rubber, with a new entrance from Dowgate Hill, came into use on
October 25th, 1964. A new buffet and stationmaster's office
were ready on November 2nd, 1965, and the left-luggage and
inquiry offices on December 13th.

In connexion with a scheme for a dual carriageway road
from Blackfriars to the Tower, the City Corporation proposed
to widen Upper Thames Street, which passes beneath the
station about one-third of the distance between Cannon Street
and the river. This entailed the removal of the existing 37-ft-
span bridge and its replacement by one of 77-ft span, with
twin box girders for each line. The work was completed in
June 1964, and was followed by the erection of umbrella type
canopies over the exposed southern sections of the platforms.
At the same time, the old side walls of the station were demolished as far as the southern abutments of the new bridge,
to be replaced by metal and glass screens.

Fourteen years after the announcement of the rebuilding
scheme, the work was still incomplete. Pending the widening of
Cannon Street, and the consequent rebuilding of the Underground station, the two-storey structure planned to form the
main entrance and booking-hall remains on paper, and the
modern ticket-issuing facilities introduced in December 1965
are accommodated in a temporary wooden building which pro-
jects from the front of the office block into the untidy rem-
nants of the 1866 forecourt. Today's railway engineers and
architects must envy their nineteenth-century forebears, who
could design a terminus to their own liking and requirements
and then get on with it, not needing to wait for the permission
and approval of others or for the commencement of non-
railway works.

Cannon Street now handles 80,000 passengers daily compared with 26,000 in the 1860s, but all this activity is concentrated in a few hours at the mornings and evenings of the five weekdays. In 1967, 40,800 arrived daily, 38,300 between 7 and 10 AM. There were 39,200 passengers leaving daily, 38,100 between 4 and 8 PM. At other times, although the trains were not infrequent, the place was dead.

SIGNALLING AND ACCIDENTS

The first signal box was a fine-looking affair, mounted boldly on a 62-ft girder bridge, 11 ft 6ins wide, spanning all the tracks over the northernmost pier of the river bridge. As with the London Bridge and Charing Cross boxes built at the same time, signal posts sprouted from the roof, and at a distance this must have looked rather like the rigging of a sailing ship. There were eight arms on each of the outer posts, and four on the two inner ones. The cabin itself, 42 ft long and 9 ft wide, contained thirty point and thirty-seven signal levers, the former black, the latter red for up, blue for down and yellow for distants. Two men worked the box on an eight-hour shift, accompanied by a telegraph clerk. All the equipment, including the striking interlocking, with its thirty-two locking slides and 1,000 locks, was supplied by Saxby & Farmer.

As the signalmen were not given any preliminary practice with the frame, great confusion existed on the opening day, so much so, that the general manager of the SER wanted the interlocking taken out. Fortunately this decision was delayed, and the men soon mastered their work.

When the widening of the bridge was finished, the station was resignalled, and two new boxes, fitted with Sykes' lock and block, were opened on April 22nd, 1893. No 1 box, 110 ft 6 ins by 18 ft 6 ins, spanned all the tracks over the second pier from the north bank, occupying almost the full width of the enlarged bridge. It had 244 levers, interlocked on Francis Brady's cam system, and arranged in one row, 100 ft long. Five

men and two lads were required for most of the twenty-four
hours. The other box, No 2, replaced the old Stoney Street
junction cabin, in the neck of the junction. It was situated
on south bank, on the west side of the line, 230 yd beyond No
1, and had eighty-seven levers. This box, together with others
in the Charing Cross–Cannon Street–London Bridge complex,
was fitted with the rotary train-describer instrument devised by
C. V. Walker. This apparatus, the earliest example of a
multiple-aspect visual train describer, was later used elsewhere
by the SER and by the SR. It consisted of a dial bearing such
indications as: *Main Line Empties, Engine, Greenwich, Empties Maze Hill, Mid-Kent, North Kent, Redhill, Tidal or Mail,
Cancel last Signal, Blackheath, via Chislehurst, Dartford
Loop,* all shown by an electrically-operated needle.

For the working of the suburban electric services and the
new track layout in the approaches to Cannon Street and Charing Cross, the Southern Railway installed track-circuited four-
aspect colour-light signalling between Charing Cross, Cannon
Street and Borough Market junction, just west of London
Bridge. This scheme, which included power-operated points
at the termini, came into use on June 27th, 1926. The Cannon
Street approaches and platforms were worked from a 140-lever
power box, 45 ft long and 12 ft wide, situated on the west
side of the bridge between the end of Platform 8 and the para-
pet. There were 46 running signals, 42 shunt signals, 41 point
movements, 1 bolt, 1 slot and 9 spare.

After surviving the ordeals of wartime, this timber box was
badly damaged by fire on April 5th, 1957, probably as the result of an electrical fault. All trains were diverted from Cannon Street until the following day when a partial electric
service was resumed under hand signals. The London Midland
Region came to the rescue of the harassed Southern, offering a
227-lever power frame which it had in store against emergency.
This was used to make up a forty-seven-lever frame, installed
in the remaining part of the old box on May 5th. Full electric
service was restored on the following day. Platforms 7 and 8

remained out of use, and the opportunity was taken to get on with the lengthening work. Steam trains were either diverted to other termini, with fast electric connexions from Cannon Street, or cut back to Chatham, with similar connexions. A new permanent box, in brick and glass, was opened at the east side of the old Stoney Street junction on December 16th, 1957. This had a Westinghouse 'C' type electrically-locked frame, also made up from the LMR apparatus. There were 124 working levers, and forty-three spare levers reserved for possible future absorption of Borough Market Junction.

Only two serious accidents have occurred at Cannon Street. The first took place on June 27th, 1914, when the driver of a down Hastings train missed his route indicator and misread the advance signals. In the resulting collision with an up Plumstead train a passenger with his head out of a window was killed. At 9.16 AM on March 20th, 1961, at the south end of the bridge, a six-car up train from Addiscombe, carrying some 600 passengers, overran the up home signals and sliced into the side of an empty twelve-car diesel-electric multiple-unit train which was leaving the terminus for Grove Park depot. Several coaches of both trains were derailed, and the station was closed for the rest of the day. The driver and ten passengers were slightly injured, and it was said that the tight packing of the suburban train protected the passengers from serious injuries. Following this accident, rail-level repeaters of the inner home signals were installed.

CHAPTER TEN

BLACKFRIARS, LUDGATE HILL AND HOLBORN VIADUCT

THREE-IN-ONE

As they were in a sense one, these three stations can be taken together. They were all owned by the London Chatham & Dover Railway, which secured Parliamentary powers for a deep penetration into the City of London, managing, alone among the Southern companies, to join hands with the Northern lines across the very centre of the metropolis. This great effort made, the LCDR sank into a parlous state, and was never able to afford the luxury of an adequate City terminus. Instead, it made do with three small stations, all nestling together along a quarter of a mile of track.

In 1859, the East Kent Railway, which was building a line from Strood to Dover, changed its name to the London Chatham & Dover. Assuming the role of competitor to the South Eastern Railway, it sought and obtained access to central London, first over other companies' lines, then constructing its own approaches to the central area, as described in more detail in Chapter 13. By its Metropolitan Extension Act of 1860, the Chatham was empowered to build from its existing approach at Beckenham through Dulwich and Herne Hill, and then westwards to Victoria and northwards over the river to a junction with the Metropolitan Railway at Farringdon Street, in the City. Capital for these costly new lines was raised in an extravagant and reckless fashion, and after the financial panic of 1866, the company was landed in Chancery for five years. Left with a burden of debt, it continued for the rest of its existence in a poverty-stricken state.

The City extension, carried on a brick viaduct through inner south London, reached the south bank of the Thames in 1864. Here, on June 1st, the LCDR opened a station called Blackfriars. Situated on the east side of the southern approach to the new road bridge (then not yet completed), it was designed by the engineer Joseph Cubitt, and was of course a through station, although it had to serve as a terminus for six months pending further progress northwards. There was delay in crossing the river because the City Corporation had dithered over the design of the Thames bridge (they managed to decide that it should have the same number of arches as the new road bridge, but couldn't make up their minds how many arches there should be).

This Blackfriars Bridge station was quite an impressive affair, with a long iron and glass overall roof and high walls which came right up to the edge of the river. On the eastern side was a range of offices and a goods shed, with a riverside wharf. There were only two public entrances, both off the inclined approach road to the City Corporation's bridge. Rows of narrow arched windows, decoration in light-coloured bricks, and sheer bulk gave it a certain dignity which contrasted with the squalid surroundings of factories and warehouses.

Cubitt carried the four tracks across the river on a 933-ft lattice girder bridge. The piers of the five spans were in sets of three, each individual pier of stone, supporting a cluster of four iron columns. At each end of the bridge were large decorative features in cast iron, displaying the arms and full title of the LCDR, the motto *Invicta*, and the royal initial surmounted by rose and crown. Stones from the old Westminster Bridge, demolished in 1861, were used in the abutments. From December 21st, 1864, trains terminated in a temporary station at Little Earl Street on the north bank just south of Ludgate Hill. This was the first railway service to the City from south of the river.

A permanent station, Ludgate Hill, was opened in an unfinished state on June 1st, 1865. This was on the east side of New Bridge Street, immediately south of Little Bridge Street (now Pilgrim Street). There was a street frontage alongside the viaduct, extending well above rail level to carry the all-over roof. This building was described in the *Illustrated London News* of June 10th, 1865, as having 'no great pretensions to dignity of style, but it presents rather a lively appearance, with its turrets at each corner, and its decorations of parti-coloured brickwork above the arched doorways'. A small forecourt in New Bridge Street was accessible to cabs through entrances in Union Street and Little Bridge Street. Placed under the viaduct, the booking-hall had a circular ticket office in the centre, one side allocated to suburban passengers, the other to main-line and Continental bookings. Twenty feet above, reached by narrow staircases, were two low and narrow wooden island platforms, the eastern for main-line trains, the other for suburban and local services. Additional staircases, only 6 ft wide, led from the northern ends of each platform into Little Bridge Street.

In the course of erection, the iron and glass roof had collapsed. Its place was taken by a timber truss roof supported by the high side walls and rough-hewn wooden columns on the platforms. This roof spanned all four running lines, the station width being no greater because of the high cost of property in the City. The four tracks extended from Ludgate Hill to a point south of the 1864 Blackfriars Station, but quad-rupling took place on the west side between there and Lough-borough Junction in 1866.

Blackfriars remained open as a passenger station until September 30th, 1885, when the whole site was made over to freight both at rail and street levels. There was no space for wagon sorting, and Herne Hill sorting sidings (between Loughborough Junction and Herne Hill) were laid out to supplement Blackfriars. Until 1968 the western side of the 1864 station could still be seen, with the characteristic LCDR parti-coloured bricks much in evidence.

ACROSS THE CITY

Seven months after the opening of Ludgate Hill, on January 1st, 1866, the Metropolitan extension was completed to its meeting with the Metropolitan Railway at West Street junction, Farringdon, and Ludgate Hill also became a through station. This final link included a wicked 1 in 39 descent from the viaduct at the north end of Ludgate Hill.

By what G. A. Sekon described as 'the remarkably hypnotic influence of the late James Staats Forbes,[1] who appeared able to induce otherwise shrewd railway officers to support, by financial aid, his schemes for the extension of the LC & DR,' the LSWR had subscribed £310,000 and the GNR £320,000 towards the cost of the Metropolitan extension in exchange for running powers. These two companies now exercised their rights.

On March 1st, 1866, a connexion was made between the LSWR at Clapham Junction (Ludgate junction) and the LCDR at Wandsworth Road (Factory junction), over which LSWR trains began to work between Kingston and Ludgate Hill on April 3rd. This service was replaced on January 1st, 1869, by one between Richmond and Ludgate Hill, running via a new line from Richmond to Kensington (Addison Road), and by another between Wimbledon and Ludgate Hill via the Tooting, Merton and Wimbledon line and a new spur opened on that day to connect Herne Hill and Tulse Hill. The LCDR also worked trains between Clapham Junction and the City. An LCDR service between Herne Hill and Kings Cross had operated from the opening of the connexion at Farringdon, and two days later, on January 3rd, 1866, GNR suburban trains began to run into Ludgate Hill. The north–south services were further developed by LCDR trains running between Herne Hill and Barnet from August 1st, 1866, and by GNR trains working on the same route, and on to Hatfield, from the same day. On March 1st, 1868, the GNR trains were altered to run Barnet–Victoria and Edgware–Ludgate Hill, the latter extended to

Loughborough Junction from June 1st.

A third user and financial benefactor was the Midland, which worked trains between South Tottenham or Hendon and Victoria via Ludgate Hill from July 1st, 1875. Reciprocal workings by the LCDR as far as Finchley Road were started on June 1st, 1869.

Finally, the cross-City connexion saw GNR trains operating between GNR suburban stations and Woolwich Arsenal, SER, from June 1st, 1878, using a new connexion between the Metropolitan extension and the Charing Cross extension, near Union Street, Southwark. As by this time the rivalry between the SER and the LCDR amounted almost to a state of cold war, the latter refused to allow passengers for SER stations to board these trains at Ludgate Hill and Snow Hill, where stops were made for setting down only. This Woolwich service was worked by the SER from August 1st, 1880, terminating on the northern side at Enfield or Muswell Hill (Alexandra Palace when open).

STATUTORY WORKMEN'S SERVICE

Of the LCDR's own services from Ludgate Hill, the most important of the local workings was that to Victoria via the connexion between Loughborough Junction and Brixton, opened on May 1st, 1863, at the time of the construction of the approach lines to Victoria and Blackfriars. On this route special provision was made for workmen, as required in the Metropolitan Extension Act. When this legislation was before Parliament, it was realized that the approach lines would cut their way through a densely built-up part of south London, destroying hundreds of houses in their path. The newly-developed social consciences of the period were duly pricked, and to meet the opposition on this account, the company had graciously offered to operate a few trains at extremely low fares for the benefit of workmen forced to move farther from their place of employment.

Parliament had made sure of this by making both service and fares statutory, the first of many such provisions in railway legislation. At first the procedure was a little fussy. The workmen 'both male and female' were required to give their names, addresses and occupations, and particulars of their employers before they were allowed to purchase a shilling weekly ticket. This was valid for six daily return journeys between Ludgate Hill and Victoria, or between any station on the route and one of these termini. Trains left each terminus at 4.55 AM, returning at 6.15 PM (2.30 PM on Saturdays). As mentioned in earlier chapters, the vast majority of those displaced did not move any great distance from their old homes, and the immediate effect of urban railway construction was an increase in overcrowding.

On September 1st, 1871, after completion of a curve to the east, some LCDR local services ran through to Moorgate Street. By agreement with the Metropolitan Railway, the LCDR was obliged to operate at least eighty trains a day over the new curve, or forfeit £30,000. There was little point in this as for many years the main business area was south of Moorgate Street Station, and after stations had been opened at Snow Hill and Holborn Viaduct in 1874, it was usually quicker to walk from them than to stay in the train.

Other local services worked through Ludgate Hill were those to Crystal Palace High Level (after the opening of a curve at Loughborough Junction on July 1st, 1872) and to Beckenham and Bromley via Penge. Main-line trains ran to Ramsgate and Dover via Chatham, and to Sevenoaks.

The concentration of all these services on the two island platforms at Ludgate Hill led to a good deal of congestion and inconvenience. Any enlargement of the station was ruled out by the high price of the surrounding property, not to mention the impoverished state of the railway company. The LCDR therefore investigated the cheaper alternative of constructing a small terminus in the new street called Holborn Viaduct. Some land here was already owned by the railway, and use could be made of the space over the lines down to Farringdon. In 1870, when the LCDR telegraphs were sold to the Post Office for £100,000, it was decided to go ahead with this scheme. A puppet, the Holborn Viaduct Station Company, was discreetly created to raise the balance of the capital required.

A MINI-TERMINUS

This new station, reached by a 264-yd spur off the viaduct, was primarily intended for main-line trains. It was a very modest affair consisting only of four short platforms (six faces), each capable of taking half a train length, the idea being that all main-line trains would have a City and a West End portion, to be split or combined at Herne Hill. The 400-ft platforms were numbered 1 to 6 from east to west, and were sheltered by iron, glass and wood ridge roofs in three sections, abutting against the frontage block at the north end, and extended at the south by individual platform canopies. A carriage roadway entered the station at the west side and ran for a very short distance alongside Platform 6, against the west wall.

This mini-terminus was opened on March 2nd, 1874. As well as the main-line trains, including the City portion of the Dover boat trains, services were worked from it to Maidstone and Ashford when the LCDR reached those towns in 1874 and 1884. Boat trains for the Flushing service began on July 26th, 1875, working first to and from Sheerness, and then, from May 15th, 1876, to and from Queenborough Pier. Some local trains were also dealt with at Holborn, but most continued to use the line down to Moorgate, on which two low-level platforms were opened on August 1st, 1874. This subterranean station was first called Snow Hill, but was renamed Holborn Viaduct (Low Level) from May 1st, 1912. To the north of it were four sidings connected at the far end by a fan table and used for turnover purposes. From the street, the platforms were reached through a small entrance on the north side of the viaduct.

An hotel designed by Lewis H. Isaacs was constructed along the front of the main terminus and opened on November 17th, 1877. It was let to Spiers & Pond, the LCDR caterers, for six per cent of its capital cost and ten per cent of its profits. After early activities in Australia, this firm had begun their long career as railway caterers with a buffet at Farringdon Street Station, opened in 1863. Their association with the LCDR started soon afterwards and lasted until 1905, when they were ousted by Lyons. In 1888 they became the official caterers to the LSWR, and in 1899, to the SER. From January 1924 until December 1930 they acted as caterers to the Southern Railway. Their stores and headquarters were in the arches of the LCDR viaduct immediately south of Ludgate Hill Station, with a frontage to Blackfriars Lane, still to be seen today. During the First World War, the Holborn Viaduct Hotel was requisitioned for Government purposes and afterwards became the main office of Henley's Wireless Telegraph Works Co Ltd. It was destroyed by German bombs in 1941.

ST PAUL'S FOR ST PETERSBURG

The final development of the LCDR'S cluster of City stations came in the 1880s, when the approach tracks on the south bank of the Thames were widened, and another bridge constructed alongside and to the east of that of 1864. This carried seven tracks and had five arched spans, from south to north, 183 ft, 175 ft, 185 ft, 175 ft and 185 ft. At the northern end, it fanned out to a width of 123 ft to carry the platforms of a terminus fronting the south side of Queen Victoria Street. Opened on May 10th, 1886, it was known as St Paul's until February 10th, 1937, when the Southern Railway renamed it Blackfriars. (This renaming followed London Transport's decision to change the name of a Central Line Tube station from Post Office to St Paul's. The new name of the SR station was not only more accurate but identical to that of the adjacent District Line station.)

St Paul's was another small terminus, and rather mean, but the best the poor Chatham could afford. In pink-red brick, it huddled apologetically against the viaduct, trying hard to look dignified by displaying stumpy towers at each corner, seeking to impress by showing, in incised letters on the stones around the street doors, the names of fifty-four towns and cities which could somehow be reached from its platforms. This catalogue was a curious mixture of the romantic and the mundane, ranging from St Petersburg and Vienna to Westgate-on-Sea and Crystal Palace.[2]

The frontage building straddled the District Railway and the situation made a forecourt and cab access to the platforms a physical impossibility. Fronting the street was a fairly spacious booking-hall with a wooden ticket office. From this a wide staircase led up to an intermediate floor where there was a small buffet (against the east wall) and the ticket barriers and stairs to the platform. At rail level were three terminal roads, one against the east wall, with a platform face on the west, the other two with a platform face either side. On the west, a pair of tracks was looped through the station from the original main lines, with a platform face on each track. The four tar-coated wooden platforms were covered at the inner end by a short all-over ridge roof of iron and glass, just adequate to disperse the smoke from the engines of terminating trains. At the outer end, the roofing was extended at a lower level in the form of linked canopies. The terminal roads had hydraulic buffers of an early pattern, which the patentees claimed would stop a 200-ton train at 6 mph 'without inconvenience', whilst at 12 mph 'no harm would happen to the buffers ...'

Alone among the LCDR's City stations, St Paul's had direct access to the Underground. The District Railway had reached Blackfriars from Westminster Bridge on May 30th, 1870, and by this time the Inner Circle was complete. Stairways and passages were opened on November 13th, 1886, to connect the District platforms with the intermediate floor at St Paul's.

Most of the main-line trains to and from Holborn Viaduct

called at St Paul's, as did all the local trains, except those between Moorgate and Victoria. It was also the terminus for the
City portions of the trains using the new Gravesend branch
opened on the same day, and for the Greenwich Park service,
when that branch was completed on October 1st, 1888.

The LSWR trains from Richmond and Wimbledon continued to terminate at Ludgate Hill, working forward to Snow
Hill sidings to reverse, and causing a good deal of congestion
in the process. Trains routed through St Paul's were obliged
to use the main-line platforms at Ludgate Hill, but those
using the original lines to and from Snow Hill and Holborn
Viaduct could be directed through either the main or the local
platforms.

Many passengers continued to use Ludgate Hill, either from
habit, or because it was more convenient for their final destination. A very generous and varied train service was still offered,
in spite of the opening of the other two stations. In the mornings and evenings the narrow platforms were dangerously
overcrowded and the evening congestion was so bad that returning workmen had been made to use Holborn Viaduct since
1875. At most times of the year, a wait on the Ludgate Hill
platforms was a distinctly uncomfortable experience, as the
all-over roof turned the place into a very effective wind tunnel.
Public dissatisfaction with this somewhat primitive station had
grown steadily over the years – even the LCDR admitted that it
was unsatisfactory.

In April 1903, the chairman of the City Corporation Streets
Committee, one Alpheus Cleophas Morton, told the Royal
Commission on London Traffic that the Corporation considered Ludgate Hill Station inadequate, inconvenient, and
positively dangerous to the large number of people using it,
and in 1898 had complained about it to the Board of Trade.
The City authorities had also met the railway company, who
did not seem either able or willing to enlarge it, although 'they
found the money to build the great useless station called Holborn Viaduct'.

Among the many who moaned about Ludgate Hill were the Fleet Street journalists, for whom it was the nearest station. It is an interesting thought that the anti-railway complex that has long been prevalent among London newspapermen may have its roots in the inadequate railway and Underground facilities of the Fleet Street area. For many years those working on morning papers sought a late train back to the suburbs; their wishes were finally granted in 1910 when they were given a 1.15 AM departure from Ludgate Hill, calling at most stations to Beckenham Junction. The *Railway Magazine* recorded (could it have been true?) 'Journalists who live in the outer suburbs on the south side of London are showing their gratitude'.

This late train was eventually supplemented by others providing service through the small hours to Orpington via Catford and via Herne Hill, and to Wimbledon (also to Sutton after the opening of the Wimbledon & Sutton line in 1930). These facilities were also used by market and Post Office men, but patronage fell off sharply in the 1950s as more night workers bought their own cars. In 1963 the four trains between Holborn Viaduct and Orpington between 1.30 and 3.15 AM, and the connecting service from Herne Hill to Sutton were carrying an average of twenty or so passengers each; BR discontinued them as an economy measure from June 17th and a replacement coach service was soon abandoned.

CAPITAL SPENT IN VAIN

Finally bowing to the criticisms of Ludgate Hill Station, the railway company set about a minor reconstruction, which lasted from 1907 until 1912. The main-line island platform, which had become superfluous since the opening of Holborn Viaduct and St Paul's, was taken out, and the resulting space used to slew over the two main lines and the down local line. In turn this made room for a more commodious island platform on the local side, 440 ft long and, at 32 ft maximum, almost twice as wide as its predecessor. This made it possible to broaden the

Ludgate Hill Station layout in the 1890s, showing the suburban and main-line platforms. From the Railway Magazine, December 1964

Ludgate Hill Station after the rebuilding of 1910 and the abolition of the main-line platform. From the Railway Magazine, December 1964

notorious staircases. As some of the roof supports were on the
old main-line platform, it was necessary to remove the roof.
When this was done, the height of the side walls was reduced,
and an umbrella canopy, supported on central columns, was
erected on the new platform. The bridges over the booking-hall
and over Union Street were renewed with steel girders. Tracks
in the station area were rearranged so that trains to and from
Holborn Viaduct could use the new platform or the main
lines; up trains for Snow Hill or beyond could pass through on
the main or local lines, but in the opposite direction, they had
to use the platform road and cross to the down main south of
the station.

As was so often the case with railway works in the early years
of the present century, valuable capital had been spent in vain.
Traffic trends were already changing. After 1901, the electric
tramcar, underground train and motor bus quickly sucked away
the cross-City and inner area business, and one by one, the
services through Ludgate Hill succumbed. Those to and from
the GNR ceased in 1907, the Midland ones in the following year,
even as the work on the new station was proceeding. After that,
passengers for Farringdon and points west and north had to
use the SECR services, changing at Aldersgate. The death blows
came with the war, when special demands were made upon the
capacity of the north–south link. From April 3rd, 1916, SECR
trains were withdrawn from Moorgate and Aldersgate, a few
still going through to Holborn Viaduct Low Level until that
station closed on June 1st. Stripped of its regular passenger
trains, the Ludgate Hill–Widened Lines connexion had a
little more room for the constant procession of freight trains
that were bringing coal, munitions and military stores south.
To facilitate the working of this vital traffic, some signalling
improvements had been carried out at the Low Level station
during 1915.

ELECTRIFICATION

The LSWR services from Richmond and Wimbledon to Ludgate Hill also disappeared in 1916, as did the once busy LCDR service to and from Victoria. The lines north of St Paul's were thus left to the trains starting or terminating at Holborn Viaduct, the freight traffic and a few special workings. As almost all the Holborn Viaduct trains called at the through platforms in St Paul's, Ludgate Hill became superfluous, and was opened only in weekday rush hours from 1919. A few trains terminated and started from there and from August 27th, 1923, the Wimbledon service was restored in rush hours only (four morning arrivals and three evening departures). After the electrification of the Holborn Viaduct local services in 1925, these seven trains were the only ones to use Ludgate Hill. When the Wimbledon service was also electrified, from March 3rd, 1929, the doors of Ludgate Hill were closed to passengers for the last time after close of traffic the previous day. It is doubtful if there was any thought of keeping it open any longer, but even if there had been, there was a considerable deterrent, for its platform was 80 ft too short for an eight-car electric train.

Four years before closure, the City Corporation had widened New Bridge Street. Shops and offices were then erected in the station forecourt, obscuring the 1865 frontage. An entrance to the station was left in the centre of this new building, and this continued in use as access to Spiers & Pond's station restaurant, which had existed in one of the railway arches since January 1st, 1866, and remained open.

Third-rail electric services from Holborn Viaduct and St Paul's were inaugurated by the Southern Railway on July 12th, 1925. The basic workings were St Paul's to Crystal Palace High Level, St Paul's to Shortlands via Catford Loop, and Holborn Viaduct to Shortlands and Orpington via Herne Hill. At Holborn Viaduct space restrictions were such that only Platforms 4 and 5 could be lengthened sufficiently to take eight-car elec-

tric trains. Tracks at St Paul's were rearranged to allow Holborn Viaduct trains from the local lines to run through the
loop platforms parallel to trains entering the terminal platforms
at St Paul's from the main line. These latter platforms were
altered so that the middle road had a face on its eastern side,
and the western road a face on its western side. All platforms
were extended to take eight-car trains, providing waiting passengers with some fascinating riverscapes downstream.

In 1934 the section from Bickley to St Mary Cray was electrified, and the Shortlands service was extended to that station
from May 1st. This was only a temporary arrangement, and
on January 6th, 1935, an electric service was begun between
Holborn Viaduct and Sevenoaks via Swanley and Otford. Nine
months later, an entirely new facility was offered in the peak
hours following the electrification of the 1929 connexions
between the LCDR Greenwich Park branch (which had been
closed from January 1st, 1917) and the former SER lines at
Lewisham; these connexions had the object of enabling
freight trains to and from the Northern lines to avoid the
congested tracks through London Bridge. Now they served a
similar purpose for passenger services, carrying, from September 30th, 1935, peak-hour electric trains between Dartford
and St Paul's via Sidcup and via Bexleyheath.

A final electrification of the Holborn Viaduct services took
place on July 2nd, 1939, when the peak-hour trains to and
from Gillingham were changed over from steam. It was
necessary to extend another platform for these trains, and after
much head scratching, what was formerly thought impossible
was achieved. By widening the bridge over Sea Coal Lane, it
was found feasible to extend Platform 1 to 520 ft. But these
platform extensions imposed severe restrictions on the working
of the station: Platforms 2 and 3 were blocked if there were
an eight-car train in 1 or 4; the electrics had to be coaxed
right up to the buffers to keep the outer ends of the platforms
clear; and the only parallel working possible with electric
trains was a departure from 1 or 4 whilst a train arrived at 5.

No damage of any consequence was inflicted at any of the City stations in the First World War, which was just as well, in view of the great reliance placed on the cross-City connexion for the movement of military traffic and coal diverted from the coastal shipping services. In the Second World War, German bombs found the Metropolitan extension, and wrought a great deal of havoc. At Holborn Viaduct the old hotel building was hit on October 26th, 1940, and then completely gutted by fire on the night of May 10th–11th, 1941. Such was the damage that no trains could use the station until June 1st. When it reopened, a temporary ticket office was provided in the passage leading from Old Bailey, in a part of the buildings which escaped damage, and this remained in use until 1963 when the new buildings were ready. On the night of April 16th–17th, 1941, a grievous blow was suffered when the important Blackfriars signal box on the south bank was completely destroyed, together with much of the railway bridge over Southwark Street. With military assistance a temporary bridge carrying two tracks was completed on September 29th, and a permanent structure came into use on October 9th, 1942. Makeshift signalling arrangements remained in force until after the war, and the terminal roads at Blackfriars station were locked out of use.

The Dartford rush-hour services via Lewisham, withdrawn from October 16th, 1939, were restored on August 12th, 1946, with the opening of a new signal box at Blackfriars and the reinstatement of the terminal roads. On that day the platforms at Blackfriars were renumbered 1 to 5 from east to west (formerly only 1 and 2, between the eastern 'bay siding' and the up and down loops had borne numbers). Outside the peak hours, the terminal roads were used for berthing empty rush-hour trains, and in connexion with the Eastern Section ten-car train scheme, alterations were made to allow these roads to accommodate ten-car trains, which were worked empty to and from Cannon Street and Charing Cross via the connecting curve from Metropolitan junction. Additional siding accommodation for these empty rush-hour trains of the Cannon Street and Charing Cross lines was provided in 1967 on the down side of the former Blackfriars goods depot.

VANISHED STEAM-AGE CHARM

Until the end of the 1950s, Holborn Viaduct retained much of its Victorian atmosphere, despite the wounds of war. Its old-fashioned buffet, with long high counter, was one of the last of its kind on any London station, and the calm, un-hurried air of the concourse and platforms, even at the height of the rush hour, was very relaxing. To the initiated, a sly push on an unlocked door on the concourse offered a special treat. Descending dark steps, one would arrive in the smoky cavern that was once Snow Hill. Here the ghosts of the nineteenth century still lingered. Daylight somehow penetrated through the ever-present smoke and the deep shadows cast by the high buildings all around, feebly illuminating the station walls, on which soot became encrusted to a depth of almost 2 ins a year. Here, as late as 1958, one could still see the elegant long-armed signals of the LCDR. Occasionally a J50 tank or an LMSR 'Jinty' would thrust through the gloom, trundling the trucks and vans of a transfer freight. Should it be going south, the train would be banked by a GNR 0–6–2T, and the resultant duet would echo from the narrow confines. The scene could also be glimpsed by peering over walls in Holborn Viaduct and in Snow Hill, but now the hole has been built over and this unique view of London's only cross-City main-line link is no more.

Also now gone is the Steam Age charm of Holborn Viaduct Station, where British Railways carried out a reconstruction similar to that at Cannon Street. The ugly ruins of the old frontage were removed, and in their place rose a ten-storey office block. Completed in 1963, this building had a 250-ft frontage, and included station facilities and railway offices on the ground and on part of the first floor.

Through the plate-glass doors of a handsome entrance under scoop arches, the trains can be seen from the street. Beyond these doors is a pleasant low-ceilinged concourse area beneath the office block, opened on September 9th, 1963. In the centre is a bookstall, on the east side a booking-office, and on the west, a combined buffet and waiting-room which advertises itself through large windows on to the street. The concourse opens out to a narrow cross-platform overlooked by a balcony serving the staff offices on the first floor of the frontage block. In the spring of 1967 the old train sheds were taken down and replaced with umbrella canopies over Platforms 1, 4 and 5. Later the platforms were pushed back into the concourse and equipped with new barriers.

After temporary suspensions in both World Wars, the Crystal Palace High Level service was discontinued for good in 1954. Main-line trains from Holborn Viaduct were severely cut in the First World War, and in 1922 there were only eight departures, including the two Kent coast residential trains. The latter were transferred to Cannon Street from July 12th, 1925. Thirteen years later, there were but three steam-hauled passenger departures, all in the peak hour, to Chatham and Gillingham, and these were electrified in 1939. There were also one or two early-morning trains, primarily for newspapers and parcels, but tolerating passengers, and these continued to run until the Kent coast electrification of 1959. By that time, Holborn Viaduct was left with but two basic services: to Sevenoaks via Catford and Swanley (connexions to Ramsgate, Dover, Ashford, Sheerness and Maidstone), and to Wimbledon, Sutton and West Croydon via Tulse Hill with a connexion to Orpington at Herne Hill. At peak hours these were supplemented by trains to Orpington and St Mary Cray via Herne Hill, and to Dartford via Bexleyheath and via Sidcup, plus a small number of semi-fast trains to Gillingham.

Since July 10th, 1967, the three effective platforms have handled twenty-two trains in the busiest hour between 8 and 9

AM, an increase of five on the previous service. Some 30,000 passengers now pass through daily, almost all of them in peak hours. Weekend traffic declined so much that after June 14th, 1964, the station was closed between 2 PM Saturday and midnight on Sunday. Until June 1965, when it was transferred to other SR termini, parcels, mail and newspaper traffic was quite heavy, and the non-electrified platforms usually stocked a few vans.

Blackfriars, with its gloomy, dusty passages and wooden platforms still has a trace of the Victorian aura. True the old buffet, with its frosted-glass windows, has been replaced by more commodious premises at street level, but the hydraulic buffers, engineering wonders of 1886, can still be seen, and the walk up to the platforms, with its unexpected glimpse of the District through a dirty window, takes one back fifty years, given a little imagination. Apart from a few trains to Sevenoaks, Wimbledon and West Croydon, and Dartford in the peak hours, Blackfriars is largely a through station with the same service as Holborn Viaduct, though of course it becomes a terminus again when the latter is closed at weekends. Very little traffic now passes over the 1864 bridge outside the station. In 1961 the engineers decided that this bridge should have its load eased by removing the two outer tracks to eliminate the possibility of four trains crossing at the same time. As the cross-London freight services have been much reduced, this has not caused any serious operating difficulties.

The fate of the Metropolitan extension north of the river is uncertain. The County of London Plan of 1944 proposed that it be placed in tunnel, but desirable as this might be on aesthetic grounds, such an operation would be fabulously expensive and is unlikely to be undertaken. At the time of writing consideration is being given to the possibility of providing main-line electrified links across the centre of London, and in any such scheme, these lines would play an important part. It is not impossible that future generations will see the construction of a new Ludgate Hill Station, replacing Holborn Viaduct and Blackfriars, and served by electric trains working between north and south London outer area stations.

SIGNALLING AND ACCIDENTS

There were originally seven boxes on the inner part of the City extension, all equipped with Sykes' lock and block: Holborn Viaduct Low Level, Holborn Viaduct, Ludgate North, Ludgate South, St Paul's Yard, St Paul's Junction, and Blackfriars Junction. Holborn Viaduct was a sixty-two-lever cabin straddling the ramp down to the Metropolitan lines. Ludgate North was over the up local line at the north end of Ludgate Hill platforms and controlled *inter alia*, a gantry on the bridge over Ludgate Hill which did much to enliven the view of St Paul's Cathedral from Fleet Street. Ludgate South was sited over the main lines at the south end of Ludgate Hill station.

Soon after the first electrification, on March 21st, 1926, the Southern Railway resignalled the section between Holborn Viaduct and Elephant & Castle, using four-aspect colour lights for the first time. Siemens–General Electric equipment was employed, and the seven manual boxes were replaced by two power frames. At Holborn Viaduct an eighty-six-lever frame was installed in the old manual cabin, but at Blackfriars junction, near Southwark Street, the overhead box was dismantled and a new box built on the up side. This contained a 120-lever power frame to control the approaches and platforms at St Paul's.

As related earlier, this cabin was completely destroyed by enemy action in April 1941. Its place was taken by a red-brick hut with a power frame controlling only the main signals, which gave indications restricted to caution and danger. A new permanent box, which allowed restoration of all the original signals and connexions, came into use on August 11th, 1946. This was situated on the west side of the line, just south of the original south bank Blackfriars Station.

A curious accident occurred at Ludgate Hill in 1870. When the Hawthorn 0–6–0 locomotive *Ajax* began to give trouble, the engine crew left the footplate in some panic. With regulator open, the little engine rolled briskly down the 1 in 39 to Farringdon, on through Kings Cross (Metropolitan). Finding her way on to the Midland, she finally came to rest in Haverstock Hill tunnel, no doubt much to the relief of the signalmen clearing the road before her.

CHAPTER ELEVEN

WATERLOO

PRIDE OF PLACE FOR HALF A CENTURY

For almost fifty years, until the recent reconstruction of Euston, Waterloo held pride of place as the most modern of the termini, the only one built in the twentieth century. Today its extrovert architecture is out of fashion, but many find its warm red bricks and Portland stone kinder to the eye than the harsh concrete of the new Euston, less drab than the grey and yellow stocks of other termini. This is a well-liked station, with a spacious, almost opulent air, commodious and convenient for both passenger and operator.

Curving along the heads of twenty-one platforms, the wide concourse is always animated by a wonderfully assorted selection of travellers. Well-padded widows for Bournemouth avoid sun-tanned soldiers from Aldershot; Pompey-bound sailors mix with the luggage-cluttered white emigrants that form the bulk of today's boat-train traffic; peachy schoolgirls, up for the hols from exclusive establishments deep in Hants, cast sulky glances at red-coated Chelsea pensioners taking wreaths to a comrade's funeral. As the rush hours fade, senior civil servants stride across, black briefcases full of last night's drafting; but the City men avoid the concourse, and are glimpsed only briefly in their impatient transfer from train to 'Drain'. In the night hours, Waterloo gives precarious shelter to London's roofless, who obstinately prefer its draughts and persistent policemen to the free bed which awaits them at the Camberwell Centre. A survey carried out by the National Assistance Board in December 1965 found 247 men and 28 women sleeping out in London, more than half of them in the large railway stations;

Waterloo, with 63 on the concourse, was the most favoured refuge.

On winter Saturdays, little wooden booking-booths appear, to be surrounded by wool-wrapped rugger watchers bound for Twickers; at other times, the same booths dispense tickets to punters and card sharpers making for Surrey racecourses. Through it all, porters and postmen derive innocent pleasure from harassing passengers with tractor and truck. (The postmen have some connexion with a mysterious beast which lurks at the York Road end of the concourse, its lair marked prominently DO NOT FEED and DANGER KEEP AWAY.)

To enter the concourse after crossing the windy wastes of the south Bank is to experience a dramatic change of scale, to feel human once again. Here, set between the arid office blocks of York Road and the ebbing Cockney life of Lower Marsh, is an oasis of civilization, whose continuous interest and activity has been superbly photographed and recorded in the prizewinning British Transport Film Unit documentary, *Terminus*.

NINE ELMS

Waterloo was preceded by Nine Elms, the metropolitan station of the London & Southampton Railway, first promoted in 1831. A 4-acre site in Nine Elms Lane, just south of Vauxhall Bridge, was chosen because it could be reached with virtually no disturbance of property and because of its proximity to a convenient berth for the lighters and steamboats that were to link the railway with the City. Seemingly remote, the situation was in fact no farther from the centre of London than Euston and a mile nearer than Paddington.

Nine Elms was opened to the public on May 21st, 1838, with the first 23 miles of the Southampton Railway, as far as Woking Common. Not until May 11th, 1840, almost a year after assuming the grander title of the London & South Western, did the company reach Southampton. On that day, just

after 8 AM, a party of directors and guests arrived at the be-
flagged terminus preceded by bands of music. Three hours
later, the special train, headed by the locomotive *Venus*,
reached Southampton, to be greeted by a salute of twenty-one
guns.

Designed in simple classical style by William Tite,[1] the two-
storey building at Nine Elms consisted of a central porch of
five arches set between rusticated end blocks. Behind the porch
were booking-office and waiting-room, the former with an
open counter over which passengers were issued with paper
tickets. (Edmundson card tickets, with the necessary arrangements for one person to appear before the clerk at a time,
were introduced in 1846–7.) Beyond the booking-office, a
cross-platform connected the arrival stage on the west side with
the departure stage on the east. Doorways from the arrival
platform opened on to a vehicle yard alongside the station.
Over the platforms and the two empty carriage roads between
them was a low wooden roof in three spans, supported on cast-
iron columns with ornamental stiffeners. The platforms, only
15 ins above the ground, were completely within the 290-ft by
74-ft 9-ins train shed.

A single track was carried over Nine Elms Lane on the level
into a ¾-acre goods yard by the river bank. Wagons were
moved into this yard by horses, and the freight was lifted on
and off the Thames lighters by a crane. Passenger steamboats
hired by the railway company ran between this wharf and the
City, leaving Old Swan Pier, Upper Thames Street, an hour
before the departure of each train, and calling at intermediate
piers. Buses worked between the station and various points in
the City and West End. Pack horses were kept so that anyone
wishing to take his private carriage on the train could have it
driven home or fetched, the charge for this service being half
a guinea, including driver.

At first there were five trains each way daily, their departure
signalled five minutes before by a bell on the roof of the
station. Life was tranquil enough for the first eight days after

the opening, but the ninth day was one the staff were to remember for the rest of their lives. As May 30th was Derby Day at Epsom racecourse, the L & SR had advertised eight special trains from Nine Elms to its station on the Kingston to Epsom road. For one guinea, passengers would be provided with a coach from the station to the course; the other excursionists, unless they were very fortunate, would have a walk of 6 miles to the racecourse after their $10\frac{1}{4}$ mile rail journey. This last information was not included in the advertisement. Much to everyone's surprise, a crowd of several thousands arrived on the appointed day, virtually besieging the little terminus. As many as possible were dispatched, but there were far more than could be carried, and soon the doors were shut. The more aggressive members of the crowd then pressed forward and soon had the doors off their hinges. In swept the angry throng, through the booking-office, on to the platform, and into the guinea train, which was waiting to leave. A messenger was dispatched to the Metropolitan Police, who arrived in due course and succeeded in clearing the station. About noon calm reigned again, as a notice went up announcing that no more trains would leave that day. Not discouraged by this experience, the company advertised a few weeks later that special trains would run to Woking Station for the Ascot Races. This time all went well.

OVER THE ARCHES TO WATERLOO

Short-distance traffic soon became a feature of the line's business. The original section had stations at Wandsworth (west of the present Clapham Junction), Wimbledon, Kingston (east of the present Surbiton), Ditton Marsh (now Esher), Walton, and Weybridge. A branch, opened from what is now Clapham Junction to Richmond on July 27th, 1846, serving Wandsworth, Barnes and Mortlake, quickly provided almost a quarter of the total number of passengers carried in and out of London. Despite its steamboat and omnibus connexions,

Nine Elms was hardly a convenient station for this local traffic, and the company was well aware of its deficiencies. In 1846, Joseph Locke, its engineer, admitted in evidence to the Metropolitan Termini Commission that its isolated situation discouraged business traffic, pointing out that road coaches were still running between Chertsey and the City even though the railway covered the distance more quickly.

Conscious that passenger traffic was of growing importance, and likely to form a substantial part of its revenue, the LSWR began to make plans for a better terminus. Another stimulant had been the proposal of the initially independent Richmond company to construct a line from near Nine Elms to a 'West End' terminus adjacent to Hungerford and Waterloo bridges. In 1844 the LSWR agreed to work the Richmond line and took over its 'West End' project, obtaining powers in 1845 for an extension to a terminus on a site in York Road, near the south end of Waterloo Bridge, with a supplementary Act in 1847 for two more approach lines and more land at the terminus.

Leaving the original line at Nine Elms junction, a short distance south-west of the L & SR station, the extension crossed an already built-up area, breaking down some 700 houses in its path. To minimize property disturbance, most of its $1\frac{3}{4}$ miles were on a brick viaduct with well over 200 arches, snaking about to avoid a gasworks, Lambeth Palace and the Vauxhall Gardens, and crossing twenty-one roads on brick arch and cast-iron bridges. The largest bridge, over Westminster Bridge Road, with a skew span of 90 ft, worried the Board of Trade inspector, who delayed the opening of the line whilst some deflection tests were carried out. There was one intermediate station, at Vauxhall.

At the annual meeting of 1848, W. J. Chaplin, the LSWR chairman, explained why four tracks had been provided:

> ... in order that we may have no trouble or inconvenience in future in the traffic; and also that, whatever may be the adventurous schemes of the age in future, whatever may be the

probability of introducing lines south of London, we may not
only have ample means of conducting our traffic, be it what it
may, but of ability to let others come and hire, that we may
benefit by their enterprise and industry on our property.

'Others' who may have come included the LBSCR. Between
1844 and 1846, the London & Brighton Railway had considered, with the LSWR, the possibility of running into the
proposed Waterloo Station, via a new line between Croydon
and Wandsworth, which would make some use of the course of
the old Surrey Iron Railway, but this had come to nothing. An
Act sanctioning a line between Croydon and Wandsworth, to
enable the Brighton to reach Waterloo, was passed in 1846.
In that year the Brighton and the Croydon companies combined to form the London Brighton & South Coast Railway;
the Croydon, under W. A. Wilkinson, regarded the Wandsworth connexion as a threat to its traffic and when, after the
amalgamation, relations between the LBSCR and the LSWR became soured over other matters (thanks to the Croydon), the
scheme was dropped. Again in 1853–5, the LBSCR had a
chance to get to Waterloo over the projected West End of
London & Crystal Palace Railway as recounted in Chapter 13.

In view of the later inadequacies of the LSWR terminus, it is
perhaps as well that the Brighton went to Victoria instead. The
SER also thought of using Waterloo, and in 1846 had a scheme
for an extension towards it from Bricklayers Arms, a Bill that
failed to pass through Parliament. In practice, the additional
pair of tracks was used from the opening day by the trains
of the Richmond line. That railway was extended to Windsor
on December 1st, 1849, and before long the westernmost pair
of tracks acquired the label *Windsor lines*, which they retain
to this day. A third (up) line was provided between Nine Elms
and Falcon Bridge (Clapham Junction) in August 1848; a
fourth (down), in August 1860.

The new terminus, built on arches about 20 ft above street
level, occupied an area corresponding approximately to the
present Platforms 7 to 12. About 10 acres of land was taken,

not all of it used at first, in an area which had been let out on
a building lease in the 1820s, the site of the station containing
parts of eight streets, miscellaneous haystalls, cow yards, dung-
heaps, and a large pond.

As the LSWR had obtained an Act in 1846 for a further
extension, to London Bridge, Waterloo was laid out as a
through station, with vehicle ramps either side. An iron and
glass roof in two 140-ft spans sheltered six tracks and four
300-ft platforms (two arrival, two departure, six faces in all).
Soon after the opening, the length of these platforms was
doubled. On the west of the site, a spur pointed towards the
river and future hopes in that direction.

Waterloo was opened to the public on July 11th, 1848, Nine
Elms closing for regular passenger trains after traffic the previous day. The old terminus came back into use temporarily on
April 13th, 1856, when Tite's timber-built Vauxhall Station
was destroyed by fire and some up trains were diverted. Apart
from this, Nine Elms, like Bricklayers Arms, was convenient
for handling royalty and other notabilities. The first royal
user of Nine Elms was Queen Adelaide, widow of George IV,
who made a return journey to Southampton in June, 1842.
Garibaldi arrived from Southampton in 1864, and the station
was regularly used by Queen Victoria, whose royal saloons were
kept there in readiness. For her convenience, some alterations,
including the installation of a movable platform, were made in
1849–50. The Queen found that Nine Elms offered her the
privacy of which she was so fond, as well as easy access to and
from Buckingham Palace, and when the company wished to
use the old station as a carriage shop, they made a new private
station for her in Wandsworth Road, south of the main lines.
Finished in 1854, this had one covered platform, and survived
until the widenings of the 1890s. Edward VII and his suc-
cessors were content to use Waterloo.

Although Robert Stephenson told the Royal Commission in
1846 that 'there is no point on the south side of the Thames
so good for a large railway station, or a combined station, as

the south end of Waterloo Bridge', the LSWR was not content with this alone and, as already mentioned, had obtained powers in that year to go on to serve the City. Chaplin explained to the Commission that goods traffic could not be handled at Waterloo, as the way to the water was blocked by Goding's Lion Brewery;[2] a City extension was needed to obtain a better site for a goods station as well as to accommodate the many passengers who wished to go there. The 1846 Act, and another in 1848, provided for a terminus just south-west of London Bridge. A considerable amount of property was purchased before the scheme was killed by the financial crisis of 1848-9. The South Western's access to the City was eventually realized only in partial and unsatisfactory forms, firstly by running powers over the LCDR (see Chapter 10), then by an almost useless connexion with the SER extension to Charing Cross, and finally, by the construction of a Tube railway.

Until 1853, probably owing to the uncertainty about the City extension, there were no really adequate buildings at Waterloo. In that year, a block was erected along the east side of what was then Platform 1 (on the extreme east side of the station). This had a cab yard outside, served by an incline from York Street (now Leake Street), and an exit into Waterloo Road. Additional timber roofing, which was to survive until the early years of the present century, was put up at the same time. On the west side of the station, a carriage loading dock was built, with turnplates providing access to all tracks in the station. Beyond this, near York Road, was an engine shed, sidings and a turntable on the river-pointing spur already mentioned.

A ONE-WAY TRAFFIC

A strange one-way traffic started in 1854, when the London Necropolis & National Mausoleum Company[3] opened a cemetery at Brookwood together with a private Necropolis station at Waterloo. The latter had two short sidings and a small build-

ing with a single platform; it was situated on the east side of
the approach tracks just north of Westminster Bridge Road.
A stairway connected the station with the company's office in
York Street, opposite All Saints' Church. Funeral trains were
operated daily, using specially-built hearse carriages.

Through the remaining years of the nineteenth century,
Waterloo was extended piecemeal, in an even more haphazard
fashion than Euston. The first additional platforms, opened
on August 3rd, 1860, were on the north-west side of the
original station, extending the area of the terminus to the
screen wall still to be seen alongside Platform 16. Four new
platform roads were provided, the centre platform having a
track on each face. This extension, intended for the Windsor,
and other local traffic, became known as the Windsor station.
It was separated from the original platforms (the Main station)
by its own cab yard, which had an inclined approach from
Griffin and York Streets. A direct vehicular approach to the
Windsor station from York Road, running parallel to Mepham
Street was opened in 1875. Included in the Windsor station
for working purposes was a dock siding of the Main station,
converted into a running road, with platform, on March 17th,
1869.

When the London Bridge–Charing Cross line was opened
in 1864, the owning company provided a 5-chain connexion
into the LSWR at Waterloo, as required by its Act. This single-
line spur was an extension of the empty carriage line between
Platforms 2 and 3 of the Main station which passed through
the end wall, crossing above Waterloo Road to form a junction facing London Bridge. The short-lived through service
from Kensington (Addison Road) over it has been mentioned
in Chapter 9. After that episode the spur saw no regular
workings, but occasional movements of vans, horse boxes and
passenger saloons continued to use it. Queen Victoria passed
this way when travelling between the LSWR station at Windsor
and Channel ports. A part of the Kensington service was resumed from July 1st, 1875, from which day about seven LNWR

trains each way ran between Willesden Junction and Waterloo, taking thirty minutes. These trains were taken off in January 1893 in response to an LSWR plea that Waterloo was too congested to accommodate them.

Under pressure from the LSWR, the SER opened a station at Waterloo, east of the junction, on January 1st, 1869. This offered no great convenience to LSWR passengers, who for a long time were forced to rebook. Later, through season tickets were issued from LSWR suburban stations to Cannon Street. There were also through fares, including a cheap-day return from Cannon Street to Windsor. Even so, as we shall presently see, this was not a very satisfactory access to the City for LSWR passengers.

CYPRUS AND KHARTOUM

More platforms were added to Waterloo in 1878. Yet another virtually separate station was opened on December 16th on the south-east side, a double-sided platform on the other side of the cab yard of the original station (now called the Central station). The two platform faces of what was known as the South or New station were used by suburban trains. Railwaymen, with their liking for naming new installations after contemporary events, called it 'Cyprus' (that island having been ceded to Britain by the Berlin Congress of 1878). About the same time, some of the tracks in the Central station were rearranged, and the platforms improved. New booking-offices and refreshment rooms were opened, and a 300-ft frontage erected in the Waterloo Road from the outer edge of the South station to the boundary line of the Central. This was supported on columns over the cab yard beneath.

The final addition to the old Waterloo was the North station, erected in continuation of the Windsor station towards York Road and completed in November 1885. As this was the year of Gordon's murder and of the abandonment of the Sudan, the staff called it 'Khartoum'. There were six new platform faces, making a total of eighteen in the terminus (two in the South, six in the Central, four in the Windsor, and six in the North). Unlike some of the other termini, all platforms could be used for arrivals or departures.

Outside the terminus, all sixteen platform tracks converged on the four approach lines of 1848. By the 1880s there were some 700 trains a day at Waterloo and there was much delay and congestion until two more running lines were added between the terminus and Nine Elms in 1886–92. An interesting feature of this widening was to be seen at the north end of Carlisle Lane. Here the additional width, mostly on iron girders, had to be carried across the vestibule and entrance to the Canterbury Music Hall. To avoid any interruption to the performances, most of the work was carried out between 1 AM and 4 PM, and on Sundays. Several of the old bridges in the viaduct were reconstructed to carry the heavier loads now imposed.

From east to west, the six tracks were worked as down main, up main, up main, down Windsor, down Windsor and up Windsor. A seventh road between the Waterloo A and B signal boxes, the down relief, was added on the east side on July 4th, 1900. In 1916 further widenings were completed between Waterloo and Queen's Road East box, giving eight tracks as far as Loco junction, and seven thence to Queen's Road. (Eight tracks already existed between Queen's Road West and Clapham Junction.) At Vauxhall in 1890 the LSWR provided tenements to rehouse the 1,041 people displaced by the widening work.

As at most other termini, platforms were originally 'open', tickets being collected at a special stop outside, in this case at Vauxhall. Here an army of ticket collectors would comb each arriving up train, passing rapidly from one compartment to another. To facilitate working, the 1892 widening had included an additional up Windsor road through Vauxhall Station, which was entirely rebuilt in the process. The introduction of corridor trains, combined with the construction of

closed platforms at the new Waterloo Station from 1910 onwards, dispersed the 'Vauxhall mob'.

GETTING TO THE CITY

Mention has been made of the SER insistence on rebooking at
Waterloo Junction. This was not the only source of irritation
to LSWR passengers. Train service over the heavily-occupied
section between Waterloo and Cannon Street left much to be
desired, particularly in the foggy weather then frequent in
winter months. Nor was Cannon Street a convenient station
for passengers requiring the western side of the City. In 1880,
Harris C. L. Saunders of the Sun Life Office led a group of
dissatisfied South Western commuters to form the Metropolitan Express Omnibus Company, which began to operate
horse buses between Waterloo and the City. A year later this
company was purchased by the Railways & Metropolitan
Omnibus Co Ltd. By the middle 1880s it was working eighteen
two-horse, twenty-six-seat buses on the route and carrying
some two and a half million passengers a year. These buses
were allowed to terminate in the cab yard at the top of the
incline from York Road.

For its part, the LSWR remained interested in schemes to
get its passengers to the City. Some 50,000 passengers were
arriving at Waterloo daily in 1892, of whom it was estimated
about 12,000 continued to the City, half by the SER, the rest
by the RMO buses, by cab, or on foot.[4] Schemes for an overhead railway were considered in 1882 and again in 1891, but
dismissed as too costly. Eventually it was decided to support a
proposal for a Waterloo & City Tube railway. This was
authorized by an Act of 1893, and the LSWR, which provided
five of the eight directors, undertook to work the line for not
more than fifty-five per cent of the gross receipts, on which
the payment of a three per cent dividend was to be the first
charge.

These terms attracted investors, and the line was opened

on August 8th, 1898, offering a frequent service of electric
trains between a station in the basement of Waterloo and
another at the Bank of England. There was no connexion with
any other line, and no intermediate station. To this day, the
Waterloo & City, popularly known as 'the Drain', remains independent of London Transport, the only Tube railway
operated by British Railways. A power station and open-air
carriage sidings were constructed east of Waterloo Station
adjacent to Lower Marsh. Coal trucks and rolling stock were
moved in via a hoist in the Windsor line carriage sidings on
the York Road side of Waterloo. The LSWR took over the Tube
completely in 1907.

Tube railway connexion to the West End was attempted in
the 1860s. Construction of a pneumatic Tube, the Waterloo
& Whitehall, was begun, but was abandoned in 1868 when the
company (which was ignored by the LSWR) ran into financial
difficulties. More successful, but also unsupported by the
LSWR, was the Baker Street & Waterloo Railway, opened on
March 10th, 1906, between what is now Lambeth North
Station and Baker Street. Its Waterloo station was reached by
lifts from a small booking-hall next to York Road, at the extreme western end of the subway running under the main-line
station. This booking-hall was also connected to the end of
the North station concourse by stairs and a subway.

WHERE THE FRENCH GOT LICKED

At the turn of the century, Waterloo was an untidy and confused collection of platforms, passages, stairways, cab yards
and offices, the despair of any stranger. To make confusion
worse, the platform-numbering system was almost beyond
comprehension; the existence of the South station was ignored,
and No 1 was the main departure platform in the original or
Central station. Beyond this, the other fifteen platform faces
had to share the numbers 2 to 10. Thus many of the platforms,
although bearing a single number, had a track either side, and

the unfortunate passenger, having succeeded in finding the correct platform, was still left in doubt as to which was his train.

Reliable information about departures was almost impossible to obtain, especially if one was in a hurry. In *Three Men in a Boat* (1889), Jerome K. Jerome made fun of the difficulties of finding a train to Kingston, telling how the destination was eventually reached only by bribing an engine driver. Two years later, Henry Wheatley, writing in *London Past and Present*[5] thought it 'probably the most perplexing railway station in London'. Another writer remembered 'a jumble of shabby, poverty-stricken buildings ... quite unique in London, although quite in keeping with the squalid neighbourhood surrounding it'.[6] A story was circulated that an old Devon farmer, turning to his wife on the footbridge after four or five unsuccessful attempts to find his train, had remarked in admiration, 'No wonder the French got licked here, Mary'.

Probably the best way to describe it is to take an imaginary tour of the premises as they were around 1900. A gloomy doorway in Waterloo Road opens on to an equally gloomy flight of steps. At the top of these, we find the small concourse of the South station. Trains leave the double-sided platform for Kingston, Leatherhead and Hampton Court, and the rather cramped accommodation is the scene of some confusion in the rush hours. A passageway on the right leads us to the 1853 cab yard alongside the offices of the Main or Central station. As we face the building, with its pavement steps down to the cab road, cabs are coming up the ramp on our left from York Street after negotiating a dark tunnel under the station 'which in those days of horse traffic, resembled for all the world some evil-smelling sewer'.[7] The pavement steps were known as 'the Bench', a name perpetuated in the title 'bench foreman', which was in use until at least 1946. After depositing or picking up passengers, cabs leave at a smart pace down a steep ramp on the right which takes them into the Waterloo Road. There is never a shortage of cabs at Waterloo as any driver may use the station on payment of a nominal toll of one penny.

Passing through the building, we find the main departure platform, No 1. A handbell is being rung to announce the departure of a train, and the platform presents a scene of great animation – all platforms in the terminus are 'open', and tend to be crowded with see-ers off and lookers-on in addition to the genuine passengers.

At the outer end of this platform, in the angle between the Central and South stations, is a small engine shed and turntable built over the top of the cab incline. The buildings alongside the departure platform contain the booking-office, waiting- and refreshment rooms, all equally mean and thoroughly grim. Even without looking up, we are conscious of the low roof at the inner end of the platform, supported by heavy timbers. As the three tracks between Platforms 2 and 3 extend farther into the station than any others, a footbridge is provided to connect the main departure platform with the cab yard that separates the Central station from the Windsor.

Crossing the bridge, we pass above No 2, another departure platform, one face of which shares the No 1 platform road. Between 2 and 3 is the centre road which goes through the end wall of the station and crosses over Waterloo Road to join the SECR. Both Platforms 2 and 3 come almost up to the Waterloo Road, and to enable passengers not using the footbridge to get round the ends, the connecting line to Waterloo Junction is spanned by a small opening bridge with two flaps. Outside, the end wall of the old station rises sheer from the pavements of Waterloo Road, with the junction line emerging from its middle.

Back on the footbridge, we can now see No 3, the main arrival platform. Then comes the last of the Central station platforms, No 4, also used for arrivals, sharing a track with the opposite face of No 3. Beyond the buffer stops, is another steep cab exit down to Waterloo Road, and alongside is the cab yard of the Windsor station. At its outer end, this yard is served by an inclined entry from York Street which rivals the other in insalubrity.

Descending from the bridge, we are now at the west side of the cab yard, and enter the Windsor station, with its three platforms, 5, 6 and 7, the centre one having a track either side. Along the inner ends of these is a small concourse, well back from the Waterloo Road; between this and the cab yard at the top of the approach from York Road is a block of offices. We can now see the wall carrying the roof of the North station, and proceeding along the concourse, we enter this, the most modern part of the terminus. The roof, with its decorated iron supports, is in elegant contrast to the crude timbers of the Central station. There are six platform roads, the two platforms in the centre (8 and 9) having a track either side. Walking to the end of the last platform, 10, we find seven sidings and a turntable in the space between the station and York Road. Behind the boundary wall of the station is the hoist used to reach the Waterloo & City Tube railway. At the other end of 10, in the angle of the cab approach and York Road, are the general offices of the LSWR, with a wing projecting along the north side of the North station concourse. We have now roamed through the whole tangle, but there are many nooks and corners we have not seen, and it would take many such rambles before one could be sure of really knowing the place.

All the military traffic for the South African war of 1899–1902 passed through Southampton, much of it entraining at Waterloo, although cavalry went from Nine Elms. In December 1899 the terminus saw the dramatic departure of Lord Roberts to the front. Waterloo always had a strong military flavour, serving as it did the great Army establishments at Aldershot, Bordon and Salisbury Plain, as well as the naval bases at Portsmouth, Portland and Devonport. As Britain's military might expanded in the years before 1914, uniforms became more and more conspicuous on its platforms.

Another speciality was race traffic. The LSWR served the race-courses at Epsom, Windsor, Sandown Park, Hurst Park,

Ascot, Kempton Park and Salisbury and the Imber Court
trotting course, all easily accessible from Waterloo. In the
1900s, on the occasion of a big meeting, as many as 14,000
racegoers would leave the terminus in regular and special
trains. Much of this traffic was gradually lost to the motor-car
and road coach, but in the 1920s and 1930s it was still heavy,
and many of the special trains included restaurant cars. As late
as 1939 in Ascot week, the concourse offered a fashion parade,
attracting suburban housewives, who came up to stand and
stare. Horse racing and other sources provided sufficient business in the 1900s to justify five daily departures of trains made
up entirely of horse boxes with connexions all over the LSWR
system.

A FRESH START

As the nineteenth century drew to a close, directors and management debated what was to be done about their ramshackle
terminus. To its lasting credit, the board eventually decided to
pull it all down and start again. Powers were obtained from
Parliament in 1899 and 1900 and about six and a half more
acres were purchased, mostly on the south side. This property
included six streets, with parts of two others, a church (All
Saints') and Church schools. Protestants greeted the disappearance of All Saints' with some elation as the services
were among the most ritualistic in Britain, and it was thought
that these popish practices could not be restarted in a new
church. Six blocks of flats were erected by the LSWR, providing
accommodation for some 1,750 people, more than the number displaced. Five of these blocks went up behind the Bakerloo
Tube station in Westminster Bridge Road, the other in Stan-
gate.

J. W. Jacomb-Hood, who became the LSWR's chief engineer
in 1901, went to the USA to study the design of terminal
stations. The new Waterloo largely followed the plans he drew
up on his return, providing a straightforward and spacious

station on this difficult site. There were to be twenty-three platforms in all under a new roof, with a wide passenger concourse across their ends, flanked on its outer side by a long frontage block, containing the amenities and railway offices. In practice this plan was modified, and some economy was achieved by Herbert Walker's[8] decision to retain the relatively modern and quite satisfactory roof over the North station, thus reducing the total number of platforms to twenty-one. Jacomb-Hood died in 1914, when the work was well advanced; he was succeeded by A. W. Szlumper, who completed the task.

Site clearing began in 1900. Among the properties demolished were the disorderly houses which had found much custom from the soldiers and sailors passing through Waterloo. (The squalid neighbourhood around the old station, *Whoreterloo*, is well described in Chapters 2 and 3 of Michael Sadleir's *Forlorn Sunset* [Constable, 1947].) A healthier, if less exciting haven for the Servicemen, the Union Jack Club, was established in the Waterloo Road opposite the terminus in July 1907. This offered 355 clean, but lonely, beds, and a billiard room.

While the preparatory work was going on, other men toiled unseen beneath the platforms, strengthening the arches to carry the new superstructure. New foundations had to be dug as deep as 30 ft to reach the clay beneath the marshy ground. Another ancillary task was the rebuilding of the bridge over Westminster Bridge Road to carry eleven tracks.

Standing in the way of the track rearrangements, the Necropolis station was demolished and replaced by a new structure on the south side of Westminster Bridge Road, opened on February 16th, 1902. This had two platforms, one for mourners, the other for coffin-loading, an arrangement which ensured that the operation was carefully screened from the eyes of the funeral party.

Once the site was cleared and the foundations prepared, work began on the roof which was to cover the South station and the area to the south-east of it, and this was completed in

1907. A cab road was built alongside and in front of the new station, starting from an entrance in Westminster Bridge Road, and curving under the full width of the approach tracks before climbing at 1 in 25 along the south-eastern boundary. At the top, it was later to turn sharply left along the outer face of the new frontage building, finally reaching an exit in York Road against the Charing Cross Railway viaduct. Two spur roads were made into Lower Marsh. Additional powers were taken in 1911 to buy land on the north side and to abandon the SECR connecting line.

Erection of the steel-framed frontage block began at the south-east corner; some parts of it were ready in time for the opening of the first five platforms in 1909, but the main-line booking-hall was not opened until June 11th, 1911. This hall was 95 ft long, 45 ft wide and 30 ft high to a curved ceiling carried on pairs of plaster columns. At one side, doors opened to the covered cab yard along the front, at the other, to the new concourse. Some changes were made in 1924, when the plaster columns were replaced with bronze-capped columns of Brèche marble and the original wood-block flooring by coloured glass tiles; at the same time, the two doors to the cab yard were converted to windows. Today the hall's appearance is sadly marred by unimaginative decoration and a clutter of ugly aluminium left-luggage lockers.

Next to the booking-hall, on its south-east side, was a large luggage hall (75 ft by 45 ft) and beyond that a cloakroom (left-luggage office) with additional storage space in the basement. This cloakroom was the scene of some macabre incidents in 1924. A certain Patrick Mahon, having murdered and cut up his mistress on the Crumbles at Eastbourne, arrived here on April 16th and deposited a Gladstone bag containing a blood-stained knife and other incriminating items. His suspicious wife, finding the cloakroom ticket in his clothes, persuaded an ex-policeman friend to withdraw the deposit. On seeing the contents, he informed the railway police, who returned the bag to the shelf, and gave Mrs Mahon the ticket to put back in her husband's pocket. A guard was then placed on the cloakroom by the police, who detained Mahon when he foolishly came back to retrieve his bag.[9]

From the concourse a wide flight of steps led to a 'gentlemen's court' beneath the frontage block. This haven of relief, 80 ft long by 40 ft wide, was enthusiastically described in the *Railway Magazine* of December 1910, as 'perhaps the finest in England'. It had the traditional white-tiled walls, relieved by a black and white marble floor, and teak doors and partitions. Supplementing the usual facilities were bathrooms, a boot-cleaning room and a hairdressing saloon. 'If desired,' the contemporary accounts coyly announced, 'the air could be changed every five minutes by the action of electric fans.' Necessity soon made such desire continuous.

THE NEW STATION TAKES SHAPE

Above platform level, the frontage building contained railway offices. These were supplied with electricity and hot water from the Waterloo & City Railway power station in Lower Marsh. Between the building and the platform barriers was the first section of the wide concourse that was to run across the full width of the new station. In the end wall, a door opened on to the cab approach alongside the station, an entrance at first reserved for royalty and other notabilities, as it permitted a reasonably private passage to and from the new Platform 1.

This initial section of the new station contained five ferro-concrete platforms, the first three of which came into public use on January 24th, 1909. Platform 4 was in service on July 25th, 1909, and Platform 5 on March 6th, 1910. (At last there was a number for each platform face.) Nos 1, 2 and 3 were sited on the new land, whilst No 4 was approximately where the first platform of the old South station had been. The name 'South station' was perpetuated unofficially and is still in use today for this part of the terminus, where the loudspeakers can occasionally be heard appealing for the 'South station shunter'.

About one-third of the way down each pair of new platforms was a flight of steps leading to an 18-ft-wide subway providing access to the two Tube stations beneath the terminus. Below this subway was a second one served by electric lifts from each pair of platforms and intended to facilitate movement of parcels, luggage and mail across the station, or between the platforms and the parcels depot in the basement arches. Claims were made that would bring a hollow chuckle from the present day user of Waterloo: 'Roundabout methods are now eliminated, lost time and congested platforms a thing of the past' (1922 advertisement) ... 'The station is so designed that very little movement of luggage and parcels can interfere with the passengers' (*Railway Gazette*, June 1922). Alas, methods of handling parcels have changed, and the electric lifts stand almost idle as tractor drivers form up long trains of the appropriately named BRUTES (British Railways Universal Trolley Equipment), setting out to corral as many passengers as they can by making enormous U turns between concourse and platform gate.

Over the next thirteen years the great rebuilding continued, gradually moving across the station site from south-east to north-west, until the bow-shaped concourse and frontage block were completed along the full width, and all twenty-one new platforms were finished.[10] All platforms up to 15 had access to the Tube subway, and all except 16, 18 and 21 had luggage lifts. Each line ended at Ransomes & Rapier hydraulic buffers, impressive beasts of 7-ft stroke, strong enough to arrest a 400-ton train moving at 10 mph. An iron screen with Bostwick collapsible gates separated platforms from concourse.

Not all was perfect at the new Waterloo. A curious short-sightedness was shown in regard to platform lengths, despite longer trains. In steam days it was not unusual for trains into Waterloo to be made up to twelve or more corridor coaches (say 750 ft), and with an engine at each end, even this unremarkable length was troublesome at most platforms. Platforms 1 to 6, used by the local services to Hampton

Court, Leatherhead, Shepperton and Kingston, were 696, 695, 683, 685, 720 and 723 ft long. Bournemouth and West Country trains usually left from 7 (728 ft) and Portsmouth trains from 8 (735 ft). Platforms 9 and 10 (756 and 765 ft) were used by main-line stopping trains, whilst 11, the longest, with the cab yard alongside, was convenient for the Southampton boat trains. This platform was originally 860 ft, but was later extended to 946 ft. At the south end of the cab yard was an incline for empty cabs entering from Griffin Street (since closed) and above this were loading docks 160 and 175 ft long. At the other side of the cab yard was No 12, 843 ft, used for arrivals and for loading mail, parcels and newspaper trains in view of its location alongside the central roadway. Most main-line trains arrived at 13 (857 ft) or 14 (860 ft). No 15 (635 ft) was also used for arrivals, but in view of its shortness was usually employed for loading and unloading van trains, including the milk and fish traffic still handled at the terminus.

Between Platforms 15 and 16 was a two-storey office block completed in 1920 and known as 'the Village'. Erected under the main roof, this building served the station's 450 staff and included the stationmaster's offices, staff dining-room, ticket collectors', porters' and guards' rooms and the lost-property office. At the concourse end were two escalators, either side of a fixed stairway. They connected the concourse with the subway to the Tube stations 26 ft below and were brought into use on April 9th, 1919.

At the other side of the Village were the Windsor line platforms, 16 to 21, all under the original roof of the 1885 North station, but served by the north-western end of the new concourse and thus fully integrated with the rest of the station. Platform 16 (570 ft) was used by electric services to Wimbledon via East Putney and to Shepperton via Richmond. Numbers 17 and 18 (600 and 612 ft) were allocated to the Hounslow loop service via Richmond and via Brentford. At No 19 (605 ft) were found the Kingston 'roundabout' trains, whilst 20 and 21 (625 and 551 ft) were used by the Reading

General Plan of Waterloo Station 1922. From the Railway Magazine, May 1922

and Windsor steam services. At the outer end of 21, on the opposite side, was a 234-ft dock for loading vans. Between this and York Road, the engine and carriage sidings, turntable and the hoist to the Tube railway remained largely unchanged. In the north-west corner of the station site the old general offices were left undisturbed, but were connected to the frontage block by a new wing.

Within the station, all that remained of the old Waterloo was the roof over 16 to 21, with its supporting walls. Over the rest of the station, 560,000 superficial feet of new roofing had been erected. This roof was of the ridge and furrow type, the ridges 60 ft above the platforms. There were nine spans at right angles to the tracks over Platforms 1 to 15, and twenty-five spans parallel with the rails over the concourse. The steel roof girders were supported by octagonal steel columns on brick piers.

The vehicle roadway from Westminster Bridge Road had been opened as far as the main-line booking-hall on December 18th, 1911, and by 1922 had reached York Road. It was roofed over between the south-east corner of the station and the bridge over Waterloo Road, and also for a short distance opposite Platforms 12 to 15.

Mention of the bridge over Waterloo Road recalls the fact that, inevitably, the connecting line to Waterloo Junction had disappeared during the reconstruction. It was taken up in March 1911, but on the far side, near the Junction station, a siding remained until May 3rd, 1925, when the connexion and ground frame were removed. The bridge remained for the use of passengers walking across from one line to the other and it was not until July 7th, 1935, that the word 'Junction' was dropped from the title of the former South Eastern through station, which then became integrated to some extent, with its platforms lettered A to D.

FOR THE BENEFIT OF MANKIND IN GENERAL

Free from pillars and other obstructions, the wide and well-lit concourse was a predominant and successful feature of the new Waterloo. It curved gracefully from one side of the station to the other, 120 ft wide and 770 ft long, serving all twenty-one platforms. There were three bookstalls, an inquiry office and a commendably clear departure indicator at Platforms 6 and 7 showing the departure time, platform number and stations served by each train. A similar, smaller indicator was placed opposite the Windsor line platforms. At each end were timetable stands, illuminated internally. Opposite Platform 9 a Bodmin & Wadebridge Railway four-wheel composite first- and second-class coach of the 1830s stood on a section of the original permanent way with its granite sleeper blocks. This coach, in use from 1834 to 1886, was brought to Waterloo from Eastleigh in 1915. It is now in the Transport Museum at Clapham.

Staircases sited opposite Platforms 8 and 12 led down to a wide subway which opened out on to the Waterloo Road opposite the Union Jack Club and the then LCC tramway terminus. Next to this opening was a low-level cab yard underneath the main vehicle roadway. In the north-west corner of the concourse, slopes and stairs to the Tube stairway and booking-hall. Opposite Platform 19 an impressive archway and flight of steps led up from the vehicle roadway near the York Road exit, forming the main pedestrian entrance to the station.

This was the Victory Arch, so called because it formed the LSWR war memorial, its walls displaying bronze tablets with the names of the 585 employees who were killed. The arch, of Portland stone, held a memorial window and was flanked by sculptural groups supported on pylons. One of these, '1914', featured Bellona, goddess of war, astride the world in scaled armour, with flaming torch and naked sword; the other, '1918', showed Peace enthroned on Earth, holding symbols of peace and victory. High above, over the cornice and the legend WATER-LOO STATION, sat a rather masculine Britannia triumphantly holding aloft the torch of liberty 'for the guidance of her children and children's children and the benefit of mankind in general'. This archway, together with the other achitectural features of the new Waterloo, was the work of James Robb Scott.[11] Scott had a great predilection for fasces, heads and swags, and these decorative features were liberally spattered about the station.

The frontage block, of which the Victory Arch was a dominant part, was in the impressively monumental style sometimes called Imperial Baroque, but was hopelessly swamped by the ugly viaduct carrying the railway from London Bridge to Charing Cross. Most people who use Waterloo arrive by taxi, bus or Tube, and do not see the frontage at all; of those who come on foot, many would find it difficult to describe the outward appearance of the terminus. It is quite impossible to stand back far enough to take it all in, except at a sharp angle, from the other side of York Road. Were there no foreground clutter, it would present a noble prospect from the other side of the river.

Apart from the centre section, which was higher than the rest, this building was flat-roofed. At the south-east end were the luggage and booking-halls already described, and the remainder of this first section contained waiting-rooms, lavatories for first- and third-class ladies, and a circular refreshment buffet opposite Platforms 10 and 11. This buffet had a crescent-shaped counter at the back and was lined with marbles of various colours. Its floor was of Roman marble mosaic. Under British Railways it has been thoroughly brought up to date, and is now the garish, noisy and very popular Horseshoe Bar, with a somewhat battered mural of the RMV *Queen Mary* looking out of place amid the modern décor. Above the buffet, and reached by a staircase and lift opposite Platforms 10 and 11, was a tea and luncheon room, and next to it, an oak-panelled dining-room seating 150. These three refreshment rooms were opened in 1913, and together with other refreshment facilities on the station, were managed by Spiers & Pond.

Next to the circular buffet was a wide central archway linking the cab yard between Platforms 11 and 12 with the vehicle road along the front of the station. Most of the building on the other side of this archway, towards York Road, was completed in 1920–21, whilst the portion already described was largely finished by 1914. Opposite Platforms 11 and 12 was another luggage hall, and next to this, a large buffet measuring 79 ft by 39 ft. Here was the most richly decorated room in the station: walls panelled with Greek Cipollino marble; fluted sienna pilasters; bays for statuary; a 'Grinling Gibbons' ornamented plaster ceiling 18 ft high; and a magnificent bar, 65 ft long, at the back, laid out for heavy traffic. At the front of this buffet, a semi-circular booking-office projected on to the concourse, matching the similar one outside the main-line booking-hall. Adjoining the buffet was a pleasant tea room with oak parquet floor, and cream walls decorated with mirrors. Now known as 'The Windsor', this room is a firm favourite with those who cherish the Edwardian atmosphere which still lingers, although the American soda fountain has long since disappeared.

The remainder of the block was taken up with waiting-rooms, ladies' lavatories, another left-luggage office, and a bank. The latter, opened in 1923 by the National Provincial, and the first on a London station, was originally open until 6 PM (2 PM on Saturdays). Another branch was opened by the same bank on Victoria (Eastern Section) about ten years later. Below this part of the building was another large lavatory for men (unlike the ladies, they were offered no class distinction). Beyond the Victory Arch, at the extreme end of the concourse, was the entrance to the general offices, now embellished with a small plaque in memory of Sir Herbert Walker (unveiled on May 27th, 1952).

The upper floors of the frontage block, apart from the tea

and dining-rooms near the central arch, were occupied by the
various railway offices. These included a communications
room, in telephonic or telegraphic contact with all the stations
on the system. Spread around the new station were some 240
synchronized electric clocks of various sizes, including a 6-ft-
diameter, four-face turret clock hung over the centre of the
concourse, and a sunray clock in the memorial window. Waterloo was now the best served of all London termini as regards
amenities, with an excellent selection of shops, kiosks and
restaurants. At the time of writing there are thirty-one shops
and service points supplementing the railway facilities, offering a range of items from theatre tickets to foreign stamps.

By the beginning of 1922, most of the reconstruction work
was completed, and the new station, covering some 24½ acres,
was formally opened on March 21st by Queen Mary, deputiz-
ing for the King, who was indisposed. After studying the
Memorial Arch, the Queen passed along the concourse.

WATERLOO AT WAR

No doubt the royal visitor was reminded of the important part
the station had played in the 1914–18 War, when millions of
soldiers and sailors, with their equipment, had passed through
the terminus, day and night. As well as the draft and leave
movements to and from the many camps and bases served by
the LSWR, there was a heavy traffic to Southampton, the port
which handled the embarkation of the British Expeditionary
Force in 1914, subsequent reinforcements until the spring of
1915, and after that, embarkations for other theatres of war.
At certain times during the war the terminus also dealt with
ambulance trains and Army overseas mail. Station officials had
often worked continuously for eighteen hours at a stretch; the
numbers of men returning from leave on Sunday nights were
so great that up to thirty special trains would have to be organized. Between December 1915 and April 1920 a free
buffet, open throughout the twenty-four hours, and staffed by

voluntary lady workers, dispensed over eight million meals. The buffet was in the long subway beneath the platforms, where a tarnished plaque records this prodigious feat.

Bomb damage in 1914-18 was limited to the night of September 29th, 1917, when explosions occurred on the down main line between A box and Westminster Bridge Road and in No 6 siding north of the station. Track damage was restored in sixteen hours. In the vast warren of arches and subways beneath the station, shelter accommodation was set aside for the railway staff, including the military control office. Elsewhere, the public responded in large numbers to the invitation of the railway company to use the basement at their own risk.

ELECTRIFICATION AND REARRANGED TRACKS

Stimulated in part by competition from the electric tramcar and motor bus, and also by threats to extend the Central London Tube railway into the Thames Valley, the LSWR had electrified some of its suburban services, using the economical and straightforward 600-volt dc third-rail system later adopted for the 'Southern Electric'. The Wimbledon via East Putney service had been electrified on October 25th, 1915, and the Kingston Roundabout and Shepperton services had followed on January 30th, 1916. Just over a month later, on March 12th, it was the turn of the Hounslow loop, and on June 18th of the Hampton Court service. The 'New Guildford' line was electrified as far as Claygate on November 20th, with a steam push-pull connecting service beyond, but to provide more rolling stock for the other electric services, this Claygate working had been suspended in July 1919. All eight running lines in the terminal approaches were equipped for electric working, but in the terminus itself only Platforms 1 to 6 and 16 to 21 could take electric trains.

After the formation of the Southern Railway in 1923, the live rail was extended from Raynes Park to Dorking North and Effingham Junction and from Claygate to Effingham Junction and Guildford. A full public service of electric trains began on these lines on July 12th, 1925. Five years later, on July 6th, 1930, the Windsor service was electrified. At that date, a total of thirty-two electric trains left Waterloo in the evening peak hour (5 to 6 PM). From January 3rd, 1937, Windsor electric trains divided at Staines, the rear portion serving Chertsey and Weybridge.

A third Tube service was available from September 13th, 1926, when the present Northern Line was extended southwards from Charing Cross to Kennington, giving the terminus direct connexion with Euston and (with one change) access to Kings Cross and St Pancras. Three escalators linked the Tube platforms with a new booking-hall beneath the Windsor side, completed in 1927. Forty years later, rush-hour traffic justified the construction of a fourth escalator.

Until 1920 the up main through line into Waterloo ran into Platforms 7 to 11 and 12 to 16, but in that year, a new lead was built to provide access to Platforms 4 to 6, making it possible for a train to run into one of these platforms parallel with one from the up main relief into 1, 2 or 3.

Further expansion of the electric services into Waterloo was hindered by the inadequacies of the track layout and the limited capacity of the manual signalling. At the beginning of the 1930s, the approach tracks inwards from C box (just north of Vauxhall Station) were worked (south to north):

down main local (serving Platforms 1 to 10)
down main through (4 to 10)
up main relief (1 to 6)
up main through (4 to 16)
up main local (7 to 16)
down Windsor local (7 to 16)
down Windsor through (13 to 21)
up Windsor (13 to 21)

Although interchange facilities at B box made it possible to route a train to or from almost any part of the station, all electric trains approaching the electrified Platforms 1 to 6 were confined to the up main relief from which they had to cross the down main through immediately outside the station.

Towards the end of 1934, the SR announced that £500,000 would be spent putting this right. At Durnsford Road, Wimbledon (the nearest suitable site), a flyover would be built to carry the up main local over the up and down main through lines so that from that point inwards, the tracks would be:

    down main local
    up main local
    down main through
    up main through

joined at Clapham Junction by:

    down Windsor local
    down Windsor through
    up Windsor through
    up Windsor local

From Vauxhall to Waterloo, an additional up main relief road would be sited between the up main through and down Windsor local, but as before, there would be only one up Windsor road on this stretch. At the terminus, Platforms 7 to 9 would be electrified, and all electric platforms up to 9 would be available to the up main local. Concurrently with these changes, colour-light signalling, with track circuits and power-operated points, would be installed between Waterloo and Hampton Court junction.

Following the Cannon Street precedent, engineers assembled and tested the new Waterloo layout in a field near Mitcham. On Sunday May 17th, 1936, the flyover, new tracks and most of the colour-light signalling were brought into use, but the signal changes at the terminus itself were delayed until October 19th, clear of the holiday season. Weekday electric services were rearranged from July 5th, with Dorking North and Effingham via Leatherhead trains running fast between Waterloo and Wimbledon (Motspur Park in peak hours), supplemented by an all-stations service from Waterloo to Motspur Park (extended to Tolworth over a new line, May 29th, 1938, and to Chessington South, May 28th, 1939). These improvements went some way towards meeting the traffic demands arising from new housing developments in the area south-west of Wimbledon.

One little nuisance remained after the layout changes. The two small turntables at Waterloo (B box sidings, 49 ft 11 ins and North sidings, 54 ft 10 ins) were inadequate for modern locomotives and engine facilities at the terminus were little used after the 1920s. To reach the 64-ft 10-in turntable at Nine Elms locomotive depot, light engines of main-line trains were obliged to cross the up and down main local lines, which could cause delays to build up on the suburban services. However, if conditions allowed, this awkward movement could be avoided by sending the engine to Clapham Junction, crossing it over there. Engines coming out of Waterloo or Nine Elms loco were often run light to Clapham yard to pick up empty stock which they would haul back to Waterloo over the up main local and (after May 17th, 1936) over the up main through. After the departure from Waterloo, they would run out behind, ready to back on to their own train. Outward empties were usually worked over the down Windsor lines to avoid conflicting movements at Clapham yard.

With the new track layout and signalling working smoothly, the way was clear for more electrification. A full service of electric trains to Woking, Guildford and Portsmouth Harbour (connexions to the Isle of Wight) started on July 4th, 1937, together with a connecting service to Aldershot and Alton. In the coming war, these trains were destined to carry a very heavy military and naval traffic as well as encouraging a strong flow of commuters from the 'stockbroker belt'. From January 1st, 1939, electric trains ran between Waterloo and Reading, shedding a portion at Ascot to serve Guildford via Camberley and Aldershot.

Little modification was required to the structure of the re-built station. Experience demonstrated that the provision for luggage and waiting-rooms was over-generous; part of the lug-gage hall opposite Platforms 12 and 13 was converted between the wars to a post office, and the waiting-room opposite Plat-forms 8 and 9 became an inquiry office. Loudspeakers were installed and used for the first time on March 9th, 1932, a memorable day when the University Boat Race clashed with a rugby football international match at Twickenham. As an experiment, light opera music was interspersed with train announcements in 1937, becoming a regular feature in 1940. During the war, planned programmes of music were broadcast, a welcome diversion in those grey years. In 1948 passengers were questioned about the music; most approved, some sug-gesting that lively marches should be played in the morning rush hours, with something more soothing for the homeward journey. It was announced that the music would continue, but vocal records would be avoided as they might be confused with train information (!).

At first the train announcer cum disc jockey was in a booth over a kiosk opposite Platforms 8 and 9, but was later banished to an eyrie on top of the Village.

Another form of entertainment was to be found in the small cinema opened by the entrance to Platform 1 on August 27th, 1934. Its auditorium, seating 250, was carried on girders over the cab road outside, and its frontage, in the brutal, jazzy style of the 1930s was the work of Alistair MacDonald, son of the famous Ramsay. An hour-long programme of news films, cartoons and 'topical features' was screened continuously from 9.45 AM to 11 PM. Announcements of train arrivals would be projected at the side of the screen on request to the cashier. In recent years the cinema has become part of the Classic chain, showing full-length feature films.

In preparation for the expected war, air-raid shelters for

some 6,500 people were constructed in the arches beneath the station. When the bombing began, those who had lost their homes took up permanent residence, bringing in bits of furniture, even laying linoleum and carpets. There was also accommodation for the station staff and a telephone room for use by the headquarters staff should they be driven out of their wartime home at Dorking by invading armies. Someone had a respect for history. Not without effort, the Bodmin & Wadebridge coach was moved from the concourse to the relative safety of the lower subway.

Waterloo felt the first effects of enemy action on September 7th, 1940, when the viaduct at John Street, just outside the station, was opened up by a bomb. All platforms were out of use until September 19th, and despite the assistance of the Royal Engineers, services were not fully restored until October 1st. During the interval, mail piled up until there were around 5,000 unsorted bags. Night newspaper trains were diverted to Clapham yard, bombed out of there, transferred to Wimbledon, and when bombs blocked the road access to that station, moved again, to Surbiton. Following damage by oil and incendiary bombs on the night of December 29th, 1940, the station was closed again. It reopened on January 5th, 1941, and on that night the old general offices in the York Road corner, already damaged by an earlier air raid, were largely destroyed by a bomb which also badly battered the Underground lifts and booking-hall.

During a very heavy raid on May 10th–11th, 1941, more damage was wrought, by high-explosive, delayed action, incendiary and oil bombs, and a furious fire was started in the basement arches where great quantities of spirits fanned flames which burned on until May 15th, when the station was partly reopened. Altogether, some fifty bombs found the station and its approaches, and one, a 2,000-pounder, lay undiscovered until office-building operations started along the York Road side in 1959.[12] The Necropolis station was obliterated by a land mine, and Tite's Nine Elms lost its roof and attic.

Waterloo has seen few changes since the war. On the traffic side, the most notable have been the disappearance of steam, which held out here longer than at any other London terminus, and the decline in the transatlantic boat-train traffic to and from Southampton following the capture of passengers by the airlines in the 1950s. A number of boat trains still survive at the time of writing, but these are almost all related to cruise and emigrant sailings. Almost gone are the days when Ministers of State, film stars and other notabilities said their helloes and goodbyes in front of Press cameras at Waterloo, although such memories did return in December 1968 when Ginger Rogers arrived in her special train.

Largely for the benefit of boat-train passengers, the roof over the cab yard opposite Platforms 12 to 15 was extended a further 135 ft towards York Road in 1948. An overhead footway, the first to serve any London terminus, was opened on October 11th, 1965, linking the concourse to the south bank walkways, Hungerford Bridge, and Charing Cross. Shortly after leaving the concourse, this walkway penetrated the new office block which was built alongside the station in the early 1960s.

During 1967 accommodation for railway staff was erected over the barrier ends of Platforms 1 to 6, partly to replace the main-line booking-on point that disappeared with the closure of Nine Elms locomotive depot in that year. This wooden structure, supported on steel girders, had a communicating gallery overlooking the platforms, a place where guards and drivers could gaze down at the rush-hour crowds with a feeling of superiority. Also accommodated here were the staff of the Thomson Newscaster, a device offering in lights a close mixture of news headlines and advertisements. Installed over the news cinema, this eventually came to life on April 4th, 1968. At least it didn't make a noise.

Until the summer of 1962, the throbs and fumes of the diesel were almost unknown at Waterloo. Steam locomotives were to be seen there at all hours of the day; BR 2–6–2T and 2–6–4T had at last replaced the venerable LSWR M7 0–4–4T on the empty stock workings, but on the main-line trains to the west, to Bournemouth and to Weymouth, Bulleid's Pacifics still shared the burden with the more handsome BR rebuilds. Even when the diesels did appear they did not sweep the board – steam survived on the ECS workings and on some main-line trains until the final completion of the Bournemouth electrification on July 10th, 1967.

That was the year when the long familiar Southern green finally began to give way to 'rail blue' and yellow front ends, but it was above all the year when Waterloo became the funeral parlour of main-line steam working in southern England. Every day until the changeover on July 9th, a band of mourners gathered at the platform ends, dressed in cameras and tape-recorders, pockets bulging with notebooks and stopwatches, in greedy struggle for mementoes. Steam railtour followed steam railtour round the same old circuits. And from the concourse, Mr McKenna's loudspeakers blared out *Colonel Bogey*. A year later, the smoke-blackened roof glass over the central platforms still remained, in memoriam.

SIGNALLING AND ACCIDENTS

During the time that Nine Elms was open to regular passenger working, trains on the running lines were controlled by the time-interval system. On arriving at the approaches to the terminus, they proceeded under the instructions of a manually-operated revolving lamp showing red (danger), green (caution), or white (all clear), or flags of the same colours. At the entrance to the station, the locomotive was uncoupled, proceeding to a siding whilst the carriages were hauled inside the train shed by rope.

Waterloo's signalling arrangements grew in the same piece-meal fashion as the station. At first each platform had hand-operated disc signals and the points were controlled by outside hand levers. At a ground hut close to Westminster Bridge Road sat the 'stop signalman' controlling a manual disc signal and an 'auxiliary' or distant signal worked by a wire. He also operated a gong which warned staff of incoming trains, providing a code description. All up trains stopped at a ticket platform south of Westminster Bridge Road (later, at Vauxhall) where a long removable coupling was placed between the locomotive and the first coach. When the train started off again, and a speed of some 10 mph had been reached, this coupling was slipped, the locomotive moving forward into a siding. The points were quickly reset as the coaches rolled on into their appropriate platform, where they were braked by the guard. Time-interval working was the rule until the criticisms of the Government inspector investigating a collision between Ascot race specials at Egham in 1864 provoked the introduction of block working. By the beginning of 1866, this system was in use from Waterloo and Staines.

A signal box was opened at Waterloo in March 1867. Erected by Stevens & Sons, this was on a gantry over all four approach tracks at the entrance to the station. The hook locking frame had twenty-four main-line levers and another twenty-three for the Windsor lines. Two tall posts, each with six semaphore arms (three for up and three for down trains, the up and down arms on the same pivot) sprouted from the gantry, one at each end. The post on the south side, by the Necropolis station, controlled the main lines, the other the Windsor lines. Disc signals remained in use for distants and for the engine roads. At first there were no starting signals, but when these were provided, a stirrup frame was fitted to work them.

Saxby & Farmer built a second box alongside the old in 1874, with rocker and grid locking frames for Main and Windsor working – 100 levers in a continuous row. It was enlarged four years later by Stevens & Sons, who added thirty-five levers for the new South station. Another sixty-five levers were added in 1885 for the North station. By the latter date, the box, which had two parallel frames, back to back, was worked by four men between 7 AM and 10 PM, and by two men on the night shift. At busy times each man was pulling over the heavy levers once every fifteen seconds. Hernia was an occupational disease of signalmen in those days.

A new and larger box was required when the approach tracks were widened in 1892. Built alongside, and to the north of the old, this was opened between May 1st–15th, 1892. It had Stevens frames, with a total of 220 levers. As triple working and gear levers were used, the 102 signal levers in this total controlled no fewer than 247 semaphore arms. The gantry which supported the box carried a magnificent display of signals, six sets of triple bracket posts, each controlling one of the six approach lines. High enough to disappear in foggy weather, the gantry had four rows of arms; at the top were the two down Windsor indicating signals, then a row of twenty up and down main-line signals. Beneath these were twenty-seven arms for Windsor line movements in and out of all platform roads, and at the bottom, a row of twelve shunt arms. At the platform ends, thirteen sets of starting signals on wrought iron brackets replaced the old wooden posts.

The box, 74 ft by 30 ft, consisted of two storeys, the upper one containing the lever frames and a mess room. The tappet interlocking supplied by Stevens was very comprehensive; some main signals were controlled by as many as fifteen levers. A large amount of auxiliary electrical equipment was installed. When the approach tracks were further widened and the station rebuilt, the number of levers was increased to 250, plus six slides. With the special levers already mentioned, this was equivalent to a total of 410 ordinary levers.

By 1922 the skyline signals over the box had all but disappeared (a photograph taken about this time shows only nineteen arms). They had been replaced by route-indicating signals for the up trains and signals at the platform ends for departures. Track circuits had been fitted to all running lines by the early 1920s, and the box equipped with illuminated diagrams showing the occupation of the circuits and the Sykes' electric fouling bars. A tentative trial of a light signal took place in 1920 when a three-position signal of the pattern used on the Pennsylvania Railroad was fixed on the girder of the box opposite Platform 16. Rows of yellow-white lights indicated danger at the horizontal, caution at the oblique and clear at the vertical positions.

At this time six men were required to work the box between 6 AM and 2 PM, and between 2 PM and 10 PM, while the night shift needed four men. There were also eight booking boys and three telegraph lads. The latter did not survive long into the SR era as the new company made a clean sweep of telegraph instruments, relying entirely on telephones.

Supplementing the main (A) box were B, C and D, and the three yard cabins. One of the latter was in the engine yard near the end of the South station platform, and another on the north side of the station by the turntable near York Road. The third, opened seven years after the first main box, and altered from time to time, was nicknamed the 'Crows' Nest' because it was situated against the gable end of the Central station roof. These yard boxes supervised the admission of trains to the platforms, and Crows' Nest also worked the connecting line to Waterloo Junction. This little box at one time controlled the bolt locks of the turnplates which connected the tracks of the original station and were used to marshal trains in the days of four-wheel coaches (and also to turn horse boxes and carriage trucks off trains). Crows' Nest disappeared in 1911, during the rebuilding of Waterloo, as did the other yard boxes.

Box B was another overhead cabin, 462 yd out from A, with a 100-lever Stevens frame. It was worked by three men at busy times, two at night. Boxes C and D were much smaller, and were between B and Vauxhall Station; C, with thirty-five levers, was on the down side 445 yd from B, and D was an overhead box with twenty-three levers another 522 yd down the line.

All the traffic of this great twenty-one-platform terminus remained controlled by this complex mesh of levers, wires, rods, slots, bolts, bells and fallible human beings without serious accident until 1936. The mental and physical strain on the men had been relieved to some extent by track circuiting and other refinements, but Waterloo A remained one of the most demanding jobs on offer for a railway signalman. As they looked through the window and saw the new concrete box going up, these fine men must have had few regrets at the passing of the old régime.

In the 'Odeon cinema' style favoured by the SR in the 1930s, the new box was built over the cab entrance in Westminster Bridge Road, on the site of the old blacksmiths' shop. It came into use on October 18th, 1936, replacing six manual boxes. There were 309 miniature levers and sixteen train and engine describers in three sub-frames, one for the suburban Platforms 1 to 4, another for Platforms 5 to 15 and the third for 16 to 21. Four track diagrams of the negative type covered all lines between the station and Vauxhall. Four signalmen were required for the early and middle turns, three for the night shift. Three-aspect colour-light signals were used between Waterloo and Loco junction, four-aspect beyond to Hampton Court junction. The three-light junction indicator was used for the first time in an SR installation.

In its short career as a passenger station, Nine Elms suffered one serious accident. On October 17th, 1840, in the hours of darkness, a train arrived very much behind time (such behaviour is not new, despite what we read in the papers). Whilst its engines were being detached, the following train came in *early*, and the confused policeman omitted to show a red light to its driver. In the resulting collision, one passenger was killed.

Serious accidents at Waterloo have fortunately been few. Soon after the opening of the new A box, on August 21st, 1896, a light engine left the locomotive yard to run into the South station under hand signals. Over-running the clearance point, it collided with a down train just leaving, derailing its engine. This was not serious, but unfortunately the sudden stop of the outgoing train surprised the driver of the light engine following up its rear; he could not stop in time, and ran into the back of the train, injuring five passengers.

On May 5th, 1904, a signal linesman carrying out some repairs accidentally stepped on to a signal wire, putting the signal to clear. A train of empty milk vans moved off and collided with a passenger train, killing one passenger.

On April 11th, 1961, about 5.30 PM, the motorman of an electric train from Effingham via Leatherhead passed a signal at danger, bringing his train into collision with Bulleid Pacific *Crewkerne*, which was crossing over to reach Nine Elms depot, after working the 1.25 PM from Weymouth. This accident, which occurred about 400 yards out of the terminus, caused the death of the motorman, who was crushed in his cab.

A bizarre incident took place on April 13th, 1948. A Drummond M7 tank was propelling four loaded coal wagons on to the Waterloo & City hoist when suddenly the lift began to sink, taking trucks and locomotive with it. Driver and fireman jumped clear as their engine tilted into the shaft. It landed upside down at the bottom, spurting steam, and resting on the smashed coal wagons. Raised piecemeal, its parts were later used as spares.

CHAPTER TWELVE

CHARING CROSS

IN THE HEART OF THINGS

'Only Charing Cross really puts you down in the heart of things, in an air melodious with the bells of St Martin's,' wrote Ronald Knox. And so it is. Although Cannon Street is ideal for the heart of the City, Charing Cross is closer than any other terminus to what is generally accepted as the true centre of London. Without doubt it is the capital's most conveniently situated main-line station. Used daily by some 120,000 passengers, it is so well-placed that many can complete their journey on foot. Yet, for all its convenience and utility, it has long been an irritant to politicians and the less-practical town planners and civic designers, who would see it swept away to give place to a new road crossing of the river into an enlarged Trafalgar Square.

Now primarily a commuter station, Charing Cross has a cramped concourse which is the scene of great activity in the rush hours. Most of the time, the miracle is achieved, and as the incoming evening tide advances from the Strand, capacious electric trains suck it away as fast as it comes, but should there be some disruption or delay to slacken the pace of the outgoing trains, the jam-packed mass will quickly solidify. Charing Cross is then no place for the weak.

The SER had promoted an unsuccessful Bill for an extension from Bricklayers Arms to Hungerford Bridge as early as 1846, and we have already seen how it had promised Parliament in 1857 that it would establish a West End terminus. After some abortive attempts to get into Victoria, the company obtained the consent of the LBSCR to a westward thrust from London Bridge. In 1857 Samuel Smiles,[1] the SER secretary, investigated possible routes and sites, concluding that the best choice for a terminus was Hungerford Market in West Strand. He also proposed that the approach line should connect with the LSWR at Waterloo. Traffic prospects were, he thought, bright; there would be foreign workings via the Waterloo link, and as well as the obvious demand for a terminus farther west (Smiles had found that some three-fifths of the passengers at London Bridge were making for the West End) a healthy local business was expected from the West End to the City (there was then no District Railway, and no Victoria Embankment). Smiles recommended two 'City' stations on the extension, one in what is now Blackfriars Road, the other just west of London Bridge.

An Act of 1859 authorized the separate, but SER-inspired Charing Cross Railway Company to construct 1 mile, 68 chains of line to the new terminus. The SER agreed to contribute £300,000 of the £800,000 capital, later increasing this to £650,000. On August 1st, 1864, seven months after the opening of Charing Cross, the little company was completely absorbed into the SER.

Apart from the thorough milking organized by St Thomas's Hospital (Chapter 8), the line proved to be far more expensive than expected. It passed through a thickly built-up, insalubrious area, and landlords were successful in forcing up prices all round. The cost was further increased when in 1862 the company decided to have three running lines instead of two, and a quadruple- rather than double-track bridge over the river.

To minimize property disturbance and maintain a reasonably level gradient throughout, the running lines were carried on 190 brick arches (fourteen of them were over streets). There were also seventeen iron bridges and two iron viaducts, including one of 404 ft over the Borough Market, which was rebuilt at the railway's expense. 'Amidst an effusion almost suffocating' well over 7,000 corpses were removed from the College Burial Ground of St Mary, Lambeth, to be reburied at Brookwood.

There were three tracks from Cannon Street West junction (now Metropolitan junction) to the Thames, worked as up, down and up. Between the junction and Borough Market junction, two tracks were thought sufficient as it had been decided to work most of the passenger trains in and out of Cannon Street to accommodate the West End–City traffic already mentioned.

The subsequent decision to build Cannon Street eliminated the need for the intermediate station near London Bridge, and this was not started. The other station was opened with the Charing Cross extension and was sited just north of the junction of Great Surrey Street (now Blackfriars Road) and Charlotte Street (now Union Street). It had a short life, closing on December 31st, 1868, in favour of Waterloo Junction. There is no sign of it now, apart from a widening on one side of the viaduct. Nearby, from Metropolitan junction, a curve was later put in to the LCDR at Blackfriars junction (June 1st, 1878). The other link, to the LSWR, has been described in the Waterloo chapter.

OVER THE RIVER TO WESTMINSTER

Beyond Waterloo, a gradient of 1 in 210 was required to gain sufficient height for the river crossing. The line was carried over the Thames on a lattice girder bridge, 61 ft 3 ins wide, with four running lines, one of which was later converted to a siding. The new bridge occupied the site of the Charing Cross Suspension Bridge, designed by I. K. Brunel, and opened on May 1st, 1845, in the hope of attracting custom to the Hungerford Market from the Surrey side. After purchase by the railway, the chains and ironwork of the bridge were sold and used for the Clifton Suspension Bridge at Bristol. Much abused by the 'scrap Charing Cross' party in later years, the Charing Cross railway bridge was a straightforward engineering job with little attempt at ornamentation, contributing nothing to the riverscape. Had the Victoria Embankment existed, there is little doubt that Parliament would have insisted on something rather more monumental.

There were six spans of 154 ft, and three of 100 ft, the last on the Westminster shore, carrying the track fan at the entrance to the terminus, as the ground available was somewhat restricted. The superstructure of the longer spans consisted of two main side girders carrying cross-girders some 30 ft above the high-water mark, and the whole was supported on cast-iron cylinders sunk into the clay beneath the river bed, and also on the two red-brick piers and the abutments of the old suspension footbridge. Except at the fan end, the cylinders were 14 ft diameter below ground and 10 ft above. There were four piers, three between the towers of the old bridge and one between the tower and the abutment on the Surrey side. Each consisted of two cylinders 49 ft 4 ins apart centre to centre, filled with concrete up to low-water level, and brickwork above. At the fan end, there were two piers; that next to the brick tower had seven cylinders, that next to the abutment, nine. The outer cylinders here were 10 ft diameter below ground, 8 ft above, the inner ones 10 ft and 6 ft.

On both sides of the bridge the cross-girders were prolonged beyond the main ones to support 7-ft 6-in wide footways which the railway company were required to provide to replace the suspension bridge. This path was reached by wooden stairs from Villiers Street, and on the south side by a wooden ramp from Belvedere Road. The suspension bridge was kept open until the footways were ready, so as not to interrupt pedestrian traffic. A halfpenny toll was exacted for the crossing until 1878 when the Metropolitan Board of Works secured its abolition on payment of £98,000 to the SER. Ten years later, the Board erected an iron staircase to link the footway with the west side of the Victoria Embankment.

Work on the railway bridge began in June 1860 and it was finished in about three years. Charing Cross Station was opened for Greenwich and Mid-Kent line trains on January 11th, 1864, North Kent services using it from April 1st, main-line trains from May 1st. Bridge and station were designed by John Hawkshaw, but the hotel forming the frontage of the terminus was the work of E. M. Barry. From its elevated approach, the line came to an end approximately at ground level, owing to the siting of the station against the gravel terrace. The substructure of the building was composed of arches up to 30 ft high, offering excellent cellarage for wine merchants, a purpose for which it is still used.

Hawkshaw's train shed, 510 ft long, was topped by an all-over arched roof of 164-ft clear span, rising 98 ft above the rails to disperse the smoke and steam. Very shortly after, Hawkshaw built another similar roof at Cannon Street; from the river, both appeared enormous, 'colossal sheds of stations ... that mar the river's banks, that soar and project like Brobdingnag poke-bonnets'.[2]

Inside Charing Cross there were single tracks along each wall, and between them, six platform faces, numbered from west to east. Between Platforms 2 and 3 were three tracks, and between 4 and 5, two. The middle road between 2 and 3 and the Platform 1 road terminated in loading docks. All platforms were wooden, and all extended some 20 ft beyond the train shed on to the bridge, the longest being about 609 ft. Platforms 1 and 2 were used for main-line arrivals and departures; between them was a cab road with an exit through the front of the station and a ramp for empty cabs coming up from a tiny yard in Villiers Street. Before the station was completed, this ramp served for a while as a passenger entrance. Beyond the cab incline, at the outer end of 1 and 2, was the customs searching-room, waiting-rooms and accommodation for customs officers, with a bedroom and sitting-room for the head officer. These latter facilities were required for the boat trains to and from Dover and Folkestone. An engine siding (the 'Gusset') was later provided at the end of Platform 1, and another opposite the end of Platform 6.

Between the buffer stops and the frontage was a small concourse, overlooked by a large clock on the inner wall of the

hotel. 'Under the clock at Charing Cross' became a favourite
meeting place, in more ways than one: 'half feminine London
used to wait there at night for its young man, and the other
half said that was who it was waiting for'.[3] Some of the latter
would be those who made such lucrative use of the Cannon
Street run.

The ground floor of the frontage building contained a cab
exit arch at the Brewers Lane (Craven Street) side, and an exit
archway of similar dimensions at the other. Between were
three separate booking-offices (the main line, near the cab arch,
the North Kent, and the Greenwich and Cannon Street) as
well as a cloakroom and waiting-rooms.

HOTEL FRONTAGE

Barry's 250-bedroom hotel formed the main 300-ft frontage,
also extending a short way down Villiers Street alongside the
concourse. It had seven storeys including attics. The architectural style, vaguely French Renaissance, was suitably pompous,
but spoilt by too much emphasis on horizontals. The cab
archway, and its opposite counterpart, distinctly elegant, were
later marred by iron and glass 'conservatories' erected immediately above them.

Inside the hotel were pleasant and richly ornamented public
rooms, some with little balconies overlooking the station concourse. The lift was quaintly described in a contemporary account as a 'rising room, fitted with comfortable seats'. Opened
on May 15th, 1865, the hotel, with its excellent appointments,
and central situation, soon became a popular resort, reaping
dividends of between ten and twelve per cent. A ninety-bed-
room annexe, connected to the main building by a footbridge
over Villiers Street, was completed in 1878.

At the front of the hotel was a cab yard, 120 ft deep, separated from West Strand by iron railings and stone pillars. A
gateway at each end was guarded by a police lodge. Later, these
two lodges were let, one to a tobacconist, the other to Hands &

Co, who operated a *bureau de change* for the benefit of Continental travellers, with sidelines in the sale and purchase of Irish and country banknotes, war medals and gold and silver. In the centre of the forecourt was Barry's reproduction of the original Charing Cross. This had marked the last resting place of Queen Eleanor's body before burial in Westminster Abbey and was erected in 1291, probably at the top of Whitehall, where the King Charles statue now stands. It had been demolished by order of Parliament in 1647. Barry completed his work in 1865 with, to quote Walford again, the 'scanty guidance of two or three scarce and indistinct prints'. This 70-ft edifice was carved by Thomas Earp of Lambeth. Unfortunately it does not stand out well against the ornate background of the hotel, and many pass without noticing it.

When opened, the West End terminus of the SER took all the main-line services which had formerly terminated at London Bridge, including the Continental boat trains. It soon assumed an international flavour, and with Victoria, was the main point of departure for travellers from London to Europe and beyond, so much so that Percy Fitzgerald was moved to describe its platform barriers as 'the Gates of the World'. Thomas Cook & Son set up an ornately decorated office (matching the style of the hotel) on the Craven Street side of the forecourt (the premises are now occupied by a wine merchant), and French and German were always to be heard around the station. After the opening of the Sevenoaks cut-off in 1868, the SER route to Dover was $1\frac{1}{2}$ miles shorter than that of its rival at Victoria. By 1913, Paris was within six and a half hours of Charing Cross.

In the winter months, Charing Cross was often wreathed by the fogs, which hung thick and low over the river when the air was still. In such conditions, working was frequently disrupted; signals blanketed from view, the trains moved very slowly, their progress punctuated by detonators and the crackling braziers of the intrepid fogmen. Viewed from the embankment on such a night, the station offered a picture to stir the imagination:

> look up at the great half-circle of the station roof, and watch the trains thunder along the bridge overhead, the lights flashing through the girders, and the torrents of dull white steam bursting out above, falling again beneath the weight of the fog, and melting into nothingness as they fall.[4]

UNFULFILLED CONNEXIONS

Not to be outdone by its competitor, the SER supported a scheme for a connexion between Charing Cross and the Northern lines. The North Western & Charing Cross Railway Act, which proposed a shallow subway line for goods and passengers between Charing Cross and the LNWR just outside Euston, was passed in 1864 soon after the terminus opened. There was a joint guarantee of five per cent from both main-line companies, but the capital could not be raised, and the scheme died in the financial crisis of 1866. A similar proposal, the London Central Railway, which also included a link to the Midland at St Pancras, was authorized in 1871. Parliament imposed obligations to construct new streets above the line and this, together with a severe vibration clause, discouraged investors; despite support from the Midland and the SER, the scheme was abandoned in 1874.

The proposal for a shallow subway between Euston and Charing Cross came up for the last time in 1885. On this occasion it foundered owing to a dispute between Watkin and Moon (the chairmen of the SER and the LNWR) as to where one-third of the capital should rank – the two main-line companies were each ready to put up a third of the £1,500,000 capital, but the outside parties putting up the remainder wanted their investment to rank in front of the other two-thirds. When the connexion was eventually established, it was in the form of a deep-level Tube railway with no physical connexions to the main lines. Just as well perhaps, for no one seems to have given much thought to the problem of handling cross-London traffic on the congested fog-ridden line between Charing Cross and London Bridge.

The difficulties of working an expanding business over this line led inevitably to widenings. The river bridge was tackled first, and in 1887 was widened 48 ft 9 ins on the upstream side to carry three more tracks. From south-west to north-east, the order of lines was then:

    up west No 1
    down west
    up west No 2
    engine road
    up main
    down main
    up local

Between Belvedere Road, Waterloo, and Metropolitan junction, another track was added to the south side of the viaduct and came into full use on June 2nd, 1901. The two inner roads were then worked as down lines, the outer ones as up, a practice which provided the minor convenience of down trains either side of the island platform at Waterloo junction. Two sets of scissors crossovers were installed east of Waterloo junction between the up lines, and between the down lines.

From the 1880s, if not earlier, enlargement of Charing Cross Station had been under consideration, and a number of freeholds were purchased either side, in Craven and Villiers Streets. Powers for enlargement of the station, and for a further widening of the bridge (on the City side) were obtained in 1900, but no action was taken, largely because of the uncertainty caused by the Charing Cross Bridge Scheme, a matter which will be considered presently. Eventually, electrification and resignalling created a substantial increase in terminal capacity, rendering physical expansion less urgent.

UNPREMEDITATED REBUILDING

A rebuilding of sorts did take place in the 1900s, but it was unpremeditated. A programme of roof-maintenance work was begun in June 1905, and for the remainder of the year, some thirty or so men toiled away above the trains and passengers. On the afternoon of December 5th, glazing and sash bars were being renewed when, at approximately 3.45, there was a sudden and unusual noise. The repair men were seen trying to escape from their precarious situation, and staff and passengers beat a hasty retreat, fearing that worse was to follow. It did. Twelve minutes later, the physical strains worked themselves out and 70 ft of the roof, two bays, with the huge windscreen at the river end, crashed down into the station with a roar, pushing the side wall outwards until it tipped over on to the Avenue Theatre at the bottom of Craven Street (now the Playhouse). About 100 men were at work on the reconstruction of that building, and three were crushed to death as the avalanche of iron and bricks thundered through its roof. In the station itself, three more men had died as the 3.50 PM train for Hastings was buried in the rubble.

The railway staff closed Charing Cross at once, shutting the forecourt gates and halting incoming trains on the bridge, whilst police sealed off Craven and Villiers Streets; medical staff from Charing Cross Hospital, alerted by the thunderous crash, tended the wounded and dying. Firemen and railwaymen were soon busy shoring up the wreckage.

The formal inquiries established that the cause of the accident was a sudden fracture in a weak wrought-iron tie rod of the main principal next to the windscreen. It was thought that a flaw in welding had occurred at the time of manufacture and that during the next forty-two years the rod had gradually weakened as the metal expanded and contracted with changes in air temperature. Some additional strain had been imposed by the weight of the repair gang and their staging, and although this was not in any way unreasonable, it was the immediate cause of the final fracture.

Although some engineering witnesses had given the remaining eleven bays of the roof at least forty more years of safe life, the railway company decided to take no chances and brought it all down. The side walls were rebuilt at slightly reduced height and a new ridge and furrow type roof was erected in place of the old single span. This had no end screen, but the girder across the outer end was decorated with a large coat of arms, flanked by the letters SE CR.

During the reconstruction, the station remained closed to traffic, but the various amenities and offices, including the refreshment rooms, were opened towards the end of December. Most trains terminated at Cannon Street, but some boat trains, and all horse and carriage traffic, were dealt with at Victoria. A partial train service was restored on March 19th, 1906.

Good came out of evil, not for the SECR, but for the Underground company, who were building a Tube station beneath the forecourt and paying £60,000 for the privilege. Before the accident, the main-line company had insisted that any temporary occupation of the forecourt for this work should be as brief as possible to avoid any interference with the cab traffic in and out of the terminus, and the engineers had therefore planned to work upwards from the Tube tunnel, by no means an easy task. When the roof collapsed, the Underground company suggested the closure of the terminus might have changed the situation. They were told that they could break up the forecourt, provided all was made good within six weeks. Good use was made of this time, and the construction of the Tube station (the present Strand) was greatly facilitated. The Charing Cross Euston & Hampstead Railway was opened to the public on June 22nd, 1907, placing the terminus in direct communication with Euston, Highgate and Golders Green. Stairs from the main-line concourse led directly to the Tube station booking-hall beneath the forecourt, whilst other entrances were available in West Strand and Villiers Street.

Following the completion of the new roof, the amenities of the terminus were rebuilt and improved. The dark and narrow booking-offices were demolished and the various waiting- and other rooms in the ground floor of the frontage building were entirely rearranged. In the centre a new combined booking-hall was built measuring 58 ft by 22 ft. On the eastern side of this was a new general waiting-room, 34 ft by 33 ft, panelled in Riga wainscot oak. Between this and the concourse was a new ladies' waiting-room 34 ft by 22 ft, its walls covered with scagliola marble; stairs led down from this to the lavatories, bathroom and dressing-room constructed in the upper space of the arches under the station. Completed in 1913, this work still survives largely in its original form, apart from the general waiting-room, which was converted to an inquiry and reservation office in the 1950s.

As the nearest English railway system to the scene of war, the SECR played an important strategic role during 1914–18. Charing Cross, close to the centre of government and administration, was in the thick of things, and in constant use by ministers, high-ranking officials and their staff on their way to and from France. A special train, coded *Imperial A*, consisting of a D or E 4–4–0, a Pullman car partly converted, or saloon, and a bogie brake composite, was held in a constant state of readiness for emergency journeys from Charing Cross to the coast. This train ran non-stop on a cleared path and 283 journeys were made by it during the war period. In addition, a military staff officers' train was dispatched daily to Folkestone at 12.20 PM. When a critical situation arose on the Western Front in March 1918, vans of small-arms ammunition were attached to this train and flown direct from Folkestone to the beleaguered sections of the front. In the opposite direction, a sad procession of ambulance trains brought back the mutilated bodies of the young men who had left their homeland in such high enthusiasm and patriotic fervour. The reception of sick and wounded was concentrated at the partially completed Dover Marine station from January

2nd, 1915, and the trains ran from there not only to Charing Cross, but to hospitals all over the country. This ambulance traffic was conducted with great efficiency and speed. An account in *British Medical Journal* for August 1st, 1917, recorded that the first wounded of the Battle of Messines, which had begun at dawn on June 7th, 1917, were brought into Charing Cross station at 2.15 PM the same day.

Precautions against air attack were taken at a surprisingly early date. At the end of October 1914, following a Zeppelin raid on Antwerp, but before any raids on England, the London district superintendent of the SECR instructed the Charing Cross stationmaster to post a responsible man to keep look-out on the bridge as soon as telephone warning of imminent danger was received from London Bridge. Should danger threaten, no trains were to be allowed on the bridge. But nothing more serious than a few panes of broken glass happened to Charing Cross.

During the war years, civil traffic to Europe was severely restricted. Dover was appropriated entirely for military purposes and there were no public boat services from August 3rd, 1914. All SECR civil traffic was diverted to Victoria from November 15th, one advantage being that the station provided more space for the rigorous passport and immigration controls that had been introduced. Restrictions were further increased in November 1915 when the SECR ceased to handle civilian boat traffic via Folkestone.

With the ending of the war, the SECR resumed its cross-Channel services; Dover–Ostend began again on January 18th, 1919; Dover–Boulogne on February 3rd, 1919 (Folkestone reopened on March 1st); and Dover–Calais on January 8th, 1920. As the stringent customs, passport and immigration examinations were continued after the armistice, the SECR made the sensible decision to concentrate all the associated boat-train services at the more spacious Victoria from January 8th, 1920.[5] The former LCDR terminus also offered the advantage of engine and carriage accommodation conveniently close to the station. (Continental empty carriage stock for Charing Cross was worked up from Rotherhithe Road, taking about twenty-five minutes, including the necessary reversal at Surrey Canal junction.)

With the transfer of the boat-train traffic, Charing Cross lost much of its character and romance. It was never the same again. But before this happened, there was a final blaze of glory, commemorated by a plaque near the entrance to the booking-hall. On December 26th, 1918, President Woodrow Wilson of the United States arrived at Charing Cross, where he was greeted by King George V and his ministers: 'at a supreme hour in human history. The war over, the future to be fashioned, the two nations significantly met.'

Slowly, the old international atmosphere faded away. The customs shed was demolished and the cab rank from Villiers Street blocked up. Signs reading HERREN, DAMES or BAGAGES were taken down. Only one reminder now exists – W. H. Smith & Son still maintains an excellent selection of Continental newspapers at the main bookstall.

THE BATTLE OF THE BRIDGES

Some people were hoping that Charing Cross would not only lose its boat trains, but would close altogether. Soon after the formation of the London County Council in 1889 there had developed within that body an entirely commendable and new-found pride in the capital city and its appearance. In the Progressive Party in particular there bubbled a healthy zeal to make London a better place to live in. A leader of this movement was John Burns,[6] who cherished dreams of a new riverscape, with a graceful road bridge in place of the Charing Cross railway bridge.

Within the LCC, the proposal to demolish the railway bridge and reconstruct the terminus on the south bank met with considerable support, as it would permit the widening of West Strand, and provide a new road bridge over the river at a

point where one was said to be urgently required. In 1901 the
Council sought the railway company's views, but the SECR
was not enthusiastic and the expense of purchasing a new site
for the terminus was enough to give the LCC pause. Discussions
were held at intervals, but no tangible scheme emerged before
the outbreak of the First World War. Meanwhile, the SECR
had a problem on their hands.

Designed for the lightweight locomotives of the 1860s, the
original bridge had a maximum live load of one ton per foot
of track, about half that required for the steam engines of the
twentieth century. While the station was closed for the reconstruction of the roof in 1906, the opportunity was taken to
make a thorough examination of the bridge. Some new main
girders were then put in to strengthen it, but this was not in
itself sufficient, and the civil engineer had been obliged to
follow the work with load restrictions, to avoid overstressing
the girders and foundations. The heavier classes of locomotives
were banned from the structure and it was ruled that not more
than two of the tracks should be under load at the same time,
and then not on adjacent lines. This produced serious delays
because trains had to be held at one side or the other whilst
another train passed in the contrary direction, and the effect
was to reduce the capacity of the bridge by twenty-five to
thirty-three per cent.

In 1916 the SECR came to Parliament seeking powers to
strengthen the bridge more substantially, so that it could be
used to the full extent of its track capacity, postponing indefinitely the need for any further widening or reconstruction.
Four new masonry piers were to be built and balanced cantilever brackets erected to take the strain from the cross-girders,
forming arched spans.

Perhaps the railway company hoped that its Bill would go
through on the nod, whilst the war occupied everyone's attention. If so, it was unlucky; the controversy erupted with
new force. In Parliament, Burns worked himself into a great
froth:

It violates all the canons of public taste, and it outrages all the amenities of a fine riverside view ... now is the hour when a discussion of this problem suggests that all the local authorities concerned, and the railway company, should substitute for the Charing Cross Station, which is cabin'd, cribb'd, confin'd on the north, a fine station on the south.

Others opposed on the flimsy grounds that the new arches would impede navigation, and the Permanent Secretary of the Office of Works was quoted as being of the opinion that the proposed works would make the bridge even uglier. This official counselled delay, pointing out that Charing Cross was unlikely to be adequate for future traffic, especially when the Channel Tunnel was built. Someone else inserted the notion that the site of the station might be required after the war for a national monument to Lord Kitchener. Despite Board of Trade support, the Bill was defeated in a thin House of Commons, when railway director MPs were otherwise engaged.

Another attempt was made in the following year. The Bill, which included abandonment of the 1900 powers to widen the bridge, was more successful, thanks to better explanations of the company's needs and intentions and a less emotive reception in Parliament. The Act, passed on August 2nd, 1917, insisted that the new spans should have curved soffits, firmly imposed a ban on enlarging the *station*, as well as the bridge, and required that no work above water level be started for three years. In the meantime, beginning at the end of October 1916, urgent minor strengthening work was undertaken between 12.30 AM and 8.30 AM each day, some trains terminating at Cannon Street during those hours.

Burns pressed on, enlisting the aid of other politicians and artists to work for the destruction of 'that ugly red-oxide Behemoth which sprawls from the north to the south', but after some meetings and pamphleteering in 1916–17, the fuss subsided. Repainted Navy grey by the SR, the Behemoth attracted less attention.

But not for long. Interest in the bridge revived in 1925 when a Royal Commission on Cross River Traffic in London considered various bridge schemes. In May, the LCC and the SR had an informal conference on the future of Charing Cross Bridge, but reached no conclusions. The report of the Commission, published in 1926, included a proposal that the monstrosity be replaced by a monster: a double-decker, 60-ft road above, six rail tracks below, with a new Charing Cross Station into the bargain, a little east of the old. To this the SR offered no objection, secure in the knowledge that it would gain improved terminal facilities, backed by adequate compensation. After consulting with the LCC, the Ministry of Transport then requested Messrs Mott, Hay & Anderson, the consulting engineers, to investigate and cost the project in detail, with the assistance of the LCC's chief engineer, Sir George W. Humphrey, and A. W. Szlumper, the former chief engineer of the SR.

In May 1928 the engineers reported, finding the double-deck scheme quite feasible, but once again throwing up the old idea of a road bridge, with the railway removed to the south bank. Szlumper naturally refused to endorse the latter proposal. The report alleged that the road-bridge scheme would be much cheaper; £10·77 million against £13·05 million for a satisfactory double-deck bridge and approaches. Promising a seventy-five per cent contribution towards the cost of an agreed scheme, the Government favoured the road bridge, and the Prime Minister (Stanley Baldwin) urged it upon the SR as a matter of national importance. After achieving a modification which brought the proposed new terminus from Waterloo junction to the river bank, the SR waited while the LCC prepared firm plans. Provisional agreement was reached between the Council and the railway company in 1929; in return for the railway viaduct beyond York Road, the bridge and all railway property at Charing Cross, the LCC offered the SR the 8½ acre Lion Brewery site (immediately south of Waterloo Bridge, bounded by the river, Waterloo Road and the line of the railway viaduct), for the new terminus.

In addition to the cost of the new terminus, the SR was to receive £325,000 as compensation for the hotel and other losses. On July 30th, 1929, after the directors had recommended these terms as the best available, and told the shareholders that the plan had been accepted with reluctance, and only because the Government had said it was of national importance, a substantial majority of the proprietors voted in favour of the agreement.

An LCC Bill was then prepared, seeking the necessary powers for a 95-ft-wide road bridge and approaches, and for railway access to the new station and hotel site. It was now Parliament's turn to influence events. No fault was found with the idea of a road bridge at this site, but the Commons Select Committee, under Sir Henry Cautley, could not stomach the idea of a railway terminus prominently placed at the bridgehead on the south bank, and the Bill was rejected on May 6th, 1930. After this, the LCC exhaustively examined a number of alternative proposals including the construction of a terminus below street level, out of sight from across the river. Still hoping for the seventy-five per cent grant, the Council was ready in July 1931 to promote another Bill, but the Government had second thoughts, and the Minister of Transport announced that in view of the controversial nature of the south bank terminus proposal, the changes stemming from railway electrification, and the serious economic situation, he was not prepared to renew the offer of a seventy-five per cent grant. That killed the scheme stone dead.

In 1936 the problem was examined by the London & Home Counties Traffic Advisory Committee, which concluded that pruning back the railway to the south side was no longer a practical proposition; a tunnel was out of the question from the engineering point of view, and the double-deck bridge scheme of 1926 seemed the only answer. The SR announced that it was willing to cooperate, and was anxious for a decision, as it wished to rebuild both the station and the hotel. The Westminster City Council and the Metropolitan Police Commissioner also expressed support for retaining the terminus on the north side. Further moves in the game were effectively stifled by the outbreak of war, and since 1945, apart from the occasional newspaper article, there has been no revival. It would be unwise to assume that the issue is dead.

BENEFITS OF ELECTRIFICATION

In spite of all the expenditure on legislation, nothing more was done to strengthen the bridge, and the working restrictions continued until 1926 when electrification of the Eastern Section suburban services presented a neat solution to the problem. With a uniformly distributed load of only 0.7 ton per foot, multiple-unit electric trains imposed no strains on the old bridge; it was therefore decided to route all the electric services over this part of the structure, reserving the stronger 1887 section for the main-line steam trains. The load on the original bridge was further relieved by reducing the running roads to two (up and down local) and using the rest of the space for sidings arranged in such a way that there could be no possibility of lines being simultaneously loaded side by side except over the short section resting on the masonry pier nearest the Surrey side. These arrangements gave the old bridge a lower level of stresses than those in Hawkshaw's calculations – the mildly alarming shudder that one experiences on the footway as a train rumbles across is no more significant than the movement of a skyscraper in a strong wind.

With the rearrangement of tracks on the bridge, the order of the lines between Belvedere Road and Metropolitan Junction, north to south, became:

down local
up local
down through
up through

At the south-east corner of the bridge, near Belvedere Road, the old turntable, water crane and coaling stage were retained, connexions being provided to the up and down local lines so that steam engines could be worked to the electrified side in emergency.

Other changes were made in Charing Cross Station. The numbering of the platforms was reversed so that 1 was against Villiers Street, and 6 by Craven Street. All platforms were lengthened, 1 and 2 to 610 ft and 640 ft, 2 and 3 to 750 ft and 5 and 6 to 690 ft and 748 ft. Numbers 1 to 3 were electrified. With the removal of the middle road between 4 and 5, a useful widening of Platform 4 was achieved. Between the outer end of Platform 6 road and the edge of the Bridge, there was a short loop siding for standing engines. As engine movements from one platform to another across the width of the station were no longer necessary, it was possible to simplify the track layout at the outer ends of the platforms.

The final changeover, including the rearrangement of tracks, was made on August 22nd and 24th, 1925, and on Sunday, August 23rd, a skeleton service of local trains ran on a single line from London Bridge, hand-signalled into Charing Cross. All work was not completed until November. Electric services to Orpington, Bromley North, Addiscombe, Hayes and Beckenham Junction started on February 28th, 1926, and those to Dartford by all four routes began on June 6th. Electrification encouraged the usual traffic increase: the terminus was handling 71,200 passengers daily in 1930, compared with 48,800 in 1925.

A gruesome discovery was made in the cloakroom in 1927. Their suspicions aroused by a foul odour issuing from a trunk, the attendants summoned the police. The case was found to contain five separate pieces of a woman, later identified as a Mrs Bonati. She had been killed in Rochester Row by a man called John Robinson, who was eventually traced and convicted.

During the 1930s some modest improvements were made to the terminus. The circulating area was enlarged in 1930 by

Plan of Charing Cross 1964. From the Railway Magazine, January 1964

setting forward the buffers of Platforms 2 and 3 some 65 ft, bringing them into line with those of Platform 1, which had been set back slightly to the eastern side of the Villiers Street steps. In 1934 the ugly and crude wooden platform gates were replaced by metal barriers; two years later, these were re-arranged to provide direct access across the ends of 1 to 3. Suburban traffic increased steadily at Charing Cross, as more offices opened in the West End. To accommodate this growth, additional rush-hour trains were provided to and from Charing Cross in 1932.

Although no longer possessing the strategic importance it had in 1914–18, Charing Cross received its share of attention in the air attacks of the Second World War. A train standing in the station was badly damaged during a daylight raid in the Whitehall area on the morning of October 8th, 1940, but the worst onslaught came on the night of April 16th–17th, 1941, when the hotel was severely damaged by fire and high explosive, and many fires were started on the bridge. Four trains were set alight, three within the station, another on the bridge, and whilst these were being dealt with, a porter discovered that a land mine had come to rest near the signal cabin, its parachute gear entangled in the girders of the bridge. A fire under No 4 platform was creeping towards this 28-cwt mine, but was brought under control when within 12 ft of the canister, which the heat of the fires had fused to the conductor rail. Throughout April 17th the station remained closed whilst the fires were extinguished in the hotel, the mine defused and debris cleared. Another bad night was experienced on May 10th–11th, and the terminus was again closed for a while.

After the excitements of spring 1941, things remained quiet until June 18th, 1944, when a flying bomb blew out a span of the 1864 bridge near the south side. The site of this damage is still marked by a missing section of the original ornamental balustrade in the footway. Access to the station was still available via the tracks on the upstream side, and trains were running over them by 11.30 AM. Normal working over the bridge was not resumed until December 4th.

Repairs to the hotel were deferred until after the war, but by 1951 everything had been restored and a new top storey added. Little or no attempt was made to match the new work with Barry's style, and its rather plain appearance tended to spoil the whole, though the incongruity has been less obvious since BR completed a thorough cleaning of the masonry and brickwork of the hotel and Cross in the early 1960s.

TEN-CAR TRAIN SCHEME

As at the other Eastern Section stations, platform lengthening was necessary for the ten-car train scheme. This involved a new track layout for the approaches to Platforms 1 to 3. Once again this was laid out and tested at New Cross before being placed in its final position on April 2nd–3rd, 1954. Ten-car trains worked on the Bexleyheath line from June 14th, 1954, and on the Dartford loop from June 13th, 1955, but the full service of the long trains did not operate until June 17th, 1957.

The widening of West Strand, planned by the LCC at the turn of the century, was at last realized in the late 1950s. The work entailed a reduction in the size of Charing Cross fore-court with the consequent disappearance of the boundary pillars and lodges (demolished in 1958). The entrance to the Tube station needed no alteration as it had been sited on the new building line in 1906!

A scheme for a pedestrian subway under the Strand to divert the rush-hour tide from the roadway was announced in 1956, but had not been started at the time of writing. Also in abey-ance is a 1963 proposal to link the station concourse with the Hungerford footbridge. When these works are finally achieved, there will be a safe footway from Trafalgar Square to the con-course of Waterloo Station.

To meet the requirements of the 1951 Festival of Britain, the 54-ft turntable at Belvedere Road was removed, after which steam engines had to run back to Ewer Street depot to turn. Steam working into Charing Cross came to an end in June 1961 upon the completion of the Kent coast electrification scheme. Before that, in June 1958, multiple-unit diesel-electric trains had taken over the service to Hastings via Tunbridge Wells.

With remarkable ingenuity, the Southern timetable men succeeded in introducing six more trains into the rush hour at Charing Cross from July 10th, 1967, making thirty arrivals between 8 and 9 AM. This was achieved by closer signalling at London Bridge, by running some trains through that station without stopping, and by reducing the number of trains travelling south over Borough Market junction in the peak hour (empty trains from Charing Cross were diverted to new sidings at Southwark depot and Blackfriars). To celebrate the occasion, BR redecorated Charing Cross with new signs, and erected bright modern barrier screens in blue and white, with departure information over each platform entrance. These platform indicators, together with a combined departure indicator on the hotel wall on the Villiers Street side of the concourse, were of the flap type, electrically controlled from a console in the train announcer's room above the concourse. The indications were transmitted by the agency of punched cards, or by manual switch operation if required.

In addition to its important suburban traffic, and the Hastings service already mentioned, Charing Cross remains the terminus for main-line trains to Folkestone and Dover via Tonbridge. These leave from Platform 6 (748 ft), the only platform usable by a twelve-car corridor train (even then, one car is off the end).

A big question mark still hangs over the future of this station. A plan for 'development', including offices, shops and showrooms, and an extension of the hotel over the platform, was produced in May 1963, but failed to obtain planning permission. The abolition of the railway from the Westminster bank is still advocated from time to time by people who never use the station and choose to ignore the convenience of the thousands who do. Renewal of the bridge cannot be postponed for ever, and when it next comes up for serious consideration, we shall no doubt have the Great Charing Cross Bridge Controversy all over again. Meanwhile Charing Cross is a clean and efficiently run little terminus handling a traffic out of all proportion to its size, and together with its popular hotel, it continues to play a lively part in the life of central London.

SIGNALLING AND ACCIDENTS

The first signal cabin sat on a gantry over the tracks just beyond the platform ends, on the same alignment as the present one. It contained a small Saxby & Farmer frame with an early form of interlocking. Like the similar cabins at Cannon Street and London Bridge, it had an array of signals on its roof, three posts, each with two sets of double arms, each set controlling one of the six platform roads in both directions. This arrangement eliminated wire runs, and its operating rods were easy to install and maintain, but there were no set stopping places and the engine drivers had to be trusted to pull up clear of the fouling points. In the foggy weather that was a frequent hazard on this riparian site, these high signals were worse than useless, and groundmen were busy. Despite these disadvantages, they continued in use for many years, and in due course four more arms were installed above the central set, making the display even more impressive.

To work the new layout which followed the widening of the bridge, a new box was erected in the same position and opened in February 1888. This cabin began life with 119 levers, but eventually had 130, all cam-interlocked, in one row across the tracks. Walker's miniature semaphore block instruments were fitted, as in the old box, but were eventually replaced by Sykes' lock and block and Walker's dial-type train describers. Safe working was ensured by Sykes' electric fouling bars, locking bolts and bars, and rod-worked scotch blocks.

Three men were required in this box during the day shifts.

At Belvedere Road, the end of the first block section, the box was on the south-west side of the line. Around the turn of the century this was replaced by an overhead box, erected above the newly-widened approach tracks at the south-east end of the river bridge. This cabin had 129 levers, tappet and spring catch interlocked.

For the electric suburban services of 1926 a colour-light signalling installation was provided. In August 1924 the old manual box at Charing Cross was disconnected and the layout in the station area was worked manually from a temporary box on the up side of the old bridge, at the station end. This enabled the old box to be demolished, and new power frame, light signals and relays to be placed in position and introduced as an entity, without interruption to traffic. Four-aspect colour lights and electrically-operated points were brought into use between Charing Cross and Borough Market junction (exclusive) during a six-hour possession on Sunday June 27th, 1926. The new box at Charing Cross, in the same position as its predecessors, had a 100-lever power frame (32 running signals, 36 shunt, 25 points, 1 bolt, 6 spare) with an illuminated track circuit diagram at the back. Constructed of wood and glass, this signal box was no thing of beauty, the style being of the garden-shed school. Its crude appearance, emphasized by its prominent position, provided good bait for the anti-railway-bridge party.

There were two other boxes in the 1926 scheme, a 60-lever mechanical frame at Metropolitan junction and the existing 43-lever mechanical frame at Borough Market junction. Both were given illuminated signal diagrams. Borough Market received a 35-lever power frame in 1928 with the resignalling of London Bridge. The Charing Cross area resignalling, by the Westinghouse Brake & Saxby Signal Company, achieved a fifty per cent increase in line capacity, and eliminated the manual boxes at Belvedere Road, Waterloo Station and Union Street (the other box at Waterloo, 'Waterloo Junction Signals', had been closed about 1914, after the removal of the LSWR connexion).

Despite the strain and difficulty of working manual signals in fog conditions, and the intensity of its traffic, no serious train accident has ever occurred at Charing Cross, but on October 25th, 1913, a Blackheath and a Mid-Kent line train collided in dense fog at Waterloo junction, killing three passengers. The inspecting officer decided that hasty and incautious use of the release key by the signalman at the Junction box had enabled his colleague in the Station box to admit the second train into the station.

At 2.15 PM on July 31st, 1925, there was a side-on collision between two 'H' class tanks both moving towards No 2 platform at Charing Cross. This revealed that some movements at the terminus were still being made without shunting signals. The incident caused a great deal of disorganization of train services and until matters were restored, some trains were terminated at London Bridge.

CHAPTER THIRTEEN

VICTORIA

WEST END TWINS

The first truly West End terminus available to the Southern lines, Victoria was for many years two quite separate stations, a fact which Lady Bracknell, at any rate, found immaterial. With an interesting mix of Continental, air-feeder, suburban and short-distance main-line traffic, present-day Victoria is a characterful if dowdy station, still retaining two distinct flavours. The Central Section side is redolent of the soft, leisured southern counties, with its theatre and racing types, its ageing *nouveau riche*, its adulterous couples and its Brighton belles. Next door, the Eastern Section station, that British fag-end of Railway Europe, has the faded grandeur of past glories; the scene of many distinguished arrivals and departures in the last fifty years, it is still the gateway to London for many foreign visitors, and in summer is thronged by those who prefer to *travel* into Europe rather than to *fly* there.

The greater bustle is usually to be found on the Central Side, with its heavy suburban traffic and popular fast electric trains to the thriving inland and coastal towns of Sussex. In summer, the other station is busy enough, with well-filled holiday trains to the Kent coast adding to the weight of the Continental traffic, but its suburban load is light. On a winter afternoon the contrast is noticeable.

Pullman is a word to be associated with Victoria. More Pullman cars were to be seen here than at any other terminus before 1914, and the Southern carried on the tradition. First-class Pullmans came to the Brighton line on November 1st, 1875, and the first all-Pullman train ran on December 1st, 1881. The SECR inaugurated Pullman service on Continental boat trains on April 21st, 1910, and on the Kent coast lines on June 16th, 1919. An all-Pullman boat train, later called the 'Golden Arrow', was started in 1924; this survives, but ordinary coaches have taken the place of some of the Pullman cars in recent years.

In the early 1850s, the Southern lines had but three London termini: the overcrowded and cramped sheds of London Bridge, the remote and unloved Bricklayers Arms, and Waterloo. Only the last was anywhere near the burgeoning West End. Dissatisfied with its situation at London Bridge, and interested in obtaining a foothold farther west, the LBSCR had already made approaches to the LSWR. When the latter company spurned the 1853 promotion of the West End of London & Crystal Palace Railway, the Brighton gave the newcomer every encouragement. This new line was to extend from an end-on junction with the LBSCR's proposed Crystal Palace branch (sanctioned in the same year) and from its main line at Norwood, to a junction with the LSWR main line in Wandsworth. The 'West End' part of its title was to be a branch from the LSWR main line nearer Waterloo to a riverside terminus on the *south* bank, opposite Pimlico. The WEL & CPR, which opened on December 1st, 1856, from Crystal Palace to a temporary terminus at the north end of Wandsworth Common, was worked from the start by the LBSCR, which operated a service between London Bridge and Wandsworth. It was nevertheless an independent and speculative promotion, looking beyond the avuncular interest of the Brighton company, and obtaining powers in 1854 for an extension eastwards to Farnborough, where it hoped to meet new lines coming up from Kent. The connexion with the Brighton main line at Norwood Junction was established on October 1st, 1857, and public traffic to and from the riverside terminus at 'Pimlico' began on March 29th, 1858, with LBSCR trains serving Brighton and London Bridge. From the new terminus there was direct road access to the West End over the Chelsea Suspension Bridge, completed three days earlier.

From Crystal Palace this substantially built line passed through Streatham Hill and Balham, and on meeting the LSWR main line near what is now Clapham Junction ran parallel with it, without a physical junction, as far as Stewarts Lane. Here it turned north to pass under the LSWR, continuing almost due north towards the river.

PIMLICO IN BATTERSEA

Some 22 acres of land were bought for the so-called Pimlico terminus in Battersea New Town, but the station itself was of wooden construction, and quite clearly of a temporary character. It was next to what is now Queenstown Road, on the east side of Chelsea Bridge, just south of the river bank, and approximately where Battersea goods depot now stands. Its precise location was determined by the position of the road bridge and the Southwark Water Works, immediately to the east.

The temporary character of the terminus building was explained by the existence of schemes to push on over the river to a more credible West End location. A Westminster Terminus Railway, which proposed connexions with the West End of London and Crystal Palace, and a terminus near the Greycoat School (at the Victoria Street end of Horseferry Road) had been authorized in 1854, but three years later, an even healthier newcomer, the Victoria Station & Pimlico Railway, had appeared on the scene. This was strongly backed by the LBSCR, and obtained its Act in 1858.

The VS & PR proposed a bridge over the river from a junction with the West End of London and Crystal Palace at Stewarts Lane, and a short line built over the course of the obsolescent Grosvenor Canal to a terminus at the western end of Victoria Street, using the site of the canal basin. Here, next door to the newly-laid-out Belgravia and Pimlico, and within a few hundred yards of Buckingham Palace, the terminus really was in the *West End*, without fear of contradiction.

Construction was begun in 1859, and to ensure security of access to the new terminus, the LBSCR took over the Crystal Palace–Battersea portion of the WEL & CPR from July 1st of that year.

The prospectus of the Pimlico Railway had suggested that the new terminus might be used by the LBSCR, the SER,[1] the LSWR, and the East Kent Railway. The latter was a line authorized in 1853 from Strood, on the SER, to Canterbury (thence to Dover, by an Act of 1855). At first this railway was regarded as a feeder to the SER, the proposal being that its London traffic should pass over that company's North Kent line. Then, in 1856, the East Kent began to look around for a surer means of access to the capital, and found the West End of London and Crystal Palace in suitable attitude. Two years later, the East Kent had obtained an Act for a line inwards from Strood to St Mary Cray, where it proposed to join the Farnborough extension of the WEL & CPR, which it arranged to purchase. Puffed with self-importance after attaining this tenuous foothold, the East Kent changed its name in August 1859 to the London Chatham & Dover Railway.

Meanwhile the West End of London had extended from Norwood to Bromley (now Shortlands) on May 3rd, 1858, and a line eastwards from there to Southborough Road (now Bickley) had been opened by the Mid-Kent (Bromley to St Mary Cray) Railway on July 5th. This last section was at first leased to, and worked by, the SER as an extension of its Mid-Kent line from Lewisham to Beckenham, but from September 1st, 1863, the lease was transferred to the LCDR. The Chatham company reached the eastern end of this line on December 3rd, 1860, and as Victoria was now open, it was able to operate a through service between Canterbury and London.

Realizing that it would have to charge fares competitive with those of the SER, and yet at the same time have to pay tolls to get into London over other companies' lines, the LCDR determined to have its own freehold approaches to the centre, and obtained powers in 1860 to construct lines to Victoria and the

Pimlico terminus, as shown on Crutchley's 'New Plan of London', 1859, indicating the extension to Victoria, then under construction. From the Railway Magazine, *March 1958*

City. This ambitious project, which nearly brought the company to financial disaster, involved a line from Beckenham to the WEL & CPR at Stewarts Lane, Battersea, via Herne Hill, with a connexion from Herne Hill to the Metropolitan Railway right across the City, as described in Chapter 10.

But this is jumping ahead. We must now return to the construction of Victoria Station and the arrangements for its use. Various agreements were made between the Victoria Station & Pimlico company, the LBSCR and the LCDR regarding the terminus and its approaches. As a result, the LBSCR, which had subscribed two-thirds of the VS & PR capital, obtained its own section of the terminus and use of the access line. The eastern side of the station was to be leased jointly to the LCDR and the Great Western Railway for 999 years, and in return for the rent, the VS & PR undertook to charge no tolls for the use of its line. As the GWR was still using 7-ft 0¼-in gauge rolling stock, mixed-gauge track was to be laid from Longhedge junction, Battersea (the GWR was to reach Victoria via the West London Extension Railway, opened in 1863) to the eastern side of Victoria, the work to be done at GWR expense.

Grosvenor (or Victoria) Bridge was the first railway bridge to cross the Thames in the London area. To reach it, the VS & PR had to climb at 1 in 50 from its junction with the WEL & CPR (which in turn had a gradient of 1 in 53 and a 15-chain curve in its passage under the LSWR main line). The 930-ft-long river bridge, which had to be high enough to clear all river traffic that was even remotely likely to appear, was designed by John Fowler,[2] who, with the assistance of Benjamin Baker and W. Wilson, was the engineer of the VS & PR. It carried a mixed-gauge double track and was 30 ft 9 ins wide between parapets. At the southern end was a land arch of 65-ft span over the eastern end of the old Pimlico premises, then followed four segmental wrought-iron arches of 175-ft span rising to 22 ft above high-water line, and finally, a land arch of 70-ft span over the Grosvenor Road. The position of the faces of the abutments was determined by the line of the river walls and that of two of the piers by the piers of the suspension bridge 150 yd upstream. Work on the bridge began on June 9th, 1859, and the first train passed over it exactly one year later.

ON RUBBER, BENEATH GLASS

Immediately on leaving the bridge, the line fell steeply (1 in 57) to reach the level of the canal. It then ran due north for a little way before curving slightly north-east over the canal alignment to reach the terminus. Although it would have been possible to avoid the awkward descent from the bridge by constructing a viaduct to an elevated terminus, this would not only have presented engineering difficulties (the subsoil was made ground), it would have offended the influential and aristocratic landowners, who whilst pocketing the compensation, wished to pretend that the railway wasn't there. It was in deference to their wishes that the tracks were covered for most of the distance beyond the bridge by a glazed roof supported on iron columns and arcaded brick walls. They also required the longitudinal sleepers to be cushioned with rubber. It is interesting to speculate what delightful restrictions these gentlemen would have imposed had they been faced with the obscene row of modern jet aircraft.

Of the 14 acres taken for the terminus, the Brighton's premises, completed first, took up 8½. Designed by its resident engineer, Robert Jacomb-Hood, this part of the station was opened on October 1st, 1860, 'Pimlico' closing the previous day.

Extending from the southern side of the present Terminus Place to Eccleston Bridge, the station was 800 ft long by 230 ft wide, with six platform faces and ten tracks under a 40-ft-high ridge and furrow roof in 50-ft spans. This roof was supported on two sets of transverse wrought-iron lattice girders, each of 120-ft span and 50 ft apart and resting on the west wall and two rows of iron columns. As a precaution

The two main-line stations at Victoria, from a survey of 1869. The Railway Magazine, *September 1960*

against a train collision causing the roof to collapse, one row, with foliated capitals and bases, stood in the middle of a 40 ft cab road which ran down the centre of the station between two platform faces; the other row ran along the east side.

Cabs entered by inclined approach from Eccleston Bridge, leaving at the Victoria Street end. Next to the platform roads either side of the central roadway were middle roads with loading docks for horse and carriage traffic at their northern ends. By Eccleston Bridge, at the south-west corner of the station, was a 46-ft engine turntable, whilst the usual turnplates were provided at the inner ends of the main platform roads. Suburban trains used the west side of the station.

At the north end, the cross-platform was narrow and the single-storey frontage building distinctly unpretentious. Discreetly hidden by a large canopy, it was dominated by the huge bulk of the 150-ft-high Grosvenor Hotel at the west corner. This massively-built edifice, 75 ft wide, extended 262 ft down Buckingham Palace Road along the west side of the station. Designed by J. T. Knowles,[3] its frontage abounded in rusticated stone blocks and crinkly-carved stonework, later to prove perfect resting places for soot. Completed in 1861, the 300-room hotel was owned by an independent company attracted to the site by the presence of the railway.

Two years after the opening of the Brighton station, on August 25th, 1862, the LCDR and GWR terminus came into use (the LCDR had been using temporary accommodation at Victoria since its arrival in London in December 1860). This second station occupied 6 acres along the eastern side of the Brighton terminus, with a main entrance and offices on the east, in a turning off Wilton Road. The latter building in yellow brick, with stone facings, was plain, even severe, in appearance. By 1869 the Chatham station had nine tracks, four of mixed gauge, with nine platform faces. Between the two westernmost faces was a cab road, and the south end of these platforms terminated in horse and carriage docks, with a locomotive turntable just beyond. The 740-ft-long iron roof, designed by John

Fowler, was in the form of two tied lattice arch spans of 124
ft and 117 ft.

GREAT WESTERN SERVICES

Whoever had sold a part-share in the lease to the GWR had a
very persuasive manner, for Victoria could not have brought
that company much income. The GWR service began appropriately on April 1st, 1863, providing connexions to the main-
line trains at Southall. Later, some trains ran through to
Uxbridge, Reading, Slough and even Windsor. In addition to
the basic service there were occasional oddities: a slip coach
off trains from Bristol and Birmingham in 1864, a Sunday train
for river pleasures at Henley between 1904 and 1913. Sunday
railcars from Victoria or Clapham Junction to the Wycombe
line via Greenford from 1905 to 1915, and, from October
1910, as a counterblast to the 'City to City' express of the
LNWR, one train each way daily between Birmingham and
Wolverhampton and Victoria via the new Bicester route. This
latter service had a very short life, and was withdrawn for
lack of patronage early in 1912. Although largely rendered
redundant by the opening of the underground line between
Victoria and Paddington in 1868, the GWR trains to Southall,
etc, continued to run from Victoria until 1915.

On the Chatham side were the trains of the Midland and the
Great Northern companies. The GNR started a service from
Barnet via Ludgate Hill on March 1st, 1868, and Midland
trains worked the same way from South Tottenham or Hendon from July 1st, 1875 (LCDR trains from Victoria ran on to
the Midland from June 1st, 1869, at first to Finchley Road, and
from July 1st, 1875, to Hendon). In the Brighton station, the
only foreign colours seen were those of the LNWR, which
operated to Broad Street via Willesden Junction and the West
London Railway from January 1st, 1869. This had begun as
Broad Street–Kensington on September 1st, 1867, and was diverted to Mansion House, District Railway, from February 1st,

1872. It was replaced by an irregular service between Willesden Junction and Victoria which lasted until 1917.

COMPLICATING THE APPROACHES

Before long the approaches to Victoria became more complicated. On December 1st, 1862, the LBSCR opened its cut-off line between Balham and Windmill Bridge junction, East Croydon, roughly equalizing the distance between Croydon and the two London termini. The Chatham's own approach lines, mentioned earlier, were opened in two sections, Stewarts Lane–Herne Hill on August 25th, 1862, and Herne Hill–Penge Junction (Beckenham) on July 1st, 1863. After that, the West End of London between Beckenham and Balham was reduced to the status of a local line.

With steadily increasing traffic, the narrow and tortuous approaches between Stewarts Lane and the terminus were revealed as a serious bottleneck. Sir Charles Fox, the eminent consulting engineer, was engaged to look at the problem. He produced designs for a complicated series of new lines and junctions. These included extra tracks over the river and into the station, and new high-level approach lines to the south end of the river bridge for both the LBSCR and the LCDR, enabling them to bypass the sharp curves and steep gradients of the original line from Longhedge to the river. In addition it was proposed to complete the South London line between Brixton and the new LCDR high-level line, provide new low-level lines for the LCDR from the bridge to Stewarts Lane and to link the LCDR and the LSWR (the Longhedge junction railway).

Fox's plans were adopted, and authorized by Parliament. On the two existing approach tracks between the bridge and Victoria, the broad-gauge rails were removed. An additional standard-gauge line for the LBSCR was laid alongside. For the other two companies, three new mixed-gauge and one standard-gauge track were built. As the existing tracks were between retaining walls, the work involved demolition of one of

these as well as extension of the statutory covered way to close
in all the new tracks with a roof of iron, glass and zinc, the
gables being left open to allow the smoke to escape.

On Grosvenor Bridge, the broad-gauge rails were removed
and the space used to provide a third line for the LBSCR. A
new bridge was constructed alongside, to the east of the old.
This bridge had wrought-iron arches with fixed bearings
corresponding to the earlier ones, and over the four arches between the abutments was placed a continuous deck, linking
the new and old bridges. The piers of the new bridge were
faced with Portland stone and Bramley Fall ashlar.

The bridge now had two standard-gauge and two mixed-
gauge tracks for the LCDR and GWR, and three standard-gauge
for the Brighton, the combined width now being 132 ft 3¼ ins
between parapets. Work began on February 22nd, 1865; the
first locomotive passed over on August 1st, 1866, and the new
tracks were opened for public traffic on December 20th.

Provision was made for a station at each end, each with two
island platforms, one 25 ft 10 ins wide between the LBSCR
and LCDR, and the other 12 ft 8 ins wide between the two
easternmost LCDR tracks. The northern one, known as Grosvenor Road, was opened on November 1st, 1867, for LCDR
trains. At the south end was the LBSCR station known as Battersea Park and Steamboat Pier, which had originally opened on
October 1st, 1860, as a substitute for the old Pimlico terminus.
This was now rebuilt and survived until November 1st, 1870,
when the LBSCR opened its own platforms at Grosvenor Road
(it had previously only used the one platform for ticket collection). This northern station was very largely used for collecting
tickets from up trains, but some local trains called in either
direction. The LBSCR withdrew its services from it from April
1st, 1907, and these windswept inhospitable platforms were
finally abandoned from October 1st, 1911, when the LCDR
also withdrew. Thereafter tickets were collected at Victoria or
Herne Hill.

The LCDR high-level line, 1 mile long, with three tracks,

Approaches to Victoria: A, Battersea Park Road 1867-1916. B, Battersea Park and Steamboat Pier, 1860-70. C, Opened 1870. LBSCR side closed 1907; LCDR side closed 1911. D, LCDR side closed 1916. E, Wandsworth Road Goods (Midland). F, Falcon Lane Goods (LNWR)

mainly on a brick viaduct, was opened on January 1st, 1867, between Battersea Pier junction at the south end of the river bridge and Wandsworth Road. It had a ruling gradient of 1 in 120 and a minimum curve of 20 chains and crossed over the LSWR just west of the original underline crossing of the WEL & CPR. The 1¼-mile LBSCR line was also mainly on a brick viaduct, with three tracks, one fast up, one local up and one down. It crossed the LSWR main line on a lattice girder bridge with a central span of 149 ft supported on 3-ft 6-in diameter cast-iron columns 14 ft 6 ins high. This bridge offered a fine railscape towards Clapham Junction as it crossed the Waterloo lines at an angle of fifty-one degrees. A double-track branch from just north-west of Wandsworth Road linked the LBSCR high-level line with the South London line, crossing the LSWR on a separate 120-ft-span bridge. The LBSCR new line between the river bridge and Wandsworth Road came into use on May 1st, 1867, and the remainder, from York Road Station (now Battersea Park) to Pouparts junction (just east of Clapham Junction) on December 1st. The year 1867 also saw the completion of the South London line, enabling a service to be worked from May 1st between Victoria and London Bridge through the densely populated inner areas of south London.

From the front, the original Victoria stations presented a shabby and unworthy appearance to the arriving passenger. Exhausted by the effort of reaching the West End and building their train sheds, neither the Brighton nor the Chatham had bothered to give any architectural treatment to the northern frontage and the ends of the train sheds were closed off with 'untidy wooden structures ... in appearance more in keeping with those of some new town of mushroom growth in the wilds of Canada or Australia than with that of the leading railway stations of London'.[4]

Of the two, the Chatham's buildings were by far the worst. It is true that the main office block was round the corner, off Wilton Road, but most people got their first impression of the station coming in from Victoria Street. Facing them, and along Wilton Road, were a shoddy pair of wooden shacks cringing under a wooden hoarding, which though huge, left the tops of the train sheds exposed. This hoarding and other notices exhibited the company's title in full, together with a confusion of destinations ranging from the High Level station at Crystal Palace to Paris and India. Above the central doorway, a modest board announced with an air of surprise, *Great Western Railway Trains From and To this Station*. The only other features of any prominence were a motley collection of homely chimney stacks topped by giant tin flue extensions. Next door, the Brighton concealed its low frontage building behind a generous canopy of iron and glass.

Inside, the Brighton's premises were not inelegant, though the Fenian Brotherhood had done its best to wreck them in February 1884 by leaving a home-made dynamite bomb in a

Gladstone bag. The explosion demolished the cloakroom and ticket office, but the police reacted in time to whisk away similar deposits at Paddington and Charing Cross.

Outside the disreputable frontages was a large cab yard shared by both companies, bounded by a 5-ft-high fence of wooden palings. On the northern side of this yard, between it and Victoria Street, was the District Railway station opened on December 24th, 1868, connected to both main-line stations by a subway beneath the yard, opened on August 12th, 1878.

In the 1890s, the Brighton company was enjoying a period of mild prosperity, its dividend on ordinary stock fluctuating between six and seven per cent. The directors decided that the time had come to widen the approach tracks to Victoria and build a station large enough to meet all requirements. Powers for the quadrupling of the Clapham Junction–Victoria line were obtained in 1898 and the work was completed in July 1907, including two more tracks on the upstream side of Grosvenor Bridge, making a total of nine and increasing the width to 178 ft. Each mild steel arch of the new river bridge supported its own deck. Grosvenor Bridge now consisted of what were in effect three separate bridges on common piers with differing foundations, and arches of similar profile but disparate design.

LENGTHWAYS STRETCH FOR THE BRIGHTON

At Victoria, the first steps towards reconstruction of the Brighton station were taken in 1892–9 when the houses on the west side, in Buckingham Palace Road, were purchased, together with the freehold of the Grosvenor Hotel. This last move was undertaken with existing statutory powers as the owners of the hotel proved un-cooperative in disposing of houses owned by them. The hotel was then let to Gordon Hotels Ltd for fifty years, and the redecorated and refurnished building was opened under the new management on December 10th, 1900. As part of the arrangements, the LBSCR promised

that a new 150-room wing for the hotel would be incorporated
in the frontage of the rebuilt station.

Although the purchased property in Buckingham Palace
Road provided another 90-ft width between Eccleston Bridge
and the hotel, and more room could be obtained south of
Eccleston Bridge by taking in the remains of the canal, this
was not in itself adequate for the size of station required.
Hemmed in as it was by Buckingham Palace Road on the one
hand, and the Chatham's premises on the other, the station
could not expand sideways, so Charles L. Morgan, the LBSCR
chief engineer, drew up plans for lengthening, as the only
practicable alternative. His proposals envisaged two stations
end to end, the North and the South, the latter between
Eccleston and Elizabeth Bridges. In its final form, the 1860
station had ten roads with eight platform faces. The new one
was to have thirteen roads and nine faces.

The necessary powers were obtained in 1899 and work began
in 1901. After the old roof had been removed, five new louvred
ridge roofs were erected side by side, parallel with the tracks,
and another similar set was to cover the South station. Trusses
of 50-ft span rested on trussed girders spanning 125 ft and
118 ft, supported on cast-iron columns 1 ft 6 ins in diameter.
The ridges of the roof were 64 ft above rail level.

Across the front, a nine-storey hotel block was built, 240 ft
long and 70 ft wide, set back 56 ft from the old building line.
This confident chunk of Edwardian monumental was in the
so-called free Renaissance style and blended well enough with
the Grosvenor. Its red-brick frontage, with Portland stone
dressings, was dominated by an illuminated clock flanked by
recumbent figures. Below, over the cab yard, an ugly iron and
glass canopy supported on iron pillars displayed on its fascia the
names of the principal towns served.

The first part of the rebuilt station was opened on June
10th, 1906; the five western platforms and a new cab exit
to Buckingham Palace Road followed on February 10th, 1907.
The Grosvenor Hotel annexe in the frontage block was finished

by the end of 1907, and the reconstruction was finally completed in 1908 when the four eastern platforms came into use, with a formal opening on July 1st.

Passing from the front cab yard, the passenger entered an impressive booking-hall, 120 ft long and 70 ft wide, with a square-shaped ticket office panelled in dark fumed oak. The hall was tiled in pale green and off-white, with small *art nouveau* motifs in green and gold mosaic.

Today it is utterly spoiled by a self-defeating muddle of advertisements, a lining of telephone booths, overall dirt and unsuitable lighting. On the east wall was the entrance to the main waiting-room, flanked by tile maps of the main line and suburban networks of the LBSCR (parts of these can still be seen today above the telephone boxes, including the long-lost route into Liverpool Street). Along the west wall was the excess luggage and baggage registration office with two lifts to the luggage subway which connected Platforms 1 to 7 (now 9 to 15). A jeweller's shop now occupies the site of the office.

Openings either side of the ticket office led out to a 25,000-sq-ft concourse across the heads of Platforms 1 to 7, alongside the top end of 7, and across the ends of 8 and 9. Facing the passenger, opposite the ends of Platforms 4 and 5, was a departure indicator of Howell's patent, displaying departure times, platforms and stopping stations of eighteen trains simultaneously. Replaced by a larger one of the 'card and key' type in 1927 (another was then erected on the Eastern Section side), this indicator went to Brighton, where it is still in use. Behind the indicator was a telegraph office, which backed on to the entrance to the underground 'gentlemen's court', with its hairdressing saloon.

This cramped little telegraph office became a post office on October 2nd, 1911, one of the first on a London terminus. Although all London termini had telegraph offices from which the public could dispatch private telegrams, and the telegraph office at Kings Cross sold stamps, there was at this time only one post office on a terminus – at London Bridge. In 1910 the

The Brighton station 1908. From the Railway Magazine, October 1960

Post Office authorities approached the railway companies about
the operation of post offices on their terminal stations. The
LBSCR and the GER responded, and post offices were subsequently opened at Victoria and Liverpool Street. Later, this
facility was also provided at Euston, Paddington and Waterloo.
At Paddington a fully equipped Crown post office was opened
on Platform 1 on May 22nd, 1935, said to be the first such on
any British railway station. The Victoria post office was closed
from November 1st, 1967, but new facilities may be provided
when the station is rebuilt.

In the buildings around the concourse were a tea room, a
buffet, waiting-rooms, a chemist shop, cloakroom and a parcels
office, the last three against the ground floor of the old Grosvenor Hotel, which had an entrance from the concourse.
Alongside the eastern wall, at the head of Platform 1, was a
large suburban booking-office and a refreshment room. Each
platform was entered through a gate with a pretty arch in cast-
iron displaying the platform number in its 'keystone'.

Middle roads, with suitably placed crossovers were provided
between the outer halves of Platforms 2 and 3, 4 and 5, 6 and
7, and throughout 8 and 9. These roads could be used to allow
trains from the North station to overtake those standing in the
South station; in other words, one long platform face could
take two trains at the same time. Platform 1 could also be used
in two sections. Thus the combined North and South stations
could accommodate up to eighteen trains at a time. The usual
method of working was as follows: the first train would run
into the North station, the second into the South, at the same
platform; then the engine from train two backed on to train
one, taking it out via the middle road; lastly the engine of train
one followed over the middle road, reversed, backed on to
train two, pushing it into the North station and leaving with
it via the middle road whilst train three was already unloading
in the South station; and so on. In the slack hours the South
station was not normally used for passengers. Before long train
lengths became such that they restricted the use which could

be made of these facilities, but it was and is still possible for
two eight-car electric trains to use the same platform face. At
Eccleston Bridge, an interchange footway between the platforms of the South station provided access to exits to the
bridge.

Platforms 1 to 4 (now 9 to 12) were allocated to local trains,
5 and 6 (13 and 14) were used by main-line departures, 7 and
8 (15 and 16) for main-line arrivals, and No 9 was used as an
excursion platform. Platform 7, the longest in the station, together with 8, its opposite face, extended some 400 ft south of
Elizabeth Bridge, and Platform 9 also extended some way
beyond the bridge. A cab road ran into the station from
Buckingham Palace Road just south of the Grosvenor Hotel,
across the heads of Platforms 8 and 9 (16 and 17), and then
through the station to Elizabeth Bridge between Platforms
7 and 8 (15 and 16).

Coaling stages were built at the ends of Platforms 3 and 4
(11 and 12) and 5 and 6 (13 and 14). Two loading docks were
available at the outer ends of 7 and 8 (15 and 16). Beyond the
station, there were five tracks; down local on the east, up local,
down main, up main and a reversible carriage road. The latter
was originally worked by Sykes' non-token instruments. At the
south end of the station, on the west side, were locomotive and
carriage sidings and a 60-ft turntable.

Outside, along Buckingham Palace Road, Parliament had
insisted upon an ornamental screen wall. This was duly
designed by C. L. Morgan and constructed of Portland stone,
and red hand-made sand-faced Reading bricks. The niches in
this wall still await their busts (who is worthy?). The cab
entrance at the north end of this wall took the form of a
massive archway, providing a suitably dignified welcome for
royalty using the station. A curious consequence of the rebuilding were the artificial humps made in Buckingham Palace Road
to meet the increased height of the Eccleston and Elizabeth
Bridges.

In size the new station was impressive; 320 ft wide, and

Ludgate Hill LCDR in 1865. A train is seen on the viaduct to the City Widened Lines at the extreme left. An engraving for the *Illustrated London News*

Ludgate Hill LCDR, c 1898. LCDR 0-4-4T 216 is entering with an up Local train

Holborn Viaduct Station and hotel in 1877. Building work is still not quite complete

Bricklayers Arms. This drawing by S. Sly for the *Illustrated London News*, contains a number of errors and renders the building more impressive than it was in reality

The old Waterloo, c 1900, looking across the concourse of the Windsor and North stations, Platforms 6-10

The new Waterloo, Platforms 1-4 on May 3rd, 1912. Main-line trains are using the suburban platforms during reconstruction. The cab yard and buildings of the old Central station are on the extreme right, background

Charing Cross signals and river bridge, c 1864

Charing Cross interior in 1864. The cab ramp from Villiers Street is seen in the centre

Interior of the old LBSCR Victoria Station, looking outwards

Continental splendour: the rebuilt SECR frontage at Victoria, c 1910.
Note the legend 'GREAT WESTERN RAILWAY' over the arch, the
spot where so many last goodbyes were said in the First World War

Interior of Paddington Station, 1843. This was the first 'temporary' station erected by Bishop's Bridge, and was replaced by the present Paddington Station in 1854

Brunel's Paddington, looking through the 'transept' from the balcony above Platform 1, July 31st, 1959

Paddington, looking outwards from the old footbridge over Platforms 3–7. The date is July 1912 and special trains for the Royal Garden Party at Windsor are drawn up at Platforms 4 and 5

Opening ceremonies at Marylebone, March 9th, 1899

Marylebone exterior on August 26th, 1967. The original Baker Street and Waterloo Railway Tube Station is seen on the extreme left; the Great Central Hotel is out of view, beyond the canopy, right

1,500 ft long, its platforms together totalled $2\frac{1}{4}$ miles (it feels all of that to the passenger alighting from the end car of a train terminating in the South station). Altogether the Brighton's new Victoria covered 16 acres compared with the $8\frac{1}{2}$ of the original. It was a commodious and comfortable terminus, with a vaguely old-fashioned air. This was particularly noticeable at night, when Sugg's patent high-pressure gas lights bathed everything in a gentle glow, a feature which remained, despite the presence of electric trains, until 1927. Another backward-looking amenity (which soon fell into disuse) was a furnace room heating water for carriage footwarmers, a comfort which might be welcomed by today's commuters on those winter mornings when the Southern's electric carriage heating mysteriously goes cold.

More up to date than footwarmers and gas lighting were the electric trains, worked regularly into the new station from December 1st, 1909, and serving the South London line to London Bridge. Platforms 1 to 5 (now 9 to 13) were electrified, together with the middle roads between 3 and 4, and between 5 and 6. This was the Brighton's 'Elevated Electric', operating at 6,600-V ac, single-phase, with bow collectors and overhead wires. Following the success of the South London electrification, the Victoria–Crystal Palace (LL) via Streatham Hill service was electrified from May 12, 1911. Next came the London Bridge–Streatham Hill–Victoria and Victoria–Norwood Junction trains, on June 1st, 1912. The overhead-wire electric system was extended by the Southern Railway on April 1st, 1925, from Balham to Coulsdon North, and to Sutton via Selhurst.

SECR REBUILDING

Not to be outdone, the SECR decided that the time had come to replace its ugly and tatty frontage buildings with something rather better. In 1907 the wooden huts were demolished, and in their stead a handsome four-storey masonry block rose up.

The style was French Second Empire, with a maritime flavour bestowed by four mermaids contemplating their well-parted bosoms. Finished in 1908, the new block projected a little from the Brighton's establishment, but was rather dwarfed by it. The main feature of the 170-ft frontage was a large central archway for the cab road, flanked by an elegant canopy (since removed) which formed a pleasing contrast to that of the Brighton station.

To the west of the cab arch was a third-class refreshment room, to the east, a first-class refreshment room and tea room. Upstairs, on the east, was the Pillar Hall Restaurant (now appropriately renamed *The Chatham*). All these establishments were originally managed by J. Lyons & Co. The new building, which extended for 200 ft down Wilton Road until it met the old station block, contained on the ground floor a cloakroom, lavatories and yet another refreshment room.

Under its double arch roof, the remainder of the Chatham station was virtually unchanged. In the old building off Wilton Road were the booking-hall, baggage office and waiting-rooms, including accommodation for royalty. This royal suite was furnished in white and gold and decorated with pictures of various royalty, no doubt discreetly reduced in number during the violent years after August 1914.

These waiting-rooms were conveniently situated alongside the main departure platform, which was at the other side of the booking-hall block. At this time (1908) the Chatham station had ten platform faces, arranged as follows:

wall of the Brighton station
single track
Platform 1 (main-line arrivals)
cab road
Platform 2 (main-line arrivals)
single track
Platform 3 (short)
single track
Platform 4 (short)
three tracks

Platform 6 (short)
Platform 7 (short)
three tracks
Platform 9 (main-line departures)
Platform 10 (a short opposite face to 9 at outer end)
single track (alongside 10)

Between the station and the river were one down line, two
up lines, and a siding, with an empty carriage or engine road
over the bridge on the down side. On the eastern side of these
Chatham approach tracks were carriage sidings (roofed over
by the SR in 1928) and a 54-ft 10-in engine turntable.

Victoria had handled the LCDR boat trains since they had
started in the summer of 1862, but it was not until the rebuilding of the Chatham station in 1907–8 that the passenger
amenities compared with those available at the rival establishments of Charing Cross and Cannon Street. After the reconstruction, Victoria, with its more spacious platforms and less
intrusive local traffic, took pride of place as a Continental
terminus. There were not only the boat trains connecting with
the Dover–Calais and Dover–Ostend services, but also
those of the Gravesend–Rotterdam route, and in the Brighton
station, those for the Newhaven–Dieppe.

The canopies of the new Chatham station proudly
announced: SHORTEST AND QUICKEST ROUTE TO
PARIS & THE CONTINENT SEA PASSAGE ONE
HOUR. The Brighton's canopy countered: TO PARIS AND
THE CONTINENT VIA NEWHAVEN AND DIEPPE
SHORTEST AND CHEAPEST ROUTE, but the LBSCR's
Continental service was little more than a side-show; the three
and a half hours' sea journey made it less popular than the
Dover and Folkestone routes – the little packet boats of the
cross-Channel services were often tossed about violently and
most people preferred to get that part of the journey over as
quickly as possible, even if it did cost a little more to do so.

As elsewhere, the cross-London services working into
Victoria succumbed to the improvements in street and under-

ground railway transport. The GNR trains, the first to go, were withdrawn from October 1st, 1907; the Midland workings went at the end of June 1908, and those of the LNWR in September 1917. (Until about 1939, the LMSR ran trains into the Central Section station at Victoria, but did not carry passengers beyond the West London line, such trains as continued to Victoria being for parcels traffic only.) Although they remained part lessees of the Chatham station until 1933, the GWR ran no regular services from Victoria after March 21st, 1915. The SECR Victoria–Holborn Viaduct trains ceased in April 1916, but the South London electrics continued to serve stations between Victoria and Brixton.

Victoria was worked very hard during the First World War. Troop traffic was heavy, as it was the main London station for leave and draft movements to and from France. Special trains between Victoria and Folkestone for leave traffic began in November 1914, increasing until there were as many as twelve a day each way. Later there were also two daily leave trains between Victoria and Dover. By October 1918 some 7,500 men were travelling each way daily to and from leave. At the cab arch of the Chatham station, almost every day, pathetic little groups of soldiers, families and girlfriends could be seen making their farewells (relatives and friends were not allowed on the platforms for fear this might delay departures). Many, too many, of these men were never to see London again. The scene was captured for all time by F. J. Mortimer's superb photograph, 'The Gate of Goodbye'.

Much was done for the welfare of the soldiers continuously moving through the station. From February 15th, 1915, to June 30th, 1919, a free buffet, staffed by lady voluntary workers, served up to 4,000 men every twenty-four hours, never shutting its doors. Voluntary bodies in profusion, from the YMCA to the Ladies' Vigilance Society (was the vigilance for the ladies or the men?) attended upon the sad procession of khaki to and from the carnage across the Channel. Money-exchange offices, manned by off-duty booking clerks, were set up along the arrival platform to change francs to pounds as soon as the men jumped off the trains.

Outward mails for the Western Front were also dealt with at the Chatham station, a train of some thirty vans remaining in the station from 11 AM to 11 PM whilst letters and parcels were loaded. Inward mail from France was received at Charing Cross and Cannon Street as well as Victoria.

The only air-raid damage to the terminus was a shell case which returned to earth through the roof, but on October 1st, 1917, about 100 ft of Grosvenor Bridge was set alight when an anti-aircraft shell pierced a gas main under the old ticket platform.

At the outbreak of war, Dover was taken over by the military, and all SECR Continental boat trains for the remaining Folkestone service ran from Victoria from November 15th, 1914. On October 14th, the Germans were in Ostend, bringing to an abrupt end the service to that port. Civil traffic between Folkestone and Boulogne was stopped from November 29th, 1915, but the Dieppe service, which had been diverted from Newhaven on August 12th, 1914, continued until April 13th, 1916. Any civilian passengers for France then had to travel via Waterloo–Southampton–Le Havre.

The war over, memorial plaques were erected on the north walls of both stations. That on the Chatham side listed names of 556 SECR men lost. In contrast, the much larger Southern Railway lost 626 employees in 1939-45.

CONTINENTAL CONCENTRATION

From January 8th, 1920, as mentioned in the Charing Cross chapter, all SECR French services were concentrated at Victoria. There was not only more room than at Charing Cross and Cannon Street, but the locomotive and empty carriage facilities were much closer to the platforms. It is true that the approaches to Victoria were bedevilled with heavy gradients and speed restrictions, but the other factors were more important. The Dover–Ostend service was restored on January 18th, 1919, when the public were able to use the new Marine station at Dover for the first time. Civilian traffic between Folkestone and Boulogne was re-established on February 3rd, 1919, and a Victoria–Dover–Calais–Paris service began on January 8th, 1920. The Newhaven boat trains resumed on June 1st, 1919, with connexions to Paris from July 15th, and a night service from March 1st, 1920. Enterprising ex-servicemen had begun the first London–Paris air services in August 1919, but as yet they offered no serious competition to the rail-served Channel ferries.

During 1921, the SECR altered the main arrival Platforms 1 and 2 (now 8 and 7), lengthening them to 764 ft and 735 ft. A year later, the stumpy little Platforms 3 and 4, 380 ft and 410 ft long and only 12 ft wide at maximum, were demolished and replaced by a new platform numbered 3 and 4, 550 ft long and 37 ft wide. The Chatham side platforms were then renumbered, and across the station from west to east the arrangement became:

single track against the wall of the Brighton station
Platform 1
cab road
Platform 2
two tracks
Platform 3
Platform 4
two tracks
Platform 5
Platform 6
three tracks
Platform 8
Platform 9 (opposite face, outer end)
single track (alongside platform 9)

Under the Railways Act, 1921, the Victoria Station & Pimlico Railway Company was taken over by the newly-

formed Southern Railway, which became the sole owner of
both Victorias, apart from the continuing rights of the GWR.
The Chatham side was then known as 'Victoria (Eastern
Section)' and the remainder as 'Victoria (Central Section)',
but the Southern Railway soon took steps to integrate the two
stations.

Early in 1924 a start was made by breaking open a hole in
the wall between the two termini. At the same time one stationmaster was appointed to look after both stations, with their
combined staff of 1,016. A second hole was made to connect the
two concourses, later in the year. This necessitated the setting
back of Platform 1, Eastern Section (now 8) by 30 ft. The concourse was then enlarged by bringing all the other platform
ends into line with No 1, and extra width was given to 6 and
8 (now 2 and 3) by eliminating the middle road between them.
A cab incline was constructed to Eccleston Bridge to remove
the congestion caused at the arch by two directions of vehicular
traffic. This work was completed in 1925, and on September
21st, the platforms of both sides of Victoria were renumbered
east to west in sequence, 1 to 17.

Then the early enthusiasm waned, and life went on much the
same as before, as if the two separate companies still existed.
Until 1938 there was no running connexion between the two
sides of the station (a transfer siding had existed for many
years between the outer ends of Platforms 8 and 9 near
Eccleston Bridge). In that year, a direct link was laid between
the Eastern Section and the Central Section down local line.

The hiatus in coordination at Victoria may have been due
in part to the Southern Railway's preoccupation with electrification. In 1926 it was announced that the third-rail 600-V dc
system would be adopted as standard, and in the next decade,
the SR filled Victoria with electric trains. The station's first
regular third-rail service started on July 12th, 1925, when
trains for Herne Hill and Orpington began to use Platforms
3, 4 and 6 on the Eastern side. 'Elevated Electrics' on the
South London line were replaced by dc trains on June 17th,

1928, and those on the Crystal Palace (LL) service on March 3rd, 1929 (the third-rail trains worked beyond Crystal Palace to West Croydon and Beckenham Junction). Also on March 3rd, 1929, electric services were started between Victoria and Epsom via Mitcham junction.

The last overhead-wire electric train left Victoria for Coulsdon North at 12.30 AM on Sunday, September 22nd, 1929; third-rail trains had begun to take over the service on the previous day. By the summer of 1930, the busiest evening peak hour saw twenty-six electric departures from Victoria.

Main-line electric services to Brighton and Worthing began on January 1st, 1933 (some electric trains had run to Reigate and Three Bridges since July 17th, 1932). There were four trains every hour throughout the day down the main line from Victoria, including a train every hour, on the hour, reaching Brighton in fifty-eight minutes non-stop. Electric trains between Victoria and Eastbourne, Hastings and Seaford started on July 7th, 1935, and Littlehampton, Bognor and Portsmouth were served, via Horsham, from July 3rd, 1938. The last electrification before the outbreak of war was that to Gillingham and Maidstone East, from July 2nd, 1939. Electrification almost doubled the rush-hour traffic at Victoria: the number of passengers arriving in the busiest hour rose from 10,200 in 1927 to 17,200 in 1937 (today it is over 35,000).

Until 1930 the customs facilities on Platform 8, the main Continental arrival platform, were somewhat primitive, passengers being obliged to wait in the open before examination. In that year, the whole of the platform was roofed over, and heated accommodation provided for the examination area. Other changes of the 1930s included a news cinema similar to that at Waterloo. Erected over the cab gateway by Platform 17, this was opened on September 12th, 1933.

An increasing clientele of newly rich, and, later, some competition from air transport, led to improvements in the Continental services. Pullman cars had been included in these trains since 1910, and in 1924 an all-Pullman boat train was started

Victoria Station in January 1960. From the Railway Magazine, October 1960

between Victoria and Dover. Four years later, on May 15th, 1929, the all-Pullman 'Golden Arrow' was inaugurated, connecting with the Calais–Paris Pullman of the same name which had run since September 12th, 1926. A train of sleeping cars, working between Victoria and Paris Nord via the Dover–Dunkerque train ferry, the 'Night Ferry', was introduced on October 14th, 1936. Its cars, of European pattern, and owned by the International Sleeping Car Company, imparted a distinctly cosmopolitan air to Victoria.

The remaining changes of note in the inter-war years relate to Victoria's associations with other forms of transport. Motor buses had followed their horse-drawn predecessors into the large cab yard, although they had not been allowed in until about 1909. The main user was the London General Omnibus Company, which set up a pioneer bus station in the yard in July 1926. In the following year, on August 28th, this was embellished with a control tower of steel and glass, a kind of bus signal box, from which the controller had a clear view of all five 'platforms' as he signalled the movements of the twenty-one terminating services by means of lights. This bus station still survives, but the control tower was removed in 1950 (the light signals had been out of use for some time before that).

Imperial Airways inaugurated its London terminal in Buckingham Palace Road, near Ebury Bridge, in 1939. In connexion with this, the SR worked Flying Boat trains to the Empire Air Base at Southampton. The first of this new type of boat train left Victoria on June 6th, 1939, and consisted of a composite coach, a Pullman car and a van drawn by a Drummond 4–4–0 (a distinctly old-fashioned-looking engine for such a train, but the weight restrictions of the route precluded the use of heavier modern locomotives). After spending the night at the South Western Hotel, Southampton, the passengers left early the next morning for the Far East, Australia, the Middle East and Africa. These specials went out from Victoria via Balham, Tooting and Wimbledon, but in the up direction ran via East Putney, Clapham Junction (Windsor side), and Longhedge junction. During the Second World War, 'Air Specials' left Victoria in the evening to connect with air services from Poole Harbour to Baltimore (USA) and for Bournemouth West for other flights from Hurn. The latter were the first trains ever to run between Victoria and Bournemouth.

Victoria had its share of bombs in 1940 and 1941, but although closed through damage to the approaches, it was not itself put out of action. On September 15th, 1940, a shot-up Dornier bomber plane crashed against the Eastern Section after its crew had parachuted into Kennington Oval. A flying bomb hit the station on June 27th, 1944, removing part of the offices alongside the Eastern Section departure platform, and damaging the booking-office.

As the train ferries were required for military use, the 'Night Ferry' ceased to run on September 4th, 1939, the cars running back to France empty from Victoria on that day. Boat trains from Victoria were rudely interrupted in May 1940 following the German invasion of northern France. After D Day, military traffic began to move across the short sea routes again, and from January 1945 there were daily leave trains, with buffets in converted Pullmans, between Victoria and Folkestone and Dover. Later in 1945, limited public facilities were made available via Newhaven–Dieppe, and a Folkestone–Ostend service started in October. Regular working of the Victoria–Dover–Calais–Paris route, with connexions to other European destinations, began again on April 15th, 1946, with a daily boat train and a restored 'Golden Arrow'. From the same day, Newhaven boat trains used the Eastern side of Victoria, crossing over to the Central Section local line just outside the station, and to the down main at Balham. The Victoria–Folkestone–Boulogne–Paris service started again in the summer of 1947, and the 'Night Ferry' came back on the following December 14th.

POST-WAR SCHEMES

These post-war Continental services soon built up a healthy traffic, although the number of destinations bookable from London was at first a mere 173 compared with over 400 in 1939. A new Continental inquiry, reservation and ticket office, with a staff of forty-four, was opened on June 14th, 1948. This was on the opposite side of the road to the Eastern Section booking-office block. It underwent considerable internal refurbishing and rearrangement in 1962 after an O & M study.

The Eastern Section booking-hall was reconstructed and opened in its new form on February 5th, 1951. The booking-office had six large windows on to the northern side of the hall, and was fitted with four Bellmatic ticket-issuing machines. With its travertine wall linings and terrazzo floor, the hall looked very much like a hangover from the 1930s, despite decorative attempts with white and orange cold cathode lighting tubes formed into squares and circles on the ceiling. It is already a period piece. A large list of station names over the booking windows contains many deletions of stations subsequently closed, forming an interesting guessing game for the railway student finding himself at Victoria with a few minutes to spare.

Other post-war changes on this side of the station included the 1960 extension of Platforms 1 to 8 in connexion with the Kent coast electrification and the operation of fourteen-car electric boat trains. Lavatories and powder rooms to a new standard of luxury, with a 500 per cent increase in entrance fee, were added to the Eastern side in 1965.

The platform extensions caused the reconstruction in single span of Eccleston Bridge, which crossed the outer ends of the lengthened 1 to 7. The little-used southern part of Platform 9 disappeared in the consequent slewing over of tracks. At the same time, the siding alongside the Eastern Section tracks between the station and the river was converted to a running line, giving four roads between Victoria Eastern and Battersea Pier junction. Another of the 1960 works was the electrification of the Eastern Section carriage sidings and the conversion of the carriage shed at Grosvenor Bridge to house the new electric trains. Full electric working to Sheerness, Margate, Ramsgate and Dover via Canterbury began on June 15th, 1959. The 'Night Ferry', which since June 3rd, 1957, had also included a Brussels portion, was hauled by electric locomotives from June 8th.

At the height of the London office-building boom of the 1950s, a number of schemes were put forward for the 're-development' of Victoria Station, which formed an attractive site for such proposals owing to its excellent transport facilities and proximity to the air terminal. No fewer than five separate plans were put to the LCC in 1956, involving the construction of offices, hotels, air terminals and helicopter stations over or alongside the railway station. At that time any scheme for using railway property for commercial purposes would have required special legislation, but in view of the profits to be made, this was regarded as a minor hurdle. All these schemes were in the event held over, as the planning authorities had doubts about increasing the road traffic congestion in the area. In 1963, exercising its new freedom to develop its property on a commercial basis, the British Railways Board produced its own plan for an office block over a reconstructed station. This too was rejected.

In the face of this lack of encouragement by the authorities, BR allowed a notable piece of private development within the existing station. On May 1st, 1962, London's first rail-air terminal opened at Victoria. Designed by Clive Pascall, the British United Airways terminal was a steel and glass building on a concrete base, held 15 ft above the cab road at the north end of Platforms 15 and 16 by reinforced concrete stilts. It was some 13,400 sq ft in area and contained an air-ticket office, passenger lounge and buffet, reached by an escalator and staircases from the ground level. Outgoing passengers used a light footbridge spanning Platforms 11 to 16 to reach trains for London Airport (Gatwick), forty minutes journey down the Brighton main line. (London Airport [Gatwick] was opened in 1958, with its own station on the Brighton main line. There were special train services on a modest scale from May 28th, 1958.) Trains calling at Gatwick now leave every fifteen minutes throughout the day and in the summer an hourly non-stop all-night service is provided. In 1962 some 40,000 BUA passengers used the rail-air facility and by 1965 this number had increased to 230,000. Another 450,000 users were Servicemen and passengers for other air lines using Gatwick. These numbers included those travelling by the unique rail-air-rail 'Silver Arrow' service from Victoria to Paris Nord in four and a quarter hours, via Gatwick and le Touquet.

In 1963 the former Imperial Airways terminal, now operated by the British Overseas Airways Corporation, was extended by the construction of an eight-storey block on a 3-ft concrete slab over the ends of Platforms 15 to 17, incorporating a new cab exit from Platforms 15 and 16. Rail connexions for BOAC passengers must await the construction of the authorized branch line to serve London Airport (Heathrow).

As at the other London termini, steam traction gradually disappeared in the early 1960s. With the electrification of the Continental station at Newhaven Harbour, most Newhaven boat trains were electrically hauled from May 15th, 1949. It was the Kent coast electrification that removed most of the remaining steam locomotives from Victoria, but some lingered on until 1963 when diesel-electric multiple-units and locomotives completely took over the services on the Oxted, Uckfield and East Grinstead lines.

Although Grosvenor Bridge had been strengthened in 1920 by reinforcement of the steelwork and the construction of relieving arches, it was in poor condition by the 1960s, and beyond economic repair. A decision was taken to rebuild it to carry twice the load, by inserting new sections over a period of some four years whilst the traffic of around 1,000 trains a day continued with virtually no interruption. Work began in mid-1963. The new bridge, completed late in 1967, consisted of ten separate arch sections in each of the four 164-ft spans, each arch carrying one line of rails, making ten tracks in all, one more than the old bridge. The approach spans were 70 ft and 64 ft 4 ins, the new piers, larger than the old, 215 ft by 45 ft.

During the greater part of the rebuilding period, only one track was out of action at a time, but for a while two tracks on the Eastern Section side were closed. After the new pier and abutment foundations had been prepared, the prefabricated, all-welded half-arch and single-track deck units were towed up the river in barges, lifted into position and connected up to the existing tracks until all the old work was replaced.

The marked difference in the traffic patterns of the two sides of Victoria has already been noted. In the slack hours of 1967, the Central side had twenty-three trains an hour, including one diesel-electric, rising to thirty-four (three diesel) in the peak; comparable totals on the Eastern side were six and thirteen. The Central not only has four main routes compared with the Eastern's one, but the outlets for the suburban traffic are much greater on the former LBSCR lines. Brighton is Britain's largest coastal resort, generating an all-year-round traffic, which is fostered by the excellent electric-train service, including the all-Pullman 'Brighton Belles'. The Kent coast and boat-train traffic of the Eastern Section is much more seasonal in character; in 1967 there were eleven booked Kent coast trains between nine and twelve noon on an August Saturday, compared with three on a winter Saturday. In the same periods, booked boat trains were eleven and six. This imbalance has survived overlong, and may soon be a thing of the past.

With the rebuilding of its cross-river approaches completed, Victoria awaits reconstruction as a combined terminal for rail, air and cross-Channel traffic, including the Channel Tunnel rail service. Much depends on the rail link between Victoria and London Airport (Heathrow), which has been talked about, planned and re-planned since 1948, but became an urgent necessity with the pending arrival of high-capacity civil aircraft (the so-called jumbo-jets). Parliament approved the rail connexion in 1967, including junctions between the former LBSCR lines and the Windsor fast lines just south of Battersea Park Station.

It is intended that the rebuilt Victoria shall absorb a greater share of the West End traffic from the south-east suburban and outer areas, including that from planned building development at Kidbrooke and the new town of Thamesmead on the Plumstead and Erith marshes. To achieve this it will be necessary to construct some new connexions in the Peckham Rye–Nunhead area.

There are to be twenty platforms, handling international, airport and main-line trains on the west side and suburban traffic on the east. On Grosvenor Bridge, the western pair of tracks will take the Heathrow airport trains; the second pair the Brighton line fasts; the third the fast trains on the Eastern Section, including those using the Channel Tunnel; the fourth, the Central Section slow trains; and the fifth, or easternmost pair, the Eastern Section suburban trains.

A development study, commissioned by the Greater London Council, Westminster City Council, British Railways and London Transport has prepared an outline plan for the new terminus, which will include a 1,000 bed hotel and airways offices. Meanwhile, the station's value as a West End terminus was much enhanced by the opening on March 7th, 1969, of the Victoria Line Tube railway, providing a direct link to the heart of the West End and the Northern termini, with connexions to all other Underground lines.

The new Victoria, with trains to European capitals, including through sleeping cars to Moscow and with its continual flow of air passengers arriving and departing for journeys all over the world, presents an exciting prospect. Night and day,

it will be one of the busiest and most interesting railway stations
anywhere.

SIGNALLING AND ACCIDENTS

The original stations of 1860–62 were signalled from a small
platform set in the eastern wall of the covered way just south
of the passenger platforms. This twenty-three-lever frame,
which was fully open to view in its 'hole in the wall', was
completed in 1861, and operated on the interlocking system
patented by John Saxby in 1860. There were separate levels
for points and signals, the locking between them being set in
motion immediately one was moved; no releasing could be
effected until the determining lever had been moved through
its entire stroke. The levers themselves acted directly on swing-
ing pieces, pushing them to one side; these pieces were connected by bars to others forming obstacles in the path of any
lever it was necessary to lock. The box also controlled some
curious route-indicating signals suspended from the roof of
the covered way nearby, with two, four and six spectacle
glasses set in a revolving disc.

All the signalling was rearranged with the opening of the
additional tracks into both stations in 1866–7. There were then
five boxes, 235 levers in all, with Saxby & Farmer equipment.
The Hole in the Wall disappeared, but another of the same
design was erected on the Chatham side and remained in use,
together with the Chatham's Yard box, until 1920. When it
became necessary to adopt shunting signals on the LCDR side
the cramped accommodation in these two boxes did not allow
the installation of additional levers. W. R. Sykes' electric
shunting signals were therefore adopted in November 1883.
These were worked by small switches in the Yard box. In 1887
a similar set was provided for the Hole in the Wall box. These
signals had a circular disc, red at front, white at back, and
were operated by energizing an electric magnet. As the disc
turned on edge it moved a small frame carrying the coloured

glass between the gas jet and a bull's-eye.

A complete resignalling of the Brighton side was undertaken in connexion with the rebuilding of 1908. Sykes' electromechanical system was chosen, with lower-quadrant semaphore and banner signals controlled and worked electronically and interlocked with the points, which, together with the bolts, were operated mechanically by normal-type levers in one long frame. The small 'slides' for the electrically-operated signals were placed above the point levers, providing a useful saving in cabin space. The banner signals controlled not only the shunting and siding movements, but also some of the running lines. They consisted of a centrally-pivoted semaphore arm of red cloth on a wire frame, enclosed in a drum-type case with clear glass in front and white glass behind, illuminated by a gas jet at the back. Indications were given in the upper and lower quadrants, to the right as well as to the left, thus distinguishing a variety of movements.

Extensive use was made of Sykes' electric fouling bars, indicated by plates carrying a blue star on a white ground. There was also an interesting arrangement of signal lamps over the platform barriers. The lamp over each gate was covered by a shade which contained a purple and a red bull's-eye, the latter showing along the platform as long as the barrier was open. When the collector closed the barrier, he turned the shade to show the purple light along the platform as an indication that the train could be started if the starting signal was off. The shade was rotated through the necessary quarter-circle by a cord working around the bull's-eye and reaching to hand level at the gate. This 'passenger signalling' system gradually fell into disuse.

In the station yard were three boxes, the most important of which was South box, with 106 mechanical levers and 163 slides. This was between the dock lines at the south end of Platforms 7 and 8 (now 15 and 16) and was 60 ft long by 14 ft wide. North box, 28 ft long and only 10 ft wide, was centrally sited on Platforms 5 and 6 (now 13 and 14), near Eccleston

Bridge. It had twenty-three mechanical levers and eighty-three slides, controlling all platform movements in the North station.

The third box, Shunting box, was on the south side of Ebury Bridge, on the up side of the line. With eleven levers and eleven slides, it was 16 ft long and 12 ft wide, and dealt with shunting movements to and from the carriage road and within the carriage sidings, which were laid out on the level alongside the main lines at the point where they were climbing to meet the river bridge. Beyond South box were Grosvenor Road (six levers, twenty-seven slides), Battersea Pier junction (twenty-three and fifty).

With traffic grown to some 650 movements every twenty-four hours, the need for better signalling on the Chatham side had become urgent by the end of the 1900s. The existing equipment was hopelessly inadequate, in particular, Hole in the Wall box, with its glorious jumble of levers made up from frames of different dates, some still with wooden quadrant plates. A scheme for working the whole station from one mechanical box was prepared and discarded; eventually, the decision was taken to resignal the platforms and the lines to Grosvenor Road with the American system of electrically-worked three-position upper-quadrant semaphores, in combination with dwarf ground signals for shunting and local movements, and electrically-worked points. The contract was let to the British Power Railway Signal Company, which ordered all the necessary equipment from the General Railway Signal Company of Rochester, NY. Delays and troubles associated with the 1914–18 War (not least the loss of the locking frame in a torpedoed merchantman) meant that it was not until January 4th, 1920, that the new signals came into operation.

It was a notable brace of firsts – the first large-scale installation of upper-quadrant signals on any British main-line railway, and the first London terminus to be power-signalled. The indications were the normal ones, viz:

horizontal and red light=danger
45 deg upward and yellow light=clear to next signal
vertical and green light=all clear; next signal off

In their forty-five-degree and ninety-degree positions, all signals were controlled by dc track circuits and by the signal in advance. Ground signals could be moved to forty-five degrees regardless of track circuits, the ninety-degree indication following automatically after the opening of the circuit. Illuminated theatre-type indicators for routes were also provided. Point locking by track circuits replaced facing point lock bars.

The two manual boxes gave way to Victoria A, on the down side, just beyond the end of Platform 1 and next to Hole in the Wall. This box had 200 horizontal pull-out slides of standard GRS pattern (107 signal and release, 47 points, 2 scotch blocks, 1 bolt block and 43 spares). Near the carriage sidings was Victoria B, with 42 levers, and beyond that, Grosvenor Road (14), and Battersea Pier junction (22), both all-mechanical boxes.

In 1924 the SR distinguished between the two Battersea Pier junction and Grosvenor Road boxes by designating the former LBSCR ones A and the Chatham ones B, in each case.

These two quite advanced signalling installations worked well for many years. In accordance with the Southern Railway's policy, they became due for conversion to colour-light signalling in the late 1930s, a change accelerated after a collision at Battersea Park in 1937, caused by a serious irregularity on the part of the signalman. The colour-light scheme was carried through with commendable speed, and the first section, south of Victoria to Pouparts junction, was brought into use on October 16th, 1938. The remaining Central Section lines were changed over on June 4th, 1939, when a new box at Victoria replaced North, South and Battersea Pier junction A. Conversion of the Eastern Section lines was completed on June 25th, 1939, when Victoria B, Grosvenor Road B and Battersea Pier junction B went out of use. Much of the existing GRS apparatus, including the Victoria A power frame, was adapted for use with the colour-light signals.

The new box, situated on the west side of the approaches, near Ebury Bridge, had a 225-lever all-electric frame in three sections, each with its own track-circuit diagram. Under the roof of the station over Platforms 9 to 17, certain colour lights were two-aspect, but elsewhere there were three and four aspects. Theatre-type route indicators and floodlit plate ground discs, together with 'on' and 'off' platform indicators, were included in the installation.

No serious accident has occurred in the immediate vicinity of Victoria, but on August 27th, 1910, a fourteen-car empty stock train and steam engine, moving out of the Brighton station on the down main line, derailed at a crossing, colliding with part of the 9.30 PM West Croydon to Victoria, in which three passengers were injured. The inquiry established that following a movement out of the platform which had been signalled by a hand-lamp (the starting signal was not used), the signalman had pulled the wrong lever.

CHAPTER FOURTEEN

PADDINGTON

SUNSET ELEGANCE

Paddington's rails go out towards the sunset, reaching the deep peace still to be found in the rural heartlands, stretching on to the relaxing West Country beyond; that they also serve industrial Bristol and the South Wales coalfield is a mere anomaly. From this favoured territory, the terminus gathers a distinguished clientele, which dispenses tips said to be the best of any London station.

This place epitomized *The Great Western Railway*, a belief you either accepted or rejected – there was no room for indifference. But few would deny that the Great Western's London terminus displayed a certain dignity. Brunel's graceful roof, Wyatt's elegant decoration, the spaciousness inherited from the broad gauge, all these contribute, but the indefinable atmosphere owes more to association with the long traditions of the only major railway company to survive the 1921 grouping, the only one which did its damnedest to survive nationalization. Standing on the hallowed ground of Platform 1, or, better still, on the balcony of Brunel's office, it is still not difficult to accept that the Great Western goes on for ever.

Various sites were considered for the terminus of the Bristol line – on the river bank at the south-west corner of Vauxhall Bridge; at Grosvenor Road, south-east of where Victoria was later built; and at Euston Square, sharing with the London & Birmingham Railway, after making a junction with it near what is now Kensal Green Cemetery. This last received statutory sanction in 1835.

To the Great Western's brilliant young engineer, Isambard Kingdom Brunel,[1] the Euston plan must have seemed a humiliating second best. A man of powerful drive and imagination combined with great practical ability, Brunel had conceived a railway on the grand scale, and it is certain that he could have had no heart for sharing a London terminus with another line. When he put his plans to the directors, he told them that the Euston arrangement was the only valid argument against the adoption of a broad gauge. On October 29th, 1835, the GWR board agreed the line should be built to broad gauge (7 ft 0¼ ins as laid), setting aside for the moment Brunel's misgivings about Euston. Then the negotiations with the L & BR over the terms of GWR tenure at Euston Square turned sour, and it must have been with considerable relief that Brunel heard, at the end of the year, that he could plan a separate entry into London.

By arrangement with landowners, some work was begun before Parliament had sanctioned the approach line. Authorized by an Act of 1837, this followed the alignment of the Paddington branch of the Grand Union Canal, coming in from Kensal Green through clay cuttings. The terminus was to be at Paddington, north of the Bishops Walk (later Bishops Road, now Bishops Bridge Road), and alongside the canal. This was then the very western edge of London.

Land belonging to the Bishop of London on both sides of the walk, was leased. Brunel had a long-term plan for a permanent station a little to the south, but lack of capital precluded an immediate start on this. Some twelve years were to pass before he was to have the satisfaction of designing a terminus worthy of his magnificent broad-gauge railway.

THE FIRST PADDINGTON

The provisional terminus was opened on June 4th, 1838, with the first 22½ miles of the Bristol line as far as a temporary station at Maidenhead, east of the Thames. Reading was reached on March 30th, 1840, and through communication between London and Bristol was established on June 30th, 1841.

This first Paddington Station was mostly of timber construction, but the various passenger amenities and offices were in the arches of the bridge under Bishops Road, which were given a simple classical treatment to form the frontage of the terminus. Inside, there was an arrival platform on the north, separated from the departure platform by a wide vehicle roadway. This was quite sufficient for the traffic – a dozen or so trains each way daily. But with the opening through to Bristol, more space was needed, and by 1845 there were seven tracks, with three arrival platform faces and two departure. At the outer end was a carriage shed, with engine shed and workshops beyond.

It was at this station that Queen Victoria arrived on completing her first railway journey (from Slough, then the nearest station to Windsor), on June 13th, 1842. Daniel Gooch[2] drove the engine *Phlegethon* at an average speed of 44 mph, which was far faster than HM had ever moved before. That she was a little shaken by the experience was evident in the Prince Consort's request that next time the train be run less quickly. Thereafter her royal progress on the railways was always sedate, until her funeral trains, of February 2nd, 1901, which Edward VII ordered to be driven at a fair lick from Gosport to Victoria and again from Paddington to Windsor. The funeral trains of King Edward VII (May 20th, 1910), King George V (January 28th, 1936) and King George VI (February 15th, 1952) also went from Paddington to Windsor.

Pending the construction of the permanent terminus, a wooden goods shed and offices had been erected on part of the land south of Bishops Road. When, at the end of 1850, the directors finally authorized a start on the work, it was the demolition of these facilities and their replacement that caused irksome delays in the programme. Spurred into activity by the imminent completion of lines to Birmingham and South Wales, the board at first agreed only to a 'departure shed', hoping that the original premises would be able to cope with arrivals for a few more years. In February 1853 they considered the matter

again, and sanctioned the remainder of the permanent
terminus.

BRUNEL'S TERMINUS

Brunel was excited at the prospect, and had no lack of ideas. He
believed himself competent to design a railway station, especially one largely of ironwork, but did nevertheless call in
an eminent architect, Matthew Digby Wyatt,[3] to provide
ornamentation. It was not in Brunel's character to take any-

*Layout of the temporary Paddington Station, north of Bishops Road, in
1845. From the* Railway Magazine, *June 1954*

thing but the major role in a project of this kind, and he made
it quite clear to Wyatt that he would act as assistant.

As it was in a cutting, the main visual impact of the new
Paddington was to be concentrated in the interior. Inspired
by Paxton's Crystal Palace (he had served on the Building
Committee) and also by the main station in Munich, Brunel
produced the first of the large station roofs in metal. Wyatt
contributed new patterns contrived from traditional Moorish
motifs, rearranging the old forms in lively manner to decorate
the supporting columns, end screens and walls. On the wind

screens his metal tracery strangely anticipated *art nouveau*; on the interior walls his work in cement deceived the eye, seeming for all the world like iron. Perhaps the most outstanding features of Wyatt's work were the two sets of delightful oriel windows looking out across the station from the first floor of the side block.

Covering an area 700 ft by 238 ft, the terminus was about 20 chains south-east of the original station. Its principal build-

The new Paddington Station in 1854. From the Railway Magazine, *June 1954*

ing, between the main departure platform and Spring Street (now Eastbourne Terrace) was 580 ft long. Served on the outer side by a cab road, it contained the main offices and amenities. An additional storey was provided in the early 1900s.

A private entrance to the departure platform was provided through this building for the convenience of royalty. This corridor was flanked by a royal waiting-room, discreetly lit by a barred, ground glass window, and filled with stuffy French furniture. Its walls were enamelled in a salmon tint, inlaid with gilt moulding and relieved by grey silk panels. Above the door of the entrance, Wyatt placed a crown design in relief, but on the platform side, one doorway was decorated with the royal coat of arms, its twin by the arms of the GWR.

Light and elegant, the roof of the station was of Paxton

glass and corrugated iron, supported on wrought-iron arched ribs. At its highest points it was 55 ft above the platforms, and it covered the station in three spans, 70 ft, 102 ft 6 ins and 68 ft, interrupted in two places by 50-ft transepts. These openings were intended to accommodate large traversers, to be used for moving carriages from one track to another, but the machines were never brought into use. Fortuitously, the spaces provided for them greatly enhanced the visual riches of the roof.

Next to the single face of the 27-ft-wide departure platform were two tracks, flanked on the other side by a double-sided subsidiary departure platform, 24 ft 6 ins wide. Beyond this were seven tracks, the five centre ones used for storing carriages. Next came a double-sided arrival platform 21 ft wide, a tenth track, and a single-faced arrival platform and cab road, together 47 ft wide. On this last platform was the up parcels office, and on the far side, parallel to the tracks, the approach road to the new goods depot on the site of the temporary passenger terminus.

Beyond the platform ends, the tracks were extended and provided with nineteen turnplates, this portion of the station being designed for the horse and carriage traffic. As the subsidiary platforms were thus true islands, it was necessary to provide some form of passenger access. Brunel solved the problem with ingenious movable bridges; each of these rested on a truck, and by means of hydraulic power, could be lowered and withdrawn under the main platforms when through rail access was required. The bridge between Platforms 1 and 2, opposite the main booking-office, remained in use until about 1920, but did not finally disappear until the scrap-metal drive of 1944, when someone remembered it.

Although the roof was unfinished, the departure side of the new terminus was opened for public use on January 16th, 1854, the arrival side following on May 29th. When the new engine sheds at Westbourne Park were completed in 1855, the old roundhouse and remaining parts of the temporary station were demolished to make room for the new goods depot.

Before 1850, the Prince of Wales Hotel, a 'Commercial Inn for Families and Gentlemen', had been opened on the south side of the line next to the temporary terminus. Observing this to be a profitable enterprise, the GWR decided to construct a much larger establishment across one end of the new Paddington. The Great Western Hotel (later the Great Western Royal Hotel) was designed by Philip Hardwick, and opened on June 9th, 1854. Obscuring the train sheds which lay quite separate behind it at a lower level, this stucco building contained 103 bedrooms and fifteen sitting-rooms, some in suites. The somewhat dreary frontage was finished at each corner with towers, each two storeys higher than the five-storey main block. As for the style, it was a mixture of classical and French-chateau, the latter evident mostly in the roof lines. Above the pediment, John Thomas contributed an allegorical sculpture, described by George Meason, in his *Official Illustrated Guide to the Great Western Railway* of 1861 as 'Britannia, surrounded by personifications of the six parts of the world, and of their arts and commerce'. Thomas' hand is also seen in minor decorations elsewhere.

Managed until 1896 by a company formed of GWR shareholders and officers, after which the GWR took over direct control, this was the precursor of London's large hotels. It was of course eminently respectable; less so were the many small private hotels which later flourished in Eastbourne Terrace, alongside the terminus, and were finally demolished after the Second World War.

The graceful roof lines of Paddington were well displayed in W. P. Frith's narrative painting, 'The Railway Station', completed in 1862. Illustrating the varied human life and incident of a large railway terminus, the 10-ft-long picture was so popular that no fewer than 21,150 people paid a shilling to see it during the seven weeks it was first on show in London. It is now in the Royal Holloway College, Egham.

PENETRATING TO THE CITY

Shortly before the opening of the new Paddington, the GWR, conscious of its far-flung isolation from the heart of London, agreed to subscribe £175,000 to the proposed North Metropolitan Railway. Arrangements were made for this underground line to be built to mixed standard and broad gauge, and to be connected to the GWR just outside Paddington. Lack of capital delayed a start on the Metropolitan Railway (so renamed in 1854), but when the work did begin, the junction with the GWR was constructed at an early stage and used for the removal of spoil and the transfer of materials. As the connecting line curved sharply away to the east to join the Metropolitan, it was not possible to use the existing station, and separate premises, known as Bishops Road, were erected just outside. Passenger traffic to Farringdon Street started on January 10th, 1863, the whole of the fifteen-minute service being worked by the GWR, but following a quarrel over money and other matters, this arrangement was terminated by the main-line company after August 10th. Until its own stock was ready at the end of 1864, the Metropolitan made do with locomotives borrowed from the GNR, and LNWR coaches, surviving with sufficient success to find the means of buying out the GWR interest.

In the following year, on June 13th, a public service began on the Hammersmith & City Railway from Bishops Road to a terminus in Hammersmith, leaving the GWR main line at Westbourne Park. This railway was designed as a feeder to the Metropolitan, and was backed by that company and the GWR (from 1867 it was operated by a joint committee of both companies). At first it was worked by GWR broad-gauge trains, running to and from Farringdon, but on April 1st, 1865, Metropolitan standard-gauge trains began to run through Bishops Road to Hammersmith.

Great Western suburban trains ran on and off the Metropolitan from the opening day of that line, eventually penetrating on mixed-gauge tracks as far as Moorgate. In March 1869, broad-gauge working over the Metropolitan ceased, but after the delivery of standard-gauge stock, GWR trains continued to share the Bishops Road connexion with the Hammersmith & City service, eventually reaching as far east as Liverpool Street. There were also the Kensington and Middle Circle services, worked via a connexion off the Hammersmith & City line at Latimer Road to Uxbridge Road on the West London Railway.

Hammersmith & City, Kensington and Middle Circle trains used the GWR main lines from Bishops Road to Green Lane Junction, Westbourne Park, until October 30th, 1871, when separate suburban lines were brought into use with stations at Royal Oak and Westbourne Park. These trains continued to cross the main line on the level until the subway between Royal Oak and Westbourne Park (H & C) was brought into use on May 12th, 1878.

On the Metropolitan, a station was opened in Praed Street, opposite the Great Western Hotel, when the railway was extended round to Gloucester Road on October 1st, 1868. Passenger connexions between the two services were not easy in the early days. It is true that slip coaches were released into the GWR terminus off trains from Windsor to the Metropolitan from 1866–8, but there was no footbridge between the main station and Bishops Road until around 1878, and no adequate subway between the terminus and Praed Street until 1887. Indeed Bishops Road, and its successor, 'Paddington (Suburban)', have always been out of the public eye, badly signposted. Even today, many users of the main-line terminus are unaware of the existence of this part of the station and its frequent service of electric trains to Hammersmith and the City.

Electric trains appeared at Bishops Road on November 5th, 1906, with the electrification of the Hammersmith & City. After electrification of the Metropolitan, GWR suburban trains were hauled to the City by Metropolitan electric locomotives.

A Tube railway station at Paddington was proposed as early as 1899, but it was not until 1911 that a firm arrangement was reached. To entice the Bakerloo out to Paddington, the GWR eventually had to offer a subsidy, much to the annoyance of the Metropolitan, which had enjoyed a similar sweetener over forty years earlier. The Bakerloo arrived from Edgware Road on December 1st, 1913, went on to Willesden Junction two years later, and ran through trains to Watford in 1917.

The Tube railway booking-hall was beneath the cab road on the arrival side, with stairs from London Street and subways from the arrival platforms. Another subway joined the booking-hall with the 1887 passage to Praed Street Station. Two escalators linked the hall with the platforms 40 ft below. So much for the connexions to the urban network. We must now return to the main story.

Brunel's broad gauge was a fine concept, but it came too late. The Great Western had to live with the rest of the British railway system, as much as it would have liked to have pretended the rest did not exist. In 1861, when an agreement was made for an amalgamation between the GWR and the standard-gauge West Midland Railway, mixed-gauge track into London became an unavoidable necessity. The work was promptly executed, the 37 miles between Paddington and Reading West Junction being relaid in time to carry a standard-gauge train into the London station on August 14th, 1861 (public service began on October 1st). From September 1870, most local trains to and from London were of standard-gauge stock, but as no mixed-gauge track was ever laid into the far west, broad-gauge trains to Plymouth and beyond were worked from Paddington for many more years. It was not until the early hours of May 21st, 1892, that the last of the giants left the terminus.

EXPANSION AND CHANGE

By the 1870s, two tracks were insufficient to handle all the traffic in the terminal approaches, and quadrupling was begun. Four tracks were available out to Westbourne Park from October 30th, 1871, to Slough in June 1879, and as far as the west end of Maidenhead bridge in September 1884. The fast lines (renamed the 'main' in 1880) were on the south side of the slow roads (renamed the 'relief').

Traffic growth also required more platform space in the terminus. In June 1878 another arrival platform (later No 9) was brought into use, together with a cab road carried in over a bridge from the goods depot approach. Platform and roadway were sheltered by a 50-ft 6-in ridge and furrow roof. A new departure platform (later 4 and 5) was added in 1885. As this reduced the amount of space available for carriage sidings in the train shed, the West London Carriage Sidings (on the south side of the main line, by Scrubbs Lane) were opened shortly afterwards.

During 1893 one of the three lines between the platforms corresponding to the present 5 and 7 was removed, to allow what is now Platform 7 to be resited in a more southerly position. This made room for a second line between 7 and 8, and the new arrival platform was double-sided (now 6 and 7). Apart from the 1878 platform, all this work was completed under Brunel's original roof, in space made available by the abandonment of carriage sidings and broad-gauge track.

In 1881 the station buildings alongside the main departure platform were extended towards the hotel over the site of the old horse dock. This marked the beginning of the disappearance of the tracks at the head of the platforms, a process completed within another decade or so.

One does not associate the post-Brunel GWR with the very latest in technical developments, but there were occasional spasms of daring, of which the most notable was probably the

large-scale introduction of diesel railcars in the 1930s. Less
well known, perhaps, is the fact that the GWR was a pioneer in
the field of electric lighting. At Christmas 1880 Paddington
was bathed in the uncertain glow of thirty-four electric lamps
installed by the Anglo-American Brush Electric Light Corporation, and supplied from plant at the east end of the down
platform at Bishops Road. Although this system proved un-
reliable, the GWR was sufficiently impressed to embark upon a
more ambitious scheme, a move perhaps not unconnected with
the fact that Daniel Gooch also happened to be chairman of
the Telegraph Construction & Maintenance Company, which
was exploiting the electric generators patented by J. E. H.
Gordon.

By April 1886 all was ready. Three generators installed on
the south side of the main line near Westbourne Bridge began
to supply a nominal 145-V ac for lighting the terminus, offices,
goods station, goods yards and the stations at Royal Oak and
Westbourne Park. It was recorded in the *Great Western Railway Magazine* of December 1906 that the voltage fell to 105
at Westbourne Park and 120 at Paddington. *The Electrician*
(May 1886) saluted it as 'the first effort to be made in England
to give a continuous supply of electric light on a very large
scale analagous to the rival illuminant, gas'. When the site of
the power station was needed in 1906 for an extension of
Platform 1, the GWR, which had purchased the TC & M installation in 1887, erected a new power station at Park Royal.
This not only supplied lighting current to Paddington Station
and area, but produced traction current for the newly-
electrified Hammersmith & City Railway. During 1907 the arc
lamps in Paddington Station were replaced by a larger number
of filament lamps.

Serving as it did the rich dairylands of the west, Paddington
had for many years an important traffic in milk. A milk arrival
dock was built in 1881 at the back of the outer end of the 1878
platform and accommodation for milk traffic was also available on the departure side. By 1900, milk trains were to be

seen in the terminus day and night, and over 3,000 churns were handled daily. Paddington also dealt with a variety of other traffics: special daily trains for meat and fish, newspapers and horses and flowers, in season.

Only one 'foreign' working was ever allowed to penetrate the sacred halls of Paddington, and even this was only a flash in the pan. In the 1900s, the Northern and the Southern companies collaborated in arranging through trains between northern and midland cities and the south coast resorts, enabling passengers to avoid the tiresome transfers between London termini. The GWR reacted by persuading the LBSCR to work a return run between Paddington and Brighton daily, using the latter's engines and stock. This train reached Brighton in 100 minutes, running via the Latimer Road spur and the West London Railway. Starting on July 2nd, 1906, it failed to attract much custom and was withdrawn in the following June. Just over three years later, another attempt was made, this time by operating a service between Wolverhampton and Birmingham and Victoria; but, as related in the Victoria chapter, this too was a flop.

Despite these minor setbacks, passenger traffic in general continued to grow; trains were getting longer, and a new direct main line to Birmingham was in prospect. The Edwardian years were the last period of real prosperity for the larger British railway companies, and in common with others, the GWR decided that it could afford improvements to its London terminal facilities, not only to relieve existing pressure, but to provide some additional capacity for future expansion. No clouds could be seen on the railway horizon in the early 1900s.

Some preparatory moves were necessary to clear the way. In March 1906 a new locomotive depot was opened at Old Oak Common, replacing that at Westbourne Park; new carriage sheds were erected at Old Oak. In 1906–7 the stationery store was moved from Paddington to Royal Oak. An extension to the main departure platform was completed in 1908. Numbered 1A, this was used for down excursion trains, and, after further extension beyond Westbourne Bridge in 1912–13, for down milk traffic. After 1923, when the milk traffic was moved to Paddington Goods, 1A became a convenient berth for stock awaiting its place in the main departure platform. Ten years later, it was converted to a double-sided parcels platform, serving the new parcels depot in Bishops Road. Other minor works in the mid-1900s included the extension of platforms 2 and 3 to about 1,000 ft and the construction of a luggage subway and lifts to serve platforms 1 to 5.

A major programme for the enlargement of Paddington was approved in 1906. This provided for the extension of the arrival side by the addition of three new platforms under a 700-ft-long steel and glass roof of 109-ft span, which was to match the original Brunel roofs as closely as possible. Platform 9 was to be extended to 950 ft, and the Bishops Road platforms were also to be extended and widened. Between Bishops Road and Old Oak Common, the old brick arch overbridges were to be replaced by long span steel structures which would give room for a rearrangement of the tracks. Lastly, a new goods depot would be built in Battersea ('South Lambeth') to relieve Paddington Goods.

APPROACHES REBUILT

The replacement of the overbridges was not finished until 1914, but before that, work had begun on the rest of the scheme. The rearrangement of the approach tracks was much needed. Separate up and down engine and carriage roads had been provided on the north side of the running lines to serve the new locomotive and carriage depots at Old Oak, but they ran only from Old Oak to Kensal Green box, and inwards from Ladbroke Bridge (up) and Portobello junction (down). Elsewhere, all empty carriage trains and light engines had to occupy running lines, and on a busy day there could be a hundred or more of each. Worse, up empties using the E & C line from Ladbroke Bridge had to cross all the running lines except the down main at Subway junction (a mile from Paddington and midway from Westbourne Park to Royal Oak), before gaining the departure side of the terminus. These arrangements proved a fruitful source of delays and unpunctual departures. Another difficulty was that between Old Oak Common and Westbourne Park, goods trains to and from Paddington depot were obliged to use the main or relief lines. And yet another; that between Paddington and Westbourne Park there was only one down line apart from the Hammersmith & City. The operating and signalling headaches can be imagined.

Work began in 1911 on a scheme to segregate all empty carriage and light-engine traffic from the running lines over the whole 3 miles between Paddington and Old Oak Common. In the following year an independent double line was completed from Old Oak to Ladbroke Bridge box, crossing to the south side of the running lines just west of Kensal Green box by means of a skew girder bridge. Work between Ladbroke Bridge box and Paddington continued slowly, hampered by the necessity to rebuild Westbourne Park Station. Under the stress of war, it petered out in 1916.

Ten years later, the task was taken up again. Good progress was made, all the new lines being completed by the end of 1927. There was now a down empty carriage line north of the relief lines all the way to the Old Oak depots, shared with goods trains beyond Westbourne Park, and provided with a junction into the down relief line at Old Oak Common East. The former up E & C line was converted into an up goods running line with a direct junction from the up relief at Old Oak Common East. On the south side of the running lines were the new up and down roads connected to the skew bridge. (The down carriage line over the skew bridge was disconnected during the changes of winter 1967.) Down light engines or ECS trains could use this route from Portobello junction box (just west of Westbourne Park), whilst up carriages and engines had an independent through run on this side all the way to Platforms 1 to 4 at the terminus. From Subway junction there was a second up empty carriage road into Paddington. After these changes, the last three-quarters of a mile into the terminus, from just west of Royal Oak Station, was worked as follows:

    up City
    down City
    down carriage
    up relief
    up main
    up carriage
    down main
    up carriage

During 1936–7, further operating flexibility was obtained by resignalling the up main and up relief lines between the terminus and Subway junction to allow their being used as required to relieve congestion on the single down carriage line. As related later, the down and one of the up carriage lines eventually became running lines.

At Paddington itself, work began in 1910. A new up parcels office was constructed, and the immediate approach tracks were levelled and remodelled to provide new and better connexions to the Hammersmith & City lines and the Ranelagh engine yard. (On the south side of the line at Royal Oak Station, this yard was used for turning engines from provincial depots.) Following extensive excavations on the arrival side, the old high-level goods yard and its approach disappeared, giving place to three new platforms and a roadway. A portion of the new Platform 12 came into use on November 10th, 1913; the remainder, and Platform 11, were ready by December 1915. The new arch roof, the only part of Paddington Station that can be seen from Praed Street, and Platform 10, were not finished until 1916.

Platform 10 was 800 ft long and 18 ft wide, 11 was 830 ft by 18 ft, whilst 12 was 750 ft long with a width varying from 15 to 35 ft. All three had Ransomes & Rapier hydraulic buffers, a new feature on the GWR. A second arrival cab road was con-

structed between 10 and 11, and brought into the station at
the country end on a bridge over 11 and 12. Cabs queued
alongside the new roof before crossing this bridge. Apart from
the main enlargement work, there were improvements to
amenities. In 1910 a space was hollowed out beneath Platform
1 for lavatories, bathrooms and a hairdressing saloon.

After the completion of the extension, platforms were normally used as follows: 1 to 4 main-line departures, 5 to 7
outer suburban trains, 8 to 11 main-line arrivals. Platform 12
was mainly concerned with inwards milk (until 1923), fish,
mails and parcels; on its opposite face, a sunken roadway
allowed a level transfer of goods between rail and road vehicles.
During the 1930s, after the resignalling of the up main and
relief roads already mentioned, it became possible to use Platforms 5 and 6 for arrivals or departures; 7 was also occasionally used for departures via the down engine and carriage line.

Paddington suffered no air-raid damage in 1914–18 other
than a few panes of glass broken by shrapnel. Although troop
movements were not as heavy as at the Southern termini, they
were sufficient to justify a twenty-four-hour free buffet,
manned by lady voluntary workers. Some ambulance trains
were dealt with, a total of 351 arriving during the war period.
T. S. Tait gave the station the most impressive of all the London termini war memorials. This was placed between the doors
of the royal suite on the main departure platform, and featured
an infantryman heavily clad in greatcoat, sheepskin and
woollen scarf, apparently reading a letter from home; naval
and RAF symbols were carved either side.

Between 1922 and 1924, the cast-iron columns supporting
Brunel's roof on Platforms 2 and 3, and between 7 and 8, were
removed and replaced by steel ones with broadly similar, but
not exact, reproductions of Digby Wyatt's decorations. The
original columns in the roadway between Platforms 8 and 9
had been renewed with steel when the new roof was erected
in 1915.

The Post Office Tube railway, opened in December 1927,

terminated alongside the station beneath the Paddington District Office in London Street. Chutes for incoming mail were installed at the head of Platforms 8, 9 and 10, and a bank of eight chutes along Platform 11. Conveyors carried the mailbags to the Tube railway platforms. Outgoing mail was brought up from the Post Office Railway by a conveyor which debouched on the departure side, just behind the hotel.

ANOTHER REBUILDING

A second major rebuilding of Paddington was made possible by the passage of the Development (Loan Guarantees and Grants) Act of 1929. This Government measure was designed to encourage major works to relieve unemployment, and enabled the Treasury to guarantee loans and make grants towards interest on capital. A £1 million GWR scheme for Paddington was approved by the Treasury, and the work, which began in May 1930, was concluded in 1934.

The project comprised the extension of Platforms 2 to 11 to beyond Bishops Road bridge; the construction of a new parcels depot in Bishops Road, releasing the space behind the hotel to form a new passenger concourse; the provision of two new office blocks and other amenities either side of this space; the construction of new cab and goods depot approach roadways; the reconstruction of all tracks for three-quarters of a mile out of the station, including the addition of a parcels line on the down side; and the improvement of the Ranelagh engine yard.

The platform extensions, which were covered with veranda-type roofing, brought the ends to the westward bend of the line by the original station, producing some very sharp curves at this point. When the work was concluded, main-line platform lengths varied from 1,200 ft (8 and 9) to 980 ft (10 and 11).

An important part of the scheme was the rearrangement of the Suburban station. Suburban traffic on the GWR had always been easy, leisurely and comfortable by the standards of other lines. Uncouth expressions such as 'rush hours' were rarely if ever heard on Great Western tongues. When Paddington first opened, there was no station before West Drayton, 13 miles out, although Ealing and Hanwell were added on December 1st, 1838. Southall followed on May 1st, 1839; Uxbridge on September 8th, 1856; Hayes, May 1st, 1864; Acton, February 1st, 1868; Castle Hill (now West Ealing), March 1st, 1871; and Westbourne Park on October 30th, 1871. For many years, tickets were collected from up trains at a ticket platform on the site of Westbourne Park Station, and the practice continued for over thirty years after the opening of that station.

In 1903 there were only eight suburban trains arriving at Paddington between 5 and 10 AM, compared with 136 at Liverpool Street (the daily total was around forty each way). But as the rush of speculative building spread over Middlesex and south Buckinghamshire in the 1920s and 1930s, the pace of suburban traffic quickened a little (there had already been some additional traffic from the new Birmingham line's suburban halts and stations). With further building expected, it was deemed prudent to enlarge Bishops Road Station so that it could be used for terminating and starting suburban trains as well as those to and from the Metropolitan. The old up and down platforms, with their middle road, were taken out, giving way to two 600-ft islands, one with two up faces, the other with two down. Each had luggage lifts linked to the subway across the station. A layby siding was added to the eastern end, by the canal wall, to serve as a stand for the electric locomotives which hauled the GWR suburban trains over the Metropolitan. A passimeter booking-office on the Bishops Road bridge was supplemented by a ticket office over Platform 8 on a new steel footbridge linking the Suburban platforms with the rest of the station.

These works, completed in 1933, involved some difficult engineering. Part of the tunnel to the Metropolitan had to be opened out and rebuilt as a covered way carrying the diverted goods approach and cab roadways over the eastern end of the enlarged Bishops Road station.

From September 11th, 1933, the name *Bishops Road* went out of use, the new platforms becoming numbers 13 to 16 of the main station, and collectively known as *Paddington (Suburban)*. Normally the electric trains to and from Hammersmith and Kensington (Addison Road) used the outside tracks (Platforms 13 and 16), the centre ones being reserved for terminating GWR steam trains. As all roads were electrified and the standing steam locomotives had a corrosive effect on the live rails, occasional electric trains were run through the centre roads to keep them usable in case of emergency. In accordance with its later policy of isolationism, London Transport removed the junction to the centre roads in 1966, making Platforms 14 and 15 dead ends from August 20th. Later still, as we shall see, the use of these platforms was changed yet again.

At the Praed Street end of the main station, the site of the track ends and turnplates of the 1854 layout was euphemistically known as the *Lawn*.[4] In latter years it had been used for mails and overflow parcels traffic as well as serving as a van approach to the hotel. Sheltered by short-span low steel and glass roofs, supported on numerous cast-iron columns, it was an unattractive spot, cluttered with barrows and reeking of cart horses and their waste products. Passengers were obliged to pass along either side of it when moving to and from the Praed Street underground station. At the platform end, it was crossed by a footbridge, with steps on Platform 1 and Platform 8, affording access to an elevated corridor passing over it into the back of the hotel.

All this was now swept away, to give place to an airy concourse under a higher, three-bay steel and glass roof. The buffers of Platforms 1 to 8 were brought into line and set back a little to provide more space. A new central entrance to the underground station replaced the old side passages, and passengers arriving this way received an altogether improved first impression of the GWR.

Either side of the Lawn, new steel-framed railway office

blocks were completed in 1933. That on the arrival side was in modernistic style, with emphasis on the verticals, and faced with Victoria patent stone. On the departure side, the new block had classical elevations to match the older buildings along Platform 1. Linking the two office blocks was a low building parallel to Praed Street, incorporating a hotel lounge on its first floor and designed to support a new hotel wing. This extension of the hotel, containing fifty-two bedrooms and increasing the total accommodation to 250, was eventually completed in the summer of 1936. The hotel itself underwent substantial internal reconstruction in 1936–8. Bathrooms were provided for most of the bedrooms, the entrance hall was much enlarged, a new entrance canopy and drive constructed, and the exterior refaced and redecorated.

The lower floors of the new buildings on the eastern and southern sides of the Lawn contained refreshment rooms and an inquiry and reservation office. As a finishing touch, an electrically-operated train indicator was installed on the Lawn in 1934. The inevitable public-address system, with twenty-three loudspeakers, came into use two years later.

All parcels traffic was transferred to a new depot beyond the end of the 1,150-ft Platform 1, on the site of the old 1A. This depot had two platforms, 930 ft and 580 ft, its own entrance in Bishops Road and a subway connexion to Platforms 1 to 8.

WARTIME WORRIES

Upon the outbreak of war in 1939, the through working of suburban trains on to the Metropolitan was abandoned, the last journeys being made on September 16th. This service was not resumed after the war. Bomb damage at Paddington was severe, but by no means disruptive of traffic. In 1941 a parachute mine demolished a section of the departure side building; three years later, a flying bomb damaged the roof and Platforms 6 and 7 below.

There were other wartime worries. Those who could afford

Plan of Paddington Station 1954. The former Bishops Road Station for Metropolitan Line trains was incorporated as Platforms 13 to 16 of the main-line station in the 1933 reconstruction. From the Railway Magazine, June 1954

to move out of London chose the West Country as the safest refuge; at the peak of the bombing attacks others spent their nights in the comparative quiet of the Thames Valley. Civilian traffic was very heavy throughout the war, notably at holiday times. With the east and much of the south coast taken over by the military, the West Country resorts were a natural objective for civilian holidays, the more expensive fares offering no discouragement in a period of high wages. In 1944 the Government imposed restrictions on the operation of additional trains and the lengthening of scheduled ones, the object being to keep the railways at peak efficiency for military traffic both before and immediately after the Anglo-American invasion of France.

Matters came to a head on Saturday, July 29th, when for the first time in its history, the terminus was closed for three hours because no more passengers could be accommodated; the concourse and platforms were jammed tight, and all Underground bookings to Paddington had to be temporarily suspended. After this chaotic morning, some relaxation in the Government restrictions on extra coaches and trains was obtained, but this was not enough, and on the August Bank Holiday weekend, gigantic queues were organized in Eastbourne Terrace, under the control of mounted police.

British Railways has made a number of changes at Paddington, not all of them attended with success. Brunel's booking-hall and ticket office on the departure side were rebuilt in 1952–3, and the new ticket office, in use from March 1953, was half as large again as the original. It possessed eleven windows, and was plastic panelled under a mahogany veneer – a combination appropriately symbolic of the new age.

To mark the centenary of the station, a bronze plaque of Brunel was unveiled on Platform 1 on May 29th, 1954. Four years later, the appearance of the master's station was sadly marred by a distracting and restless barrier screen bearing the arms of counties served from Paddington. This screen was placed across the heads of Platforms 1 to 8, and was not only

ugly in itself, but successful in damaging the precious vista
of the roof from the back of the station. In 1963, in slight
penance for this desecration, the roof was repainted in what
were thought to be the original colours – terracotta and grey;
at any rate, it was a much more pleasing combination than the
somewhat dreary chocolate and cream of the GWR.

RETREAT OF STEAM

Steam working into Paddington began to retreat before the
diesel advance in the late 1950s. Between 1959 and 1961, the
suburban services were changed over entirely to multiple-unit
diesel cars, an exercise that proved all but disastrous. Despite
the modest service (a mere ten departures in the busiest hour),
a batch of troubles (rolling-stock difficulties, staff shortages,
overburdening of the main line with traffic diverted from
Euston) caused late running and serious overcrowding. There
were even allegations that the bodies of the cars had been dis-
torted by the mass of humanity packed within, making it impossible to shut the doors properly. Barely had all this been
overcome, when in September 1964 a new suburban timetable
was bravely introduced. This made maximum use of rolling
stock, provided more trains, and gave a regular pattern of
departures, offering a fifteen-minute peak service to most
stations between Reading and Paddington. Conscious that they
were still operating the lightest-loaded of all the London
suburban networks, the Western Region men sought more
customers with a publicity campaign for their *Western Com-
muteroutes*, but they were to be harassed by troubles and
delays for another two years or so. Meanwhile, regular steam
working of main-line and ECS trains ceased in 1965.

During 1961 the No 2 up carriage road between the terminus and Subway junction was converted to a fully-signalled
running line, and the down carriage road was similarly dealt
with in 1963. Although this provided four tracks with in and
out signalling between those points, the restrictions on the

approach tracks still hampered punctuality and efficient work-ing.

With the object of providing greater turn-round flexibility by abolishing the traditional division of the station into arrival and departure sides, a £2 million scheme for track rearrange-ment and resignalling was begun in September 1967. The tracks between Subway junction and the terminus were then set out as follows:

Hammersmith & City eastbound
Hammersmith & City westbound
down relief No 2
up relief
down relief No 1
up main
down main
up engine and carriage

The four engine and carriage sidings in the yard between the up and down lines were removed, apart from a small dead-end section which was retained for holding locomotives. Three new sidings were built south of the line beyond Royal Oak. The sharp curves at the platform approaches were eased, and the general speed limit in the immediate vicinity of the terminus raised from 10 to 25 mph as a result.

From November 12th, 1967, Hammersmith & City electric services used Platforms 15 and 16 instead of 13 and 16, Royal Oak Station was confined to these trains, and all connexions between the electric lines and the Western Region were re-moved. Concurrently with the track alterations and resignal-ling, the engineers undertook partial rebuilding and resurfac-ing of Platforms 1, 4 and 5, and installed ninety-six point heaters in the station approaches.

Between October 15th and November 19th, 1967, whilst

the major part of this work was going on, Birmingham trains
were diverted to Marylebone, and about half the West Country,
Hereford and Worcester services were worked from Kensington (Olympia), where LT provided a shuttle service to and
from Earls Court. Some suburban trains were terminated at
Ealing Broadway.

These improvements were followed in 1968–9 by an enlargement of the concourse, achieved by replacing the unlovely
barrier screen with a lighter one, incorporating a train indicator, set 40 ft back. At the same time new 'daylight' lighting
was installed in the train shed, and the booking-office was rebuilt. Other new offices and amenities will complete the
scheme, including a postal sorting office with facilities designed
to remove the mail-traffic nuisance from the passenger areas.

Although these changes are still in progress at the time of
writing, it is evident that care has been taken to ensure they
will not detract from the splendour achieved by Brunel and
Wyatt. For that we must be grateful, as Paddington is a most
precious inheritance from the proud age of iron and steam.

SIGNALLING AND ACCIDENTS

The first signals at Paddington were of the disc and crossbar
type, set on revolving posts. Semaphores did not appear until
April 1st, 1865. A year later, block working was in operation
as far as Ealing, using Spagnoletti's instruments.

Eventually there were two large station boxes, one for the
arrival side, with 70 levers, one for the departure side, with
65 levers, and a 26-lever box at Bishops Road station. Beyond
there was a 53-lever cabin at Westbourne Bridge, and another
box at Royal Oak Station.

Arrival box was situated at the end of Platforms 8 and 9,
and when these were extended, it had to be moved to a new
site. Opened on April 19th, 1914, the replacement box had
horizontal tappet locking and a 70-lever frame. Platform
home signals for the up main and relief lines installed at the

same time were of the route-indicator type, with four and six positions respectively.

Between 1929 and 1932 the semaphore signals on all lines between Paddington to Southall West junction were replaced by ac electric power signals, mostly in the same locations; dc electric motors were installed for point operation, and there were track circuits throughout. On the running lines, the coloured spectacles of the new signals, moving in front of searchlights, gave the same indications as the old semaphores, but on the engine and carriage roads, three aspects were displayed (green, yellow and red). On the Hammersmith & City lines, two-aspect colour lights were provided. Most of the existing signal boxes and block telegraphs remained in use, but at Paddington three new power boxes were built, and equipped with specially-designed miniature block instruments. The new Arrival and Departure boxes had 184 and 96 slides in General Railway Signal Company mechanical interlocking frames, all slides being approach locked, and all signals detecting each set of points in the route. Illuminated spot diagrams were placed above the frames, two red lights indicating the occupation of each track circuit.

Arrival box opened on August 13th, 1933, replacing Bishops Road and Royal Oak Station mechanical boxes, as well as its namesake. It was worked by two men, one on the main locking frame, the other on the Suburban lines frame. Departure box was in use from July 2nd, 1933. At Westbourne Bridge, the new box, with its eighty-eight-slide all-electric locking frame, was opened on January 10th, 1932, controlling the parcels depot, Ranelagh yard, the down main, and Nos 1 and 2 carriage roads.

Not long after its installation, this equipment was partially destroyed by two fires. The first started at 2 AM on November 25th, 1938, in the Arrival box, putting it completely out of action. Great difficulty was encountered in improvising signalling arrangements, and the Suburban station was closed. Until the opening of a new box on July 2nd, 1939, traffic was worked from a makeshift 141-lever frame composed of spare equipment supplied by London Transport and erected on the roof of the old battery house. Suburban services were resumed when this temporary frame came into operation on December 13th, 1938, but the City through trains were not restored until July 3rd, 1939. Main-line signals were worked from the temporary frame from December 18th, 1938.

No sooner had this frame been set up than a second fire broke out, this time in the Westbourne Bridge box, putting it out of action from 5 AM on December 23rd, 1938. The new boxes, and others at Bristol and Cardiff, were wisely fitted with carbon-dioxide fire control and master switches to cut out the entire frame in an emergency. One wonders why these simple and inexpensive precautions were not taken in the first place.

Normal multiple-aspect colour-light signalling was installed in the Paddington approaches as far in as Ladbroke Grove during the 1950s. This scheme was planned on economical lines, and most of the existing boxes and equipment were retained. Train approaching indications were given by audible warning as well as on the illuminated diagrams. Through working could be made automatic when circumstances permitted.

The signalling on the section between Paddington and Ladbroke Grove remained basically as installed in 1933. Although it offered many advantages over the traditional manual-semaphore system, it was nevertheless ill-suited to modern traffic requirements, and served as a monument to the cautious conservatism of the GWR signals department. With the expectation of an increase in suburban traffic, and in conjunction with the major rearrangement of approach tracks planned for the winter of 1967–8, a revolutionary change was decided upon. Paddington was to be the first London terminus remotely signalled from a power cabin several miles away.

This installation, completed in May 1968, placed all operations at Paddington and its approaches under the surveillance of five men standing at a 40-ft entrance-exit route-setting console in Old Oak Common box, 3 miles out of the terminus. Designed by the Western Region's chief signal engineer, A. A. Cardani, this panel was accommodated in a 50-ft by 25-ft operating-room served by the relay room measuring 45 ft by 25 ft. The Paddington area interlocking provided 228 routes, embracing 77 point machines, 96 ac track circuits, 45 position-light and 34 multiple-aspect signals (4 aspects on running lines) and 4-character train describers. Old Oak Common box then controlled all 11 miles between Paddington and Hayes.

Concurrently with the resignalling, the signalling of the Hammersmith & City line between Paddington and West-bourne Park was converted to automatic operation and came under LT control. (The signalling between Westbourne Park and Hammersmith had been transferred from GWR to Metro-politan control on January 1st, 1913.)

Perhaps the most spectacular accident to occur at Padding-ton was that of May 5th, 1864, when a GNR 0–6–0 locomotive suffered a boiler explosion on starting from Bishops Road with the 9.5 AM to Farringdon Street. Several persons were injured, two seriously; severe damage was inflicted on the station, and to a train in the opposite platform. Debris fell up to 250 yd away, one piece penetrating the roof of the main-line station.

An engine hauling a down empty carriage train was derailed outside the station, near the parcels depot, on October 16th, 1944. Shortly afterwards, two coaches of the down 'Cornish Riviera' express were derailed at the same point. There were no casualties, but blockage here was bound to cause great difficulties, and it was not possible to resume normal working until the following morning.

CHAPTER FIFTEEN

MARYLEBONE

THE LAST MAIN LINE

There is a touch of romance about Marylebone, the terminus of the last main line to enter London. A bold, if irrational venture, the London extension of the Great Central was almost the swan-song of unrestricted railway competition in Britain. Optimistically arranged to allow for future expansion, the half-finished terminus had little difficulty in accommodating in its four platforms all the traffic on offer; indeed, three would have been enough. Even after the rapid suburban growth of the 1930s and the post-1950 building boom beyond the Green Belt, there is still ample capacity, and the rush hours are rest cures compared with those of Charing Cross and Liverpool Street.

Marylebone has always been a quiet place, with a strong provincial flavour, a station where the twittering of birds in the roof is heard as often as train noises. Only on Cup Final Day, when there are departures every few minutes for Wembley Stadium, does it really come to life.

This terminus, and the whole concept of the owning company's assault on London came to fruition through the drive of one man. Sir Edward William Watkin,[1] a dominant influence in the nineteenth-century railway scene, was a railway administrator and politician who manoeuvred the affairs of a number of railway companies. One of these was the Manchester Sheffield & Lincolnshire Railway, of which he became chairman in 1864. A straggling cross-country system, its main line ran from Grimsby through Retford and Sheffield to Manchester. Very much a second-rate affair, it gave up its London traffic to the Midland and the GNR, with which it had working agreements. This was not enough for Watkin, and after he had become chairman of the Metropolitan Railway in 1872, he determined that if he could not get the MS & LR amalgamated with the GNR or the Midland, he would carry it to London, using the Metropolitan for the final approach. At the back of his mind were further links, first with the SER, later with the proposed Channel Tunnel.

But the MS & LR was not rich, and for all his drive, Watkin was no company doctor; its highest dividend, three and a half per cent, occurred in the year he took the chair. There was little hope of attracting capital for large schemes, nor did anything emerge from negotiations with other companies, including a move to get the Lancashire & Yorkshire Railway interested in a shared line to London. At the close of the 1880s, Watkin was trying to persuade his fellow directors to go on alone, tempting them with the suggestion that dividends as high as six per cent might appear as soon as London was reached. He persuaded them; a survey was ordered, and a Bill deposited for the 1891 session.

From the southernmost point of the authorised MS & LR (Annesley, north of Nottingham), the line was to run $92\frac{1}{4}$ miles to a junction with the Aylesbury & Buckingham Railway, passing through Nottingham, Leicester and Rugby on the way. The A & BR had opened in 1868 from Verney Junction, on the LNWR Oxford to Bletchley line, to Aylesbury, and had been worked by the GWR until shortly after its transfer to the Metropolitan Railway on July 1st, 1891. The latter company was pushing up towards Aylesbury, and arrived there on September 1st, 1892. After using the Metropolitan for 42 miles, the MS & LR trains were to reach their London terminus over a new 2-mile line from Canfield Place, near Finchley Road Station.

Both the Midland and the GNR were in fierce opposition, as were the artists and other occupants of the pretty villas in London's St John's Wood. But most formidable of all was the wrath of the cricketing interests, which rose as one, scarlet

with anger at the imagined threat to the sacred turf of Lords.
Not surprisingly, the Bill was thrown out.

A year later Watkin tried again, having softened up other
main-line companies with running powers and other arrangements. By now Watkin was well aware of the almost religious
fervour generated among the English middle and upper classes
by the cricket game – it is surprising that he could have overlooked it before – and realized that if he was to get his railway
beneath the Temple, the homage must be substantial. His
proposals (of which more in a moment) proved acceptable.
Alongside cricketers, artists hardly mattered, but even they
were given a promise that everything would be decently
covered in and that no spoil would be carried through the
dainty streets of St John's Wood. These manoeuvres accomplished, Watkin achieved his victory, and after a delay caused
by the dissolution of Parliament, the Act was passed on March
28th, 1893. With the assistance of a subscription from the
Metropolitan and of the financier Alexander Henderson, the
necessary capital was mustered, and work began in 1894.

In that year, possibly as a result of the strain of getting the
extension moving, Watkin had a stroke and was forced to re-
sign his chairmanships. His successor on the Metropolitan was
John Bell, who took a strongly independent line, refusing to
allow the MS & LR its own way. It was clear that the Met, with
its busy suburban traffic, could not accept the newcomer without more tracks, and although it was not quite as Watkin had
planned, powers were obtained in 1895 and 1896 for a second
pair of lines, for the exclusive use of the new arrival between
Harrow South junction and the beginning of the terminal spur
at Canfield Place, Finchley Road.

With the London extension well under way, something had
to be done about the company's name. After some deliberation,
the title was changed to the more resounding *Great Central
Railway* from August 1st, 1897.

The London terminus was to be constructed on the site of
Blandford and Harewood Squares, just west of the south-west

corner of Regent's Park, a good $\frac{1}{2}$-mile farther from Charing
Cross than Euston, but a little more convenient than Paddington for the residential West End north of Oxford Street.
Some 51 acres south of St John's Wood Road were purchased
for the passenger terminus, goods and coal depots. Not all of
it was occupied by pretty villas; these came to an end just
south of the Regent's Canal, and much of the rest of the area
consisted of some of the most insanitary and overcrowded of
London's tenements. From these warrens a total of 4,448
'persons of the labouring class' were evicted. Some were found
homes in existing property, but for the 2,690 remaining, the
GCR, in the form of the Wharncliffe Dwellings Company,
erected six five-storey apartment blocks (Wharncliffe Gardens)
off St John's Wood Road. (Lord Wharncliffe had succeeded
Watkin in the chair.) Near the passenger terminus, two new
60-ft roads, Harewood Avenue and Rossmore Road, were cut
through the demolished property. A school and vicarage were
rebuilt for St Paul's Church.

Sir Douglas and Francis Fox were the engineers for the 2
miles of terminal approach. A large part of it was in tunnel or
covered way threaded under the St John's Wood streets.
Despite difficulties, the ruling gradient was kept down to 1
in 100. Soon after its junction with the Metropolitan Railway
200 ft north of Canfield Gardens, the double-track line entered Hampstead tunnel, a 691-yd covered way which took it
to the south side of Hilgrove Road. At first it was quite close
to the Metropolitan, at a lower level, but shortly it curved due
south although still remaining roughly parallel to the older
line. To avoid disturbance should the line later be quadrupled,
a second double-track tunnel was built beneath Hampstead
Baths. Emerging from the tunnel, the line was then in the
open for 125 yd whilst it crossed the LNWR main line at the
western end of Primrose Hill tunnels, above the south end of
Loudoun Road (now South Hampstead) Station. The bridge
here was 118 ft long in three girder spans.

Beyond the bridge, the double track passed under St John's

Wood in a 450-yd covered way, a 723-yd tunnel through London clay, and a 67-yd covered way. At Wellington Place there was an open area, 240 ft long by 121 ft 6 ins wide, between massive retaining walls 35 ft 10 ins high. This space was large enough to accommodate seven parallel tracks and became the terminus of the slow lines out of Marylebone and of two shunting necks.

Next came the three parallel Lords tunnels, 213 yd, the easternmost of 40-ft span for three tracks, the two double-track ones of 26 ft 3 ins span. The MCC did well. All that the railway required was a strip 42 yd wide and 110 yd long, none of it used for cricket purposes. To the south was the Clergy Orphan Asylum, which was purchased by the GCR, demolished, and rebuilt at Bushey, releasing 1¾ acres. All this land was given to the MCC, allowing them to extend Lords ground right up to Wellington Road. On the original strip, the turfs and soil were laid aside (one hopes with due reverence), to be replaced as soon as the tunnel arches beneath were finished, supplemented by new turf from Morley's cricket ground at Neasden (purchased by the GCR to form part of a locomotive depot and carriage yard). This delicate operation was begun on September 1st, 1896, and completed with commendable speed. The strip was handed back to the cricket club on May 8th, 1897, together with the free gift of 1¾ acres. Not a day's cricket had been lost.

After passing under St John's Wood Road and Lodge Road, the seven tracks fanned out to a fourteen-track bridge over the Regent's Canal. This structure included a second span of 26 ft to accommodate the proposed Regent's Canal, City & Docks Railway. (Authorized in 1882 and kept alive by subsequent Acts for extension of time, this 16⅜-mile line was to run from Royal Oak, GWR, to the City and to Royal Albert Docks along the course of the Regent's Canal. The scheme was revived in 1903 when F. B. Behr proposed a monorail line along the same route under the title of the North Metropolitan & Regent's Canal Railway.) Beyond the canal, lines curved away to the west to serve the extensive goods and coal depots on both sides of Lisson Grove. Continuing in a southerly direction to the terminus, on a slight gradient to allow platforms at street level, were the down slow, up slow, down main, up main, and, on the east side, a siding road. Also on the east, just before Rossmore Road bridge, were carriage sheds, a locomotive yard and a fish and milk wharf. Provision was made in Rossmore Road bridge for sixteen tracks and five double-faced platform ends, but, as will be seen, only part of this layout was built.

THE MODEST TERMINUS

So impoverished was the GCR after its great effort to get to London that the extra locomotives and rolling stock required could only be obtained by setting up a Rolling Stock Trust Company which sold them to the railway company under a hire-purchase agreement. Small wonder then that the passenger station was a modest affair, not in the least monumental, and hidden behind a vast hotel, the responsibility for which was gladly handed to other parties. No architect was employed. With proper regard to economy, the 'architectural details' were allotted to H. W. Braddock of the engineer's staff. The result would have been creditable as council offices for a minor provincial town, but was hardly worthy as the London terminus of a railway that aspired to be in the first rank.

Two new 60-ft approach roads were constructed either side of the hotel to serve the 341-ft, three-storey frontage block of the terminus. Dominated by gables in a vaguely Flemish style, the roof was well broken up, and even had a feeble tower. The initials 'GCR' appeared everywhere; in the railings, and in the Doulton buff terracotta dressings that relieved the Redbank pressed bricks. A vast *porte-cochère* of iron and glass spanned the 90-ft road joining the main doorway of the station with the hotel. With its delicate ironwork, this was really rather elegant and pretty, quite the best of any London terminus. BR has enhanced its appearance by painting it white.

Inside the main doors was a booking-hall, 63 ft by 40 ft 6 ins, its walls lined with Doulton terracotta to 12 ft, cream enamel bricks above, all under a white-panelled plaster ceiling (now gone, the girders exposed). Oil-polished wainscot oak clad the ticket office, with its four booking windows (one window now suffices, a sad indication of declining traffic). Teak blocks covered the floor. To the east were waiting-rooms and cloak-room, on the west, restaurants and parcels office. Above were committee and board rooms surrounded by railway offices which were occupied by the headquarters staff when they moved from Manchester in 1905. Provision was made for more storeys if required.

Beyond the booking-hall was a concourse 100 ft wide by 289 ft long, over twice the width of the platforms and tracks, which were at the eastern end. Each of the five tracks ter-minated in hydraulic buffer stops. Against the east wall were two tracks, then came Platforms 1 and 2, each 25 ft wide and separated by a 30-ft carriage roadway. The latter was fed from a 1 in 20 U-shaped ramp from Rossmore Road bridge, the cabs leaving through an arch in the frontage block. Two more tracks followed, with the departure Platforms 3 and 4, 35 ft wide, beyond. Alongside 4 was a single track. That was all. The platforms were 950 ft long, covered for 495 ft by a ridge-type roof in three spans (east to west these were 50 ft 4 ins, 50 ft 4 ins and 40 ft 9 ins). The height to the apex of this roof varied from 37 to 40 ft and it was supported by columns at 33-ft intervals along each platform. A 'temporary' cantilever roof, 16 ft 6 ins wide, sheltered Platform 4 pending completion of the station.

The remaining land westwards from Platform 4 as far as Harewood Avenue, enough for another ten tracks, with six platform faces, is now partly occupied by a modern office block (Melbury House) accommodating the British Waterways Board, the British Transport Docks Board, and some British Railways Board staffs.

Over the concourse was a roof with ridges parallel to the

frontage in five equal spans carried by rows of girders. The general effect of the low roof, with its profusion of steelwork, was rather depressing, detracting from the appearance of the spacious concourse and platforms.

Quite separate from the station, but built on railway land, was Sir Blundell Maple's red-brick Hotel Great Central. Surmounted by a be-turreted clock tower, it dwarfed and successfully obscured the station. Designed in Jacobean style by Robert William Edis,[2] the hotel had a main frontage of 215 ft set back 50 ft from Marylebone Road, seven storeys, and 700 bedrooms. Edis used that favourite nineteenth-century material, terracotta, to decorate this tall, steeply-gabled building. Over the main entrance he placed reliefs portraying two females, one with helmet and iron brassière, the other hatless and draped, one breast negligently exposed. Goodness knows what should be read into this little bit of symbolism, or what lessons it may hold for the present occupants of the building. A further touch of the bizarre was the cycle track on the roof. Presumably this was intended as a spectator diversion, not as as exercise ground for overweight executives (for in 1899 a large belly was still the sign of successful maturity).

Hotel Great Central was opened to the public on July 1st, 1899. It is doubtful whether it ever paid more than a small dividend – certainly those 700 bedrooms could not have been filled by the GCR's regular London clientele. In 1916 it was requisitioned by a grateful Government to be used as a convalescent home for wounded officers. It was again taken over for Government use in the Second World War. Just before nationalization, an optimistic LNER purchased it for central offices, but with the arrival of the British Transport Commission in 1947 it became the headquarters of that body (in 1953) under the mundane title – '222 Marylebone Road'. After the dissolution of the BTC, the British Railways Board filled up the converted rooms. One wonders what it has done with the cycle track.

A connexion between the terminus and the Metropolitan

Railway had been authorized in the 1893 Act. This would have passed beneath the hotel, carrying passengers and freight to the City and the Southern lines. Exercising its new-found independence under Bell, the Metropolitan made difficulties about the number of GCR trains it could take and the times when they could be run. There was also strong opposition from the hotel company. Beneath all this the impoverished GCR gladly gave in, and the connexion was never started.

Traffic on the London extension began on July 25th, 1898, when the first coal train left for Neasden. Marylebone goods yard opened on the following April 10th. A ceremonial inauguration of the extension and passenger terminus was performed on March 9th, 1899, by C. T. Ritchie, President of the Board of Trade, who aptly remarked that it was an event London was not likely to see again. Among the 700 guests who sat down to luncheon in the decorated train shed was the ailing Watkin. Three special trains brought notabilities from Manchester, Sheffield and Nottingham. Public traffic started on March 15th, 1899, the first train leaving at 5.15 AM with but four passengers. The heaviest loading that day was on the 1.15 PM, which carried away thirty-four fare-paying customers. During the first few weeks only two platforms were in use.

From July 1st, 1899, there were eleven trains each way on weekdays, seven of them expresses to and from Manchester. Until the track had settled down, and for some time afterwards, running times were leisurely (five hours for the 212 miles to Manchester), but the GCR set new standards of comfort from the first. All the expresses were composed of electrically-lit corridor coaches, and all but the first and last trains of the day had buffet or restaurant cars.

FAY ARRIVES

In these early days many tales were told of the porters outnumbering the passengers or of the booking clerks dozing or

playing cards among piles of unwanted tickets. Things began
to change in 1902 when the energetic Sam Fay[3] was appointed
general manager of the GCR. Fay inaugurated successful and
continuous publicity, backing it up with a high standard of
passenger service. Hard work was needed to attract traffic from
the older lines. The GCR route to Manchester was $23\frac{1}{4}$ miles
longer than that of the LNWR, and the GNR offered a quicker
service to Sheffield. Only for Leicester and Nottingham was the
GCR really competitive. By 1904 the Manchester time was
down to three hours, fifty minutes, Sheffield was reached in
three hours, and Leicester in 105 minutes. Through services
were operating to Huddersfield and Bradford via the Lancashire & Yorkshire Railway, and to Stratford-upon-Avon via
the Stratford-upon-Avon & Midland Junction Railway. At
Marylebone, Fay had buses waiting to take his passengers on
to the West End and City. But despite all this, it was freight
that mattered to the GCR, and after the excitements of the early
1900s the passenger services eventually settled down to a less
dramatic level of performance.

The quadrupling of the Metropolitan Railway between
Canfield Place and Harrow was finished in 1900. Whilst the
old line was rebuilt, there was a short period of mixed use, but
from March 31st, 1901, the GCR had a double track to itself
all the way from Marylebone to Harrow. In 1906 the new line
between Canfield Place and Harrow was leased to the GCR, and
the Metropolitan lines north of Harrow, including the branches
to Chesham, Brill and Verney Junction (but not that to Uxbridge) were leased to a Joint Committee of the Great Central
and Metropolitan Railways, the two companies taking turns
every five years to manage and staff the line. The Metropolitan stipulated that the GCR must not seek local traffic between Marylebone and Harrow, but the agreement allowed
the main-line company to develop suburban traffic on the Joint
lines. This it proceeded to do without delay, working local
trains as far as Chesham and Aylesbury from March 1st, 1906,
using John G. Robinson's 4–4–2T and new four-coach bogie

sets. For its part, the Metropolitan retained GCR receipts it might otherwise have lost, because the latter now had a second string to its bow.

ANOTHER WAY IN

Even before the opening of the London extension, the GCR had not been happy to have the Metropolitan route as its sole entry to London. This line presented great difficulties to express trains; compared to the GCR's own new main line, with its ruling gradient of 1 in 176, it was a nightmare. Not only was there the severe reverse curve at Aylesbury (which derailed a GCR express taking it too fast on December 23rd, 1904), but south of that station came a long climb of 1 in 117 to Dutchlands summit; after Amersham, there was a 6-mile descent at 1 in 105, but no advantage could be taken of it as another severe curve lay in wait at Rickmansworth. Onwards to London, the line was a series of undulations with a climax of 1 in 90 and 95 up for $1\frac{1}{4}$ miles east of Neasden.

A healthy interest was therefore aroused by the Great Western's proposed new main line to Birmingham via High Wycombe. Approaches were made, and acceptable arrangements reached. By the simple device of constructing link lines from Grendon Underwood (north of Quainton Road) to Ashendon (between Brill and Princes Risborough), and from Neasden to Northolt, the GCR obtained a much more easily graded route at the expense of only four and a half miles running. The shared section of the new main line was transferred to a Joint Committee of the Great Western and Great Central Railways. As a *douceur*, the Great Western secured the abandonment of GCR schemes to reach Birmingham.

On the $6\frac{1}{4}$-mile line between Neasden and Northolt, three suburban stations were opened, served by a steam railcar working between Marylebone and South Harrow from March 1st, 1906. The remainder of the new route was opened to passenger traffic on April 2nd, 1906, when a second group of suburban services was inaugurated, between Marylebone and High Wycombe.

It was these suburban services which provided a justification for Marylebone. New five-coach sets in varnished teak, with shoulder lights and foot stools in the first class, hauled by Robinson's excellent 4–6–2T, came into use in 1911. A vigorous publicity campaign was conducted from Fay's office, and discerning businessmen were soon buying villas in the lovely hill country of south Buckinghamshire. By the 1920s a fair traffic had been established.

The isolation of Marylebone was somewhat alleviated when the Bakerloo Tube was extended from Baker Street on March 27th, 1907. The booking-hall of the Bakerloo station, below street level, and entered from Harewood Terrace, was connected to the main-line concourse by a subway opened on the following day. In deference to the wishes of the railway company, the Tube station was named Great Central, but this was changed to Marylebone on April 15th, 1917. From February 1st, 1943, the lifts to the Bakerloo platforms were replaced by two escalators from the concourse.

The events of the First World War made little mark on Marylebone, where the motto was 'business as usual', or even 'more business than usual'. It was a popular station for journeys north because the GCR retained restaurant cars after the GNR and LNWR had withdrawn them, nor did it decelerate its services to anything like the extent its rivals did.

Towards the end of the war, LSWR engines and stock were seen when the Army overseas mail trains were diverted from Nine Elms to Marylebone at the request of the War Office. As the Army Mail Office was in Regent's Park, these workings, which lasted from early 1917 until 1918, offered greater convenience coupled with the opportunity to economize in petrol.

LNER DAYS

After the grouping, Marylebone passed to the LNER, which, having acquired a West End terminus, did little to change the station's character or appearance. In GCR days, most of the best trains had taken the Great Western and Great Central Joint route, but the LNER restored many to the older line. In general the pattern of services remained very much the same, the suburban traffic continuing to grow.

From 1923 onwards, heavy crowds were handled at Marylebone on the occasion of sporting events at Wembley Stadium, which was opened for the Cup Final on April 28th that year. Special services were arranged for the British Empire Exhibition at Wembley Park in 1924 and 1925, and the working of this traffic prompted a limited modernization of the signalling between Marylebone and Wembley. During the Exhibition season of 1924, a ten-minute service of non-stop trains was operated, each consisting of a 4–6–2T and a five-coach bogie set, offering a much more comfortable journey than the Metropolitan. The less frequent service of 1925 was worked by N7 0–6–2T.

With the opening of the joint Metropolitan and LNER branch to Watford on November 2nd, 1925, half the service was worked from Marylebone. These Watford trains ceased in the General Strike (from May 4th, 1926) and were not resumed.

During 1939–45, there were no direct hits on Marylebone, which was troubled only by a few incendiary bombs, soon brought under control. But the rest of the old GCR's London complex was not so fortunate. The vast goods depot was razed to the ground on April 16th, 1941, and the tunnel approaches through St John's Wood proved vulnerable. When Carlton Hill tunnel was breached, Marylebone had to close (October 5th to November 26th, 1940). After the lines had been cleared, this section was left as open cutting. Until permanent repairs were completed in August 1942, single-line working was in operation. Later a flying bomb damaged Marylebone signal box, killing two men.

SHAVED TO A SLITHER

One of the first moves of British Railways was to concentrate all the High Wycombe and Princes Risborough services at Marylebone. From July 4th, 1949, a time-interval basic service was introduced, with a slow and a fast train each hour. This lasted only until January 24th, 1951, when the slow push and pull trains to West Ruislip were taken off, leaving virtually no off-peak service for the stations inward from Northolt.

Diesel multiple-units were introduced gradually during 1961, restoring first class to the suburban service. After the completion of a diesel depot at Marylebone in 1962, the diesel multiple-unit sets took over completely (from June 18th). An hourly service was worked between Aylesbury and Marylebone (fifteen minutes in peak hours), the journey taking fifty-nine minutes, thirty-one less than the slowest steam trains. On the High Wycombe line, the diesel cars also ran hourly with peak-hour additions, again providing a slack-hour service to Wembley Hill, Sudbury & Harrow Road, Sudbury Hill and Northolt Park, although this lasted only until 1964.

On the main line, BR made a brave start by introducing two named trains, the 'Master Cutler' (to Sheffield, from October 6th, 1947), and the 'South Yorkshireman' (to Bradford, from May 31st, 1948), but after a decade or so of slumber, the economists and accountants began to stir. In January 1960 the Sheffield, Manchester and Bradford services disappeared, leaving only three semi-fast trains each way daily to Leicester and Nottingham, shorn of refreshment facilities, and single night trains to and from Manchester. This move led to speculation that Marylebone, the last London terminus to be constructed, would be the first to close, but this BR sternly denied. Patronage of the Nottingham service slowly declined, not surprisingly, as punctuality was poor and breakdowns were frequent, circumstances which took no turn for the better when diesel traction was introduced for some workings in 1963. At last the brutal but logical decision was taken; the line between Ayles- bury and Rugby had to close. Steam working survived until the very end, the engines seeping at all joints, rusty and begrimed, and loved by none but the lineside observers. Marylebone ceased to be a main-line station at 5.23 AM on September 4th, 1966, with the arrival of the 10.50 PM passenger and parcels train from Manchester Central.

But not quite. In the winter of 1967, during the signalling and layout alterations at Paddington, the Western Region's trains to and from Birmingham were briefly diverted to the old GCR terminus, in truth a preparation for its own funeral.

Few changes have been made to the station in recent years. The dining-room has been modernized to form a pleasant self- service cafeteria, but next door, the charming little Victorian buffet still survives. With its mirrors, dark varnished wood, and old-fashioned light bowls, it offers a cosy retreat at the end of a busy day.

Marylebone seems unlikely to last much longer. Already much of the goods yard has been sold for building. The temptation to dispose of the rest, which is on higher-value land, must be very strong. The old hotel will no longer be needed when the new BR offices at St Pancras are ready. After its modernization, Paddington will absorb the High Wycombe line trains without difficulty and the stations north of Amer- sham could then be served by a shuttle, or an extension of the London Transport electrification. All the stations on the Neasden–Northolt loop are close to Tube or BR stations offer- ing a more frequent service. The killing could be done without too much pain, but when it comes, there will be a certain sadness.

SIGNALLING AND ACCIDENTS

When the line opened, three cabins were provided in Marylebone yard – Platform box, Station box and Goods junction
box. At first the line inwards to Goods junction was signalled
by the Metropolitan Railway's Spagnoletti lock and block
instruments, but after the transfer to the Joint Committee in
1906, GCR block instruments of the three-wire needle type
were installed between Marylebone Station and Harrow South
junction.

Platform box, with thirty-one levers, was at the outer end of
Nos 3 and 4, controlling the starting signals. Station box was
between the milk wharf and the running lines, just north of
Rossmore Road bridge. It was 54 ft long by 12 ft wide, with
100 levers in its tappet-locking frame. This was the beginning
of block working and communication with Platform box was
by ringing code.

Goods junction box, just north of the Lodge Road over-
bridge, on the east side of the line, marked the end of the first
block section. It was one of the largest cabins on the GCR,
56 ft by 11 ft, with provision for 100 levers, and controlled the
junction of the fast and slow lines as well as the entry into
the goods yard.

Beyond Goods junction, the second block section ended at
Canfield Place box (a Metropolitan cabin until the Joint line
agreement), but in the early years there was an intermediate
box at Hilgrove Road.

When the construction of Wembley Stadium and prepara-
tions for the British Empire Exhibition began at Wembley
Park in 1922, the GCR decided that the special traffic would
warrant headways as close as three minutes, with a running
time of twelve minutes for the $6\frac{1}{2}$ miles from Marylebone. To
work such a service it was necessary to resignal the line between Marylebone Goods junction (inner home and advance
starters) and Wembley Hill Station and loop. The Westing-

house Brake & Saxby Signal Company was asked to install the automatic and semi-automatic colour-light signals and selective illuminated speed indicators. The latter, indicating 10 and 35 mph, replaced splitting distants at Marylebone Goods junction and normally displayed the lower speed, changing when the inner home to fast-line signal showed yellow or green.

This installation, which included ac track circuiting throughout, came into use on April 8th, 1923, and was the first daylight and three-aspect colour-light signalling on a British main line. The single lens signals were of Hall's pattern; those with two and three lenses were Westinghouse. Platform, Canfield Place and Willesden boxes were all closed, but Canfield Place was available in an emergency. Marylebone Goods junction box had an illuminated diagram controlled by the track circuits, and track-block working was instituted. At Marylebone Station, the semaphore signals were retained, but the running lines were track circuited.

With the removal of the down slow running lines and the closure of the goods yards, a great deal of the signalling became redundant. The installation was therefore considerably simplified in 1967, when a new box was built to replace Goods junction and Station boxes. Opened on October 8th, and situated just south of the Station box, this new cabin contained fifty-five working levers and five spares, controlling the station, the diesel depot and power station sidings. It had an illuminated diagram showing the up lines from Neasden South and the down lines to Canfield Place. The only semaphores remaining were the platform starters.

A fatal accident occurred outside Marylebone in the afternoon of March 28th, 1913. As a train from Leicester was crossing from the up main to enter Platform 4, a High Wycombe train left Platform 3, where the intermediate starter, controlled from the Platform box, was off. The driver of the local train was under the impression that his fireman was looking out for the starter, which was 75 yd away on Rossmore

Road bridge and obscured by the smoke of the Leicester engine. Realizing his situation at the last moment, the driver slipped as he went to apply the brake, and his engine collided with the last coach of the up train, killing one passenger and injuring twenty-three others. Five passengers in the local train were also slightly hurt. The inspecting officer made the rather obvious comment that the company might consider whether the intermediate starter should not be lowered until the starter was off; certainly the existing procedure, which allowed a down train to draw up to the starter, did not appear to save any useful amount of time for the risk involved.

APPENDICES

APPENDIX I

Opening Dates

LONDON BRIDGE	December 14th, 1836
EUSTON	July 20th, 1837
Nine Elms (Vauxhall)	May 21st, 1838
Paddington I	June 4th, 1838
Shoreditch	July 1st, 1840
Minories	July 6th, 1840
FENCHURCH STREET	August 2nd, 1841
Bricklayers Arms	May 1st, 1844
WATERLOO	July 11th, 1848
Maiden Lane	August 7th, 1850
KINGS CROSS	October 14th, 1852
PADDINGTON II	January 16th, 1854
Pimlico (Battersea Pier)	March 29th, 1858
VICTORIA	October 1st, 1860
CHARING CROSS	January 11th, 1864
Blackfriars (Bridge)	June 1st, 1864
LUDGATE HILL	June 1st, 1865*
BROAD STREET	November 1st, 1865
CANNON STREET	September 1st, 1866
ST PANCRAS	October 1st, 1868
LIVERPOOL STREET	February 2nd, 1874
HOLBORN VIADUCT	March 2nd, 1874
ST PAUL'S (now BLACKFRIARS)	May 10th, 1886
MARYLEBONE	March 15th, 1899

* Temporary station in Little Earl Street December 21st, 1864.

Traffic Statistics 1903 (1)
Trains arriving daily (Weekdays)

	Suburban	Total
LIVERPOOL STREET	380	416
BROAD STREET	322	322
VICTORIA	306	370
WATERLOO	256	303
LONDON BRIDGE	243	293
FENCHURCH STREET	232	233
CANNON STREET	211	249*
ST PAUL'S AND LUDGATE HILL	171	171
CHARING CROSS	152	187
KINGS CROSS	60	101
HOLBORN VIADUCT	50	71
PADDINGTON	39	103
ST PANCRAS	38	66
EUSTON	36	78
MARYLEBONE	—	13

Source: Royal Commission on London Traffic, 1905, Volume
III Appendices, Appendix 6, Table 33.

* Includes trains going on to Charing Cross.

Traffic Statistics 1903 (2)

Season-ticket journeys in year (millions)		Total journeys in year (millions)	
Liverpool Street	20·0	Liverpool Street	65·3
London Bridge (both)	11·7	Waterloo	31·0
Broad Street	9·8	London Bridge (both)	29·8
Victoria (both)	9·4	Victoria (both)	29·4
Waterloo	8·7	Broad Street	26.7
Kings Cross	8·3	Fenchurch Street	23·9
St Pancras	7·3	Kings Cross	15·4
Fenchurch Street	5·5	Cannon Street	13·5
Cannon Street	4·3	Holborn Viaduct	10·7
Holborn Viaduct	3·5	Charing Cross	10·2
Charing Cross	3·3	St Pancras	9·8
Paddington	2·7	Paddington	9·2
Euston	1·9	Ludgate Hill	4·8
Ludgate Hill	1·5	Euston	4·5
St Paul's	1·2	St Paul's	3·8
Marylebone	0·1	Marylebone	0·5

Source: Royal Commission on London Traffic, 1905, Vol I, para 133.

Traffic Statistics 1967–8 (1)

	Trains in and out daily	Passengers daily (weekdays, nearest 100)
LIVERPOOL STREET	1,001	204,700
WATERLOO	1,214	195,900
VICTORIA	1,031	182,900
LONDON BRIDGE	645*	168,900
CHARING CROSS	729	119,900
CANNON STREET	261	80,000
FENCHURCH STREET	253	67,300
PADDINGTON	287	43,000
EUSTON	410	40,000
KINGS CROSS	297	39,900
ST PANCRAS	187	30,000
MARYLEBONE	126	15,000
BROAD STREET	146	9,000

Source: British Railways Regions (Southern Region figures are for October 1967, all others for October 1968).

* Does not include trains passing through to Cannon Street and Charing Cross.

Traffic Statistics 1967–8 (2)

Passengers and trains arriving 7 to 10 AM at the busiest stations

	Passengers	Trains
LIVERPOOL STREET	79,904	167
WATERLOO	70,108	152
LONDON BRIDGE	61,467	105
VICTORIA	57,669	107
CHARING CROSS	42,230	71
CANNON STREET	38,320	63
FENCHURCH STREET	30,728	41
PADDINGTON	10,500	42
ST PANCRAS	8,326	37

Source: British Railway Regions (Southern Region figures are for October 1967, all others for October 1968).

APPENDIX VI

SOURCES AND BIBLIOGRAPHY

A fully annotated reference for each of the many hundreds of
facts and dates in this book would fill almost as many pages as
the text itself, pages which would be of value to only a small
minority of readers. The following notes and bibliography
should provide an indication of sources as well as serving as a
guide to further reading.

Much basic information is given in the Acts of Parliament for
the works concerned, and in the unsuccessful Bills, with their
deposited plans (adequately indexed in the London and
Middlesex County Record Offices). Detail is available in the
minutes and reports of the various railway companies (British
Transport Historical Records, Porchester Road, W2), in contemporary public timetables and travel guides, working timetables and their appendices, and in contemporary maps and
plans (notably the large scale Ordnance Survey and the in-
valuable Railway Clearing House Junction Diagrams). Of
major importance as a source are the contemporary accounts
and comments in the daily and periodical press, especially:
*The Times, The Daily Telegraph, Illustrated London News,
Railway Times, Railway News, Railway Engineer, Railway
Magazine, Railway & Travel Monthly, Railway Gazette,
Railway Club Journal, Railway World, Trains Illustrated,
Modern Railways* and *Modern Transport*. Of the various
company magazines, the *Great Western Railway Magazine* is
particularly useful on Paddington, the *Southern Railway
Magazine* on the southern termini; the others are less reward-
ing. Architectural detail is to be found in *The Builder, Build-
ing News* and *The Architect*. Much is to be gained from

magnification of old drawings and photographs, not forgetting the picture postcards of the 1900–14 period.

Some statements in the text are derived from the author's own observations and field work in the past thirty years, and that of friends, particularly Mr G. T. Moody, whose notebooks go back over fifty years.

The following books, magazine articles, and reports are suggested to those seeking further background and detail:

1. General

Acworth, W. M., *The Railways of England*, various editions from 1889, John Murray.

Clunn, H., *London Rebuilt 1897–1927*, John Murray, 1927.

Clunn, H., *The Face of London*, Spring Books, 1956.

Course, E. A., *London Railways*, B. T. Batsford, 1962.

Crump, N., *By Rail to Victory, the story of the LNER in wartime*, LNER, 1947.

Darwin, B., *War on the Line: the story of the Southern Railway in wartime*, SR, 1946.

Dyos, H. J., 'Railways and Housing in Victorian London', *Journal of Transport History*, 2 (1955–6).

John, E., *Timetable for Victory: a brief and popular account of the railways and railway-owned dockyards of Great Britain and Northern Ireland, during the six years' war, 1939–45*, The British Railways, 1946.

Knight, C. (ed), *London*, Henry G. Bohn, 1851 (chapter by Saunders, J.).

London County Council, *Survey of London*, Vols 21, 23, 24.

Nash, G. G., *The LMS at War*, LMSR, 1946.

Pratt, E. A., *British Railways and the Great War* (two vols), Selwyn & Blount, 1921.

Sekon, G. A., *Locomotion in Victorian London*, Oxford University Press, 1938.

Thornbury, W. and Walford, E., *Old and New London* (six vols), Cassell & Co, 1897.

Wheatley, H. B., *London Past and Present*, John Murray, 1891.

White, H. P., *A Regional History of the Railways of Great Britain, Vol 3, Greater London,* David & Charles, 1971.

State Publications

Report of the Commissioners on Railway Termini within or in the immediate vicinity of the Metropolis, and Evidence, 1846.

Report of the Select Committee of the House of Commons on Metropolitan Communications, and Evidence, 1855.

Report of the Select Committee on Metropolitan Railway Communication, and Evidence, 1863.

Report of the Joint Committee on Railway Schemes (Metropolis), and Evidence, 1864.

Royal Commission on the Housing of the Working Classes, and Evidence, 1885.

Report of the Joint Select Committee on the Housing of the Working Classes, and Evidence, 1902.

Royal Commission on London Traffic, Report, Evidence, Appendices (eight vols), 1905.

2. Architecture

Hitchcock, H. R., *Early Victorian Architecture in Great Britain* (two vols), Architectural Press, 1954.

Hitchcock, H. R., *Architecture: 19th and 20th centuries,* Penguin Books (Pelican History of Art), 1958.

Meeks, C. L. V., *The Railway Station: An Architectural History*, Architectural Press, 1957.

3. The Stations (order as in text)

EUSTON

Anon, 'Old Euston', *Country Life*, 1938.

Barrie, D. S., 'The Story of Euston', *Railway Magazine*, July and September, 1937.

Head, F. B., *Stokers and Pokers*, John Murray, 1849.

ST PANCRAS

Barlow, W. H., Proceedings, Institution of Civil Engineers, Vol 30.

Barnes, E. G., 'The Midland Drive for London', *Railway World*, September 1962.

Scott, Sir G. G., *Personal & Professional Recollections*, Sampson Low, Marston, Searle & Rivington, 1879.

Lee, C. E., 'St Pancras Station, 1868–1968', *Railway Magazine*, September and October 1968.

Simmons, J., *St Pancras Station*, George Allen & Unwin, 1968.

Williams, F. S., *The Midland Railway, Its Rise and Progress*, Bemrose & Co, 1877.

KINGS CROSS

Gairns, J. F., 'Notable Railway Stations and their Traffic: Kings Cross', *Railway Magazine*, August 1914.

Grinling, C. H., *The History of the Great Northern Railway, 1845–1902*, 1903.

Johns, C. A., 'One Hundred Years at Kings Cross', *Railway Magazine*, October and November 1952.

BISHOPSGATE

Evill, W., Proceedings, Institution of Civil Engineers, Vol 3.

LIVERPOOL STREET

Gairns, J. F., 'Jubilee of a Great London Terminus', *Railway Magazine*, May 1924.

FENCHURCH STREET

Gairns, J. F., 'Notable Railway Stations and their Traffic: Fenchurch Street', *Railway Magazine*, June 1919.

BRICKLAYERS ARMS

Fellows, R. B., 'The Failure of Bricklayers Arms as a Passenger Station', *Railway Magazine*, July/August and September/October 1944.

LONDON BRIDGE

Reed, B. A. and Lee, C. E., 'London Bridge, the Oldest Terminus', *Railway Magazine*, December 1936, February 1937.

CANNON STREET

Ellson, G., Proceedings, Institution of Civil Engineers, Vol 223.

Lee, C. E., 'Cannon Street Station 1866–1966', *Railway Magazine*, August and September 1966.

Wolfe Barry, J., Proceedings, Institution of Civil Engineers, Vol 27.

LUDGATE HILL

Lee, C. E., 'Useful but Unloved, the story of Ludgate Hill Station', *Railway Magazine*, December 1964.

WATERLOO AND NINE ELMS

Anon, 'The New Waterloo Station, LSWR', reprinted from the *Railway Gazette*, June 9th, 1922.

Davis, H. G., *Waterloo Station Centenary, 1848–1948*, British Railways, 1948.

Fay, Sam, *A Royal Road*, W. L. Drewett, 1883.

Gairns, J. F., 'The Largest Railway Terminus in Great Britain', *Railway Magazine*, May 1922.

Szlumper, A. W., Proceedings, Institution of Civil Engineers, Vols 107, 111.

CHARING CROSS

Ellson, G., Proceedings, Institution of Civil Engineers, Vol 223.

Hayter, H., Proceedings, Institution of Civil Engineers, Vol 22.

Lee, C. E., 'Charing Cross Station 1864–1964', *Railway Magazine*, January 1964.

Wolfe Barry, J., Proceedings, Institution of Civil Engineers, Vol 27.

VICTORIA AND PIMLICO

Fox, C. W., Proceedings, Institution of Civil Engineers, Vol 27.

Gairns, J. F., 'Notable Railway Stations and their traffic: Victoria (London)', *Railway Magazine*, April 1927.

Lee, C. E., 'The First West End Terminus', *Railway Magazine*, March 1958.

Lee, C. E., 'Victoria Station London in the 19th century', *Railway Magazine*, September 1960.

Lee, C. E., 'Victoria Station, London in the 20th century', *Railway Magazine*, October 1960.

MacDermot, E. T., *History of the Great Western Railway*, GWR, 1927.

Wilson, W., Proceedings, Institution of Civil Engineers, Vol 27.

PADDINGTON

MacDermot, E. T., *History of the Great Western Railway*, GWR, 1927.

Lee, C. E., 'The Centenary of Paddington Station', *Railway Magazine*, June 1954.

MARYLEBONE

Hobson, G. A. and Wragge, E., Proceedings, Institution of Civil Engineers, Vol 143.

REFERENCES

CHAPTER 1 (pp 1–17)

[1] 1801–65. Landscape gardener, engineer and architect, designer of the building for the Great Exhibition of 1851, later called the Crystal Palace and removed to Sydenham.

[2] In Standing Orders of 1884, following a recommendation of the Royal Commission on the Housing of the Working Classes, 1884. Earlier Standing Orders (1853, 1874 and 1875) failed to ensure any provision of permanent accommodation for the displaced, although they secured some modest compensation for people turned out of their homes, and, in some cases, temporary shelter.

[3] For a fully-detailed study of these as they existed in the late 1950s, just before they ceased in their traditional form, see Alan Rannie, *Railway Magazine*, Vol 104, p 751, and p 864, 'Empty Stock Working at London Termini'.

CHAPTER 2 (pp 18–46)

[1] 1792–1870. Architect to the Duke of Wellington. He designed the warehouses at St Katharine's Docks, London (1827–8), Goldsmiths' Hall (1835) and the Stone Buildings, Lincoln's Inn (1835–42).

[2] 1822–92. He shared a great deal of his father's later work.

[3] *An Apology for the Revival of Christian Architecture in England*, 1843.

[4] 1810–74. Civil and consulting engineer, knighted in 1851 for his work on the Great Exhibition building, practised in London from 1857, together with his two eldest sons Charles and Francis.

[5] 1813–62. Sculptor and architectural draughtsman. Thomas was also responsible for the rather comic lions that guard the Britannia Bridge over the Menai Straits; the pediment and other decorations on the Great Western Hotel, Paddington; the en-

trance piers of Buckingham Palace; the royal dairy at Windsor; and the National Bank, Glasgow.

[6] This description is largely taken from Saunders in *London* (1851).

[7] Samuel Sidney, *Rides on Railways leading to the Lake and Mountain Districts* etc (1851). William S. Orr & Co, 1851.

[8] *Railway Magazine*, October 1930.

CHAPTER 3 (pp 47–66)

[1] William Henry Barlow, 1812–1902. He practised as a consulting engineer from 1857 onwards after working for the Midland and constructing the Leicester–Hitchin line. A member of the Tay Bridge disaster inquiry, co-designer of the new Tay Bridge and of the Forth Bridge, he was the inventor of the self-supporting broad-flanged wrought-iron rail. He is sometimes confused with his brother, Peter William, also a railway and civil engineer.

[2] 1811–92. General manager of the Manchester Sheffield & Lincolnshire Railway 1850–3, of the Midland Railway 1853–7 and 1860–80. He died appropriately in the Midland Grand Hotel, St Pancras.

[3] *Proceedings, Institution of Civil Engineers*, Vol 30, discussion on Barlow's paper.

[4] 1811–78. His other buildings included the Albert Memorial in Hyde Park, Glasgow University, St Mary's Cathedral, Edinburgh, and the Foreign and India Offices in Whitehall. The quotation is taken from his *Personal and Professional Recollections* (1879).

[5] *Personal and Professional Recollections* (1879).

[6] D. T. Timins, *Railway Magazine*, June 1902.

CHAPTER 4 (pp 67–86)

[1] 1799–?. Brother of Thomas Cubitt, the founder of the famous building firm. Lewis designed houses for his brother in Bloomsbury and Belgravia and was also responsible for the frontage of Bricklayers Arms Station.

[2] Sir William Cubitt (knighted in 1851 for his work as a Commissioner for the Great Exhibition) was engineer of the Great

Northern Railway, assisted by his son, Joseph. They were not directly related to Lewis.

[3] Norman Crump, *By Rail to Victory*, London & North Eastern Railway, 1947, pp 139 and 173.

CHAPTER 6 (pp 98–123)

[1] 1797–1870. He manufactured the first practical steam fire engine, and, with John Ericsson, the locomotive *Novelty*, which ran in the Rainhill trials. He laid out the ECR with C. B. Vignoles, but ceased to be engineer for that company in 1843. Braithwaite also surveyed several lines in France, and was the joint founder of the *Railway News*.

[2] Evidence of the Rev Timothy Gibson to the Royal Commission on Metropolitan Termini, 1846.

[3] 1843–1925. Director of the GER 1872, deputy chairman 1875, chairman 1893–1923.

[4] For a full account of Fryatt's exploits see Edwin A. Pratt, *British Railways and the Great War*, London, Selwyn & Blount, 1921, pp 907–12.

[5] Ashbee was also responsible for Norwich Thorpe, Colchester, Hertford, Felixstowe, Southend and Wolferton stations.

[6] For a fuller account, see Norman Crump, *By Rail to Victory*, London & North-Eastern Railway, 1947.

CHAPTER 8 (pp 140–71)

[1] 18?–1876. His other work included model housing (he was architect to Lord Shaftesbury's Society for Improving the Dwellings of the Working Classes), Camberwell Grammar School and Fishmongers' Hall.

[2] See for example the photograph on p 355, *Railway Magazine*, Vol 48 (June 1921).

[3] 1786–1851. Beazley combined his architectural activities with play writing. He designed many theatres, including the Lyceum and St James's in London. Most of the stations on the North Kent line were his work.

[4] Since 1928, below Spa Road, these tracks have been worked as: No 2 up, No 3 down, No 1 up, down local, down through and up through. On the London Bridge side of Spa Road, the first two are the present No 3 down and No 2 up.

[5] 1820–1900. He designed the new St Thomas's Hospital on the Albert Embankment, also hotels at Buxton and Eastbourne, and P & O offices in the City of London, houses at Eastbourne, and various churches.

[6] Loudspeakers had been introduced at Paris, Orsay, and Paris, Austerlitz in the early part of 1925, and in the following year, the GWR installed five at Newport (Mon). The LCC had used horn-amplified telephone equipment in their Blackfriars tram shelter as early as 1911.

[7] 'London Bridge Railways' was a terminus for buses from the 1840s, and has remained an important bus centre ever since. At present eight services terminate there, some of them still following, in part, the old horse bus routes.

CHAPTER 9 (pp 172–91)

[1] 1811–91. One of the foremost engineers of the nineteenth century, responsible for the design and construction of the Manchester & Leeds Railway, East London Railway, the Severn tunnel, and the Charing Cross and Cannon Street stations and river bridges. Knighted in 1873.

[2] 1830–80. Son of Sir Charles Barry, architect of the Houses of Parliament, Edward also designed the railway hotel at Charing Cross, the Birmingham Public Library, the Hospital for Sick Children (Great Ormond Street, London) and the Inner Temple buildings.

[3] Edwin A. Pratt in *British Railways and the Great War*, London, Selwyn & Blount, 1921, p. 1085.

[4] For a full account of this hectic night see Bernard Darwin, *War on the Line*, Southern Railway, 1946, pp 74–6.

CHAPTER 10 (pp 192–212)

[1] 1823–1904. After a successful few years in managerial posts with the GWR and the Dutch-Rhenish Railway, Forbes became general manager of the LCDR in 1861, was appointed a director ten years later, and was chairman and general manager from 1873 until the formation of the SECR in January 1899. In 1870 he became a director of the Metropolitan District Railway, and was its chairman from 1872 until 1901.

[2] The full list was: (*East Door*) Bale, Genoa, Milan, Lyons,

Naples/Antwerp, Baden Baden, Berlin, Boulogne, Bremen, Brindisi, Brussels, Calais, Cannes, Cologne, Dresden : (*Centre*) Ashford, Beckenham, Bickley, Broadstairs, Bromley, Canterbury, Chatham, Crystal Palace, Deal, Dover, Faversham/Gravesend, Herne Bay, Maidstone, Margate, Ramsgate, Rochester, Sevenoaks, Sittingbourne, Sheerness, Westgate-on-Sea, Walmer : (*West Door*) Darmstadt, Florence, Frankfort, Geneva, Lausanne, Leipsic, Lucerne, Marseilles, Vienna, St Petersburg, Wiesbaden/Nice, Paris, Rome, Turin, Venice.

CHAPTER 11 (pp 213–53)

[1] 1798–1873. Tite, who was knighted in 1869, also designed the new buildings at Mill Hill School, the Royal Exchange, and a large number of stations, including Blackwall, Windsor Riverside, Carlisle Citadel, and Southampton Terminus (the rather more pretentious opposite number of Nine Elms).

[2] The Lion Brewery was again under consideration for railway use eighty-three years later. In 1929 the LCC offered it to the SR for a new terminus on condition the company gave up Charing Cross (see p 270). The brewery was eventually demolished in 1950 under the South Bank Improvement Scheme, and, at the suggestion of King George VI, one of its artificial stone lions was preserved, and re-erected at the York Road entrance to Waterloo Station. In 1965 the lion was displaced by a new office block and moved this time to the east end of Westminster Bridge.

[3] The company was incorporated by an Act of 1852. Its name was changed in 1927 to the London Necropolis Company. Brookwood Cemetery, which still exists, was served by a single-track branch with two stations designed by Tite.

[4] Charles Scotter, general manager, LSWR, to the Parliamentary Joint Committee on the Electric and Cable Railway Schemes for the Metropolis, 1892.

[5] John Murray, London, 1891.

[6] C. de Brio, in the *Railway Magazine*, Vol 68, No 406 (April 1931).

[7] Harold Clunn, *London Rebuilt, 1897–1927*. London, John Murray, 1927.

[8] Herbert Ashcombe Walker, 1868–1949, general manager LSWR 1912, chairman, Railway Executive Committee 1914, knighted 1915, general manager SR 1924–37, and largely respons-

ible for the highly successful electrifications of the 1920s and 1930s.

[9] For a full account see J. R. Whitbread, *The Railway Policeman*, London, George G. Harrap & Co Ltd, 1961, pp 192–6.

[10] The main dates are: platforms renumbered in sequence, October 1st, 1912; new road 5a, March 9th, 1913; new Platform 6, June 29th, 1913; platforms serving roads 5a, 6, 6a became 6 to 8, October 1st, 1913; new Platform 11, existing 9 to 17 became 12 to 20, December 7th, 1913; new locomotive yard, March 1st, 1914; new Platform 19, June 14th, 1914; new Platform 20, February 14th, 1915; new Platform 21, February 28th, 1915; new Platforms 17 and 18, April 11th, 1915; new Platform 16, June 13th, 1915; new Platform 12, August 20th, 1916; new Platform 13, August 27th, 1916; new Platform 14, October 29th, 1916; Windsor side booking-office, July 22nd, 1918; new administrative offices, February 1920.

[11] Chief architectural assistant, LSWR.

[12] For a full account of Waterloo's war, see Bernard Darwin, *War on the Line*, London, Southern Railway, 1946.

CHAPTER 12 (pp 254–80)

[1] 1812–1904. Author of *The Life of George Stephenson* (1857), *Self-Help* (1859), *Lives of the Engineers* (1861–2), *Character* (1871), *Thrift* (1875), *Duty* (1880), *Life and Labour* (1887), in early life a medical practitioner.

[2] A contemporary writer quoted in Edward Walford's *Old and New London*, Cassell & Co, London 1897. Vol III, p 130.

[3] John Gibbons, *Railway Magazine*, Vol 75, p 159.

[4] F. T. Jane, *The English Illustrated Magazine*, June 1893.

[5] The boat trains for the Folkestone–Flushing service, resumed in 1919, did not move to Victoria until 1921. Flushing was served from Harwich and Liverpool Street from January 1st, 1927.

[6] 1858–1943. Burns was a socialist, later a 'radical liberal'. A member of the LCC from 1889 to 1907, and MP for Battersea from 1892 to 1918, he was the first member of the working class to serve in the Cabinet, becoming President of the Local Government Board in 1905, and holding that post until 1914, when he was appointed President of the Board of Trade. As he was unable to support the declaration of war on Germany in August 1914, he resigned from the Government.

CHAPTER 13 (pp 281–321)

[1] SER access was not a practical proposition. The company was effectively precluded from taking running powers over the WEL & CPR by the 'territorial' agreement made with the LBSCR in 1847–8. Some correspondence took place between the two major companies in 1858 because SER proposals for running powers to Victoria and LBSCR proposals for running powers over the WEL & CPR Farnborough line both conflicted with the spirit of the agreement and subsequent understandings. Eventually, both companies retracted, and the LBSCR did not oppose the SER extending to a West End terminus of its own at Charing Cross.

[2] 1817–98. Knighted 1885, Fowler was a consulting engineer, the designer of the Metropolitan Railway and, with Benjamin Baker, of the Forth Bridge.

[3] 1831–1908. Better known as the founder and editor of *The Nineteenth Century*. His other architecture included churches at Clapham and Albert Mansions, Victoria Street. He was made KCVO in 1903.

[4] Harold Clunn, *London Rebuilt 1897–1927*, John Murray, 1927.

CHAPTER 14 (pp 322–50)

[1] 1805–59. Son of Marc Isambard Brunel, the designer of the Thames Tunnel. He was engineer in charge of his father's tunnel works, the designer and builder of the early Great Western Railway, the South Devon Railway and of the pioneer ocean-going steamships, *Great Western*, *Great Britain* and *Great Eastern*.

[2] 1816–89. Gooch was appointed the first GWR superintendent of locomotives by Brunel when only twenty years of age. He became a director of the Great Eastern Steamship Company in 1860 and supervised the laying of the first Atlantic cable. He was chairman of the GWR from 1865 until his death in 1889. Baronet 1866.

[3] 1820–80. Wyatt was secretary of the Royal Society of Arts Executive Committee for the Great Exhibition of 1851 and superintendent of works for the building of the Crystal Palace at Sydenham. With Sir George Gilbert Scott, he designed the

interior of the India Office. His other works included the Adelphi Theatre, the chapel and hospital at Warley Barracks and the Crimean memorial at Chatham. Knighted 1855.

[4] The origin of this name is obscure. It may be derived from the grass slope that existed alongside the entrance to the original station, on the site of the present terminus and hotel. This slope is referred to in a letter published in *The Times*, of May 24th, 1839, describing the somewhat barbarous treatment of a ten-year-old girl by railway officials after she had been seen picking a wallflower through the fence.

CHAPTER 15 (pp 351–68)

[1] 1819–1901. Secretary of the Trent Valley Railway 1845, general manager, Manchester, Sheffield & Lincolnshire Railway, 1854–61, director MS & LR, 1863, chairman MS & LR 1864–94, chairman SER 1866–94, chairman Metropolitan Railway 1872–94, also a director of the GER, GWR and Channel Tunnel companies; MP for Stockport 1864–8, for Hythe 1874–95; knighted 1868, baronet 1880.

[2] 1839–1927. His other work included three London clubs (Constitutional, Junior Constitutional and Badminton), the Conservative Club, Glasgow, the ballroom at Sandringham and the Inner Temple Library. He was knighted in 1919.

[3] 1856–1953. General manager, Midland & South Western Junction Railway 1892–99; traffic superintendent LSWR 1899–1902; general manager, GCR 1902–16 and 1919–22; Director of Movements, War Office 1917–18; Director-General of Movements and Railways, and member of the Army Council 1918–19; Fay was knighted during the opening of Immingham Docks in 1912.

INDEX

David and Charles Railway Series

These and other PAN Books are obtainable from all booksellers and newsagents. If you have any difficulty please send purchase price plus 5p postage to P.O. Box 11, Falmouth, Cornwall.
While every effort is made to keep prices low, it is sometimes necessary to increase prices at short notice. PAN Books reserve the right to show new retail prices on covers which may differ from those advertised in the text or elsewhere.